Leadership Skills

APLED 123

SPOKANE COMMUNITY COLLEGE

HUMAN RELATIONS

create.mheducation.com

ISBN-13: 9781307361216

ISBN-10: 1307361218

Contents

Contents

authors

Lowell Lamberton is an emeritus business professor with an extensive background in both writing and business. He has worked as an expert consultant to many businesses, especially in the area of human behavior, specializing in organizational behavior and management. Prof. Lamberton has had many years of experience teaching management, human relations, and business communications classes at Central Oregon Community College and at Linfield College. He lives in Bend, Oregon, with his wife, Ruth, who is an artist.

He holds two degrees in English, one from Walla Walla University and the other from the University of Nebraska. He also holds an MBA and an advanced professional certificate (APC) in management from Suffolk University in Boston, Massachusetts.

Besides this textbook, he has also coauthored *Working with People: A Human Relations Guide* with Leslie Minor.

©Leslie Minor

Leslie Minor is a social psychologist and sociologist with a bachelor's degree in psychology from the University of Washington (Seattle), and M.A. and Ph.D. degrees from the School of Social Ecology at the University of California (Irvine). Her teaching career spans more than 20 years, with teaching experience at large and small colleges, public and private, rural and urban, two-year and four-year institutions, in online and traditional formats, in the United States and in Singapore. She also has several years of experience in college administration. Dr. Minor believes that her most rigorous and satisfying on-the-job training in teaching and administration came from rearing her three sons, Demitrius, Zamir, and Jawan.

©Lowell Lamberton

Demitrius Zeigler is a freelance project manager and enthusiastic urban farmer currently residing in Southern California. He completed his undergraduate studies in urban and regional planning at Cornell University, and a master's degree at the University of Southern California. Demitrius is currently a small business owner, and has worked as an urban planner, middle school teacher, and business and land use consultant, among other things. But his favorite role is as project manager for his rambunctious young daughter.

©Demitrius Zeigler

Throughout our years of teaching and consulting in the fields of social science and organizational behavior, we have become increasingly aware of the need for a textbook that is down to earth, experience based, and grounded in sound research and theory. We believe strongly in the importance of understanding the relationship between self-esteem and human relations, and, by extension, the relationship between human relations skills and ongoing career success. On the other hand, we do not condone the approach of the "self-esteem peddlers" who encourage self-esteem building outside of a context of the real world. What realistic strategies and techniques can we teach our students to encourage their growth in human relations success, on and off the job site? How can students tap into the power that comes from working well in one-on-one situations, in groups, and in organizations large and small?

Human Relations: Strategies for Success attempts to provide answers to these questions and guidance in developing human relations skills that transfer from the classroom to the real world of work. Our commitment to the creation of a book that is at once interesting to read, motivating to study, and relevant to a wide variety of students has been the driving force behind *Human Relations: Strategies for Success.*

This text covers time-tested, research-based social science and management principles, as well as newer theories and philosophies of human relations drawn from management theory, group theory, personality theory, and relationship theory. More than ever, effective human relations skills are crucial to business success as organizations grow and compete in a global business environment. Employees must have the knowledge and skill to adapt to a workplace where change is as frequent as it is inevitable.

FEATURES OF THE SIXTH EDITION

This sixth edition features the following changes from previous editions:

Chapter 1
- New introductory vignette is more workplace-related, current, and better sets the tone for the book
- Updated figures and diagrams
- Updated demographic data
- New, more contemporary "Case Studies" to reinforce Chapter 1 themes
- Minor textual edits throughout the chapter to update contemporary understanding of issues

Chapter 2
- New text revisions and inserts throughout the chapter to promote understanding and clarity

PREFACE   v

- Revised figure(s)
- Minor textual edits throughout chapter to update contemporary understanding of issues from late second-decade perspectives

Chapter 3

- Two new, more contemporary "Case Studies" provided to reinforce Chapter 3 themes
- Minor textual edits throughout the chapter to update contemporary understanding of issues
- Updated "Real World Examples" for better continuity

Chapter 4

- Minor textual edits throughout the chapter to update contemporary interpretation of issues
- Condensed and consolidated material on attitudes and values to concentrate a focus on the most relevant aspects of values and attitudes in the workplace
- Updated historical references and research study results
- New case study on "Relationships in the HR"

Chapter 5

- New text revisions and inserts throughout the chapter to promote understanding and clarity
- Improved presentation of figures, along with other layout improvements
- New figures provided to illustrate changing demographic and workplace realities
- Minor textual edits throughout the chapter to update contemporary understanding of issues
- New cases to reflect realities of motivating new generations of communicators

Chapter 6

- Updated opening vignette to reflect more contemporary workplace scenario
- Subsection on "Online Communication" has been included to provide students with strategies for successful online communication, as well as the pitfalls that can occur with these transactions
- New "Real World" examples connect students' learning about communication with a prominent contemporary workplace scenario
- Improved presentation of figures, and other layout improvements

Chapter 7

- Minor textual edits throughout the chapter to update contemporary understanding of issues
- Updated discussion of quality organizations, more in keeping with current practice
- Consolidated material on corporate/organizational culture and the "new" corporate culture

Chapter 8

- Updated discussion on Gardner's "Ninth Intelligence"
- Minor textual edits throughout the chapter to update contemporary understanding of issues
- Added section on positive intelligence and inner saboteurs
- Streamlined "The Games People Play" section
- Streamlined "Working It Out" section
- New "Strategy" on positive intelligence and defeating inner saboteurs

Chapter 9

- Updated discussion on organizational changes resulting from technology, (i.e., the rise of the Internet as a critical business tool)
- Minor textual edits throughout the chapter to update contemporary understanding of issues
- Improved presentation of figures, and other layout improvements
- New "Real World" example included to enhance students' connection between conceptual ideas and real-world scenarios
- Streamlined "Real World" examples to promote clarity
- Revised section on international and intercultural business practices

Chapter 10

- Improved presentation of figures, and other layout improvements
- Minor textual edits throughout the chapter to update contemporary understanding of issues
- Enhanced discussion of creativity in the workplace
- Enhanced discussion of Csikszentmihalyi ("big C/little c"), creativity theory, along with enhanced discussion on "Four C's of Creativity"
- New, more contemporary "Real World" examples included.
- Substituted one case for another with greater appeal to students

Chapter 11

- Updated demographic data
- New figures provided to illustrate changing demographic and employment (workplace) trends
- Improved presentation of figures, and other layout improvements
- Minor textual edits throughout the chapter to update contemporary understanding of issues
- Two new cases added for greater interest and variety

Chapter 12

- New information on stress management reflecting the latest research on the topic
- New images and figures provided to illustrate changing demographic and employment workplace trends
- Improved presentation of figures, and other layout improvements
- Streamlined and updated "Real World" examples for continuity
- Textual edits throughout the chapter to update contemporary understanding of issues

Chapter 13

- New and enhanced "More About" sections provide information on ethics in the workplace
- New section, "Customer Service Ethics," provides a more contemporary discussion of ethics in the workplace, including the evolving ethics of the Internet
- Minor textual edits throughout the chapter to update contemporary understanding of issues
- New case on ethics in the workplace

Chapter 14

- Updated demographic data
- New text revisions and inserts throughout the chapter reflect changing U.S. economic and political climate
- New figures provided to illustrate changing demographic and employment (workplace) trends
- Improved presentation of figures, and other layout improvements
- Minor textual edits throughout the chapter to update contemporary understanding of issues
- Expanded section on LGBT issues in the workplace

Chapter 15

- Improved presentation of figures, and other layout improvements
- Minor textual edits throughout the chapter to update contemporary understanding of issues
- New "Real World" examples illustrates contemporary business ethics issues surrounding technology and use of the Internet as a business tool
- New "More About" section discusses the role of and potential ethical issues involved with "hacktivism" in the discussion on whistleblowers
- New "Critical Thinking" question about the role of business ethics in our technologically advanced society

Chapter 16

- Minor textual edits throughout the chapter to update contemporary understanding of issues
- Material on family and individual issues leading to lower productivity in the workplace, with a focus on the most relevant issues occurring in the workplace
- Condensed time management information and movement of applied exercises on time logs to the Online Learning Center
- Maintained and moved all job search material to the Online Learning Center for instructors to allow access to the information
- New "Real World" examples, "More About" sections, and a new "Strategy" on goals definition
- A new case study addressing career preparation

TEXTBOOK-WIDE FEATURES

Each chapter includes the following pedagogical features to facilitate student comprehension and to show how chapter concepts apply to the real world:

> **Strategies for Success.** To highlight the connection between human relations theories and their real-world applications, this textbook contains a unique series of strategies that are integrated into all of the chapters. These strategies offer concrete guidance on how to use human relations skills to address situations that all people face.
>
> **Opening Vignettes.** Each chapter opens with a short vignette to set the tone of the chapter. These vignettes use the narrative approach to make the chapter concepts more real to students at the outset, before they begin to absorb concepts and terms.
>
> **Key Terms.** Important terms are highlighted within the text and called out in the margin. They are also listed at the end of each chapter and are defined in the glossary.

Review Questions and Critical Thinking Questions. Each chapter closes with thought-provoking questions. These questions call on students to go beyond simply reading the chapter, by asking them to consider its implications for their lives in the classroom and beyond. Many questions tap students' creativity and problem-solving abilities as they encourage students to think beyond the boundaries of the book.

Case Studies. Two realistic, job-based case studies (each with questions) are presented in every chapter. These classroom-tested case studies are drawn from familiar experiences in a wide variety of workplace settings. These cases allow students to resolve realistic human relations problems for which there is usually more than one viable solution. Each case study can be used as a springboard for classroom discussion and group problem-solving activities.

"Working It Out" Exercises. For most students, active participation is motivating, rewarding, and crucial to reinforcing learning. In a variety of classroom-tested Working It Out exercises, students are encouraged to build on their human relations skills as they role-play, interview each other, assess their own and each others' strengths and weaknesses, work on setting goals and developing strategies, practice giving and receiving feedback, and explore other applications of chapter topics.

acknowledgments

Many people were involved in the writing and production of this book. We especially would like to thank Jennifer Blankenship, our product developer, and Laura Hurst Spell, our associate portfolio manager from McGraw-Hill Higher Education, for their help, kindness, and patience. Also, our project manager, Danielle Clement, worked very hard with problems, many of them unforeseen. Mike Ablassmeir, our director, has also been hard at work behind the scenes. Thanks, Mike. At home, too many students to mention have offered suggestions and help since the last edition.

We would also like to thank our colleagues and co-workers, friends, and family members for the help they have offered by presenting real-life situations involving human relations issues. This real-life material has been incorporated into opening vignettes, Real World examples, and some of the case studies. A special thanks goes out as well to our families who provided ongoing support and assistance: Lowell's wife, Ruth Lamberton; and Leslie's sons, Demitrius Zeigler, Zamir Zeigler, and Jawan Davis.

Solid previous editions have made this one possible. In the first edition, Betty Morgan, our adjunct editor, created the "Strategies" approach, for which we are extremely grateful. Heather Lamberton spent many hours doing research for nearly all of the chapters. Brian Dement contributed material for the Instructor's Manual and Test Bank. And without Carla Tishler, our first editor, we would never have completed the project. In the second edition, we were helped greatly by Cheryl Adams, adjunct editor for Glencoe/McGraw-Hill. Tammy Higham was invaluable in the creation of the third edition. Of course, the instructors and students who have used the textbook over the past decade have a special place in our hearts as well.

We would also like to thank the following people for their feedback and guidance as reviewers of this edition of the manuscript:

Daniel Bialas, *Muskegon Community College*

James B. Davis, *Pierpont Community & Technical College*

Norma Johansen, *Scottsdale Community College*

CHAPTER ONE

HUMAN RELATIONS
A Background

LEARNING OBJECTIVES

After studying this chapter, you will be able to:

- Define human relations
- Explain the importance of human relations in business
- Discuss the challenges of human relations as these factors affect success in business
- Identify what the study of human relations does not include
- Describe the areas of emphasis for human relations in today's workplace
- Discuss a short history of the study of human relations

STRATEGIES FOR SUCCESS

- Develop Mutual Respect
- Build Your Communication Skills

CHAPTER ONE

1

HUMAN RELATIONS
A Background

≪ ≪ LEARNING OBJECTIVES

After studying this chapter, you will be able to:

LO 1-1   Define human relations.

LO 1-2   Explain the importance of human relations in business.

LO 1-3   Discuss the challenges of human relations as these factors affect success in business.

LO 1-4   Identify what the study of human relations does *not* include.

LO 1-5   Describe the areas of emphasis for human relations in today's workplace.

LO 1-6   Discuss a short history of the study of human relations.

≪ ≪ STRATEGIES FOR SUCCESS

Strategy 1.1   Develop Mutual Respect

Strategy 1.2   Build Your Communication Skills

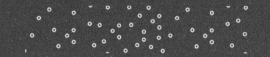

Social Media Meltdown

SITUATION

This had been a long day for Kelly. In her job as an administrative assistant at the county's Small Business and Entrepreneurship Program, she dealt with dozens of people each day, often at a dizzying pace. Now that the

©KieferPix/Shutterstock

work day was ending, she felt frazzled, tired, and angry. The last client of the day had been rude and insulting to her. The client, Mr. Petrov, blamed Kelly for problems with his new business. He wouldn't listen when Kelly tried to explain that she was there as clerical support, not as a consultant; that she could not give him business advice; and that she was not responsible for his business failure. Voices were raised as tempers flared on both sides.

As a public employee, Kelly had signed confidentiality and ethics agreements with her employer agreeing that she would not disclose private information related to the program, and that she would not make public statements that put the organization in a bad light. But this terrible, horrible day ending with Mr. Petrov made her forget about all that. After everyone else had left the office, she logged into her Facebook account and started venting. She posted about her frustrations with the difficult client, called out other clients who had treated her badly, her supervisors, and had a few choice words for county administration in general. She really let them have it.

The next morning as she arrived at work, her supervisor immediately called Kelly into her office and closed the door. "Kelly," she began, "as a public agency, we hold high standards for our office. We work hard to keep our community's trust. With your venting session on your social media page, you violated confidentiality and ethical behavior policies, and tore down the basic integrity of our work here that has taken years to build. Just this morning, I have heard from dozens of people who saw your post and called to complain. I'm going to have to ask for your resignation."

Kelly was in complete shock. She felt sick, and could barely speak. "But . . ." she stammered, "those were my private opinions! I have free speech rights, don't I? Those weren't public statements, it was just my own personal Facebook account! And anyway, I didn't really mean what I said, I was just upset!"

DISCOVERY

As Kelly gathered her belongings and prepared to leave, the seriousness of the situation began to sink in. There was no way she could explain away what she had posted. She had mocked Mr. Petrov, his business, and even his accent. She had made sarcastic and hostile remarks about other clients and county administrators by name, and in detail.

Kelly felt terrible about what she had said. The bitter irony was that she was proud to work for an organization that helped people work toward achieving their dreams. She was filled with remorse and regret. She wished she could apologize to everyone, on the spot.

"It's going to take a miracle for me to make this right with everyone," Kelly thought to herself. Kelly's impulsive behavior had become a human relations nightmare for the organization, clients, staff and administrators, and Kelly herself.

THINK ABOUT IT

Consider the situation Kelly now finds herself in—at what point did her situation became problematic?

As you read through Chapter 1, ask yourself, "Which of the areas of major emphasis in human relations arise with Kelly's situation?"

How can human relations knowledge and skills be used to resolve this situation?

» WHAT IS HUMAN RELATIONS?

The importance of human relations in our personal and work lives cannot be exaggerated. The skills that are necessary for good relations with others are the most important skills anyone can learn in life. Human relations decisions may not involve life-or-death outcomes, but they can have very serious impacts.

human relations

The skill or ability to work effectively through and with other people.

Human relations is the skill or ability to *work effectively through and with other people*. Human relations includes a desire to understand others, their needs and weaknesses, and their talents and abilities. For anyone in a workplace setting, human relations also involves an understanding of how people work together in groups, satisfying both individual needs and group objectives. If an organization is to succeed, the relationships among the people in that organization must be monitored and maintained.

In all aspects of life, you will deal with other people. No matter what you do for a living or how well you do it, your relationship with others is the key to your success or failure. Even when someone is otherwise only average at a job, good human relations skills can usually make that person seem better to others. Sadly, the opposite is also true: Poor human relations skills can make an otherwise able person seem like a poor performer. A doctor who respects patients, a lawyer who listens carefully to clients, a manager who gets along well with others in the workplace: all of these people will most likely be thought of by others as successful.

» THE IMPORTANCE OF HUMAN RELATIONS SKILLS

The ability to create and maintain effective relationships with others is the most important reason to understand human relations. Other reasons for studying human relations include the following:

more about...

Internal customers can be defined as a department's employees, or as employees in other departments within an organization.

trust

Firm belief in the reliability, truth, ability, or strength of someone or something.

1. **Human rights.** Today, managers and employees have a greater awareness of the rights of employees. This awareness calls for more skillful relations among employees, using tact, **trust,** and diplomacy with greater skill. The rights of all others involved in the dealings of an organization must be respected and protected as well. In today's workplace, the term *internal customer* is often used. This identifies a new attitude toward employees as the other customers in a company. Companies must also protect the human rights of traditional customers, managers, and even competitors.

2. **The global marketplace.** The United States seems to have fallen into disfavor in many countries—even countries we had long considered to be our friends. Often, when anti-American stories are told, they involve Americans using poor human relations skills when doing business with people from other cultures. Improving interpersonal skills (the skills

associated with getting along with others) can be a factor in fighting the widespread anti-Americanism that sometimes seems to be growing worldwide.[1]

3. **Emphasis on people as human resources.** Two decades ago, many forecasters predicted that by this time in history, strong computer skills would be the number one factor in the workplace. However, now, perhaps more than ever, managers and corporate planners are placing great emphasis on the human factor. The two sets of behaviors now considered the most important for new job applicants are communication skills and human relations abilities.[2] This trend, emphasis on what are often called business "soft skills," will likely continue in the future.

4. **Renewed emphasis on working groups.** Today's employees tend to like working as teams and being involved in making decisions as a group. Helping groups work well together in such endeavors (as either a team member or leader) requires a great deal of human relations skill. Both managers and employees need to understand the dynamic of group interaction if such participation is to be effective.

5. **Increasing diversity in the workplace.** Few countries on earth contain the diversity of race, religion, and culture that exists in the United States. The number of foreign-born Americans in the United States in 2000 was estimated at 28 million. By the year 2014 the number had grown to 42 million (about 13 percent of the total population), and the number is projected to reach 78 million by the year 2060.[3] The United States gains an international migrant every 33 seconds.[4] In addition to this reality, the number of women in the workplace globally has increased over the past decade, and more employees are staying in the workplace past typical retirement age.[5] Experts predict that the number of older workers will increase more than five times faster than the overall labor force over the next several years, and that ethnic and racial diversity will continue to increase as well.[6] A deep understanding of the differences that diversity brings is one of the most important skills in human relations.

Group work is a necessity in today's workforce.
©Uber Images/Shutterstock

Human Relations and You

The study of human relations can help you in several ways. Human relations skills can help you get a job, enjoy your work, be more productive at it, and stay there longer with better chances for advancement. An understanding of yourself and others can help you be happier and more productive in all areas of your life.

You, the Manager

A percentage of students who read this book will one day become managers. For a manager, no skill area is more important than human relations abilities. A manager with good human relations skills will retain employees longer, be more productive, and provide employees with an enjoyable environment. The most common reason for failure in the job of manager is faulty human relations skills.[7] Because interpersonal skills are so important, experts often suggest that new managers should put as much effort into studying people as they put into developing technical skills.[8]

You, the Entrepreneur

In the 21st century, an increasing number of today's business students are entering the exciting realm of entrepreneurship: owning their own businesses. When you are the owner and operator of a business, your people skills—or human relations—are the most important factors in your success. In an e-commerce business, although there is less face-to-face contact with customers and suppliers, the ability to work with people and to fulfill their needs remains extremely crucial to success. For example, in 2011, an employee of a firm known as Ocean Marketing single-handedly destroyed the integrity of his firm with his lack of human relations skills in dealing with a customer inquiry.[9] This led to a public outcry on the Internet which wreaked havoc for both the employee and the company, illustrating that, even in e-commerce business, human relations skills matter immensely.

In a larger sense, your knowledge of human relations helps the work you do—or the business you own—provide fulfillment. Famed Russian author Fyodor Dostoyevsky wrote, "If it were desired to reduce a man to nothingness, it would be necessary only to give his work a character of uselessness."[10] Many entrepreneurs become business owners to escape the feeling of uselessness associated with their former jobs. The entrepreneur is in the position of being able to control the human climate of the business he or she owns and operates.

> **more about...**
>
> An **entrepreneur** is someone who organizes and assumes the risks of beginning a business enterprise.

You, the Employee

Underdeveloped interpersonal skills represent the single most important reason for failure at a job. This is especially true in the early days and weeks on a new assignment.[11] Making a good impression on your superiors, your peers, and all other co-workers will set you on a good track. Developing interpersonal skills is extremely important to the advancement of your career and will affect the ways in which your fellow employees, supervisors, and customers view your overall performance.[12]

» CURRENT CHALLENGES IN HUMAN RELATIONS

Young Millennials entering the job market for the first time can find that good, sustainable-wage jobs are hard to come by, and that advancement can be difficult at first. The problems faced by this group, and by the slightly older "Generation X," are often blamed on the "Baby Boomers," the late-middle-aged people who are mostly in management positions above them. Although a "generation gap" is nothing new in the American workplace, the potential friction between up-and-coming Millennials and not-yet-ready-to-retire Baby Boomers is one that may have a direct and profound effect on relations in the workplace.[13] You will learn more about this topic in Chapter 14, which discusses issues of workplace diversity.

Generation X is the generation of Americans born between 1965 and 1984, following the Baby Boomers who were born during the years 1946–1964.

Millennials generally refers to Americans born after 1984, (but has been used on those born as early as 1978 or 1980), until around 2004. This term especially applies to students who are now graduating from high school and either going to college or entering the job market. The Millennial Generation is a fast-growing segment of today's workforce.[14]

more about...

Increased Competition in the Workplace

Competitiveness reaches into all geographic areas—urban, suburban, and rural—and affects all businesses, large and small. Small businesses may feel pressure to meet the high international standards of the foreign market, and of the huge multinational companies that dominate the economy. When a chain retailer such as Walmart moves into a small town, the competition felt by local business owners is very real. Likewise, the increasing number of people doing business on the Internet has created a source of competition unlike anything else in human history.

Secure, well-paid jobs are more competitive than ever before. Having a college degree is no longer a ticket to a meaningful career, as it was just a generation ago. This new reality causes a great deal of frustration for many people in the workplace, and many human relations problems can result.

Another very important factor in competition is the current strength of some of America's trading partners in Asian countries, especially China, which have an ever-increasing share of the world economy. For example, China—which will surpass the United States to become the world's largest economy by 2024—has had an average annual growth rate of 9.69 percent from 1989 until 2017.[15]

Contrast that with an average annual growth rate of not more than 4 percent in United States during the same time period, and it becomes easier to understand American workers' general anxiety about their role in an increasingly competitive "global workplace."

Experts predict that emerging nations such as China, India, Brazil, Russia, and South Africa will continue to have a major impact on world markets, and continue their growth and competition with the traditionally dominant West.[16]

Most families now need income from both adult members to survive comfortably. This reality has placed a strain on the family and its members—a strain that is felt in the workplace in several ways. First, additional financial pressures cause workplace stress. Second, the time needed for the everyday realities of child rearing—such as visits to the family doctor and transportation to and from school—create difficulties for everyone involved.

Divorce: a heavy impact on employees' lives

©Latin Stock Collection/Corbis

Single-Parent Families and Divorce

Two important factors have contributed to the existence of a higher number of single parents than was prevalent among the Baby Boomer generation: a high divorce rate and an increase in the number of never-married parents. The parent—often the mother—must be the provider, taxi service, spiritual guide, and emotional support source. These many roles often result in a spillover effect of frustration and stress in the workplace. This type of worker can be truly overloaded.

A divorced person typically has to go through a period of emotional recovery, during which many emotional issues can form. Such issues often negatively affect job performance and attitudes, harming relationships with co-workers, bosses, and fellow employees. Besides the already-heavy burdens of single parenthood that divorced, single workers have, they are often dealing with challenging issues of self-worth and self-esteem.

Two Generations of Dependents

People are living longer now than in previous decades.[17] This rise in life expectancy, along with fewer high-income jobs for senior citizens, and cuts to pension funds and post-retirement health insurance, means that many middle-aged adults now find themselves helping to support their own children along with their aging parents and parents-in-law—all at the same time. These middle-aged adults who find themselves squeezed for time and finances are often referred to as the "sandwich generation" (with the elderly dependent parents as one piece of bread, and the dependent children as the other, and the middle-aged adults in the middle). The added responsibilities exist when parents or in-laws live with the adult children and their families, but also when elderly parents live alone or in retirement homes. The emotional impact affects all involved, including the dependent parent who usually would prefer self-sufficiency.

» WHAT HUMAN RELATIONS IS *NOT*

Now that you know what human relations is, how it has developed into what it is, and challenges within human relations, it is time to look at some characteristics it *does not* have. First, human relations is not a study in understanding human behavior in order to manipulate others. Good human relations means being real, positive, and honest. Practicing effective human relations means *being yourself at your very best.*

Second, learning better human relations skills is not a cure-all. Nor is it a quick fix for deep and ongoing personal problems. The skills you will learn in this book are skills to be built upon, developed, and tried out whenever you can as part of your own experience on the job and throughout your life.

Last, human relations is not just *common sense.* This argument is often used by people who think a book like this in unnecessary. "Common sense," they may say, "will carry you through!" In the area of human relations, however, common sense (meaning ordinary good sense and judgment) is all too *un*common. The abuses of many workers on the job today, the misunderstandings that cost thousands of companies millions of dollars every year, the unhappiness of many workers with the jobs they have: all of these factors illustrate the need for a strong foundation in human relations—even if much of it seems like simple common sense.

Despite all of the progress in human relations during the past decades, the 21st century has produced some "nay-sayers" who will argue that mistreating employees actually works. According to *Bloomberg Businessweek* magazine, Dish Network's boss, Charlie Ergen, makes that claim. He has said that "ruling with an iron hand" is one of his success secrets.[18] Perhaps, then, it is not surprising that his company was named "America's worst company to work for" by a watchdog website.[19] It remains to be seen how successful this approach will be for Dish Network in a highly competitive global industry.

》 AREAS OF MAJOR EMPHASIS

In the broadest sense, the study of human relations has two goals: personal development and growth, and achievement of an organization's objectives. (See Figure 1.1.) All of the following areas of emphasis take both of those

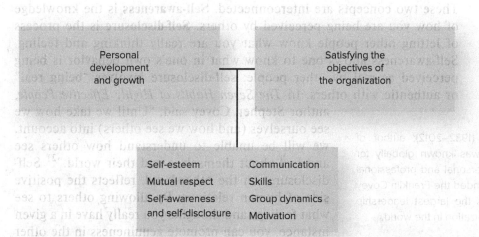

figure 1.1

MAJOR GOALS AND EMPHASIS AREAS OF HUMAN RELATIONS

Which of these areas do you personally consider most important to effective human relations?

goals into consideration. You will notice that each of the areas is further developed in the following chapters of this book. Most of them overlap, and some are dependent upon others. Those relationships will become clearer as you read further.

Self-Esteem

self-esteem

The regard in which an individual holds himself or herself.

Self-esteem is your feeling of confidence and worth as a person. Psychological research has shown that lower self-esteem is related to a variety of mental health problems, including alcoholism, anxiety, and depression—all of which cause problems on the job. Higher self-esteem, on the other hand, improves attitudes, job morale, and overall quality of life. In the workplace, healthy self-esteem is the key to top performance and high-quality work—especially when the work directly affects other people.

Self-esteem is a buzzword in many business circles today. Most Americans seem to have discovered this important part of themselves and its influence on every other factor in their lives. More than a mere buzzword, though, self-esteem is at the core of most issues in human relations. Because it is so important, Chapter 2 is dedicated to that subject.

Mutual Respect

mutual respect

The positive consideration or regard that two people have for each other.

Notice that this isn't simply respect, but *mutual* respect. **Mutual respect,** the positive consideration or regard that two people have for each other, can exist only when your self-esteem is stable. If your self-esteem is too fragile, you will have little energy left for cultivating mutual respect. Also, without trust, mutual respect is meaningless. Many human relations specialists rate trust as the single most important element in human relations.[20] People at all levels of an organization need trust and mutual respect to perform at their best.

Self-Awareness and Self-Disclosure

self-awareness

The knowledge of how you are being perceived by others.

self-disclosure

The process of letting other people know what you are really thinking and feeling.

These two concepts are interconnected. **Self-awareness** is the knowledge of how you are being perceived by others. **Self-disclosure** is the process of letting other people know what you are really thinking and feeling. Self-awareness allows one to know what in one's own behavior is being perceived as real by other people; self-disclosure involves "being real" or authentic with others. In *The Seven Habits of Highly Effective People,* author Stephen Covey said, "Until we take how we see ourselves (and how we see others) into account, we will be unable to understand how others see and feel about themselves and their world."[21] Self-disclosure, on the other hand, reflects the positive side of human relations: By allowing others to see what feelings and thoughts you really have in a given instance, you can promote genuineness in the other

more about...

Stephen Covey (1932–2012), author of numerous books, was known globally for his emphasis on personal and professional integrity. He co-founded the Franklin Covey Company, which is the largest leadership development organization in the world.

person. A positive side effect is that your relationship with the other person is likely to become closer.

Communication Skills

Communication is the process of sending ideas, thoughts, and feelings from one individual or group to another, and having them received in the way you intended.[22] The communication process is at the heart of all managerial functions, and it is directly related to success or failure at the managerial level. It is also a vital part of all personal interactions. When a human relations problem emerges, miscommunication is usually involved.

If you are to grow either as an individual or in groups, effective communication is essential.[23] Much of your success depends on your ability to express ideas and concepts precisely. Part of that ability is based on your listening level, which includes listening for feelings and emotions as well as for objective content.

communication

The giving and receiving of ideas, feelings, and information among people.

Group Dynamics

Whenever two or more people form a relationship, there is, in effect, a group. Once a group is formed, it immediately requires understanding, planning, and organizational tactics appropriate to groups. Thus, understanding **group dynamics**—the ways in which groups operate—is a cornerstone in the study of human relations.[24]

As important as our individuality is, nearly everything that people value in life can be achieved only through groups.[25] For success, people learn how to make group processes more effective. In *The New Realities,* well-known management expert Peter Drucker said, "Management is about human beings. Its task is to make people capable of *joint performance,* to make their strengths effective and their weaknesses irrelevant."[26]

Knowledge of group dynamics includes understanding conflict management. Much of good human relations involves preventing negative conflict.

Peter Drucker (1909–2005), a management expert for over 60 years, authored several books that still carry the same strong impact as they did when he was still alive. His first influential work was the 1945 study *The Concept of a Corporation,* which compared his ideal of management with the management of General Motors.

group dynamics

The set of interpersonal relationships within a group that determine how group members relate to one another and that influence task performance.

Motivation

People often use the term **motivation** to describe the force that gets them to do their tasks. It is no longer enough to threaten punishment or even to reward a job well done. Motivation derives from the needs of an individual and of a group. It is also a major element in understanding human relations.

motivation

The force of the need or desire to act.

» A BRIEF HISTORY OF HUMAN RELATIONS

One cannot fully appreciate the present state of human relations without at least a partial understanding of the past. The history of human relations is essential to a thorough understanding of its place in today's world.

Human relations has been important ever since human beings began to live together in groups. Of course, attitudes toward power—especially the sharing of power—have changed through the centuries. Most societies no longer tolerate slavery, nor do most cultures blindly follow powerful leaders as they once did. Thus, the history of human relations problems can be viewed in different ways during different times.

The Early Years

Human relations began to be an issue as we know it today around the early to mid-1800s. Figure 1.2 gives a thumbnail view of major events in the field. The Knights of Labor, founded in 1869, was an organization much like the labor unions that came later. The founders of this group denounced the bad working conditions and unfair treatment in many workplaces of the time.[27] The labor union movement might never have started if human relations between managers and workers had been better, and if working conditions had been more tolerable. Anyone who is blindly anti-union needs to understand that negative management and poor working conditions pushed workers to organize into unions.

In early 19th-century England, a man named Robert Owen came up with the amazing idea that treating workers better would actually increase productivity and, thus, profits. Owen introduced many reforms in the industry of the time. For example, he stopped employing young children in his factory. He also encouraged his workforce to stay sober. Although by today's standards these measures might seem quite basic, Owen was quite progressive for his time.[28]

Like Robert Owen, Andrew Ure (also from Great Britain) was interested in human relations in manufacturing companies. In 1835, Ure published a book called *The Philosophy of Manufacturers*. This book suggested that workers should have medical help, hot tea on a regular basis, good ventilation, and even sick leave—again, all ideas that were advanced for their time.[29]

Owen and Ure were definitely not typical. Both in Europe and in the United States, the first decades of the Industrial Revolution were full of abuses by bosses against workers, especially workers with few skills. Many of the immigrants to America during that time were forced to face inhumane working conditions.

Some of the better employers built "company towns." These were settlements, owned by the company, where workers would live in standard housing built by the company, buy supplies at the company-owned store, and even

---

more about...

Robert Owen (1771–1858) was a Welsh-born social reformer who influenced both English and American employers. His philosophy was known as "Owenism" and his followers Owenites.

more about...

Andrew Ure (1778–1857) was, like many of his time, an avid enthusiast of the Industrial Revolution. He was the first person to write a detailed study of manufacturers and their management processes.

Max Weber (1864–1920), who was a sociologist, philosopher, and political economist, is best known for writing *The Protestant Ethic and the Spirit of Capitalism* (1904).

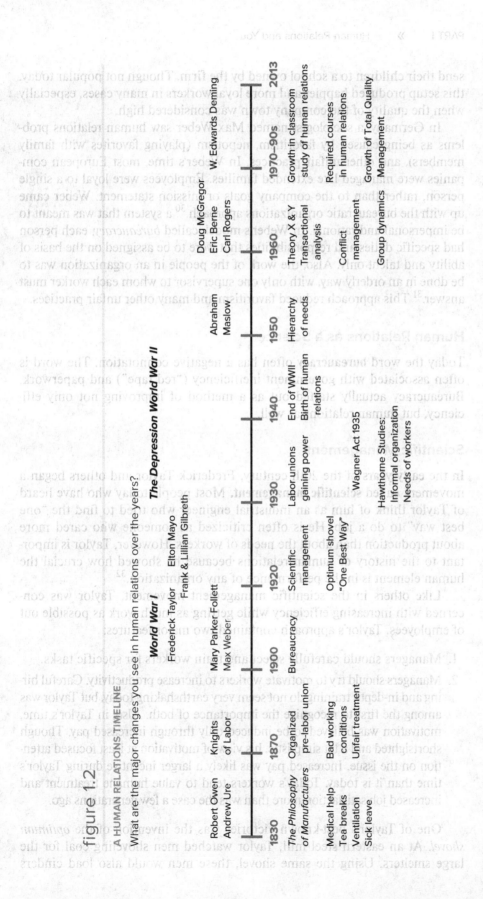

figure 1.2

A HUMAN RELATIONS TIMELINE

What are the major changes you see in human relations over the years?

1830	1870	1900	1920	1930	1940	1950	1960	1970–90s	2013

The Philosophy of Manufacturers | *World War I* | *The Depression World War II* |

Robert Owen
Andrew Ure

Knights of Labor

Mary Parker Follett
Max Weber

Frederick Taylor
Frank & Lillian Gilbreth

Elton Mayo

Abraham Maslow

Doug McGregor
Eric Berne
Carl Rogers

W. Edwards Deming

Medical help
Tea breaks
Ventilation
Sick leave

Organized
pre-labor union

Bad working
conditions

Unfair treatment

Bureaucracy

Scientific
management

Optimum shovel
"One Best Way"

Labor unions
gaining power

Wagner Act 1935

Hawthorne Studies:
Informal organization
Needs of workers

End of WWII
Birth of human
relations

Hierarchy
of needs

Theory X & Y

Transactional
analysis

Conflict
management

Group dynamics

Growth in classroom
study of human relations

Required courses
in human relations

Growth of Total Quality
Management

send their children to a school owned by the firm. Though not popular today, this setup produced happier and more loyal workers in many cases, especially when the quality of the company town was considered high.

In Germany, a sociologist named Max Weber saw human relations problems as being caused by favoritism, nepotism (playing favorites with family members), and other unfair practices. In Weber's time, most European companies were managed like extended families. Employees were loyal to a single person, rather than to the company goals or mission statement. Weber came up with the bureaucratic organizations approach,[30] a system that was meant to be impersonal and rational. In Weber's model, called *bureaucracy,* each person had specific duties and responsibilities that were to be assigned on the basis of ability and talent only. Also, the work of the people in an organization was to be done in an orderly way, with only one supervisor to whom each worker must answer.[31] This approach reduced favoritism and many other unfair practices.

Human Relations as a Science

bureaucracy

A formal organization in which each person has specific duties and responsibilities and is assigned to only one supervisor.

Today the word **bureaucracy** often has a negative connotation. The word is often associated with government inefficiency ("red tape") and paperwork. Bureaucracy actually started out as a method of improving not only efficiency, but human relations as well.

Scientific Management

scientific management

A system based upon scientific and engineering principles.

In the early years of the 20th century, Frederick Taylor and others began a movement called **scientific management.** Most people today who have heard of Taylor think of him as an industrial engineer who tried to find the "one best way" to do a job. He is often criticized as someone who cared more about production than about the needs of workers. However, Taylor is important to the history of human relations because he showed how crucial the human element is in the performance of any organization.[32]

Like others in the scientific management movement, Taylor was concerned with increasing efficiency while getting as much work as possible out of employees. Taylor's approach contained two major features:

1. Managers should carefully select and train workers for specific tasks.
2. Managers should try to motivate workers to increase productivity. Careful hiring and in-depth training do not seem very earthshaking today, but Taylor was among the first to recognize the importance of both. Also, in Taylor's time, motivation was believed to be induced only through increased pay. Though shortsighted and a bit simplistic, his view of motivation at least focused attention on the issue. Increased pay was likely a larger incentive during Taylor's time than it is today. Today's workers tend to value humane treatment and increased job satisfaction more than was the case a few generations ago.

One of Taylor's best-known victories was the invention of the *optimum shovel.* At an eastern steel mill, Taylor watched men shoveling coal for the large smelters. Using the same shovel, these men would also load cinders into waste containers. After carefully studying both processes, Taylor came up with two shovels: a much larger shovel for the light cinders and a smaller shovel for the heavier coal. This shovel was exactly the right size and weight to allow the maximum work without the need for frequent rest periods. The productivity of the steel mill rose immediately, making Taylor and scientific management both very popular.[33]

Frank and Lillian Gilbreth

Living around the same time period as Taylor, Frank and Lillian Gilbreth were a married couple who were both industrial engineers—and scientific managers. The Gilbreths became especially well-known for their research study of bricklayers. Frank Gilbreth identified 18 different motions that had been used by bricklayers, apparently for as long as people had been laying bricks. By inventing some labor-saving devices and by changing the basic routine, the Gilbreths reduced those 18 motions to 5. The result was a system of bricklaying with more than double the productivity of the old system.

Lillian Gilbreth was especially interested in studying workers and their reactions to working under stressful conditions. She taught the importance of standard work days, relaxed and regular lunch breaks, and periodic rest periods. Her life's work helped influence Congress to pass child labor laws. The mother of 12 children, Lillian was among the first women in America to receive

Frederick Winslow Taylor (1856–1915) was also renowned as an inventor; the optimum shovel is perhaps his best-known invention. By experimenting with different materials, he was able to design shovels that would permit workers to shovel for the whole day.

Frank Gilbreth (1868–1924)

Lillian Gilbreth (1878–1972)

Frank and Lillian Gilbreth were pioneers in time and motion study. Besides their early work refining the bricklaying process, they had a great impact on medicine by significantly reducing the amount of time patients had to spend on the surgical table. Thus the Gilbreths were also responsible for saving many people's lives.

Source: Daniel A. Wren, *The Evolution of Management Thought,* 2nd ed. (New York: Wiley, 1979), p. 171.

more about...

more about...

FRANK AND LILLIAN GILBRETH

Pioneers in scientific management, especially time and motion study, in the late 1800s and early 1900s.

©George Rinhart/Corbis/Getty Images

a Ph.D. in psychology. In her later life, she became known as "The First Lady of Management." She was an important early force in the human relations movement as well.[34]

Mary Parker Follett

In the early years of the 20th century, Mary Parker Follett became known for her lectures and writings on what we would now call human relations issues. Follett was a member of the upper class—not someone with a work-related background.

She lectured widely on issues of human relations among workers, however, and was quite influential.

Follett taught three concepts that were ahead of their time. First, she held that workers should be allowed to be involved in decisions affecting them. To her it was logical that the people closest to the action could make the best decisions. Second, she stressed that the workplace is dynamic—that is, constantly changing. She felt that inflexible, static rules were potentially harmful to maintaining a productive workforce. Finally, Mary Parker Follett believed that the main job of managers at all levels was to maintain positive relationships with workers. Happy workers with a sense of belonging, she said, would end up making more money for the company and would remain at the same job for a longer time.

These three concepts define Follett as a very important early pioneer of the human relations movement, and definitely ahead of her time.[35]

> **Mary Parker Follett (1868–1933)**
>
> Mary Parker Follett attended the college known today as Radcliffe. She studied philosophy and political science but became deeply interested in management. Always the advocate of humanizing the workplace, she stressed people over technology. One of her pieces of advice to engineers was "Don't hug your blueprints!"
>
> Source: Henry Metcalf and Lyndall Urwick, eds., *Dynamic Administration: The Collected Papers of Mary Parker Follett* (New York: Harper & Row, 1940).

...more about...

The Hawthorne Experiment

Hawthorne Experiment
A five-year study conducted at the Western Electric plant in Hawthorne, Illinois, that showed that workers performed better when someone was paying attention to them.

In the late 1920s, a group of scientific management scholars went to a factory in Hawthorne, Illinois, to study the effects of physical factors on workers and their productivity. Each time they would try an experiment, productivity would go up. However, when they reversed the experiment, productivity would still increase. The most popular of these experiments was with lighting. When the lights in this Western Electric assembly plant were brightened, productivity increased. However, when the lights were dimmed, productivity went up again.

The researchers were really confused. Why would workers work even harder under such poor conditions as very dim lighting? The problem confronting these scientific management scholars attracted the attention of Elton Mayo, a social psychologist from Harvard University. He traveled to Hawthorne and stayed. For nearly five years, from 1927 to 1932, he and his Harvard colleagues studied the **Hawthorne Experiment**.[36]

...more about...

Elton Mayo (1880–1940) was born in Australia and relocated to the United States in 1922. He was the driving force behind the Hawthorne Studies, and translations of his work appeared in German, Spanish, Italian, Japanese, Arabic, and other languages.

Two important discoveries came from this five-year study. First, Mayo showed that the workers at Hawthorne performed better because someone was paying attention to them. This attention was more than they had been accustomed to receiving at work, and they responded with extra motivation. Second, Mayo found that the relationships that had formed naturally in the workplace made up what he called the **informal organization.** On days when a worker would not be as motivated as usual, the expectations of the group would make up the difference, and productivity would remain high.

Recent research has suggested that the Hawthorne workers were very likely motivated by fear as well as by attention. Whether or not this new interpretation is true, the findings of Elton Mayo influenced decades of thought on the role of human relations on the job. Whether reacting to fear or attention, human relations issues are still the driving force in the workers' behavior. Much of what has been written and practiced since Hawthorne has been influenced by what Mayo himself concluded—and although the findings have been reexamined, the original shape of those findings still influences people today.[37]

Human Relations and Management

Probably the most important improvement Elton Mayo brought about was to change the way management looked at workers. Rather than seeing workers mostly as people who need wages, managers now began to understand that the complex needs of workers include a unique combination of values, attitudes, and desires.

By the time Elton Mayo left Hawthorne, the Great Depression was several years old. Although the interest in human relations still existed, the stubborn fact was that a ruthless manager could mistreat workers now without much fear of losing them. After all, jobs were very hard to find.

During the Great Depression, labor unions began to gain power. Congress passed the Wagner Act in 1935, giving unions and union members more rights than they had enjoyed before. For example, businesses were now forced to negotiate contracts with union representatives.[38] Although this new union activity was good for workers, it did not necessarily mean that human relations issues were being emphasized. Many managers still had the attitude that one needed only to "fire the problems and hire the solutions." Unions usually emphasized salary and benefits for workers rather than the more abstract issues of employee treatment and workplace morale.

By the time the Japanese bombed Pearl Harbor in 1941, the Depression was showing some signs of lifting. Once the country began gearing up its manufacturing sector for World War II, the workplace was affected drastically. With hundreds of thousands of young workers going overseas to fight, employers were forced to hire nearly anybody who would work. Sadly, human relations in the workplace always seems to be affected by the job market, and

informal organization
The ever-changing set of relationships and interactions that are not formally put together; they form naturally in the workplace.

The Wagner Act, also called the National Labor Relations Act, made it illegal for employers to use scare tactics or other techniques to prevent employees from forming or joining unions.

more about...

The Great Depression: an era of human relations setbacks

Source: Courtesy of the Franklin D. Roosevelt Presidential Library & Museum, Hyde Park, New York.

Theories X and Y

Theory X managers see workers as lacking ambition, disliking work, and wanting security above all else. Theory Y managers see workers as enjoying work, being able to assume responsibility, and being creative.

Total Quality Management (TQM)

A management organizational philosophy that was very influential in the 1980s and 1990s, which stated that quality must be present in the product or the service produced, and in the process itself of producing the goods or service. **See quality movement**.

more about...

Douglas McGregor (1906–1964) was a pioneer in industrial relations. His creation of Theory X and Theory Y allowed management to understand their influence on employee morale and productivity. Although well-respected in his lifetime, his peak popularity did not come until the 1990s, 30 years after his death.

the onset of World War II was no exception. Managers knew their employees would be very hard to replace, so treatment of workers temporarily improved. Cases of sexism, racism, and sexual harassment, however, were all too common.

Throughout the war, and in the years immediately following, many studies were being done on human relations factors. The noted psychologist Abraham Maslow devised a "hierarchy of needs," which teaches that people tend to satisfy their needs in a certain order; you will read more about this in Chapter 5.

Studies continued through the 20th century, and in 1960, psychologist Douglas McGregor wrote *The Human Side of Enterprise,* considered by some to be the most important book on human relations ever written.

McGregor introduced the concepts of **Theory X** and **Theory Y**. These two theories are held by different types of managers, based on their ways of looking at workers. Theory X managers see workers as lacking ambition, disliking work, and wanting security above all else. Theory Y managers, on the other hand, see workers as happy to work, able to assume responsibility, and overall quite creative. These two theories—especially Theory Y—have influenced thinking in both management and human relations since the year of their creation.

Human Relations, History, and the Individual

The second half of the 20th century brought a great deal of attention to the study of the workplace from psychologists and other social scientists. In the early 1960s, Eric Berne had created his famous *Transactional Analysis* method of understanding interpersonal communication. Carl Rogers published his findings on the development of the personality, group dynamics, and conflict management. Some managers began experimenting with participative decision making and other human relations-based management.

By the late 1960s, an era had started that would affect human relations for years. A new emphasis was placed on the rights and needs of the individual person. For the first time, it was popular in this culture to "do your own thing." Perhaps even more importantly, other people were allowed to do their own thing as well. Also new was the revolutionary attitude toward success as having to do with people, rather than just with money. Many of today's middle managers were members of an emerging youth subculture at that time, sometimes referred to as hippies. As many of those young people grew into leadership roles, influence from that era grew and has still not yet peaked.

By 1980 **Total Quality Management (TQM)** had been introduced in the United States as it had been three decades earlier in Japan. The man responsible for this new movement was an American named

W. Edwards Deming. This important school of thought held that the *process* of whatever happens in an organization is more important than the *product*. Doing away with targets, "zero defects" programs, and slogans, the TQM people concentrated on the process—which inevitably includes people and relationships. The work that was pioneered by Elton Mayo and others became refocused with a process emphasis. People in organizations participated at work to an extent unimagined before. Working conditions had come to be seen as the most important single issue in many companies.[39]

By the late 1980s, Total Quality Management had changed industry both in the United States and abroad. From the mid-1990s to the present, the label "TQM" has been heard less frequently. However, the process of TQM survives under other names—sometimes simply "quality"—and remains an important part of many successful organizations. There must be quality in the process itself, as well as in the final product. Of course, TQM covers many other organizational issues besides human relations, but the positive effect of the quality movement on human relations promises to be lasting.

The 1970s through the 2000s saw a tremendous growth in the academic study of human relations. Today, an increasing number of college business and industrial education departments require courses in human relations. This trend reflects the growing awareness of the importance of understanding, and working with, others effectively. As the global economy continues to develop, human relations assumes a broader significance.

STRATEGIES FOR SUCCESS

Strategy 1.1   Develop Mutual Respect

1. Develop your self-esteem.
2. Develop your self-awareness.
3. Develop trust.
4. Learn to self-disclose.
5. Cultivate mutual respect.

Although these are big tasks, they can be achieved by anyone with a clear understanding of human relations.

1. **Develop your self-esteem.** First, you must develop your self-esteem. Self-esteem can be encouraged or damaged very early in life, and some people who have self-esteem problems do not even realize it. However, no matter what your age or self-esteem level, you can always learn to like yourself more. Chapter 2 will cover self-esteem in great detail and provide tips on how you can build your own self-esteem.

2. **Develop your self-awareness.** Without self-awareness, you will find it hard to develop self-esteem or any of the other issues that are important to successful human relations. This is because you must know yourself before you can value yourself highly and express yourself honestly to others. You will learn more about how to develop self-awareness in Chapter 3.

3. **Develop trust.** Without adequate self-esteem, you will find it difficult to trust. With trust, however, you will find that your relationships will grow deep and meaningful, and that you will be able to tell other people what's in your "gut" without unnecessary fear.

4. **Learn to self-disclose.** As you develop trust, you will be able to disclose more about yourself. Self-disclosure and trust are areas that you can develop simultaneously: As you learn to self-disclose appropriately, you will develop deeper trust in your relationships. Chapter 3 will cover self-disclosure in greater detail.

5. **Cultivate mutual respect.** Developing trust will lead to mutual respect, as you forge relationships that are based on honesty. You will learn more about talking "from your gut," also called self-disclosure, in Chapter 3.

Strategy 1.2   **Build Your Communication Skills**

1. Learn to communicate honestly.
2. Learn what effective communication is and how to develop this skill.
3. Know what you are communicating to others by increasing your self-awareness.
4. Know what you are communicating to others by your nonverbal signals.
5. Learn to deal effectively with conflict.

1. **Learn to communicate honestly.** When you communicate honestly by learning to say what you feel, by establishing trust, and by using effective and appropriate self-disclosure, your listeners will learn to respect and trust you more.

2. **Learn what effective communication is and how to develop this skill.** Effective communication is communicating so that your listener receives the message you intended to send. When you use honesty and appropriate self-disclosure, and state your message in a clear way that shows high self-esteem, you will send your message more effectively.

3. **Know what you are communicating to others by increasing your self-awareness.** If you have low self-awareness, you may communicate so that your true meaning is unclear. By working on your self-awareness, you will improve your communication skill.

4. **Know what you are communicating to others by your nonverbal signals.** If you give nonverbal signals that are unintended, your message will be different than what you expect. This can lead to confusion and mistrust. Nonverbal communication is covered in more detail in Chapter 6.

5. **Learn to deal effectively with conflict.** Effective communication skill involves the ability to deal with conflict. Chapter 11 will show you how to deal with conflict to restore trust and mutual respect.

CHAPTER ONE SUMMARY

Chapter Summary by Learning Objectives

LO 1-1 Define human relations. Whatever direction your life takes—whether you become a manager, an entrepreneur, or an employee—you will always have to deal with other people, and human relations skills will be essential. Human relations is the skill or ability to work effectively with and through other people.

Human Relations: A Background 《 CHAPTER 1 21

LO 1-2 **Explain the importance of human relations in business.** Human relations skills are especially important today for several reasons: greater awareness of human rights, current fluctuations in international markets, growing emphasis on the human resource in companies, current emphasis on teamwork, and increased diversity in the workplace.

LO 1-3 **Discuss the challenges of human relations as these factors affect success in business.** Today's problems make workplace survival an even greater challenge. Increased workplace competition, the rise of the dual-career family, the divorce rate, and the problem of two generations of dependents: All of these factors increase personal stress and complicate the issues of human relations.

LO 1-4 **Identify what the study of human relations does not include.** Skill in human relations does not mean being phony or manipulative. It is neither a quick fix nor a cure-all, and it is not just common sense. It is a skill area that is learnable, though growth continues for a lifetime.

LO 1-5 **Describe the areas of emphasis for human relations in today's workplace.** The main areas of human relations are self-esteem, mutual respect, self-awareness and self-disclosure, communication skill, group dynamics, and motivation.

LO 1-6 **Discuss a short history of the study of human relations.** Starting with the scientific managers in the early part of this century, and finding a focal point in the Hawthorne Experiment, the human relations movement began in the 1800s and spanned the entire 20th century. Names to remember include Robert Owen, Andrew Ure, Max Weber, Frederick Taylor, Frank and Lillian Gilbreth, Mary Parker Follett, and Elton Mayo. In 1960 Douglas McGregor wrote about Theory X and Theory Y managers, showing the latter as both more effective and more humane.

key terms

bureaucracy 14	informal organization 16	self-disclosure 10
communication 11	motivation 11	self-esteem 9
group dynamics 11	mutual respect 10	Theories X and Y 18
Hawthorne	scientific	Total Quality
Experiment 16	management 14	Management (TQM) 18
human relations 4	self-awareness 10	trust 4

review questions

1. In your own words, write a one- or two-sentence definition of human relations as you would have defined it before reading this chapter. Then, assuming your definition has changed a bit, write a new one.

2. Consider the importance of Elton Mayo and his work in the Hawthorne Studies to the history of human relations. Fear was noted as a possible driver for productivity in the studies. Do you think fear is a good long-term motivator for employees? Why or why not? How would human relations skills affect a fear motivation?

3. How can the development of human relations skills help you on the job as a manager? As an entrepreneur? As an employee?

4. Consider the information on Theory X and Theory Y. Which theory do you think is more useful, and why? If you chose Theory X, why do you think some people who win the lottery continue to work anyhow, or do volunteer work? If you chose Theory Y, why do you think some employees seem unhappy with working no matter what they are doing?

5. List three reasons why human relations issues are more important today than ever before.

6. Why is self-esteem important to the development of human relation skills?

7. List the six "areas of emphasis" in the study of human relations and explain each one briefly.

8. Why did the human relations movement not make much progress during the Great Depression? Discuss the relevance that experience might have to today's workplace.

critical thinking questions

1. Explain the importance of the work of Frederick Taylor and Frank and Lillian Gilbreth and the scientific management movement to the development of modern industry.

2. What are the problems of today's society that cause greater stress on the job, thus increasing the need for human relations skills? List and explain the importance of each.

3. Consider Peter Drucker's statement that "Management is about human beings. Its task is to make people capable of joint performance, to make their strengths effective and their weaknesses irrelevant." Can you think of examples in your own life where a leader helped facilitate this for a group you were part of (whether or not you were the leader)? Did this help you feel more motivated to complete the task your group was working on? Why or why not?

working it out 1.1

COMMUNICATING WITH A SUPERVISOR

School-to-Work Connection: Interpersonal Skills, Thinking Skills, and Personal Qualities Skills

Situation: Doris Johnston is the president of Elko Manufacturing Company.

Workers are in short supply in the town where Elko is located. Doris noticed that the turnover rate has been extremely high in one department. The supervisor in this department, Janet Kent, has been having problems relating to her workers. Janet has become known as someone who abuses her power by intimidating her workers and purposely conducting herself in a way that makes them constantly concerned that they will lose their jobs. Many workers never voice their complaints and simply find work elsewhere.

Doris has asked Janet six times during the past five months why the turnover is so high in her department. She also tells Janet that she has overheard workers complain about the way Janet treats them. Janet answers that the workers leave because they can't handle her demands and maintains that she is "tough, that's all, not unreasonable."

Procedure: Four volunteers should play Doris and Janet in two separate role plays. The first will present how Doris should *not* confront Janet with her concerns. Then, without class discussion, play the second role play, showing a better way that Doris can communicate her concerns with Janet. Finally, the class should discuss both role plays, sharing what they have learned from the process.

a. How could those differences create human relations issues?

b. How can effective human relations prevent or solve misunderstandings related to these differences?

case study 1.1

The Fighting Carpenters

Alan McKenzie's department was in trouble. Of all the departments in the construction company, Alan's remodeling division was showing the lowest profit margin. Yesterday his boss had called him on his cell phone from a job outside of town. "Alan," he exclaimed, "I drove out here to double-check on the sheet rock work, and I found a big fight going on between your carpenters. They are about three days behind schedule on this job, and they're holding up three subcontractors who are mad at you—and the company. Get over here and straighten things out!"

The boss wasn't telling Alan anything he didn't already know. Alan knew what the problem was; the question was what to do about it. He had two groups in his crew who kept sabotaging each other's work and hurling insults at each other. Last week, a fistfight had broken out between the leaders of the two groups, and now, apparently, the same people were at it again. When he had

arrived at the job site, the fight had ended, but the atmosphere was still very tense, and Alan was frankly scared about what would happen next. If only he could solve his human relations problem, his other problems would be much more easily solved.

"I'll drive out there and get hold of the situation right away," he told his manager.

"You'd better," the manager snapped back. "The company can't keep losing subcontractors because your crew would rather fight than work."

Case Study Questions

1. Which emphasis areas of human relations does this case mostly address?

2. What steps should Alan take to solve the conflict in his department?

3. Could Alan have done anything to prevent this problem from occurring in the first place? If so, what?

case study 1.2

The Buzz at B&B.com

While Jenny Wilson was a sophomore at Portland Community College, she started her own web-based business. It was an international electronic brokerage for bed-and-breakfasts. Her business obtained listings with elaborate photos and descriptions from the owners of the B&Bs. She would then sell travel packages to customers, making her profit on the percentage paid by the owners and—depending on the package type—often a small fee from the customers as well.

At first, business was good. Jenny found herself spending long hours online. Her area was undergoing a tremendous worker shortage, however, and she was forced to get by with a few part-timers. B&B.com, as the business was known, had succeeded largely because Jenny was so good with the owners of the bed-and-breakfasts, selling her ideas by phone and Internet, even to owners who had a poor concept of marketing.

Now, with five new people she had hired, that element was often missing. In fact, she began to get messages from well-established clients that they had been "treated rudely" on the phone or by text messaging. One day, Jenny walked into her new downtown office to hear one of her workers in a heated argument over an unpaid bill. As it turned out, the bill had been mailed to the wrong web address, and the B&B owner had not even received it.

"Henry," she said to the employee, "we need to talk."

Case Study Questions

1. What should Jenny say to this employee during the talk she has with him?

2. Should Jenny call a meeting with her entire crew to train them in some of her own human relations policies? What other steps could she take to improve relationships?

3. What could have been done to prevent this from happening in the first place?

CHAPTER SIX

COMMUNICATION AND HUMAN RELATIONS

LEARNING OBJECTIVES

After studying this chapter, you will be able to:

LO 6-1   Explain the crucial role of communication at work and what occurs when miscommunications happen.

LO 6-2   Compare and contrast successful and unsuccessful listening skills.

LO 6-3   Explain the importance of timing with regard to messages.

LO 6-4   Examine the role of nonverbal communication.

LO 6-5   Identify the functions of nonverbal communication.

LO 6-6   Outline strategies for communication within an organization.

LO 6-7   Explain the importance of intercultural communication in today's professional world.

STRATEGIES FOR SUCCESS

Strategy 6.1   Become a Better Listener

Strategy 6.2   Practice High-Context Communication

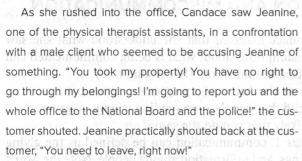

In the Workplace: Candace's Jump to Conclusions

SITUATION

Office Manager Candace Kim-Jenkins was running late to her job at a physical therapy office. A severe winter storm had dumped a foot of snow and ice onto her driveway overnight, blocking her car in the garage. Taking the bus had caused her considerable delay in getting to work that morning.

©PhotoTalk/Getty Images

As she rushed into the office, Candace saw Jeanine, one of the physical therapist assistants, in a confrontation with a male client who seemed to be accusing Jeanine of something. "You took my property! You have no right to go through my belongings! I'm going to report you and the whole office to the National Board and the police!" the customer shouted. Jeanine practically shouted back at the customer, "You need to leave, right now!"

"You know what, I've had it," Candace thought to herself. She motioned for Jeanine to follow her to her office, where she slammed the door closed and said harshly, "You're out of here, Jeanine. We can't have our staff treating clients with that level of disrespect."

"But, but . . ." Jeanine stammered.

"Just get your things" was Candace's only response.

DISCOVERY

A few minutes after a distraught Jeanine left the building, Jack, one of the physical therapists in the office, walked up to Candace. "Uh, hey, would you like to know what was really happening here a few minutes ago? Well, that guy," he pointed to the male client, "left his cell phone in the changing area and started accusing Jeanine of stealing it. He smelled of alcohol and even tried to push me away when I went to Jeanine's defense. Even after she gave him his phone, he got more and more agitated as Jeanine and I tried to calm him down. Jeanine was only trying to restore some order by asking the man to leave. I was just going to call the police when you arrived. The guy was totally out of control."

"Oh my gosh!" Candace responded. "That's not what I thought I was seeing at all. I hope I can catch up with Jeanine before she leaves the parking lot!"

THINK ABOUT IT

Have you ever misinterpreted something that you observed? Have you ever been misunderstood? What were the results?

REAL WORLD EXAMPLE 6.1

A supervisor at a science museum announces that she wants all employees who have questions about the new online timesheet app to come to her office at any time without an appointment, and she will be happy to help them. However, when employees *do* approach her in her office with questions about recording their hours in the new software, the supervisor fidgets, frowns, and looks at her watch frequently.

With her first statement about being open and available, compared with her actual behavior when employees do approach her, the supervisor has sent two messages: one of openness, another of irritation. She has made the false assumption that only the first message was communicated to staff members, when in fact both were very clear—and contradictory.

» COMMUNICATION AND MISCOMMUNICATION

In the opening story, Candace *assumed* that she understood what she saw and heard. Making false assumptions about what is being communicated can be a crucial problem in miscommunication. (See Figure 6.1.)

False assumptions lie at the heart of many miscommunications. How many times have you noticed that people were sending you messages without being aware of it? Isn't it likely that you do the same?

As discussed in Chapter 1, communication can be defined as the giving and receiving of ideas, feelings, and information among people. Note the words *and receiving*. Communication includes listening as well as speaking. In fact, good listening skills and effective communication are critical to success in work. This chapter examines the process of successful communication. Why is this important at work? Without effective communication, no workplace can function properly. Miscommunication not only strains relationships and wastes time, but it also wastes billions of dollars a year in American industry.

The importance of communication in the business world cannot be overstated. In Real World Example 6.2, a CEO of a major corporation used a

figure 6.1

FACTORS OF COMMUNICATION

Several factors go into communication. Major factors include attitudes and values, conscious and unconscious communication, and timing. *Who do you think plays a more important role in effective communication—the sender or the receiver?*

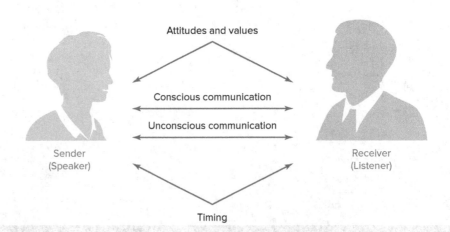

Attitudes and values

Conscious communication

Unconscious communication

Timing

Sender (Speaker)

Receiver (Listener)

REAL WORLD EXAMPLE 6.2

In early 2017, United Airlines found itself reeling from a series of communications disasters at the highest levels. The most serious occurred after the airline forcibly removed a fare-paying passenger from an oversold flight in order to make room for a United employee. After refusing to give up his seat, the passenger was violently removed from the plane while other passengers watched in horror at his rough treatment, cell phone cameras in hand. Recordings of the scene quickly went viral on social and mainstream media, with the resulting PR disaster falling squarely on the missteps and miscommunication of United's CEO, Oscar Munoz.

In his first public response to the incident, Munoz apologized through Twitter for having to "re-accommodate these customers," but was conspicuously silent on the violent incident that had prompted such public outrage in the first place. In a follow-up post a day later on the company's official Twitter account, Munoz better acknowledged the rough treatment of the bloodied and screaming passenger, but by then, the damage had been done.

In the days that followed, the public outcry against the airline was deafening. Due to a lack of confidence in him resulting from his epic communication failure, Munoz was denied the Chairman of the Board position he had been tapped to fill within the coming year. The great irony of the story: CEO Munoz had, just weeks earlier, been honored as *PR Week*'s *Communicator of the Year*. "Munoz has shown himself to be a smart, dedicated, and excellent leader who understands the value of communications," the *PR Week* announcement read. Notably, within days of the incident, *PR Week* demurred on its choice in selecting Munoz to receive its highest honor.

social media platform to amplify his message, and communicate his company's regret over the incident. But the timing and tone of his message fell short, causing irreparable damage to his professional reputation and that of the airline, making them the frequent target of late-night comedians.

The ability to communicate well with others in your professional role is perhaps the most important universal job skill for employees. Everything else about a specific job can be taught. This means that being able to speak well and to listen well are probably the most important assets you—or anyone—can bring to a job.

Online Communication

Connecting with others quickly, and more often, is the hallmark of online communication. In our society we are able to freely share our ideas about culture and business through e-mail and instant messaging apps. Online communication is an indispensable business tool for both internal and external communication.

This type of electronic messaging allows users to communicate with one another from nearly any location, at any hour, eliminating the barriers of time and distance (though cultural or other barriers may persist!). And online communication can encourage more flexibility for workers, who may use communications technology when working in the field, or may have the option of "telecommuting" from home periodically during the workweek.

The use of e-mail and social messaging apps to share ideas, feelings, and information has likewise grown tremendously in recent years. Ideas that

Epic Communication Failures

1. MISHAP TO MARS

In September 1999, NASA's Mars Climate Orbiter broke into pieces before crashing unceremoniously onto the surface of the Red Planet, all because of a simple conversion error: one engineering team had measured in metric units, and another used feet and inches. After nearly 10 months in space, the essential communication mishap pushed the Orbiter too close to the planet's surface, causing it to crash and effectively ending the mission to study water on Mars. NASA's associate administrator for space science said in a written statement at the time, "People sometimes make errors." This elementary mistake cost $125 million, and pushed scientists' understanding of water on Mars back more than a decade.

2. THE RUMSFELD TECHNIQUE

Communicating your ideas effectively so that the listener understands you is essential in business communication. And then there is the "Rumsfeld Technique." Championed by the former Secretary of Defense under George W. Bush, Donald Rumsfeld, he perfected a technique of communicating using as many words as possible to say nothing at all. A classic example:

"There are known knowns; there are things we know we know. We also know there are known unknowns; that is to say, we know there are some things we do not know. But there are also unknown unknowns—the ones we don't know we don't know."

The Rumsfeld technique became synonymous with obfuscation (unclear, obscure, unintelligible communication), and did little to calm the American public's anxiety during the wars in Iraq and Afghanistan.

3. NORTH KOREA'S SEXIEST MAN ALIVE

In 2012, *The Onion*, an American satirical newspaper, published an article declaring North Korea's newly elected leader, Kim Jong-Un, to be the sexiest man alive. Soon after the article ran, the Chinese state newspaper, *The People's Daily*, mistook *The Onion*'s satire for a genuine poll and proceeded to run a 55-page photo spread on him, directly quoting the *Onion* article's assertion that he was a "Pyongyang-bred heartthrob." Misunderstanding and international hilarity ensued. For several reasons, this example highlights cultural differences in communication—including that humor and satire do not always translate well across international boundaries and cultures, and in this case were mistaken for praise and flattery.

were once exchanged in person or in small groups are now sent digitally to co-workers, friends, and family members via computers and wireless devices.

But the same things that make online communication so popular, such as the speed and efficiency, can sometimes become problematic for the sender or receiver. For example, a note may be sent too soon, before it is checked for mistakes, and lead to unnecessary delays. Another potential problem is that the personalization and "tone" of messages can get lost in brief e-mail or text messages, which can cause misunderstandings and time lost in clearing up confusion. Also, technical glitches and human error can delay messages, or reroute them to unintended recipients. Miscues in online communication can lead to major and minor misunderstandings and can cost a person or company valuable time and resources.

When using electronic communication, a great strategy for success is to be *disciplined*. This discipline includes reading, waiting—and re-reading—e-mails or text messages rather than just plunking out a response and sending it right away. It requires a professional mindset, and sharp focus on the topic at hand. Likewise, successful online business communication requires that we remain professional, and try to reserve our personal opinions. Ask yourself if the message you are ready to send is professional enough in tone and content to be forwarded to anyone in the company, knowing that messages are often forwarded. And finally, we must have the discipline to decide when and how to convey information: do the people with whom you're communicating all require the exact same information? Does everyone have the appropriate information that he or she needs to complete his or her job? And does everyone need to be cc'd (copied on the message), or should the message be more targeted?

» LISTENING—AND HOW IT CAN FAIL

What do you really want when you communicate with someone else? You might need a question answered, or for someone to affirm that a job is being done correctly. Maybe you just want to be heard. This tremendous need to be listened to is crucial to human relations. Most people have a very strong need to have others hear them, understand them, and process the information they receive. This need is so strong that when listening is purposely withheld, the speaker's self-esteem can suffer.

Everyone needs to know they can be heard. You will probably be amazed at the results you can get once you become tuned in to other people and their needs. The need to be a good listener to others is often ignored by people who consider themselves good communicators.

In *Harvard Business Review*, Ralph Nichols and Leonard Stevens wrote, "Immediately after the average person has listened to someone talk, he remembers only half of what he has heard—no matter how carefully he thought he was listening. . . . Two months after listening to a talk, the average listener will remember only about 25 percent of what was said."[1] Other recent studies have reached very similar conclusions.[2] What makes people miss so much of what they hear?

Selective Listening

There are some legitimate reasons for poor listening. For instance, in modern society everyone is constantly bombarded with messages. No one could possibly give full attention to every message, so many people practice **selective listening,** which is when you deliberately choose what you want to hear. If you are in a personal environment with even more demands on your attention, the problem is greater. For example, picture a home with young children chattering and constantly trying to get attention; or a busy office with phones ringing, people talking, and keyboards clattering. In these circumstances, people often become selective listeners by default. The main cause of selective listening is **information overload.** Another form of information overload has increasingly come from our own fast-paced tech-driven culture. For example, with a person's smartphone now serving as her conduit for all of her calls, e-mails, texts, social media platforms, calendar alerts, and more,

selective listening

The type of listening that happens when a listener deliberately chooses what he or she wants to pay attention to.

information overload

The type of listening that happens when a listener is overwhelmed with incoming information and has to decide which information will be processed and remembered; this is a common cause of poor listening skills.

REAL WORLD EXAMPLE 6.3

Choon-Lan was explaining impatiently to Rick, for the umpteenth time, how to fill out the requisitions forms correctly. In the process, she was also scolding him for not paying better attention to her directions. Meanwhile, Rick seemed to be lost in space. "Are you listening to me?" she asked bluntly. "No," he replied, "to be honest, I was thinking of the next thing I was going to say to you to defend myself."

The **"Ebbinghaus Curve of Forgetting,"** or the "Ebbinghaus Curve," developed by Herman Ebbinghaus (1850–1909), shows that we remember less than half of what we've heard after an hour and about one-fourth after two months.

Source: H. E. Ebbinghaus, *Memory: A Contribution to Experimental Psychology* (H. A. Ruger and C. E. Bussenius, Trans.) (New York: Dover, 1964). (From original work published 1885.)

more about...

it can be difficult to choose when, and on what, to focus one's attention. Sometimes better listening may simply be a matter of taking a break from technology—by going "offline" and refocusing on face-to-face communication. With information overload, you are overwhelmed with incoming information and must decide which information will be processed and remembered, which can lead to poor listening skills.

In addition to turning off technology in order to listen more effectively, some of us may need to remember to turn off our own responses while the other person is still talking. *Rearranging the letters of the word "silent" gives us the word "listen."* Take time to hear the other person out in order to reduce miscommunication.

Many other reasons for poor listening come from bad communication habits. For example, when many people assume a subject will be too difficult for them to understand, they fail to listen. If they had listened, they may have seen how clear and understandable the subject was, or they could have narrowed down the difficulty with the subject. The opposite often happens, too. A listener might reject a speaker because the message seems too basic and beneath the listener's level of knowledge. In either case, the message is lost.

When you are in a group, listening to a single speaker, you can easily allow your mind to wander. If you are attending a business meeting or conference, the success of the meeting can be destroyed by this habit. One reason for this tendency is that most humans have a capacity for listening at a speed that far exceeds the ability of the fastest speaker. You *could* listen and comprehend up to 500 words per minute; the average public speaker travels through a message at about 125 words per minute. How you spend that extra time and energy often determines your effectiveness as a listener.[3] If you can keep your focus on the speaker and use the free time to take notes or think about what is being said, you will hear more and remember more.

FAILURE TO COMMUNICATE

Actions on the part of the listener can contribute to miscommunication. *What are some of the causes of poor listening?*

©Ariel Skelley/Getty Images

REAL WORLD EXAMPLE 6.4

In a busy office environment, Stefanie was responsible for sending out a weekly e-mail reminder, and updates on important office business. Always pleasant and outgoing, Stefanie had a quirky fashion sense, and her own distinct communication style—including the use of ALL CAPS in outgoing e-mail messages. She figured she could type notes more quickly this way; that by using all capital letters she would catch people's attention, and ensure that what she communicated was made a priority.

However, most people reacted a little differently when they received Stefanie's notes. Some felt as though she were angry, constantly SHOUTING AT THEM by e-mail, while others questioned her writing skills and deleted her notes before reading them, because this communication style was too jarring for them. After several people asked Stefanie if she was angry with them, she finally got the hint and adjusted her written correspondence.

Tuning Out

Some people may refuse to listen to co-workers or other people due to **prejudice;** such people may elevate their bias to the point where they refuse to listen to someone from the other gender, or to people from different ethnic backgrounds or social classes, or from different parts of the world. Prejudice can be more subtle than these examples, though, and it can also overlap with jealousy. Some people won't listen to a speaker who seems to "act better than them" or be "a little uppity," a bit too perfect. These perceptions can, of course, be flat-out wrong. Successful business communicators should observe their personal listening habits to ensure that they are not hampered by personal biases or prejudice. Prejudice will be covered more fully in Chapter 14.

Red flag words and expressions are those that bring an immediate emotional response (usually negative) from the listener, generally because of strong beliefs on the subject. Some red flag words have implied meanings beyond their literal meaning. Words such as *terrorist* or *communist* might begin a flood of emotions that would prevent some people from hearing anything else for quite a while. The word *sex* might get similar results, although the emotions may be different.[4]

People do not hear what their co-workers really say for a variety of reasons. Listening expert Anthony Allesandra says that one major cause underlies most poor listening habits. From childhood, most people have been taught that talking requires energy, attention, and organization, but that listening is a passive, compliant behavior. Starting from kindergarten, children in Western society are taught to be assertive and to express themselves effectively. Until recently, though, little has been done to teach what Dr. Allesandra calls **active listening,** which is listening with greater concentration, less tolerance for distractions, and more feedback to the speaker.[5]

When you improve your listening skills, as you can learn to do from Strategy for Success 6.1 you will find that you learn more from speakers than a poor listener does. You will also gain more speakers' respect as someone who understands their messages and cares enough to actively listen.

prejudice

The outcome of prejudging a person. Prejudice in communication is the unwillingness to listen to members of groups the listener believes are inferior, such as other ethnic groups or women; it can also take more subtle forms; how you feel as a result of the stereotypes you believe in.

red flag words

Words that bring an immediate emotional response (usually negative) from the listener, generally because of strong beliefs on the subject.

active listening

Listening with greater concentration, less tolerance for distractions, and more feedback to the speaker.

REAL WORLD EXAMPLE 6.5

Toni, an executive, had just delivered a speech. She was still nervous and wanted to be sure that her talk was well received. Then her boss called her to his office to discuss a problem in their department, making no reference at all to the speech that Toni had just presented. To Toni, her boss's comments seemed off-the-wall and irrelevant. In the sense of "relevance timing," they were.[7] This could create further miscommunication if she feels (right or wrong) that he is avoiding the topic because he disliked something she said, or she had done a poor job in delivering the speech, or he thought the talk was not important enough to mention.

» THE TIMING OF MESSAGES

Many other factors can explain poor communication. Some are psychological, and others depend on the listening situation and circumstances. Timing can be a major factor when a message becomes distorted and misunderstood.

Emotional Timing

Emotional timing refers to the emotional readiness of the listener to hear a message. Sometimes a message gets to the receiver when the mood is inappropriate. "Time talks," wrote anthropologist Edward Hall in *The Silent Language*.[6] Have you ever received a phone call in the middle of the night? People who hear the phone ring at 2:00 a.m. may feel dread before picking up the phone. "The message must be urgent," they think, "otherwise the phone wouldn't ring at this hour."

The amount of time you take to return calls also communicates a message. For example, when a manager fails to answer a message until three days later, the employee who left the message may feel that the manager is either inefficient or is showing off power or status. This situation is not universal. As mentioned in Chapter 4, people in different cultures maintain different attitudes toward time. Americans sometimes forget this and make false assumptions when dealing with people from another culture.

Situational Timing

Situational timing refers to the listener's situation when a message is received. Privacy is usually a key element. For example, most people wouldn't want to discuss intimate details of their lives in a crowded bus or subway. If two people are enjoying an emotional reunion, they will probably put off the more intimate parts of the meeting until they are alone. Often, communication that would

TIMING IS EVERYTHING

Good communication depends on making sure that your audience is listening. *How can you make sure that you are communicating your ideas to a receptive listener?*

©Blend Images

REAL WORLD EXAMPLE 6.6

The supervisor's performance review for Helen contained both positive and negative elements, written as commendations and suggestions for improvement. However, the negative material was threatening to Helen's self-esteem, so she really heard only the good parts. Helen had filtered the message to make it fit what she wanted to hear. When her colleagues asked her how her performance evaluation had gone, she was upbeat and replied that everything had gone really well.

be totally appropriate in one situation is out of place in another. Because of this, a listener usually can't fully hear the message unless the situation is appropriate.

Bad situational timing can also ruin an otherwise good business undertaking. For example, a crowded elevator would be a poor setting for introducing an important new idea to your boss. Your idea would require careful and focused listening that your boss would not be able to give in an elevator.

Relevance Timing

Relevance timing is similar to situational timing. It simply means that communication should fit the other topics being discussed. If a corporate manager in a weekly planning meeting veers from the listed agenda items to talk about company landscaping updates, the relevance will be lost.

Filtering

When listeners engage in **filtering,** they may fail to receive messages correctly because they are *hearing only what they want to hear.*

Sometimes the listener wants something to be true so badly that he or she interprets the message to make it true.

filtering

A method listeners use to *hear only what they want to hear,* which may result in failing to receive messages correctly.

Filtering works both ways. It reflects what a person decides to *hear* and what he or she decides to *say.* In communicating to others, be sure that your filtering is appropriate and that you are not sharing too much or too little.

more about...

›› COMMUNICATING WITHOUT WORDS

Nonverbal communication is also related to communication skills. Much of what people say is expressed by **nonverbals**—which are ways of communicating without speaking, such as gestures, body language, and facial expressions—rather than words. Next time you attend a class, look around the classroom to see if you can interpret the nonverbal communication around you. Notice the way your fellow students dress, the way they look at each other and the instructor, and the amount of interest they seem to have in the course. These factors send messages that can be read by nearly anyone around them.

nonverbals

Ways of communicating without speaking, such as gestures, body language, and facial expressions.

REAL WORLD EXAMPLE 6.7

Kiran was jazzed. She had just finished presenting the latest design module to her software development team, which today included team leaders and a senior designer. She found herself smiling as the group concluded its discussion and everyone went back to their desks. Kiran felt the presentation and subsequent Q & A discussion had gone well.

Since starting in her new job six months earlier, Kiran had studied the communication style and "culture" of her new office environment, and had worked tirelessly to learn all she could about the design module she'd been assigned to create. Now that she'd shared her design and ideas with her colleagues, she felt a certain satisfaction. Well, she hadn't *actually spoken* with any of her colleagues in the brief moments since the presentation ended, but

she still *knew* it had been received well. For example, she had seen the senior engineer nod vigorously when she reached her important conclusions (which he was known to do when he was pleased), and she had seen several of her colleagues smile broadly and give her the *real* thumbs up—not the fake one—as she drew to a close.

When she called her mother later that night to share the good news, her mother asked what kind of feedback she had received—what had they said about her presentation that showed her they valued her ideas? "Well, mom, they didn't actually say anything. I can't quite explain . . . I just know it. Everyone paid such close attention, and you could tell by the looks on their faces as I was talking, and their nods and smiles. I'll probably get some written feedback tomorrow, but I'm feeling real good about it, mom!"

Note the nonverbal cues that Kiran picked up on as she was assessing her own performance. Even though she hadn't yet received any written or verbal comments on her ideas, she was convinced that what she'd presented had been well-received. But how could she know? Through her reading of nonverbal behaviors and gestures that her team members exhibited as she spoke, the responses seemed clear. Had she been less prepared, or given a poor presentation, nonverbal responses to her would have been notably different. Have you ever found yourself encouraged, or discouraged, by nonverbal cues directed at you? What did you perceive, and what was the outcome?

» FUNCTIONS OF NONVERBAL MESSAGES

What is the purpose of nonverbal communication? Basically, nonverbal messages reflect the *relationship* between speaker and listener. Nonverbal messages:

1. **Show the Speaker's Attitudes and Emotions**

   The words you choose can say a great deal about the way you feel. However, nonverbal signals in this area tend to be both more powerful and more honest. If a speaker's nonverbal signals disagree with the words being said, which do you believe? Which *should* you believe? Both questions have the same answer: the nonverbal ones.

   Understand your feelings and emotions. They will show themselves when you communicate with others, since much of what you communicate is done unconsciously. People often communicate feelings and opinions to others without any awareness they are doing so. And sometimes, people will communicate feelings and opinions that they didn't even consciously realize exist. These feelings may be buried somewhere beneath the

REAL WORLD EXAMPLE 6.8

Jerry was a salesperson who had been hired via a series of telephone interviews by a company a thousand miles away. After being hired, he was required to attend a session for new recruits at company headquarters. At that session, he met dozens of salespeople from all across the country who were similar in ability, age, and even somewhat in looks. The company had gotten the type of sales staff it wanted, although all of them had also been hired by telephone. During one of the sessions, Jerry asked how such a feat had been accomplished.

With a knowing grin, the company sales manager replied, "You'd be amazed at how many nonverbals you people gave us on the phone."

consciousness, but can appear clearly in nonverbal signals. When you communicate unconsciously, your *internal climate*—the way you feel within yourself—is likely to give you away. Self-esteem is the key to internal climate. If you are feeling bad about yourself, it will show. If you are feeling good about yourself, that too will show. If you have other issues on your mind, your lack of complete attention could get in the way of real communication.

2. **Convey Meaning**

   Nonverbal gestures can be very meaningful and brutally honest. When a gladiator lost in the Roman arena, a thumbs down from the emperor signaled his demise. In sports like baseball, entire plays are scripted through brief nonverbal gestures.

3. **Clarify Messages Between and Among People**

   When used together with *verbal* communication, **nonverbal communication** allows you to understand and interpret meaning in context. **Context** is a point of reference, a place from which to begin.

   Have you ever been forced to ask for directions in an unfamiliar city? If the person were to give you only verbal signals, without offering any nonverbal cues like pointing and gesturing "that way" or "left over there around the corner," your brain might not fully process the directions, and you might even feel slighted by the direction-giver. You may be more likely to get the directions wrong. When a direction-giver points the way using gestures, along with a decent verbal explanation, the two-way communication should be more successful.

4. **Show the Speaker's Reactions to the Listener**

   Watch someone walk down a hallway, greeting people along the way. You might be surprised at how many different ways there are of saying things as simple as "Hi" or "How are you?" Although the words are the same, variations in facial expression, tone and pitch of the voice, amount of time spent in the greeting, and eye contact are all likely to show at least some differences in emotional reaction. These differences include variations in acceptance, approval, and comfort level.

   If you were to say, "Nice to meet you" to someone in a fairly neutral tone of voice, that statement could easily be taken as something casual.

nonverbal communication
communication that allows you to understand and interpret meaning in context.

context
A point of reference (or a place from which to begin) when communicating.

An employee moves around his office hanging his head, speaking in a soft voice, and shuffling his feet. What do these behaviors tell you? You will likely perceive more about the message the employee is about to give you than the message itself. Your nonverbal reactions to such a speaker can also be important.

intensity

The degree to which an individual shows serious concentration or emotion; another dimension of nonverbal communication.

illustrators

Gestures that are used to clarify a point, such as pointing when giving directions.

However, try shaking hands with the same person while saying, "Nice to meet you." The difference in intensity alone would be quite obvious. **Intensity**, the degree to which you show serious concentration or emotion, is another dimension of nonverbal communication.[8]

Over the years, many people have commented that the English language should have a least a dozen different words to express various types and intensities of love. For example, "I love chocolate" certainly means something totally different from "I love my mother." Because of gaps such as this in the English language, nonverbal expressions are often necessary to help communicate feelings more completely.

Nonverbal Messages about Self-Esteem

Nonverbal communication signals your *self-esteem level*. Does this mean you should try to act in ways that cover up low self-esteem? Indeed, when attempting to make a good first impression, such a tactic might be useful. Also, your own apparent dislike of yourself can trigger actions in other people that might actually threaten your self-esteem. In the end, though, there is no substitute for genuinely building up your self-esteem. When your self-esteem is high, it will be evident in your nonverbal behavior. You will be listened to more effectively, and the overall communication process will improve.

Gestures and Their Meanings

What about gestures—the movements you make with your arms, legs, hands, fingers, feet, face, and shoulders? By observing gestures, you can tell a great deal about how open or closed people are in their attitudes. Gestures also indicate the true leader of a group, and how open a person is to physical contact.[9] Another way of looking at gestures is to divide them into four categories. Every gesture you use falls into one of these four categories:

©Graham Bell/Corbis

- **Illustrators** are gestures people use to clarify a point they might be making. Pointing the way

Communication and Human Relations   《   CHAPTER 6   **149**

down the street when giving directions, and pounding a fist to emphasize a point, are both illustrators.

- **Regulators** are used to control the flow of communication. When you
  raise your hand in class to get the instructor's attention, you are using
  a regulator. Perhaps you have seen someone point to someone else who
  hasn't been allowed to speak. With proper eye contact, the message
  is: "Please let this person say something." Regulators can also include
  raised eyebrows, head nods, or any other nonverbal indications that say,
  "Please let me (or this other person) into—or out of—this discussion."

- **Displays** are gestures that are used like nonverbal punctuation marks.
  These are gestures that show the emotions going on inside a person,
  and they effectively reveal just how strongly people mean what they say.
  Clenched fists displayed during a committee meeting would likely indicate emotional tension. Displays usually augment another type of nonverbal behavior, such as facial expressions and general body movements.
  If someone is saying, "Yes, that's a pretty good idea," yet the displays
  don't agree (arms are crossed, the speaker is frowning), the listener will
  likely not believe what the speaker is saying.

- **Emblems** are gestures used in a specific manner because they have
  a specific meaning, usually one understood by both sender and
  receiver. The peace sign used by war protesters in the 1960s would
  be one example. Another would be the "O" formed by the thumb and
  forefinger, which means (in American culture), "Everything is okay."
  Several obscene gestures would also fall into this category of emblems,
  as well. Remember, though, that emblems are culture-specific: An
  emblem we assume is universal can easily mean something quite different in another culture. This is especially important to remember
  when traveling and doing business in different parts of the world; many
  embarrassing blunders have occurred when travelers did not know the
  local meanings of nonverbal gestures.[10] In Figure 6.2, see if you can
  determine what the gestures indicate.

regulators

Gestures that are used
to control the flow of
communication; eye contact
is a common type of
regulator.

displays

Gestures that are used like
nonverbal punctuation marks,
such as pounding your fist on
the table.

emblems

Gestures that are used in a
specific manner because
they have a specific meaning,
usually one understood by
both sender and receiver; the
peace sign is an example.

figure 6.2

**WHAT DO THESE
GESTURES MEAN?**

Look at these gestures.
*How would you interpret
each gesture?*

Source: John Stewart and
Carole Logan, *Together:
Communicating Interpersonally*
(New York: McGraw-Hill, 1993),
p. 167. ©JGI/Blend Images
LLC, ©Di Studio/Shutterstock,
©McGraw-Hill Education/
Mark Dierker, photographer,
©Ingram Publishing/
Alamy Stock Photo, ©George
Doyle/Getty Images, ©JGI/
Blend Images LLC, ©Ilya
Akinshin/Shutterstock, ©Grant
Terry/Shutterstock, ©Ingram
Publishing/Alamy Stock
Photo, ©Barbara Penoyar/
Getty Images, ©Matthias
G. Ziegler/Shutterstock,
©geargodz/123RF

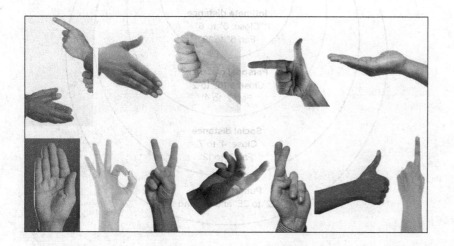

In a small travel agency, one of the co-owners is very friendly and tries to make her clients feel at ease by standing very close to them and putting her hand on their arm or making other similar types of physical contact. Some clients are fine with this "space invasion" while others are very uncomfortable and do not understand her intentions. She may be losing more business than she is gaining, without even realizing it, due to unintentionally violating their distance zones.

Distance Between Speakers

distancing

The distance of physical space you maintain between other people and yourself.

Another area of nonverbal communication is called *proxemics,* or **distancing,** which can be defined as the distance of physical space that you maintain between other people and yourself. Most people carry around a *bubble of space,* or several bubbles. These are illustrated in Figure 6.3. The first bubble is reserved for intimate relationships, such as with mates, romantic partners, and children. It extends from physical contact out to 18 inches or so. The next, from about 18 inches out to 4 feet, is the area saved for close friends. The third bubble, from about 4 to 12 feet, is used for communicating with business contacts and casual acquaintances. The last one, from 12 feet on out, is used for the general public.[11]

When any one of the first three bubbles is violated, most people feel very uncomfortable. Even when Americans ride subways and crowded elevators

figure 6.3

THE ZONES OF DISTANCING

Everyone has different zones to communicate with different people in their lives. These four zones—intimate, personal, social, and public—can vary, depending on the person and the culture. *Which is the most common zone for you?*

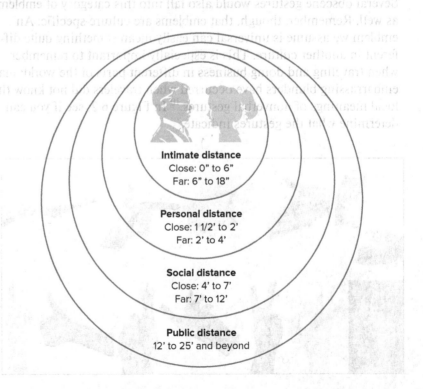

Intimate distance
Close: 0" to 6"
Far: 6" to 18"

Personal distance
Close: 1 1/2' to 2'
Far: 2' to 4'

Social distance
Close: 4' to 7'
Far: 7' to 12'

Public distance
12' to 25' and beyond

every day of their lives, they usually never learn to like the daily violations of their personal space. Next time you are in a crowded public vehicle or elevator, notice your fellow passengers' facial expressions. On most of their faces you will see looks of resignation, or else they are showing an unemotional mask—which both show that they have accepted this invasion of their space as necessary, although they don't like it.

This distancing issue varies geographically. In some cultures, being very close to another person is much more acceptable than in the United States or in many European cultures. In most Middle Eastern countries, two businesspeople will typically stand about 18 inches from each other while talking. Most people in East Asian and Southeast Asian societies also feel more comfortable at closer distances with strangers than most Americans do. As the world becomes more and more an international community, learning the norms of other societies is becoming increasingly important.

» COMMUNICATING IN AN ORGANIZATION

Organizational communication has both formal and informal dimensions. In traditional organizations, most messages that need to be communicated must go through the chain of command. In other words, the flow of messages has to follow the organizational chart, both upward and downward. These are **vertical communication** channels. Also, the policies of most firms include formal methods of communicating in oral, electronic, and written form. These policies should be followed closely, because the formal dimension of organizational communication is important. If you went to your manager's boss, for example, to discuss something important, you could very likely be seen as jumping rank or going over your manager's head.[12]

Even in **horizontal communication,** which refers to messages between you and your equals in the formal organization, you should take care to communicate without causing problems for yourself and others in the company. In this type of communication, be sure that you are not intruding into someone else's area, and that you are not setting yourself up to be accused of causing trouble in someone else's department or division.

Grapevines

Probably even more important than a formal organization is the informal organization within it. When communication takes place in an informal context, the rules are less formal but still very real. Every company that has employees contains an informal organization. The informal organization is made up of friendships and friendly relationships that establish themselves naturally in any situation. You may have joined groups like this when you

organizational communication

Oral and written communication in an organization. It has formal and informal dimensions and travels vertically and horizontally.

vertical communication

Messages that are communicated according to an organization's chain of command by flowing both upward and downward.

Hooked Up to the Grapevine

By forming friendships with people on various formal levels of your firm, you can get an expanded version of the grapevine and you might be able to get a more accurate picture of what is really happening in your organization.

more about…

horizontal communication

Messages that are communicated between you and your equals in the formal organization.

In a county community services agency, Mary was always coming into another department to make sure that the needy members in her own family and circle of friends were being provided for. In some cases, she even made requests of members in the other department, such as:

"Make sure Debbie gets three boxes of apples." Needless to say, Mary was violating a basic rule of horizontal communication: Don't communicate orders in a department where you have no authority.

COMMUNICATION IN INFORMAL NETWORKS

The rumor mill and grapevine are two types of networking you may find in a work environment. *What can you learn by joining either network?*

©Frank and Helena/Getty Images

grapevine

A network within the informal organization that communicates incomplete, but usually somewhat accurate information.

rumor mill

A gossip network that produces mostly false information.

were in elementary school; the more exclusive ones were known informally as cliques. This can continue through high school and college right into the workplace. Informal groups are apparently something humans never outgrow.

The informal organization is made up of small groups based on particular interests, beliefs, and activities. These groups tend to communicate among themselves and with each other through a network known as the **grapevine.** The grapevine is not exactly the same thing as the **rumor mill,** which is a gossip network that produces mostly false information. When the informal organization communicates *incomplete* but somewhat accurate information, it is called the grapevine.[13]

You can learn a great deal by staying in touch with the grapevine. One of the most important characteristics of grapevines is that they are often selective: everyone doesn't always get all of the information, and everyone doesn't always get the same information. If you are a supervisor, the grapevine might leave you out of touch with information about your employees. If you are an employee, you might not hear what is happening in the world of the managers.

When companies have very poor formal lines of communication, the informal grapevine becomes even more important. Employees often complain that if it weren't for the grapevine, they would have no idea about what was happening. Grapevines are also usually slanted. Often, a grapevine will tend to be pro-employee, pro-manager, or in some other way biased, especially when other forms of communication are poor.[14] It is wise, then, to keep these biases in mind when listening to a grapevine; this will help you determine what to believe.

>> INTERNATIONAL AND INTERCULTURAL COMMUNICATION

As the global economy continues to expand, and different countries' economies become more integrated—think the United States and China, or the United States and Mexico, as examples—the odds are good that at some point you will find yourself in a profession that is touched by, or participates in the global economy. This international web of business has created many changes in the American workplace.

Yet despite all of the changes, the average American is ill-equipped to communicate with people from other cultures. Do you know your profession's key terms or lingo in Spanish, or in Mandarin Chinese? Are you aware of the nonverbal cues and messages you may be sending to a colleague from a different culture, with different "communication expectations"? Here are some common body-language mistakes to consider when communicating with others from a different culture:

Pointing the sole of your shoe at someone. In many Middle Eastern and Asian cultures, the bottom of your foot is regarded as the lowest part of your body, and it's rude to show the bottom of your foot. *Solution: Keep your feet flat on the floor during business meetings and avoid crossing your leg onto your knee. Best to tuck your feet underneath you if sitting on the floor.*

Coming on too strong in initial meetings. In Western business culture, we value a strong handshake combined with strong eye contact. We usually do these to signify a certain level of trust, particularly when we first meet someone. But depending on the specific country, these measures may be seen as overly aggressive, overpowering, or dominating. *Solution: Relax your eye contact and soften your handshake when meeting someone from these cultures for the first time.*

Standing too far from the listener, outside his or her personal space. During conversation between two or more people, speakers in Western cultures tend to need a large amount of space around them to feel comfortable when talking to others. In the United States, the United Kingdom, and Canada, this distance is usually an arm's length. However, this distance in Asian or Latin American nations is often much smaller. When traveling to or interacting with people from those regions, standing a full arm's length away is probably too far. *Solution: Close the gap and stand a little closer to that person so they feel more comfortable connecting with you.*

Using your index finger to point out people. In the United States and some other Western cultures, pointing someone or something out with the index finger is a natural gesture. However, in some other cultures, pointing to an object or a person with your index finger is seen as overly direct and blunt, and can be quite offensive. *Solution: Use an open palm with all of your fingers grouped together when gesturing toward the object or person.*[15]

Anthropologist Edward T. Hall identified different cultures as being high context and low context (see Figure 6.4). In a **low-context culture,** a written agreement, such as a contract, can be taken at face value. In other words, one can assume that it means what it says and that it is in itself binding. Low-context cultures include German and Scandinavian

low-context culture

A culture in which a written agreement, such as a contract, can be taken at face value.

Punctuality: A Global Issue

Many people from European and Asian countries value punctuality as much as, or even more than, people from the United States. In Hong Kong and Tokyo, the trains are famous for always being on time, and people often show up early for appointments rather than risk being late.

more about...

figure 6.4

HIGH- AND LOW-CONTEXT CULTURE EXAMPLES

Cultural anthropologist Edward T. Hall (1914–2009) illustrated how high- and low-context cultures are different, as well as their reasons for being this way. *Is the United States a low-context culture or a high-context culture? Why?*

Source: Edward T. Hall, "How Cultures Collide," *Psychology Today* 10 (July 1976), pp. 66–74.

These excerpts are from "How Cultures Collide," an article by Edward T. Hall:

"In some cultures, messages are explicit; the words carry most of the information. In other cultures, such as China or Japan or the Arab cultures, less information is contained in the verbal part of the message, since more is in the context. That's why American businessmen often complain that their Japanese counterparts never get to the point. The Japanese wouldn't dream of spelling the whole thing out. To do so would be a put–down; it's like doing your thinking for you."

"Several years ago I was traveling in Crete and wanted to visit the ruins at Knossos. My traveling companion, who was from low-context, fast-moving New York, took charge of the arrangements. He bargained with a taxi driver, agreed on a price, and a deal was made. We would take his taxi. Without warning, just as we were entering the cab, he stopped, got out and asked another driver if he would take us for less money. Since the other driver was willing, my friend said, 'Let's go.' The first taxi driver felt he had been cheated. We had made a verbal agreement, and it had been violated. But my friend, from a low-context opportunistic culture, felt no moral obligation at all. He had saved the equivalent of 75¢. I can still see the shocked and horrified look on the face of the first driver."

figure 6.5

HIGH- TO LOW-CONTEXT CULTURES

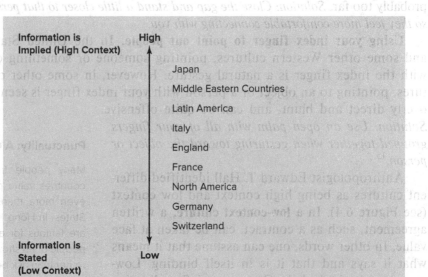

WORKING WITH PEOPLE IN HIGH-CONTEXT CULTURES

Americans who work in high-context cultures have to understand that success with their clients will depend on several factors other than the products or services being offered. *What makes a high-context culture different from a low-context one?*

high-context culture

A culture in which the *social context* surrounding a written document is far more important than the document itself. One must be very careful about cultural norms, nonverbal behaviors on both sides, and anything else involving the overall atmosphere of the communication.

cultures. North American business culture tends to lean heavily toward the low-context end of the scale.

In a **high-context culture,** on the other hand, the *social context* surrounding the writing is far more important than the writing itself. In a high-context culture, one must be very careful about cultural norms, nonverbal behaviors on both sides, and anything else involving the overall atmosphere of the communication. Notice in Figure 6.5 which countries have the highest- and lowest-context cultures. Do any of them surprise you?

Figures 6.4 and 6.6 show examples of communication problems that take place when high- and low-context cultures collide.[16] Obviously, the lower-context countries are not likely to cause trouble in communication when they are communicating only with each other.

figure 6.6

INTERNATIONAL COMMUNICATION TRAPS

Every culture is different. What is okay in Mexico may be considered rude in Saudi Arabia. When traveling or working abroad, it might be best to prepare oneself beforehand, by learning about the country's norms and customs. If that is not possible, then one should still enter open-mindedly, without expectations that norms and behaviors are the same everywhere. *Is there any other rule for doing business in differing cultures?*

Source: Lennie Copeland, "Training Americans to Do Business Overseas," *Training* (July 1983), p. 12.

International Communication Traps—Some Examples

In **Japan,** the practice of giving small gifts is nearly an obligation in most business situations. In **China,** on the other hand, gift-giving to an individual in a business situation is strictly forbidden.

In the **United States,** "tabling" an agenda item means putting it off until later. In **England,** "tabling" means "putting it on the table" right now and discussing it immediately.

In most of **Latin America,** no offense is taken when someone is late for an appointment. In fact, tardiness is somewhat the norm. In **Sweden,** to-the-minute promptness is expected.

In **Mexico,** it is courteous to ask about the spouse and family of a customer. In **Saudi Arabia,** you should never ask about such things.

» **STRATEGIES FOR SUCCESS**

Strategy 6.1   **Become a Better Listener**

1. Stop talking.
2. Get rid of distractions.
3. Try to enter into the speaker's reality.
4. Use pauses for reflecting.
5. Listen for main ideas.
6. Give feedback.
7. Listen for feelings as well as for facts.
8. Encourage others to talk.

What can you do to become an active listener? With time and effort, you can change your listening habits!

1. **Stop talking.** If you are talking, time and opportunity to talk are being taken away from the other person or people. In many ways, this is the most important rule. Remember that most humans have a strong need to be heard—to be listened to.

2. **Get rid of distractions.** Distractions can be external (such as noise, or electronic devices), or internal (such as your thoughts and emotions). Move closer to the speaker, change your physical position so that you face the speaker directly, put away your phone, and put any nagging personal problems out of your mind. All of these steps will help eliminate distractions.

3. **Try to enter into the speaker's reality.** Even before beginning to listen, prepare yourself to enter the world of the speaker. If the conversation is one-on-one, while you are listening *try to make your own needs temporarily less important than those of the other person.* Understand that the other person has very real needs. With a public speaker, listen and watch for clues about the world of the speaker.

4. **Use pauses for reflecting.** When a speaker pauses, use the time to make associations in your mind with other things he or she has said. Think of your own past experiences in order to see relationships among the ideas being offered. In all cases, avoid the temptation to let your mind wander.

5. **Listen for main ideas.** When listening to a public speaker, jot down key words and phrases. Try as early as possible to see the outline headings the speaker is using. When talking one-on-one, make sure you understand each point made by the speaker. In many cases, this involves asking questions to make certain you have understood.

6. **Give feedback.** Many people mistakenly think of feedback only as communication in a one-on-one situation. Eye contact and facial expressions are also examples of feedback. When talking with another person, you should respond with "I" statements. This way, it is clear that you are expressing your feelings, not placing blame. Rather than saying, "Your ideas on this project are hard to understand," say something like, "I feel that an important step has been left out. Why don't we examine the marketing plan before you proceed?" or "I'm having trouble understanding your point here; could you explain to me again?"

7. **Listen for feelings as well as for facts.** Watch for nonverbal messages that communicate how the speaker *feels* about the subject. Eye and body movements, vocal tone, and posture are examples. By listening for feelings, you will also become more aware of your own feelings about what you're hearing.

8. **Encourage others to talk.** Encouraging others to explain their ideas in more detail can make you more responsible for what you say yourself. In a public speaking situation, this means allowing

more about...

Active Listening

Empathy is when you attempt to feel another person's feelings, attitudes, or thoughts. It can play an important role in effective active listening.

others to be involved when the speaker calls for questions and listening carefully to both sides.

Notice how many of these eight steps involve self-esteem. If you feel good about yourself, implementing all eight of these strategies will be easier and more effective. People who are comfortable within themselves tend to be better listeners. This is because they are less likely to need attention and can listen to others without an excessive need to be heard.

Strategy 6.2   Practice High-Context Communication

1. Recognize that people in high-context cultures need to know how to put you into context, to help them understand you better.

2. Speak slowly and clearly.

3. Sprinkle your conversation with at least a few words and expressions from your listener's native language—but only if you are sure what they mean, and know how to pronounce them.

4. Be careful about your nonverbal signals.

1. **Recognize that people in high-context cultures need to know how to put *you* into context, to help them understand you better.** They need to know not only about you, but also about the company or organization that you represent. Without that knowledge, any agreement could be meaningless.

2. **Speak slowly and clearly.** Stay away from American jargon, slang, clichés, and too many idioms. When nonnative speakers learn English, they often learn a textbook version of the language. Expressions such as, "Let's get all of our ducks in a row" will likely be lost on them. Since Americans use a great deal of informal language, expressions like this slip out even when you are careful.

3. **Sprinkle your conversation with at least a few words and expressions from your listener's native language—but only if you are sure what they mean, and know how to pronounce them.** In nearly all language groups, it is considered to be good manners to learn some of the other person's language. Such an attempt shows the listener that you care and are interested enough to do a little learning. Of course, you must be sure you understand the meaning before using such phrases, and be careful not to mispronounce the words and phrases—at least not beyond recognition.

4. **Be careful about your nonverbal signals.** If you are communicating through a translator and the listeners are listening to you for periods of time without understanding, your listeners are even more likely than usual to pick up on gestures, tone of voice, and all of the other nonverbals.[17]

These rules should help greatly in high-context situations. Most of these, though, would be good to follow when dealing with companies from any other cultures. Even when context is low, thoughtfulness always pays off.

CHAPTER SIX SUMMARY

Chapter Summary by Learning Objectives

LO 6-1 **Explain the crucial role of communication at work and what occurs when miscommunications happen.** Communication takes place even when speakers and listeners do not realize that it is happening. When people communicate unconsciously, feelings are projected outward. If you are feeling bad about yourself, that emotion will show. When miscommunication happens, the results include bad decisions, damaged feelings, and loss of productivity,

LO 6-2 **Compare and contrast successful and unsuccessful listening skills.** Listening skills are important for anyone who wants to communicate effectively. Reasons for poor listening include selective listening, information overload, perceived difficulty of the subject, prejudice, daydreaming, red flag words, and the misunderstanding of listening as a passive position. Good listening is related to self-esteem. It is also a matter of priorities. People who like themselves and understand the importance of good listening tend to be better listeners.

LO 6-3 **Explain the importance of timing with regard to messages.** Messages need not only to be carefully planned in terms of content, but in terms of timing. A message that would otherwise be clear and well received can be destroyed when it is delivered at a bad time. The areas of possible timing mistakes include emotional, situational, and relevance timing.

LO 6-4 **Examine the role of nonverbal communication.** Without nonverbal communication, effective exchange of ideas and thoughts is more difficult. Gestures are an important part of the communication process. They include illustrators, regulators, displays, and emblems. Proxemics, or the study of distancing, states that people carry around several bubbles of space. When any of the first three bubbles is violated, the violated person feels uncomfortable.

LO 6-5 **Identify the functions of nonverbal communication.** Nonverbal messages exhibit attitudes and emotions, help clarify the verbal message, and show something about the emotional reactions of speaker and listener.

LO 6-6 **Outline strategies for communication within an organization.** In any organization, communication has both formal and informal dimensions. Everyone who works in an organization also needs to understand the different requirements of vertical and horizontal communication channels. Within the informal organization, the grapevine is the informal channel of information. It includes information that is largely accurate, but incomplete. When the information is distorted, the channel is called the rumor mill.

Communication and Human Relations   «   CHAPTER 6   **159**

LO 6-7 Explain the importance of intercultural communication in today's professional world. International and intercultural communication become more important as the world becomes smaller. One can see international cultures as either high-context or low-context. Doing effective business with other cultures requires some knowledge of context expectations.

key terms

active listening 143

context 147

displays 149

distancing 150

emblems 149

filtering 145

grapevine 152

high-context
 culture 155

horizontal
 communication 151

illustrators 148

information overload 141

intensity 148

low-context culture 153

nonverbals 145

nonverbal
 communication 147

organizational
 communication 151

prejudice 143

red flag words 143

regulators 149

rumor mill 152

selective listening 141

vertical
 communication 151

review questions

1. What is communication? In your definition, use an illustration from your own life.

2. Explain why your internal climate is so important to communicating effectively. Explain the importance of self-esteem to the communication process.

3. Are you usually an active listener? If not, do you know anyone who is? What qualities set an active listener apart from other people?

4. Think of people you have been around who are poor listeners. Do they all have certain qualities in common? If so, what are they?

5. How does nonverbal communication help people understand each other? How can nonverbal cues be negative, especially in the workplace?

6. What are the main differences between communication in the formal organization and in the informal organization? What cautions should you use in each area?

7. What is meant by filtering? Do you ever find yourself filtering a message being sent to you? How can one reduce the filtering of messages in the workplace?

8. What are the major differences between a high-context culture and a low-context culture? What steps could you take to prevent misunderstandings when dealing with a culture that is opposite in context from your own?

critical thinking questions

1. Do a brief self-evaluation. Ask yourself, "How effective am I at communicating with people from cultures that are higher-context or lower-context than my own?" Have you ever been guilty of ignoring such differences? Most of us have been. If so, what were you doing that could be done more effectively?

2. Think of an incident in your life when someone you were listening to was sending nonverbal messages that seemed to contradict the verbal message. Perhaps it was a public speaker or someone on television. What was your reaction to the mixed message?

working it out 6.1

GRAPEVINE OR RUMOR MILL?

School-to-Work Connection: Information Skills

This exercise graphically illustrates how quickly distortions of facts can take place, even when they are communicated in a controlled environment.

This exercise requires seven volunteers from the class. Six of the volunteers must leave the classroom, taking their places in the hallway. The other volunteer will remain in the classroom. The instructor will choose a very short story that contains several characters and a bit of action. The instructor first reads the story to the entire class, including the first volunteer. When the reading is finished, the second volunteer will be allowed to enter the room.

Volunteer number one will then retell the story he or she has just been read, without any coaching from either the instructor or the rest of the class. Then, one by one, each volunteer will be ushered into the room to hear the story retold by the last person who heard it. When volunteer number seven has heard the story, he or she must retell it to the rest of the class. Finally, the instructor will ask the seventh volunteer to read aloud the story in its original form, for the benefit of the volunteers who have gotten only distorted versions of it.

Although degrees of distortion will vary from class to class, you will readily see how messages become muddled, sometimes to ridiculous extremes. If most of the facts are correct, but the story is incomplete, the class has created a grapevine example. A rumor mill example that includes gross distortions is much more likely.

Note: This exercise has also been done successfully with a photograph or drawing that contains many different elements and/or people to remember. The picture should be shown on a screen or copies should be distributed to all class members—except six of the seven participants. Let the first participant have one minute to observe the picture; follow the same procedure as for the story.

working it out 6.2

THE IMPORTANCE OF FEEDBACK

School-to-Work Connection: Information Skills

This exercise illustrates the importance of two-way communication that includes feedback from all communicators.

A volunteer from the class will study a geometrical figure provided by the authors of this textbook to the instructor. (The other class members will not be allowed to see the figure.) Then, with the student's back to the class, he or she will describe the figure exactly enough so that each class member can reconstruct it on a piece of notebook paper. Fifteen minutes will be allowed for this portion of the exercise. During this phase, only the volunteer will be allowed to speak. No questions are allowed, except for one request to repeat each instruction. The volunteer is not allowed to explain any single descriptive instruction more than twice, and the second time is allowed only if requested by a class member.

The same volunteer will face the class and will describe the geometric figure, while classmates start over with another sheet of notebook paper. This time, the members of the class are allowed to ask questions. They may ask any question that will help clarify an accurate drawing of the figure. After 15 minutes, compare the results from the two phases. You will very likely see a vast improvement in the second part of the exercise. This is probably because the person who gave the instructions was able to provide helpful nonverbal clues while facing the class. Did the first exercise—with the student facing away—cause any frustration or confusion? If so, give specific examples. Perhaps the more complex instructions left a lot of people unsure the first time, but were somehow easier to comprehend the second time.

To the instructor: The geometrical pattern can be found in the *Instructor's Manual.*

case study 6.1

The Mysterious Strangers

When Jan came to work on Monday morning, she noticed a group of people she had never seen before at the insurance company where she was a claims supervisor. "Who are those people?" she asked one of her co-workers. Nobody seemed to know. The presence of these strangers seemed especially suspicious because they talked quietly among themselves. They would stop talking as Jan, or anyone, walked past them.

For the week that the mysterious visitors were there, rumors spread throughout the building. Since Jan was a supervisor, her crew found it hard to believe that she didn't know what was really happening. But none of the "suits" (upper-level managers) had spoken about the strangers, and she really didn't know. The more questions her employees asked her, the more frustrated she became. When Jan approached her own manager, Ron, several times, she was met only with vague answers.

Finally, on Friday morning, she caught Ron alone and demanded a straight answer. "I'm looking like a fool here, Ron," Jan complained. "Now, come on. As a supervisor I really need something to tell my workers. It's gotten so they spend more time talking about the mysterious visitors than they spend working on claims."

"Okay, Jan," Ron replied. "The top brass have hired a management consulting firm. Mostly, they're just looking at cost cutting. It wasn't supposed to be a big deal."

"Does the cost cutting involve cutting people's jobs, by any chance?" was Jan's automatic response. "No," said Ron. "In fact, we've kept quiet about this because we were afraid a panic might start on that very issue." "Well, the panic has started anyway, and I think it's time to get everyone calmed down," said Jan, shaking her head.

The next morning, Jan held a briefing with all of the employees in her unit in which she explained what Ron had told her. Most of her 14 employees were still skeptical. They found it hard to understand why they hadn't been told the truth from the start if, in fact, there was nothing to fear. Top management had still not sent even a brief memo to all the employees telling them that no positions were being cut. Several weeks later, Jan's two best claims workers left for other companies. Three others admitted that they had also considered looking for work elsewhere.

Case Study Questions

1. How could the company have handled this situation differently? What principles of effective communication have been broken in this case?

2. If you were Jan, what would be your next step? Why?

3. If the company decides to explain the situation, what form of communication should they use? Meetings, memos, personal letters? Why?

case study 6.2

Un-Gorgeous George

George had been working for the same company, a local television cable installation business, for 11 years. During that time, he had completed an apprenticeship program and had made it through the required entry-level training programs. He had also applied for promotions four times—and had been passed over each time. George simply could not understand why he was not getting promoted. He worked hard, was never late to work, and often helped others after his own assignments were finished. He thought of himself as competent and deserving of promotions, and he wanted more than anything to move into a supervisory office position.

What George didn't know was that behind his back his co-workers called him "Gorgeous George"—but not because he was so good-looking. His nickname came from the way he presented himself, which was the opposite of gorgeous. George dressed more like he was getting ready to work in the yard than to work in an office. He also seldom made eye contact during conversations. He had a tendency to mumble, and he looked down at the ground while talking or interacting with others. He seldom smiled, and usually did not speak to people in the office unless they spoke to him first. His friend at work, David, offered to help him with practice interviews to increase his prospects for promotions, but George was uncomfortable with the offer and declined.

Case Study Questions

1. How are George's nonverbal behaviors contradicting the message he is trying to get across about wanting to be promoted? What is each message channel (verbal or nonverbal) saying, and which will you most likely believe?

2. How do others likely respond to his nonverbal behaviors? How would *you* respond?

3. David may be able to convince George to do the practice interviews if he can convince George to listen to him. How might he work with George to help his active listening skills?

CHAPTER SEVEN

7

PEOPLE, GROUPS, AND TEAMS

<< << **LEARNING OBJECTIVES**

After studying this chapter, you will be able to:

LO 7-1   Discuss the characteristics and purposes of formal and informal groups.

LO 7-2   Discuss development of groups.

LO 7-3   Examine barriers to group effectiveness and their resolutions.

LO 7-4   Define leadership, leadership styles, and types of power.

LO 7-5   Explain the steps in team building.

LO 7-6   Improve the organizational climate of the workplace.

LO 7-7   Understand the new organizational or corporate culture.

<< <<   **STRATEGIES FOR SUCCESS**

Strategy 7.1   Watching for Hidden Agendas

Strategy 7.2   Building a Successful Team

In the Workplace: To Team or Not?

SOLO, OR TEAM?

Pete had been doing great design work for the company since the early days, when the start-up had grown out of a converted garage. For years he had worked mostly alone on projects, since the staffing had been too lean to rely on others. Recently, his company was expanding, and had bought out a local rival in the same field. Because they respected his past work, and his value to the company, his bosses asked him if he wanted to continue to work on projects by himself, or join one of the new permanent work teams that were being created as part of the company's restructuring.

Pete chose to continue to work alone. He just didn't see the value in wasting time talking to other people about getting something done. He figured he could just do it himself and get finished a lot faster. Besides, what if he didn't like the team members he was assigned to work with? Then he would be miserable, he thought, caught in a bad situation.

©Caiaimage/Glow Images

DISCOVERY

But today as he looked around the office, he wondered if he'd made the right choice. He was stuck on how to finish an individual project and he didn't know whom to ask. The others in his original office staff had all joined work teams. He listened in as Amy and her team were brainstorming ideas, and coming up with a lot more creative possibilities than Pete could have thought of alone. His new colleague Jasmine and her team were deciding how to divide up the project tasks; they would have their individual tasks—and the project—done in no time. Haruto's team was in deep discussion on the progress of the second phase of their work. Now, the idea of a team seemed to Pete both more efficient and more pleasant. As he struggled with his project, he wondered if it was too late to reconsider the teamwork idea.

THINK ABOUT IT

Can you think of a time when you worked alone on a work or school project, when a team approach would have been more successful?

» PEOPLE IN GROUPS

Why Do People Join Groups?

Most people begin joining groups when they are in elementary school or earlier, and group membership becomes even more prevalent as we grow and mature. Depending on the context or situation, groups can take different shapes, and can be composed for different purposes.

A **formal group** is one that is usually governed by the formal structure of an organization. In school, formal groups can include athletic teams and student government. In the workplace, it might be the planning committee or an internal work group. In these groups, members don't necessarily have the final say about whether or not they can become members, and they often do not have the choice to leave.

In contrast, **informal groups** happen naturally over time. As Elton Mayo found in the Hawthorne studies (see Chapter 1), informal groups tend to form around common interests and habits, as well as personality traits. Informal organizations can be defined as the ever-changing relationships and interactions that can be found within an organization, but they are not formally put together by anyone. Informal groups in an office setting are typically made up of people who come together based on similar experiences they may have in common. In an informal group, there is no stable membership *per se*, and members may come and go.

People join groups to fulfill needs that can't be met alone. Those needs and their fulfillment generally fit the following categories:

- *Affiliation.* Everyone has a basic need to be with other people and relate to them. Some people have stronger affiliation needs than others.
- *Attraction.* Normally, we tend to be attracted to people who are like us, or who are the way we would like to become. We are drawn to others with similar attitudes, values, personalities, and economic positions as our own.
- *Activities.* We often join groups because they are involved in interesting activities we would like to pursue.
  - *Assistance.* Sometimes people join groups because of the advice or assistance the group can give them in some area of their lives.
  - *Proximity.* People often form groups just because they tend to form close ties with people they see frequently, such as the people they work with, attend classes with, eat with, and so on.[1]

What Makes a Group?

All groups have certain qualities in common. A **group** is defined as two or more people who

---

formal group

A group that is usually governed by the formal structure of the organization.

informal group

A group that tends to form around common interests, habits, and personality traits.

group

Two or more people who interact, share common goals, have unspoken or formal rules or norms, maintain stable role relationships, and form subgroups.

GROUPS IN THE WORKPLACE

Groups help people to work more effectively and find satisfaction through interaction. *What are some of the ways that groups form in the workplace?*

©Guerilla/Alamy Stock Photo

interact with other members on either an individual or network basis, and share common goals. In defining a group, note that they are governed by *formal* rules and *unspoken* **norms** (standards of behavior) as a system of attitudes and behavior. Groups maintain relatively stable role relationships or tasks within the group, and subgroups often form through various networks of attraction and rejection.[2]

》 GROUP DEVELOPMENT

When a group forms, it has a number of issues to resolve before it can operate effectively. As a group grows and evolves, there are usually four distinct stages in group development. All four of these stages focus primarily on two behaviors of the group: **task activity** and **group process**. *Task activity* is the assignment of tasks within the group to get a job done. *Group process* is the way group members deal with each other while working on a task.[3] If you have been assigned small-group activities in a classroom, you may have been graded on both the quality of the task output, and the group process itself.

1. **Forming.** The first stage, taken when the group is new, is also called *orientation*. During this phase, members take a close look at their task, adjust themselves in terms of what behaviors are expected of them, and begin accepting one another.
2. **Redefining.** At this point, group members reexamine the task as a group problem. The group also tries to define itself in relation to solving this problem. Members will usually reveal different levels of enthusiasm. Greater differences in this enthusiasm tend to predict greater internal conflict during this stage.
3. **Coordinating.** This stage often lasts the longest, as the group starts collecting information and translating it into group objectives. Discussion about issues from the redefining stage brings feelings out into the open in this stage, and more conflicts take place here than in any other stage. This conflict can be so strong that it destroys the group.
4. **Formalizing.** This is the point where the group works smoothly in its roles and can accomplish its objectives. New roles are assigned as needed. Group members have accepted the role of both the group as an entity, and their role in the group. The group is now at a point where it can perform meaningfully, and where it is much more likely to last.[4]

When you are a member of a newly formed group, keep these four stages in mind. When conflicts begin, consider them to be normal parts of the group development process. Don't allow them to hurt your self-esteem or reduce the group's effectiveness. Remaining open yet assertive increases the chance that the group will form and evolve realistically and successfully.

norm

A standard of behavior expected of group members.

task activity

The assignment of tasks to get a job done.

group process

The way group members deal with one another while working on a task.

» BARRIERS TO GROUP EFFECTIVENESS

Many barriers to a group's effectiveness can arise from its members' interaction. Status differences between specific group members may create divisiveness or negativity. Team members may not understand their colleagues'—or their own—roles on the team. Some members of the team may seem less invested in its success, or resistant to changes that others feel would make the group more successful. And yet another barrier might be the reaction of some members of the group to its domination by one or more members. A group's effectiveness may even suffer from the phenomenon known as **groupthink**, where over-conforming can discourage creativity and/or personal responsibility. Besides the above examples, there are many potential pitfalls, or barriers, to a group's success. By studying these barriers we can better identify them, and remove them.

When group norms have been established and status issues have been sorted out, conformity becomes an issue. **Conformity** is acting in coordination and agreement with one's group. One reason members of groups conform is to avoid pressure or rejection by the rest of the group. Other reasons may include a desire to meet the group's shared objectives, or to be rewarded for their work. For a group to function effectively, a certain amount of conformity is necessary.[5] You may have heard the expression "it's like herding cats" used to refer to the difficulty of getting people in a particular group to conform to group norms and act as a unified group. This expression reminds us how difficult it can be to coordinate group tasks without the members of the group conforming to the group.

Conformity also has an ugly side. Too much conformity can kill creativity and discourage people from saying what is really on their minds. *Groupthink* is a type of well-intended, but ultimately warped thinking that results from groups "getting along too well." Likewise, groupthink gives members the illusion that the group is based on what is good and moral. "We're the good guys; who has a right to oppose us?"

Picture a group in which members know each other very well and are used to working together closely. When a well-liked leader of the group offers an idea for discussion that you immediately recognize as unworkable, yet you notice polite nods and smiles around the table, you may hesitate to offer your critical opinion out of fear of not being a team player. When groupthink invades a group or project, otherwise critical or incisive members of the group may say nothing at all.

Status is the rank an individual holds within a group. It comes from a variety of different sources, some based on formal factors and others on informal ones. Sources of status include a person's formal position in a company, effective interpersonal skills, personal charm or charisma, educational level, physical appearance, persuasive ability, and other values shared by the group. Group members with high status will usually have a high impact on the group's morale, and on its output.

---

groupthink

A problematic type of thinking that results from group members who are overly willing to agree with one another because of time pressure, stress, and low collective self-esteem.

conformity

Behaving in a way that meets a specified standard, in coordination with a group.

status

The rank an individual holds within a group.

Epic Groupthink Fiascoes

Irving Janis believed groupthink affects a group's decision-making to the point that loyalty to the group or its values overrides realistic and necessary points of view. Insider groups such as private clubs and fraternities, religious groups, as well as corporations and governmental institutions are particularly prone to groupthink. Actions made through groupthink can have grave consequences; consider the following ill-fated examples.

PEARL HARBOR

When American intelligence services intercepted Japanese secret messages indicating that an attack in the western Pacific was imminent, Navy and Army leaders ruled out Hawaii as the target, rationalizing the decision with a number of questionable assumptions. On December 7, 1941, the Japanese attacked Pearl Harbor, catching the American military unprepared to respond. Postwar studies have concluded that the American military overestimated its strength in the region; that it stereotyped the Japanese military as being too weak or scared; and the military's culture of conformity meant that different opinions of lower generals regarding risk assessment may not have been evaluated robustly.

SPACE SHUTTLE CHALLENGER DISASTER

After the loss of Challenger and its crew in 1986, the official inquiry into the disaster found that the direct cause was the malfunction of an O-ring seal on the right solid-rocket booster, which caused the shuttle to explode 73 seconds after launching. The commission also found "a serious flaw in the decision-making process leading up to the launch," noting that prior to the launch there had been questions about the O-ring seal's safety, but after months of internal discussion about the product's safety "NASA appeared to be requiring a contractor to prove that it was not safe to launch, rather than proving it was safe."[6] In this case, NASA's remarkable earlier achievements in space exploration had caused it to dismiss its own engineers and data regarding the likelihood of failure. This defective decision-making doomed the mission.

PENN STATE SANDUSKY SCANDAL

Former Penn State president Graham Spanier, former vice president Gary Schultz, and the University's former athletic director Tim Curley were sentenced to jail in 2017 for their role in the scandal at the university in which they and the former head football coach covered up multiple accounts of child abuse committed by a former assistant football coach, Jerry Sandusky.

Among other reasons, the tragedy has been explained by the groupthink phenomenon, whereby sound decision-making was impaired by the bigger concern of group unity and preservation. The tragedy of this case study was amplified by the officials in charge, who became complicit by doing, and saying, nothing.

An important related factor is degree of *status acceptance.* If you have lower status in a group than you feel you deserve, then your own morale, and in turn, the group's morale, may be badly affected. Even the opposite—giving people more status than they deserve or feel they deserve—can cause problems such as resentment from other group members, or guilty feelings in the person with higher status than is deserved. People with healthy self-esteem may be more content with the status level the group has given them and may attain higher status than those who have trouble liking themselves.

Solutions to Group Effectiveness Barriers

Three steps help improve group effectiveness:

1. *Changing ineffective norms.* Making a group more effective can be done most efficiently by changing its norms. Since most groups haven't ever

REAL WORLD EXAMPLE 7.2

The student government team at a small community college was made up of seven students, all of whom wanted to be student body president. The group was torn because everyone wanted to be a leader, and no one wanted to work as equals on a team. Not until most of the members either graduated or quit was the group replenished with a more balanced composition. Then the group could identify and pursue its goals.

discussed their norms, examining norms is the first step. The group leader must get the group to agree on the purpose for the group's existence, the role each member can play in achieving that purpose, and why a specific norm needs to be changed.[7] In the case of specific barriers to group effectiveness, the group will need to set norms for an environment that does not allow for continued conflict, where creativity is encouraged, all members are expected to participate, and change is encouraged.

2. *Identifying problems.* Try to identify problems the group is facing so that members can discuss ways to solve them. Is one person dominating the discussion? Are some group members in conflict over status differences? Are members resisting change and new ideas? Are they conforming too much, without questioning goals or process? Once the specific problem is identified, group members or the group leader can bring attention to the problem, then create a solution to address it. The solution should be designed so that it uses the full potential of each group member.[8] New job assignments given to members may make them feel they are contributing in a more useful way to the project, using their individual talents and abilities in the process.

3. *Improving the composition of the group.* Some groups are ineffective because their composition is poor. For example, they may have members whose abilities, interests, or personalities clash, or simply do not meet the needs for which the group was formed. The group may include members who actively resist change, or those who insist on dominating the group; and are not willing to change their behavior. They may have members who do not have the right mix of expertise to solve a problem they are assigned. The group itself may be too large or too small for the task. In these cases, group leaders should try to change the group's composition, if possible, to make it more effective. The leader should look for a balance of skills and knowledge to allow the group to be effective. Whenever a group's composition is changed, it will again go through the group process stages described earlier. The group will improve, but this growth toward improvement won't happen without some "growing pains." The leader must be ready to help in the readjustment that will be necessary when group composition changes.[9]

hidden agendas

The secret wishes, hopes, desires, and assumptions hidden from the group. People often try to accomplish hidden agendas while pretending to care about the group goals.

leadership

The ability to influence others to work toward the goals of an organization.

autocratic leaders

Leaders who make all the decisions and use authority and material rewards to motivate followers.

REAL WORLD EXAMPLE 7.3

Kerry joins committees and attends their meetings for only one reason: She wants to get to be known by the people on each committee so she will have political power in the managers' association to which she belongs. Her hidden agenda is to network and look good to others, and she doesn't truly care about any of the groups' goals. When group leaders and members can identify and confront hidden agendas, the strength and integrity of the group increase.

Hidden Agendas

Have you ever been in a group where nothing seemed to be getting done? **Hidden agendas** may have been part of the problem. Hidden agendas are individual members' secret wishes, hopes, desires, and assumptions that they don't want to share with the group, although they will work hard to accomplish them without being discovered. Often, people try to get these agendas accomplished even as they pretend to care more about the goals of the group. They might also try to persuade the group to make its agenda fit their own.[10] As with other barriers to group effectiveness, hidden agendas may be uncovered and reduced through good communication, good group composition, and creation of norms that discourage them.

» LEADERSHIP: WHAT IT IS AND WHAT IT REQUIRES

Leadership is broadly defined as the ability to influence people toward the attainment of goals.[11] Effective leaders in business exhibit characteristics of honesty, integrity, trustworthiness, and ethics while leading their group toward successful fulfillment of the group's goals. Leadership is a critical factor in the study of human relations.

Leadership versus Management

In his popular books on leadership, management expert Warren Bennis distinguished between a manager and a leader. According to Bennis, good managers *do things right,* whereas effective leaders *do the right things.*[12] The manager who is also a leader is the most effective of managers.

There are different thoughts as to what exactly makes a leader effective. Some argue that leaders are simply born with *traits* that make them effective. Others argue that leaders have mastered different sets of *skills* that nearly anyone can develop. Still others emphasize the *situation* in which a leader finds himself or herself. Which position do you agree with?

consultative leaders
Leaders who tend to delegate authority and confer with others in making decisions, but who makes the actual decisions independently.

participative leaders
Leaders who encourage the group to work together toward shared goals.

free-rein leaders
Leaders who set performance standards, then allow followers to work creatively to meet standards.

LEADERSHIP STYLES
Leaders may interact with others differently depending on their leadership styles. *Which style of leader would you prefer?*
©Hero Images/Getty Images

more about...

Peter Drucker once wrote the "Leadership is lifting a person's vision to high sights, the raising of a person's performance to a higher standard, the building of a personality beyond its normal limitations." Consider the following famous leaders:

Abraham Lincoln

The 16th president of the United States, a towering figure in U.S. history, kept the Union together during the American Civil War, and he effectively ended slavery in the United States by signing the Emancipation Proclamation. His greatest traits were his determination, persistence, beliefs, and courage.

Nelson Mandela

Nelson Mandela was the first South African president elected in fully democratic elections after decades of apartheid in the racially divided country. Mandela served nearly thirty years in prison for his political views, becoming an international hero for his tireless work to dismantle South Africa's apartheid regime, which created a system of institutionalized racial segregation and discrimination. Mandela's main characteristics were his determination, persistence, focus, and will.

Mahatma Gandhi

Mohandas Karamchand Gandhi, better known as Mahatma Gandhi, is considered to be the father of India because of his efforts to end the British occupation of India. Born in 1869, Gandhi pioneered the nonviolent resistance movement, and he inspired civil right movements for equality and freedom across the planet. His main characteristics were resilience, knowledge, people skills, motivational approach, and leading by example.

Do you identify with any of the above historical figures? Why? Who are some people, past and present, who have leadership qualities that you admire?

Patrick Alain, *Industry Leaders*, "Leadership and 10 Great Leaders from History." April 15, 2012.

» LEADERSHIP STYLES

One popular method of understanding leadership is to examine the four common styles used by most leaders. These styles are based mostly on the extent to which the leader includes others in the process of making decisions. They are usually called *autocratic, consultative, participative,* and *free-rein.*

Autocratic leaders make it very clear that they are in charge. The power and authority autocratic leaders have from their position in the organization are important to them, and followers usually have little or no freedom to disagree or to disobey. Although this style sounds arrogant and dehumanizing, autocratic leaders are often neither. Many simply operate in an environment where the leader is not questioned.

Consultative leaders will often spend a great deal of time and energy consulting with followers to get information about what decisions should be made for the good of the organization. This behavior sets the consultative leader apart from the autocratic leader. However, when the actual decision is to be made, the consultative leader makes it alone, usually accepting responsibility for the decision regardless of how much input on that decision has been provided by others. Consultative leaders are comfortable delegating authority.

Participative leaders have both concern for people and concern for getting the job done.[13] This type of leadership invites subordinates to share power with the leader. This style is very popular in organizations that use teams and team building. Although a participative leader encourages others to help make decisions, he or she can and will act decisively, even when not receiving the amount or quality of participation asked for. The effective participative leader will hold company needs equally with group morale, placing emphasis on both factors.[14]

Free-rein leaders often have subordinates who don't complain about the leadership; however, these leaders are not really leading at all in any strict sense. This approach is often called *laissez-faire*

REAL WORLD EXAMPLE 7.4

Major Uber Problems

The story of Uber is not unlike many Silicon Valley success stories. As a ride-sharing pioneer that upended the traditional taxi cab business when it was introduced in 2012, Uber quickly emerged as a leader in the new "gig" or "shared" economy.

Uber experienced exponential growth in its first few years, with stock prices exceeding analysts' expectations. But Uber's first several years in business were also rocky even by start-up standards, and marred by scandals both internal and external. Uber found itself in trouble not only with regulators for its aggressive business practices in new markets, but also for its dysfunctional corporate culture that seems to have permitted, or turned a blind eye to, the harassment of female employees and sometimes clients,

and lower pay for females and targeted groups of ethnic minority drivers. After a wide-sweeping audit by former United States Attorney General Eric Holder in early 2017, numerous changes to the company's business practices were recommended, particularly changes at the company's top leadership positions.

It has been widely believed that Uber's corporate culture reflected the notions of its embattled founder, Travis Kalanick, who, by mid-2017, stepped down from his role as CEO because of the widening scandal and mounting dissatisfaction with the corporate culture he had built. In Uber's case, the CEO's leadership style colored the company's early success, but also contributed to major, systemic flaws that threatened the fledgling company's very existence.

---

leadership. Laissez-faire is a French term that means "allow them to do as they will." In other words, let workers do as they please. This type of leader usually acts as a representative for the group members, while allowing them to plan, control, and complete their tasks as they wish. For success with this leadership style, followers must be self-directed and motivated to act without intervention, and have a clear vision of goals and how to accomplish them.

Which of these four styles of leadership is best? That depends on two variables. First, the *situation* will usually determine the most effective style. High-ranking military personnel may expect a consultative style, whereas musicians in large orchestras will more likely expect the autocratic approach. College and university professors, on the other hand, will often expect either a free-rein approach (since they expect to be treated as independent professionals) or the participative style in their work environments.

The second variable focuses on the personality and skill level of the leader. Many managers seem unable to use more than one type of leadership style. This often has to do with the flexibility of the leader. Even when the situation calls for a different style, then, the leader will "default" to the style he or she is accustomed to, sometimes with negative results.

Laissez-faire also refers to a system of government in which industries and other economic influences are controlled very little. The term translates from French as "allow to do," or allowing events to happen as they will, or let people do what they choose.

more about...

DIFFERENT WAYS TO LEAD

There are several different leadership styles. *What are some of the factors that determine the success of a particular style?*

©John Fedele/Blend Images

Leaders and the Use of Power and Authority

The effectiveness of a leader also depends greatly on the leader's attitude toward power. **Power** can be defined as the ability of one person to influence another. This is not to be confused with **authority**, which is the power vested in a specific position within an organization.[15] Some leaders have authority, but little or no power. Other people—sometimes not even designated leaders—have power despite having very little authority.

Sources of Power

The way followers respond to power largely determines its effectiveness. How a leader's power is received can depend on where the power comes from.[16] Power is derived at least in part on the position of the person using it. Therefore, there are different forms of position power, as follows:

- **Legitimate power.** This source of power is based on the position the person holds in the organization. This type of power is effective only when followers believe in the legitimacy of the leader's position.
- **Reward power.** This type of power comes from the user's ability to control or influence others with something of value to them, such as praise or a promotion. The reward must be obtainable, and the potential receiver of the reward must believe in the other person's ability to bestow it.
- **Coercive power.** Coercive power depends on the threat of possible punishments, and is commonly used to enforce policies and regulations. When a leader has a great ability to intimidate followers, this type of power is often used.
- **Networking power.** This source of power is sometimes also called "connection power." You have probably heard the expression "It's not what you know; it's who you know." Gaining contacts to help influence others allows a leader to use this power source in many different situations. Often, other people's perception that a leader has that connection or network of connections is just as powerful as the fact itself.
- **Expert power.** Expert power comes from a person's knowledge or skill in areas that are critical to the success of the firm. The employee or manager with expert power has a power source that can often be amazingly strong.
- **Charismatic power.** This power source is based on the attractiveness a person has to others. To produce genuine power, though, the user of charismatic power must also be respected and have characteristics that others admire. Someone with a great deal of charismatic power can often compel others to do favors simply on the basis of positive personal response.[17]

STRENGTHENING YOUR NETWORK POWER.

This source of power comes from gaining contacts. *Can networking help you strengthen other areas of power?*

©Dave and Les Jacobs/Blend Images

power

The ability of one person to influence another.

authority

The vested power to influence or command within an organization.

legitimate power

Power based on the position a person holds in an organization that is effective only when followers believe in the structure that produces this power.

reward power

Power that comes from the user's ability to control or influence others with something of value to them.

coercive power

Power that depends on the threat of possible punishment.

networking power

Power that is attained by gaining contact and knowing the right people.

REAL WORLD EXAMPLE 7.5

Tanna quit her job as a systems analyst at a small manufacturing company because of sexism, expressed as significantly lower pay than her male co-workers received. After frantically searching for a replacement, they hired her back as a systems consultant. Now, the company was forced to pay her nearly three times what she had been paid before she quit. They had underestimated the strength of this woman's *expert power*.

» TEAM BUILDING

Groups and teams in an organization can improve their performance through what is known as **team building**. With sustained, conscious effort, a manager can build a team of employees who will function effectively as a unit and achieve group goals. Such a group is known as a **work team**. In building a work team, many of the qualities of informal groups that have already been discussed are created by the team leader. Team building can be a difficult, time-consuming process that requires effort from everyone involved.

Despite the difficulty and time, many organizations are willing to put the necessary effort into building the efficiency of work teams. There are many good reasons to do so, but from the position of management, the best reason to make any improvement is the "bottom line." Effective teams save companies money by reducing the need for middle management, increasing productivity, doing work that individuals or normal work groups can't do, and making better use of resources.[18] And in a global workplace, people located in different parts of the world may need to "team up" to get a product through production and onto store shelves.

Some employees, including Pete in our opening vignette, are not sold on the idea of work teams; they may even be downright hostile to the idea. They may see working in teams as a challenge to their individual expertise or abilities. Some employees may not want to do things in a "new" way; others think teamwork causes a duplication of effort or a waste of time. But these fears are not borne out by research on effective work teams.

Work teams actually allow individuals to have more say in their jobs, because they can discuss ideas with peers rather than just following instructions from a supervisor. Job satisfaction is then improved. When job satisfaction is improved, morale and productivity rise. Most people who work in teams say they would not want to go back to the "old" way of doing business. The use of work teams typically improves the company's "bottom line" while producing a higher-quality workplace atmosphere for employees.

In the more traditional approach to management, companies are run in a traditional management style—often with no pretense about groups and work teams. The traditional manager is more like the dictatorial captain of a ship than the player-captain of a basketball or football team.

expert power

Power that comes from a person's knowledge or skill in areas that are critical to the success of the firm.

charismatic power

Power that is based on the attractiveness a person has to others.

team building

The process of creating and encouraging a group of employees to work together toward achieving group goals and increased productivity.

work team

A group of employees with shared goals who join forces on a work project.

If you want a team-building approach to work in your company, several guidelines should help. First, good intentions are not enough. A formal training program should be used, preferably with a leader who has had some experience with team building elsewhere. People who have spent most of their work lives dealing with tasks individually will likely need training to learn new skills and habits.

If you are a manager, you may need to learn to let go. Team building involves delegating responsibilities to the group—responsibilities that were once only the manager's business. Such delegation often makes managers feel threatened by a loss of authority. The new management role they must learn is more like a coach or captain of a sports team than an absolute ruler. Whatever the manager says or does, the responsibility to get the job done still ends up with the group.

Implementation

When a team-building consultant starts working to create a work group, he or she will ask the following questions:

1. What do you want from this team? What can your membership in this group do for you personally—what do you want it to do?
2. What skills, abilities, or talents do you bring to this team?

These questions will often be asked in writing. From the answers, the team builder can learn a great deal about the needs and concerns of the people who will make up the team. The answers to these questions will determine the complexity of the task of building the team. Suppose, for example, that several people responded to the first question above, "I want the team to leave me alone and let me do my work." This might have been the answer given by Pete in the opening vignette. Those members would require some selling on the idea of team building before any real progress could be made.

Trust

Building trust is one of the first steps in creating a team. Without trust, there can be no team building. Imagine a basketball team whose members didn't trust each other enough to pass the ball. Whoever had the ball would only dribble and shoot. Winning games in this way is unlikely. Often, a great deal of group interaction must take place for a beginning level of trust to develop. Whatever method of trust building is used, it must get members' feelings out in the open so issues of trust can be resolved.

Goals

Finally, the team needs to review and agree upon goals, both individually and collectively. Establishing and refining goals can be aided by using two questions: "What do you want the team to accomplish, and what can you give?"

BUILDING TRUST

Trust among team members is essential for a team to be successful. *What are some of the consequences of lack of trust among team members?*

©Andersen Ross/Blend Images

Goals must be clear and attainable, and they must be considered important by all members of the team.[19]

» ORGANIZATIONAL CLIMATE: THE WEATHER OF THE WORKPLACE

The interaction of groups within the workplace aids in the formation of **organizational climate**, a term introduced in Chapter 5. Climate in the workplace has some qualities in common with climate in the context of weather. Climate can change rapidly, without warning. A manager with a negative attitude can change a positive climate to a stressful one just by walking into the room. Climate in the workplace can be influenced by environmental factors such as the color of the room, the noise level, and the way people dress. It also affects—and is affected by—the attitudes, stress levels, and communication of the people in the organization.

organizational climate

The emotional weather within an organization that reflects the norms and attitudes of the organization's culture and affects worker morale, attitudes, stress levels, and communication.

Major Qualities of Organizational Climate

The way people see things as individuals, their interactions, and the way an organization is put together produce the climate that all perceive with similar eyes. *Perception* is a very important part of organizational climate, as are *structure* and *interaction*.[20] Organizational climate involves the way members of an organization see it in terms of trust, recognition, freedom to create, fairness, and independence. The climate is produced by the way members relate to each other. It reflects the norms and attitudes of the organization's culture. It also influences and helps to shape the behavior of individuals. Perhaps most important, organizational climate is a basis for understanding any situation in the organization.[21]

A manager has a heavy responsibility to lead the organization in a way that will produce a good, or positive, organizational climate.[22] Everyone in the workplace can affect the climate, but the manager's position allows more influence than managers themselves often realize.

Maintaining a Climate

What is a good organizational climate? The best organizational climate is one that allows the highest efficiency and productivity over the longest period of time. That type of climate will almost always include qualities such as high trust levels, a reasonable level of freedom or autonomy in work tasks, high standards of fairness, and appropriate recognition for the work of each person, The best way to communicate these qualities is to set a conscious example. A good place to begin is just basic respect, courtesy, and ethical treatment. A manager can also show appreciation to individual employees for work done well, while allowing them the time and freedom to be creative.

The large hospital where Farid works is old and noisy. Everyone who works there wears the same type of uniform. The walls are painted standard pale green, and the floors are covered with a dreary gray linoleum. The institution's employee policies have not been changed in decades. It is no wonder than Farid finds the hospital to be an oppressive and stressful place to work. Patients have the same reactions. There are no plants in the waiting room, and the attitudes of the employees are stiff and cold, just like the hospital.

» ORGANIZATIONAL OR CORPORATE CULTURE: SHARED VALUES

How does an organization's *culture* differ from organizational climate? Organizational culture refers to the collection of deeply held values and assumptions a group of people share. Climate is different in that it reflects the day-to-day norms and attitudes of the organization's culture, i.e., how it "feels" to be in the office. Culture is found in every type of organization, from small individual companies to large, multinational corporations. Some industries have their own corporate culture regardless of geography, so that a person working as a medical assistant, programmer, or veterinary technician, for example, would know what to expect in a career field if they moved from one region to another.

Organizational or corporate culture is the system of shared values and beliefs in an organization. Values are more deep-seated than attitudes. As mentioned in Chapter 4, values also tend to involve a rank order. In other words, the very nature of values places them naturally in a list of varying importance. The values of an organization will set a pattern for its activities, opinions, and actions.[23] The trend today is to build a strong, positive culture that motivates employees to work harder, to feel greater loyalty, and to stay with the company and remain productive.

While every organization has a culture, sometimes it is difficult to see, especially if you look at it from the outside. Some cultures are loyal to management; some are loyal to the union. Some are very close-knit, with a great number of culture stories or myths inspiring loyalty and enthusiasm. Others are weaker, and lack the togetherness and team spirit enjoyed by the stronger cultures. Any culture, be it a corporation, a nation, or a family, is preserved and defined by *oral history* or *culture stories*.[24] **Culture stories** are miniature myths. The culture of an organization can be understood more fully by listening to these stories and finding common themes in them.

In addition to culture stories, leaders transmit organizational culture in many other ways. The way they react to crises at work, divide up limited resources, train and coach employees, even recruit and select employees—all of these actions tell employees what is important to the person in charge.

organizational or corporate culture

An organization's network that includes the shared values and assumptions within it.

culture stories

Stories that illustrate the values of the people who make an organization work.

REAL WORLD EXAMPLE 7.7

Huge transformations are occurring in the American workplace. Companies are taking more serious looks at employee satisfaction as business leaders have come to understand its direct correlation to job performance and the bottom line. Of any company, Alphabet, Inc. (parent company of Google) has been one of the most successful large companies in addressing employee happiness, and fostering a distinctly creative, competitive, productive business environment for its workforce.

One of the principal ways Google is able to maintain its success with employee satisfaction is by reinforcing its core values to employees as new hires, and in subsequent training. It also provides generous perks to employees, with free chef-made, organic meals throughout the day; onsite physicians and masseuses; nap pods; free dry cleaning; free haircuts, and more. By meeting their employees' material *hygiene* needs, Google feels that it will attract top talent and lead to happier, more productive employees who will stay longer with the company.

But even Google is not immune to the challenges that all businesses, large and small, face when creating and implementing the corporate values, or culture of the organization. After a male employee wrote an opinion piece contending that women are underrepresented in technology jobs because of psychological differences between men and women, Google fired the employee, then faced a storm of strong opinions from those supporting and those criticizing the company's decision.

To see what is valued at an organization, employees also look at the design and layout of the physical work space, the leadership structure of the organization, its systems and policies, rites and rituals, and reinforcement for employee behavior. In a well-run organization, these will all be consistent with the company's formally stated mission and philosophy or paradigms—which in itself is a public summary of its culture and values.[25]

The "New" Organizational or Corporate Culture: A Focus on Fairness

These days, many companies are working on developing an organizational or corporate culture that is more humane, more closely knit, and above all, more profitable and productive than in the past. The so-called new corporate culture is made up of a set of new assumptions about how people should be treated. Much of this new thinking is based on a deeper understanding of the importance of employee self-worth on the job. This is moving well beyond the early findings of Elton Mayo, discussed in Chapter 1, which influenced decades of thought on the role of human relations, and have since been re-examined.

Here are some of the commonly accepted qualities that an organizational or corporate culture should have. All of them are directly related to human relations and self-esteem issues.[26]

1. Instead of bullying or shouting, or otherwise being autocratic, a manager should avoid making an employee feel intimidated or overly uncomfortable. The autocratic approach may result in immediate obedience, but it will not inspire the dedication that is needed in a strong organizational culture.

2. Among the shared values of the culture, *fairness* is very high. Managers need to respond to the same behavior by different people in a consistently equal and just manner.

3. An emerging element of the new culture is *participative management*. A participative culture is open and nonthreatening. It allows everyone to give input when decisions are made that affect the whole group. The manager acts like the player-captain of an athletic team, and everyone feels free to discuss issues openly.[27]

4. The new culture allows for the *self-esteem development* of all members of the organization. Management experts have shown that few factors in the workplace are more damaging than those that decrease or threaten people's self-esteem. Membership in a closely knit group helps, along with giving encouragement and authentic praise.

5. The new organizational culture is goal-oriented. Individual goals and group goals are combined to produce a sense of direction and purpose that, ideally, is the most important of the culture's set of shared values.

A strong corporate culture must contain a sense of justice, equality, and balanced emotion in its treatment of people. Figure 7.1 is part of a questionnaire that has been used to study the fairness level of an organization.

more about...

Fairness

"In all people, without exception, there lives some instinct for truth, some attraction toward justice."

—Former U.S. President Franklin D. Roosevelt

Trust in the workplace is the main tool for employees' confidence in management, and management's confidence in employees. One's actions provide a record of trustworthiness. Building trust can be difficult, especially where there has been a record of unfairness or other untrustworthy behavior.

Consistency means remaining predictable and fair. Stability is threatened when there are apparent contradictions in the behaviors of people whom others are depending on, especially managers. With unpredictability and lack of stability come high stress levels.

Truth is one of the most obvious necessities for fairness. Yet the temptation can be great to tell "white lies," withhold information, and tell people what they want to hear.

Integrity is a way of describing the extent to which managers and others are truly willing to put the shared values and expectations of a culture into action. It also means maintaining an ethical code—which is basic to all cultures, as well as to organizations.

Expectations, as used here, refer to those that come from management. Through their expectations, managers allow the employees to know exactly what is expected of them both individually and in groups.

Equity means treating everyone with the same rules. If a culture has both consistency and equity, all are treated in a way that is fair and just, under all conditions.

Measuring the Fairness Level of an Organization

Check which sentences apply to you. Does your selection reveal what kind of climate you have at work?

Trust

☐ My manager follows through on and carries out promises.

☐ My manager often hides his or her true feelings from others.

Consistency

☐ My manager tells the same story no matter who is asking.

☐ My manager acts inconsistently.

Truthfulness

☐ My manager sometimes tells white lies to help others.

☐ My manager does not change facts in order to look better.

Integrity

☐ My manager keeps his or her word when he or she has made an agreement to do something.

☐ My manager is concerned more with watching out for himself or herself than with helping others.

Expectations

☐ My manager has clear ideas about expectations of employees.

☐ My manager makes sure employees know what is expected of them.

Equity

☐ It is obvious by my manager's actions that he or she has definite favorites among employees.

☐ My manager takes a person's work contributions into account when giving praise recognition.

Influence

☐ My manager makes sure that those who have a "stake" also have a "say."

☐ When an employee is capable of dealing with a job independently, my manager delegates appropriately.

Justice

☐ My manager administers rewards and discipline that fit the situation.

☐ My manager does not give rewards that are out of proportion or inappropriate.

Respect

☐ My manager shows with actions that he or she really cares about employees.

☐ My manager recognizes the strengths and contributions of employees.

Overall Fairness

☐ My manager is fair in how he or she treats employees.

☐ My manager always deals with employees equally.

figure 7.1

MEASURING FAIRNESS

Factors such as trust, consistency, and honesty—among many others—shape the overall fairness of an organization, and in turn shape that organization's climate. *Which factor do you consider most important?*

Source: Marshall Sashkin and Richard L. Williams, "Does Fairness Make a Difference?" *Organizational Dynamics*, Autumn 1990, pp. 56–71.

Influence means allowing each member of the organization to have a stake in a wide range of activities, including goal setting, problem solving, and helping to make changes.

Justice means that the reward must fit the achievement; the punishment must fit the crime. The two extremes in violation of this quality are overkill (strict zero tolerance, while looking for infractions to punish) and "looking the other way" by ignoring the situation when an infraction occurs.

Respect, or a deep sense of high regard for people, is the basis of all fairness. When you believe that others truly value you, you tend to consider their actions fair. Nonverbal signals, such as looking away or walking away while the other person is talking, often show lack of respect for others.

Overall fairness means much more than simply treating people nicely. Fairness is a central issue in the **psychological contract** between managers and subordinates. This contract is not a piece of paper; it is a sometimes unconscious, usually unspoken, agreement between two people to behave in certain ways toward each other.[28]

Psychological contracts are a part of all cultures. Although they may not be written down or discussed, they are understood between people. When fairness is implied by managers, employees expect such behaviors from them. Without fairness, the employee usually feels betrayed. A healthy organization will not violate employees' psychological contracts; rather it will respect agreements and expectations set up among management and staff.

psychological contract

An agreement that is not written or spoken but is understood between people.

more about...

The violation of a **psychological contract** is the most obvious and painful violation of the principles of fairness.

Source: Marshall Sashkin and Richard L. Williams, "Does Fairness Make a Difference?" *Organizational Dynamics*, Autumn 1990, pp. 56–71.

« STRATEGIES FOR SUCCESS

Strategy 7.1   Watching for Hidden Agendas

1. Be aware of strong emotions in other members.
2. Note contradictions between verbal and nonverbal signals.
3. Pay attention to themes that keep coming up, perhaps disguised, even after the formal topic has been changed.
4. Recognize agenda conflicts that involve a group member's self-esteem.

The key to eliminating hidden agendas from your behavior in groups is self-knowledge. Before you join a group, ask yourself, "Am I too focused on what I personally want from this group? Do I know how to keep personal needs from blocking my judgment?"

A tougher problem is dealing with the agendas of other group members. As the group leader, you have the power to prevent people's agendas from hurting the group. Even as a member, you can help by watching your behaviors and those of other group members. Important signals include the following:

1. **Be aware of strong emotions in other members.** A hidden agenda will often go beyond the immediate problem. What are those emotions based on, and how appropriate are they? Are they based on a prejudice against the group's real agenda? On fear? On jealousy? On a desire to intimidate other members? On a need for power or dominance?

2. **Note contradictions between verbal and nonverbal signals.** Group members may show hidden agendas through gestures, eye contact (or lack of it), head nods, frowning, and other body movements.

3. **Pay attention to themes that keep coming up, perhaps disguised, even after the formal topic has been changed.** If it's a deeply personal agenda, it could become an underlying issue in any discussion. Note discussions that keep coming back to a topic that someone in the group has brought forward that was not favorably received.

4. **Recognize agenda conflicts that involve a group member's self-esteem.** Often, these are the easiest to spot. Self-esteem issues are behind all or part of nearly any agenda issue in a group. The issue is often personal self-esteem versus the esteem of the group as a whole. Note decisions that go against what a particular group member advocated, that seem to be taken personally by the group member.

Strategy 7.2 Building a Successful Team

1. Train the team.
2. Manage the team as a team.
3. Delegate authority specifically.
4. Be a clarifier.
5. Be a communicator.

As is any new method of dealing with people, team building is full of possible areas of error. These possible errors should be examined carefully by anyone attempting team building before the first implementation step is attempted. Each of the following steps will help avoid common pitfalls in the team-building process.

1. **Train the team.** An untrained team might be an informal group; it may be several other things, but it is not a work team. By definition, a work team must be aware of the steps that are to be taken, and the members must be sold on the idea of team building. Often a would-be "team" will feel victimized by management unless each member receives training and understands the role he or she is expected to play.

2. **Manage the team as a team.** The manager has to allow the group to be managed as a team. Any traditional manager will be tempted to continue many of the management functions on an individual basis. Some managers may not be able to break the habit of calling each team member into their office privately to discuss major group problems that arise. They will need to work harder at using cooperative coaching as their model, addressing the group as a whole.

3. **Delegate authority specifically.** The team leader needs to make it very clear what parts of the management responsibilities are to be given over to the group and which are to be retained. The team builder often makes the mistake of thinking that since the team is in place, the leader needs only to sit back and watch.

4. **Be a clarifier.** A major role of the team leader is to clarify the nature of a task and the implementation of the solution. A particular manager, thinking he or she is a team leader, will tell the team to "work out the details" of plans and goals. The team leader needs to be attuned to details, allowing the group to work together but coordinating those efforts through careful monitoring.

5. **Be a communicator.** Whether you are the team leader or a member, you need to listen, write, and speak carefully. Of the three skills, listening is the most important.

To appreciate the usefulness of a successful work team, one needs only to examine a company that has made the concept work. Morale is high, turnover is less, and productivity is higher.

CHAPTER SEVEN SUMMARY

Chapter Summary by Learning Objectives

LO 7-1 Discuss the characteristics and purposes of formal and informal groups. People join groups for many reasons, including affiliation, attraction, activities, assistance, or proximity. Formal groups are created for a specific purpose, while informal groups come together on their own and are more voluntary and fluid in their membership. A group is two or more people who interact with each other, are governed by norms, maintain stable role relationships, and form subgroups.

LO 7-2 Discuss development of groups. Usually, four stages of group development occur, in a specific order: forming, redefining, coordinating, and formalizing.

LO 7-3 Examine barriers to group effectiveness and their resolutions. Groupthink, status differences, hidden agendas, one-person domination, resistance to change, continued conflict, and lack of creativity can all lead to an ineffective group. Strategies to resolve barriers include changing the group's norms, identifying the specific problems, and changing the group's composition.

LO 7-4 Define leadership, leadership styles, and types of power. Leaders are able to influence others toward attaining goals. Leadership styles include autocratic, consultative, participative, and free-rein. Sources of power among leaders include legitimate, reward, coercive, networking, expert, and charismatic power.

LO 7-5 Explain the steps in team building. Effective team building requires time and effort. Trust building and identification of goals are necessary steps. Implementation and purpose must be defined. Good communication and clarity are essential.

LO 7-6 Improve the organizational climate of the workplace. The climate of a workplace is the tone of its day-to-day functioning. Climate includes physical environment of the workplace, attitudes of managers, communication between employees, and norms of the organization.

LO 7-7 Understand the new organizational or corporate culture. Every organization and corporate entity has a culture. Culture includes deeply held values that are used to set goals. Culture stories help transmit and describe the culture. The "new" organizational or corporate culture focuses on fairness, respect, equity, justice, balanced emotions, truth, integrity, shared influence, and trust. This type of culture promotes a more humane, loyal, and productive workplace.

key terms

authority 174
autocratic leaders 170
charismatic power 175
coercive power 174
conformity 168
consultative leaders 170
culture stories 178
expert power 175
formal group 166
free-rein leaders 170

group 166
group process 167
groupthink 168
hidden agendas 171
informal group 166
leadership 171
legitimate power 174
networking power 174
norm 167
organizational climate 177

organizational or
 corporate culture 178
participative leaders 170
power 174
psychological contract 182
reward power 174
status 168
task activity 167
team building 175
work team 175

review questions

1. Think of groups you have joined, both formally and informally. What were the benefits you expected to receive upon joining? Were those expectations fulfilled?

2. Recall a group to which you have belonged and identify the major norms the group followed. What were the penalties for breaking from a group norm?

3. Recalling groups to which you have belonged, how did they assign status in the group? Was it easy to see who had higher and lower status in the group? Did you agree with the statuses that seemed to be assigned within the group? Explain.

4. Recall a leader whose direction you once followed. Do you recognize that leader's style as autocratic, consultative, participative, or free-rein? Provide examples of behaviors that showed that style. Explain whether you liked or disliked this style of leadership.

5. Imagine a leader in any setting with whom you have worked using more than one of the styles of leadership explained in this chapter. Would this improve his or her abilities as a leader? How can flexibility influence a leader? Are there any drawbacks to flexibility?

6. Think of an ideal version, in your opinion, of a perfect organizational climate. What characteristics would be included? Why?

7. Fairness is an important quality of a positive, or warm, organizational climate and culture. What qualities are necessary for a perception of fairness to exist throughout an organization?

8. Explain the "new organizational or corporate culture." In your opinion, would this type of culture lead toward success for America as an international competitor? Why or why not?

9. At a national conference attended by one of your authors, a facilitator introduced a workshop topic as "How to Work in Teams, and Other Raising-Morale Crap." The audience reaction included dismay and surprise at the speaker's negativity toward the announced topic. Based on information from this chapter, what type of corporate culture would you guess this facilitator worked in? How well does it fit with the "new" corporate culture?

10. Imagine yourself as (a) a ship captain, and (b) a football team player and captain. How would you describe the advantages and disadvantages of each? Considering these advantages and disadvantages, why do you suppose that the team captain, rather than the ship captain, is a more popular analogy for management styles today in the United States?

critical thinking questions

1. Which of the leadership styles is yours or would most likely be yours? Why did you choose this particular style? Does your profession of choice match with this style? How does this leadership style reflect your personality?

2. Is an organizational or corporate culture necessary? That is, can we all just go to work and get our tasks done in an organization that does not have a shared culture? How important is it for an organization to have a shared corporate culture? Why is this such a common—practically universal—phenomenon? Think about an organization that has no corporate culture: What would that be like? Would people get as much accomplished?

working it out 7.1

HOW IS THE "WEATHER" IN YOUR ORGANIZATIONAL CLIMATE?

School-to-Work Connection: Resource Skills, System Skills, and Interpersonal Skills

Organizations have a pleasant or unpleasant climate, whether it is stated or not, whether it is admitted or not. The corporate culture that may be captured in a company's mission statement can sometimes give you clues about the organizational climate. Even though an organization may formally state its climate goals, and these are then agreed upon by an organization as a whole, the intended organizational climate may be interpreted in different ways by different members of the organization.

In this exercise, think about three different offices you have visited within the same organization (your own workplace, or somewhere else), or think about three different instructors' offices at the college you are attending. What differences do you note in pleasantness or unpleasantness of the organizational climate?

Consider these factors in your descriptions of each of the three offices:

1. How is the furniture arranged? Does the desk act as a barrier between the office occupant's chair and the visitor's chair? (Are there even any chairs for visitors?)

2. Is the office stark or inviting? Are there personal effects in the office, such as plants, pictures of family members, or artwork?

3. Is the office cluttered and disorganized, or neatly arranged?

4. How is your interaction with the office occupant? Does he or she make eye contact, or avoid it? Does the person do other tasks while talking with you—take phone calls, look at his or her watch or cell phone while talking—or give you full attention? Does the person smile and act inviting, or frown and act annoyed to see you?

Compare your evaluations of the three offices and discuss your findings in a small group of classmates. What does this exercise tell you about how you will set up, or modify, your own office?

working it out 7.2

ROLE-PLAY

School-to-Work Connection: Interpersonal Skills

Procedure: Break the class into groups of five or fewer. One person will be the team leader, and the others will be the team members. The team leader will read the following script while the team members respond where they think appropriate, correcting the team leader on his or her misunderstood concepts of work teams.

Scenario: You are working in a company that has just now enthusiastically embraced the idea of work teams. Your former supervisor, now "Team Leader," hasn't been to the team leader training yet, but really likes the idea of working as a team. The team leader delivers the following pep talk on teamwork one Monday morning.

As you listen, decide what your response will be whenever you think your team leader is saying the wrong thing. Try not to interrupt the team leader as he or she speaks.

"Hey, Group! Team of mine! Good morning! Wow, we're all together again after a great weekend! Hey, how about that Seahawks-Giants game?

So, this morning we're going to start working as a team, just like the Golden State Warriors. You all know what to do, you know your parts, so get out there and play ball! I'm going to be calling each one of you into my office, one at a time, to talk about this team thing. Now, when I call you in, bring in a pad and pencil, because I'm going to be giving you all the team directions. Don't worry about thinking up stuff to say or making any decisions, I've got it all figured out how this is going to run. In the meantime, if you need me, I'll be in my office; but try to make an appointment, because I'll be doing my regular administrative stuff. Okay? Then here we go, team! *Go team, go!*"

When the team leader is finished with the pep talk you may do the following:

1. Ask any questions you have about the pep talk.
2. (Gently!) Correct his or her misconceptions about working as a team.

working it out 7.3

GROUP COHESION

School-to-Work Connection: Thinking Skills, Personal Qualities Skills, Information Skills, Interpersonal Skills, and Systems Skills

"NASA: Survival on the Moon" is a famous exercise by Dr. Jay Hall that demonstrates the effectiveness of group interaction. Following is a list of 15 survival-related items. On your own, rank them from highest (what you need to survive on the moon) to lowest (what you want or need the least). At this time you will not be sharing your list with your group. Place number "1" by the most important item, number "2" by the second most important, and so on through number "15," the least important.

_____ Matches, 1 box

_____ Food concentrates

_____ Nylon rope, 50 feet

_____ Parachute silk

_____ Portable heating unit, solar-powered

_____ Pistols, two .45-caliber

_____ Dehydrated milk, 1 case

_____ Oxygen, two 100-pound tanks

_____ Stellar map

_____ Life raft, self-inflating

_____ Magnetic compass

_____ Water, 5 gallons

_____ Signal flares

_____ First-aid kit (w/injection needles)

_____ FM receiver–transmitter, solar-powered

- Form into groups of four to six. Each member should have his or her own list of survival-related items completed.

- Each group should arrive at a consensus on each rank. Don't use a democratic vote or try to change someone's vote. Consensus means that each team member must at least agree somewhat with each conclusion, so the decision will be unanimous.

- Next, the instructor will provide the numbers that go into the "Survey Score" section. The "Survey Score" section is in the *Instructor's Resource Manual.* These rankings are the result of an official survey of astronauts' opinions.

- Subtract the difference between the rankings in the individuals' core column and the survey score column, and add up the total at the bottom. Ignore plus and minus; what you are measuring is the degree of difference in either direction.

- Next, subtract the difference between the group score column and the survey score.

- Add up this total at the bottom.

Answer the following questions:

1. Did any individual have a total lower than the team? If so, either the group was not working as efficiently as it could have, or the individual member was not being sufficiently assertive with his or her knowledge.

2. Also, describe the group processes of each group.

   a. Did any of the groups function without a leader? If so, how did they make decisions?

   b. If the group had a leader, what style of leadership did the leader use?

   c. Were there any disagreements? If so, how were they resolved?

Reprinted with permission from Leadership Management International, Inc.

case study 7.1

Mariko's Promotion

Part of Mariko Koide's promotion in the advertising firm where she worked was a transfer to another division of the company. The promotion seemed like a totally positive experience for her, and she was very happy—at least initially. Her first day in the new division was one of handshaking, smiles, and welcoming comments. Things looked really positive.

However, after a few weeks had passed, it became apparent to Mariko that this division had a different "feeling" to it. In her old office, her fellow employees had spent a great deal of time on what they called "idea creation." Some nights, when ideas were a bit slow in coming, everyone would work two or three hours late. Throughout the process, everyone had seemed positive and upbeat and not at all resentful of the long sessions.

The new division was not like that at all. It seemed that a great deal of conflict was always afoot. One worker was always complaining about what a "jerk" someone else was. Overtime sessions were rare, and when they happened, they were resented and typically resulted in dozens of oral and written complaints. The walls of the restrooms had insulting caricatures of some of the managers on the walls, with equally insulting comments written below them.

Also, all of the employees seemed to be heavily involved in outside activities that had nothing to do with company business, or even with the talents needed to work there. The very idea of working late *voluntarily* was laughable.

Mariko began wondering whether she should have accepted the promotion. Instead of being excited and happy, she began finding it difficult to get up in the morning and drive to work. "I wonder if I could get back to the other division," she found herself thinking one day.

Case Study Questions

1. If you knew Mariko as a friend, what would you advise her to do at this point?

2. Is Mariko helpless in her new position? If you don't think so, suggest some courses of action she could take.

3. Evaluate Mariko's situation in terms of norms and status.

case study 7.2

Through the Ranks

Daura had been promoted through the ranks of her company to her present supervisory position in management. The president of the company recently asked her to create another administrative position—one that would report directly to Daura—which would be filled internally. The president was aware that a lot of recent conflict between administration and nonadministrative staff members had led to low morale and high employee turnover, and she had decided one way to reduce this was to create the new position to bridge the gap between these two employee groups. Seven people applied for the newly created position, and Daura sent each of them an e-mail saying that she would be interviewing only the top two or three candidates.

Soon, grumbling among applicants and other employees interested in the process began to be heard, based mainly on the decision to interview only a few candidates. Since interviews for seven applicants could be managed pretty easily, and employee morale was already low, they reasoned, *all* applicants deserved at least a "courtesy interview." Before the final candidates were announced,

Daura's administrative assistant approached her and asked her if it would be possible to schedule interviews for all seven candidates as a way to reduce growing resentment among employees.

Daura's response was straight to the point as she snapped: "If they don't like the process, they can quit. They'd better be happy I even agreed to go along with the decision to open this position. I'm in charge here, and none of you had better forget it. Anyone who wants to stand up to me on this had better do it now, so I know who the troublemakers are and I can make sure they don't get promoted."

Case Study Questions

1. What leadership style does Daura seem to be using?

2. What are Daura's sources of power? Are these the most appropriate ones she should be using in this situation?

3. If you were Daura's manager, would you try to change behaviors in her leadership methods? Which ones? Why?

CHAPTER ELEVEN

CONFLICT
MANAGEMENT

« «   **LEARNING OBJECTIVES**

After studying this chapter, you will be able to:

LO 11-1   Identify the types of conflict.

LO 11-2   List sources of conflict.

LO 11-3   Define conflict analysis.

LO 11-4   Give examples of potential solutions to a conflict.

LO 11-5   Compare and contrast styles of conflict management.

LO 11-6   Explain how to deal with special conflict cases.

« «   **STRATEGIES FOR SUCCESS**

Strategy 11.1   Negotiate Win-Win Solutions

Strategy 11.2   Make Collaboration Work

Strategy 11.3   Stop Conflicts before They Start

Conflict on the Job

SITUATION

"I feel so conflicted about my job," Mary said to her friend over coffee. She had come home that Friday evening frustrated—again—from her job in customer service for an automotive manufacturer.

©Big Cheese Photo/SuperStock

"I love helping people in my job, but I feel that what I'm asked to do is not really fulfilling that promise of customer service." Mary's friend looked confused and asked what she meant by that. "Well, I am expected to tell customers things that I know for a fact are not true. Lying to people just doesn't seem right to me; that's not how I was raised."

"What kinds of things are you expected to lie about?" her friend asked.

DISCOVERY

"Well," Mary said, "I think the worst thing is that I'm supposed to tell them that someone will contact them about the problems they're experiencing with their cars, and we will make sure the problems are fixed. But I know for a fact that will not likely happen. Sometimes they never get a call back, and I know their cars are not always getting fixed. I am supposed to tell them that their satisfaction is guaranteed, but I don't even know what that means—we have nothing to back it up with. I need this job, but it makes me feel horrible about myself doing it."

THINK ABOUT IT

Mary's situation is an illustration of one type of conflict discussed in this chapter. What other sources of conflict can you think of that might exist in a workplace like Mary's? What would you do if you were in Mary's position in terms of keeping your job, and in terms of the false promises made to customers?

» TYPES OF CONFLICT

Wherever there are people, there is conflict. Mary's frustration with her own company is quite typical. The results of conflict can range from minor inconveniences to major losses, even company failures. In American business, the workplace contains a greater amount of conflict today than in the past, mainly because of the movement of the United States from an industrial economy to a service-dominated economy. In a service economy, work tasks depend much more on successful interactions between people. Service industries account for roughly 77 percent of employment in the U.S. overall, and 70 percent or more of employment in 49 out of 50 states (Wyoming is the exception). Four out of five jobs are found in the service sector, and this sector makes up 70 percent of gross domestic product or GDP.[1] Everywhere, business leaders are striving to increase the productivity of services. Since conflict nearly always damages productivity, the U.S. workplace is in need of both workers and managers who can deal with conflict in a realistic and helpful way.[2]

Several common aspects are involved in all types of conflict:

- Conflict must be perceived by all people involved in it, because whether or not there is a conflict is often a matter of perception.

- Nearly all definitions of conflict involve opposition or incompatibility.

- Some type of interaction is going on, or all parties would be avoiding conflict.[3]

conflict

A process that begins when one person sees that another person has damaged—or is about to damage—something that the other person cares about.

For the purposes of this chapter, **conflict** will be defined as a process that begins when one person sees that another person has damaged—or is about to damage—something that the other person cares about.[4] Someone might perceive that damage is a possible outcome, and that perception itself can begin a conflict. The damage or perception of attempted damage does not have to involve a physical object; it also can mean threat or damage to ideas, values, or goals.

Conflict is usually seen as a negative factor in the workplace. However, it can be both beneficial and constructive when approached correctly. One way to classify conflicts is by seeing them as either **functional** or **dysfunctional,** that is, either constructive or destructive. For example, when a group of employees meets to make a decision that affects all of them, some conflict can be good because too much unity and agreement can result in a poor decision (groupthink). When people focus more on getting along well than on coming up with creative solutions in decision making, they may not generate as many ideas as they would have otherwise. However, if the same group generates so much conflict that fighting and polarization result, that decision could also be faulty. A manager should try whenever possible to change a dysfunctional (destructive) conflict into a functional (constructive) one.

functional conflict

Constructive conflict.

dysfunctional conflict

Destructive conflict.

Another way to classify conflict is by the participants in the conflict.

Inner conflict is conflict within an individual. It might involve values, loyalties, or priorities. Suppose that your manager wants you to do something, but you will feel immoral, or your co-workers will call you a "fink" or infor-

inner conflict

Conflict within an individual; it might involve values, loyalties, or priorities; the pressure you feel when you are forced to make a choice.

REAL WORLD EXAMPLE 11.1

Ed works as a community health worker. His purpose for working is to help people, and he puts in a lot of time and effort in doing so. Robin also works for the organization, but she spends more time at her desk than helping clients. Ed perceives her to be a time waster—someone who doesn't hold the values he holds. Values, personalities, and loyalties could all be involved in the conflict that may occur between Ed and Robin.

mant if you do. Or suppose that you have two job offers, both with attractive qualities that pull you in opposite directions.

A **person-versus-person conflict** involves two people who are at odds over personality differences, values conflicts, loyalties, or any number of issues. When only two people are involved in a conflict, the focus tends to be personal on both sides (see Real World Example 11.1).

Intergroup conflict takes place when already-formed groups have conflicts with each other. When this type of conflict takes place, the conflict often becomes widespread. War provides an extreme example of intergroup conflict.

Intragroup conflict occurs when a conflict arises among group members, and they choose sides and split off into factions within the existing group (see Real World Example 11.2). Sometimes intragroup conflict evolves from person-versus-person conflict because people take sides with the two opposing individuals.

Person-versus-group conflict occurs most often when a member of a group breaks its rules, or norms. It also can involve someone who never was a member of the group, but who opposes it (see Real World Example 11.3).

» SOURCES OF CONFLICT

The preceding four types of conflict describe in general terms *who* is involved in each type, but not *how* conflict starts. No two disagreements are alike; each one starts at a different point over different issues. If you know what type of conflict you are involved in, that knowledge can help you discover how best to resolve it.[5] Figure 11.1 shows the sources of conflict and their potential solutions.

Content Conflict

When disagreements stem from a **content conflict,** they tend to focus on disagreements over what a statement or concept means. The only real issue is whether or not an idea is right. The rightness of an idea usually focuses on one of two factors: existence or meaning. For example, if the argument is about whether or not there is a Loch Ness monster, the disagreement is over existence.

person-versus-person conflict

Conflict that involves two people who are at odds over personality differences, values conflicts, loyalties, or any number of issues.

intergroup conflict

Takes place when already-formed groups have conflicts with each other.

intragroup conflict

Conflict that occurs when two groups form and take sides.

person-versus-group conflict

Conflict that occurs most often when a member of a group breaks its rules, or norms.

content conflict

Conflict that tends to focus on disagreements over what a statement or concept means.

REAL WORLD EXAMPLE 11.2

Several medieval monks were having a heated discussion about how many teeth a horse has. After the discussion had gone on for nearly an hour, a young monk offered to go out to the post where his horse was tied and count the horse's teeth. He was promptly scolded and called a troublemaker. Because the young monk wanted to solve the debate, he indirectly showed the others that their arguing was pointless—and they were angry.

figure 11.1

SOURCES OF CONFLICT

These are the four basic sources of conflict. *Which of these sources do you feel is easiest to confront and resolve?*

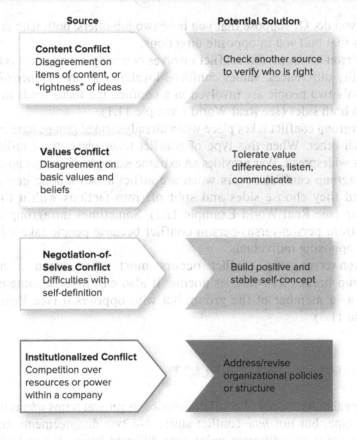

Source	Potential Solution
Content Conflict Disagreement on items of content, or "rightness" of ideas	Check another source to verify who is right
Values Conflict Disagreement on basic values and beliefs	Tolerate value differences, listen, communicate
Negotiation-of-Selves Conflict Difficulties with self-definition	Build positive and stable self-concept
Institutionalized Conflict Competition over resources or power within a company	Address/revise organizational policies or structure

If the conflict is over existence, it helps to have some way of verifying whether or not something is real. The Loch Ness monster is real to a few people, so the conflict over its existence still abounds—as it does over the conspiracy theories of President Kennedy's death, the existence of UFOs, and many other issues that are difficult to prove or disprove to everyone's satisfaction. However, when an original or reliable factual source can settle the dispute, arguing is pointless. Many existence issues are more like the number of a horse's teeth. Both sides should wait until proof is available.

More commonly, content conflicts are over meaning and interpretation. If the argument is about whether or not the task you were just assigned is included in the vague wording of your job description, you have probably moved into a disagreement over meaning. You might find a copy of your

REAL WORLD EXAMPLE 11.3

The six mechanics from Nello's Paint & Body Shop had a tradition of shooting pool together at a local bar every Friday evening. After this continued for over a year, one of the six quit the body shop and was replaced by Raffi, a non-pool player. Interpersonal conflicts resulted from Raffi's unintentional breaking of this group norm, as the other mechanics regularly asked him to come and shoot pool, and he declined, saying that he was not interested in wasting time and money in a bar or in learning to shoot pool.

job description and discover that it contains wording so ambiguous that your present task may or may not be appropriate to it, according to different interpretations. Even the interpretation of certain laws by different attorneys would fall in the category of content conflicts over meaning, as Americans witnessed in the very close presidential election of 2016.

Values Conflict

A **values conflict** usually goes very deep. For example, a Democrat, a Republican, a Green Party member, and a Libertarian Party member would likely disagree on many issues related to politics. In the workplace, managers may have deep disagreements with each other over management practices. These disagreements may be rooted in their values and the basic beliefs they hold about people and how they should be treated.

Values conflicts can be solved, rather than avoided. The solution is that many people need to develop a greater tolerance of values differences. By listening carefully and communicating your values cautiously, you can often create a sense of trust and mutual respect for differences. You will find that if you think carefully about your own values, examining them regularly, you will feel less threatened by someone with values unlike your own. Often that security becomes contagious!

values conflict

Conflict that occurs when one set of values clashes with another, and a decision has to be made.

Negotiation-of-Selves Conflicts

This type of conflict erupts over differences in self-definition. Individuals generally define who they are based on their own self-concepts. Many people see themselves as less worthy than they really are, while some see themselves as superior to others. Employees are likely to see themselves differently than the manager sees them; children see themselves differently than their parents see them, and so on.

Many interpersonal conflicts are based on a **negotiation-of-selves conflict.** Part of being human is being constantly involved in the process of defining yourself to others and responding to their implied definitions of themselves. Most of this activity goes on unnoticed. A rude bank loan officer will hardly say, "Well, I'm responding this way to you because I feel that I'm superior to you." Even the nonverbal cues in such a case might not deliver the correct message, because people try to play the roles that society has constructed.

negotiation-of-selves conflict

Conflict that is involved in the process of defining yourself to others and responding to their implied definitions of themselves.

REAL WORLD EXAMPLE 11.4

A state government agency was planning its annual budget when factions formed behind two rival leaders who were both perceived as powerful, and disliked each other. The conflict continued at a high level until members of the majority "winning" side were running the agency and in charge of the funds. The opposing members gradually quit and found other jobs, or lost interest in the conflict and focused on other tasks of the agency.

more about...

Values Conflicts

Often, many people exaggerate the number of **values conflicts** they have. A conflict may seem to be over values but is actually over the other person's perception of you and your perception of yourself, with neither side identifying the real issue.

Consider the following real-world negotiations-of-selves conflicts.

Employee: Why is it always my job to take messages? I'm not good at things like that. I get messages wrong and mess up a lot.

Boss: I ask you to take messages because you are, in fact, very good at it.

Mother: What on earth are you thinking, coming home at this ungodly hour? You're not old enough to be trusted out this late.

CONFLICT ON THE JOB

Conflict comes in more ways than many people imagine. Like Mary at the beginning of the chapter, you may expect conflict from certain aspects of your job—such as dealing with customers. However, conflict among employees, or between levels of employees, can also be very destructive. *What conflict do you feel is most common in organizations?*

©Marcus Clackson/Getty Images

Conflict Management   «   CHAPTER 11

Daughter: I'm only two years younger than you were when you met Dad. Lighten up. I can take care of myself.

Employee 1: What do you think of this report? I'd really like some input on it.

Employee 2: Don't look to me for approval. I'm not your boss.

All three of the preceding brief exchanges have something in common. They express conflicts that originate from the speakers' self-concept and self-definition. Conflicts such as these can focus on power or authority (as the first two do), on personality traits (as all of them do), or on questions of duty and obligation.

Institutionalized Conflict

Institutionalized conflict occurs when a conflict factor is built into the structure or the policies of the organization. Some organizations encourage conflict, just by the way they are structured. One example of institutionalized conflict is sports at the professional or even high school or college level, where competition for a starting position on the team is built into the organizational structure, and competition among teams is the purpose of the organization. A second example is a sales organization where competition for the most sales is a company's policies, with rewards and benefits going to the top sellers.

institutionalized conflict

Conflict that occurs when a conflict factor is built into the structure of the organization.

» CONFLICT ANALYSIS

Anyone wishing to manage a conflict should begin by looking closely at what is really happening. When strong emotions are involved, there is a temptation by conflict managers to jump to conclusions before examining the interests of those in conflict—and their own interests, as well.[6] Instead of making this common mistake, try focusing on these questions instead:

- **Who is involved?** How many people are taking part in this conflict? How well do they understand the basic issues? Are any of them repeatedly involved in conflicts, or is this a unique situation? By knowing these details, a leader can do a better job of designing a conflict management process that addresses everyone's interests.

- **What is at stake?** Do all or both sides in the dispute agree about what is really at stake? If duties and responsibilities are at stake, does everyone agree on exactly what those issues are? If money is involved, is everyone talking about the same amount? Does the issue center on assigning blame for misconduct, or could the issue be expressed as a desire to define proper conduct for the future? Without this step, the entire issue can become blurred.

- **How important is time?** Does this dispute have to be settled right away? If so, why? Does one side benefit from stalling? Would both sides benefit from a thoughtful, measured analysis of the situation that may take more time? A conflict manager should consider if the time factor will cool tempers on both sides, or if the passage of time will simply aggravate the issue.

- **What are the tie-ins with other issues?** What relationship does this dispute have with other disputes between the individuals or groups involved? What working relationships will likely be affected by the outcome of the conflict?

After these questions are answered (and assuming you decide that the issue is worth resolving), a solution can be negotiated.

» POTENTIAL SOLUTIONS

Generally speaking, there are three possible solutions to a conflict: win-lose, lose-lose, and win-win. The first two tend to produce a negative, side-taking mentality and are not likely to solve the problem permanently. Yet sometimes, because of time constraints and the other side's unwillingness to work toward a win-win solution, you may be forced to use win-lose or lose-lose tactics.

Win-Lose

win-lose strategy

A strategy that allows one side of a conflict to win at the expense of another.

The **win-lose strategy** allows one side of a conflict to win at the expense of the other.[7] It works as a quick-fix conflict solution that sometimes must be chosen when a win-win approach isn't feasible. One win-lose approach is the *democratic vote*. Democracy sounds like a wonderful approach to conflict resolution, and it is the approach on which our political system is based. Unlike a political system, though, most organizations don't contain a series of checks and balances, political rallies, or campaigning. In these situations, the majority vote will leave a minority of unhappy people without any real recourse. Especially when a vote is very close, many people on the losing side will potentially be unhappy. These are the people who are likely to bring the problem back, perhaps in another form.

Another win-lose approach is the *arbitrary approach* (arbitration). With this method, the conflict manager decides which side is right and which is wrong, then considers the issue to be resolved. Like the democratic vote, this approach produces a situation in which the losers tend to have hard feelings against both the winning side and the conflict manager. A skillful conflict manager or arbitrator can soften the effect of the arbitrary approach by using persuasive explanations. Usually, however, the gains from win-lose are short-term ones only, and problems will very likely continue.

more about...

Win-Lose

The American legal system takes a **win-lose strategy** (also called an *adversarial system*). What are the benefits of this? The drawbacks? Is there a better approach for certain situations?

REAL WORLD EXAMPLE 11.5

In a negotiation of labor union contracts, labor and management had been unable to reach agreement on a new contract for several months. After a grueling six-hour meeting with a neutral external professional negotiator, both sides left the negotiation table smiling. Both sides felt they had won their major points. In a true win-win strategy, a negotiator will find the most critical points of conflict for each side, and work to settle those in a resolution that both sides find acceptable.

Lose-Lose

In the **lose-lose strategy,** everyone gives up something. The main approach in lose-lose is compromise. That is, nobody gets what they want, but everyone can live with the decision. Like win-lose, this method usually fails to solve the underlying causes of the conflict. *Unlike* win-lose, the lose-lose strategy produces unhappy people on both sides of the issue. In the lose-lose strategy, the arbitrator typically gives little attention to tracing the development of the conflict, resulting in solutions that are mostly short term.[8]

Win-Win

A **win-win strategy** is one in which both sides feel they have come out on top. One might ask how both sides in a conflict could end up feeling like winners. The reason is that most conflicts stem from multiple sources and reasons. Because of this complexity, win-win can be accomplished. The key to the success of the win-win strategy is to satisfy as many of each side's needs as possible.[9] People in conflict almost always have more than one reason for being involved in the dispute, and they tend to attach different priorities to each of those reasons. They will, as a rule, be satisfied with less than the entire package if they feel their main goals are achieved. (See Strategy for Success 11.1.)

≫ STYLES OF CONFLICT MANAGEMENT

Everyone has his or her own style of managing conflicts, usually divided into five common approaches, discussed in the following list (also see Figure 11.2). The style you use will have a tremendous impact on the outcome of a conflict and will determine whether it has negative or positive consequences (see Figure 11.3 for effective conflict resolution strategies). Before you read any further, take the Conflict Management Style survey at the end of this chapter in Working It Out 11.1 to find out what your preferred style of conflict management is.

lose-lose strategy
A strategy in which everyone gives up something, and the focus is on compromise.

win-win strategy
A strategy that leads to a solution in which both sides feel they have come out on top.

DIFFERENT STYLES OF MANAGING CONFLICT

People have many different styles of managing conflict. They include the competitor, the avoider, the compromiser, the accommodator, and the collaborator. *Why might the collaborator require the most skill and diplomacy of all the styles of managing conflict?*

©Jeanette Dietl/Shutterstock

REAL WORLD EXAMPLE 11.6

Williams Home and Auto Insurance has five departments, all bidding for a portion of a limited company budget. Whatever one department gains, the other four see as a loss. In the end, it is very possible that none of the five will be completely content with the outcome. Conflict, it seems, is built into the way the company allocates funds.

figure 11.2

THE THOMAS–KILMAN CONFLICT MODEL

These are the five styles of conflict management. Each has a different level of assertiveness and cooperation. *With which style do you identify?*

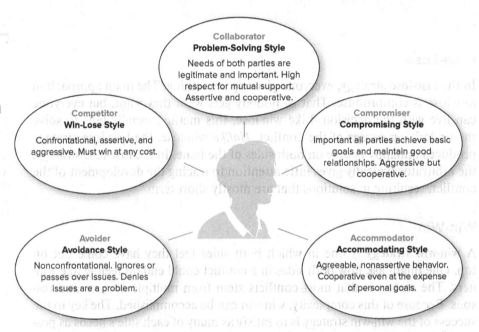

Collaborator
Problem-Solving Style
Needs of both parties are legitimate and important. High respect for mutual support. Assertive and cooperative.

Competitor
Win-Lose Style
Confrontational, assertive, and aggressive. Must win at any cost.

Compromiser
Compromising Style
Important all parties achieve basic goals and maintain good relationships. Aggressive but cooperative.

Avoider
Avoidance Style
Nonconfrontational. Ignores or passes over issues. Denies issues are a problem.

Accommodator
Accommodating Style
Agreeable, nonassertive behavior. Cooperative even at the expense of personal goals.

competitor

Someone who is most likely to try a win-lose approach to conflict resolution, especially if he or she is personally involved in the conflict.

avoider

Someone who would rather not be around conflict at all and values neutrality highly.

compromiser

Someone who uses his or her skills to blend differences and form a workable alternative.

1. **A competitor** is the most likely to try a win-lose approach to conflict resolution, especially if he or she is personally involved in the conflict. The ideals of teamwork are foreign to competitors, and they rarely move to a win-win solution. If the conflict manager (who should be neutral) is a competitor, he or she might use the lose-lose style to resolve the issue. In this role, competitors are afraid of the disruption that could result from other people's conflict, so they work rapidly and energetically to eliminate the potential disruption.

2. **An avoider** would rather not be around conflict at all. Remaining neutral is very important to an avoider. When the avoider is a manager, he or she will often mistakenly assume that if a conflict involves only other people, it should be left only to them. However, if any conflict is causing even the slightest morale problem at work, *it is the manager's business to resolve it.* Some avoiders will say positive things about the conflict if someone else does bring it up; others will pretend that nothing significant has happened. In either situation, though, the avoider often feels great internal stress.

3. **A compromiser** uses his or her skills to blend differences of both sides together and form a workable alternative. Although allowing the issue

CONFLICT RESOLUTION METHODS: A TOOK KIT

Conflict Resolution Skills

The *Conflict Resolution Network* has mapped 12 skills to develop and include in a tool kit for resolving conflicts. Effective use of these skills will result in a more cohesive workplace, where people feel they can trust each other and experience more satisfying communication and relationships. Using this took kit, we can pull out the skills that are appropriate for specific situations. The 12 skills include:

1. **Develop a Win-Win Approach.** Work together as partners, rather than as opponents, to decide how a conflict can be minimized and resolved. Shift your attitude from adversarial and defensive positions to cooperative positions. Start by understanding the needs each side brings, and the outcomes each wants to reach.

2. **Use Creative Responses.** Transform a problem into a creative opportunity. Choose to see what can be done in regard to an issue, rather than being stuck in how terrible the situation is. See issues as learning opportunities, rather than insurmountable problems.

3. **Communicate with Empathy.** Build rapport. Develop effective communication skills including active listening to clarify your understanding of a problem. Ask questions to get information on the issue. Check back, summarize, and make sure both sides agree on the facts. Listen, reflect, and explore for clarity.

4. **Be Appropriately Assertive.** Focus on the problem, rather than the person. Use "I" statements, rather than accusations. Phrase these, for example, as: "When you order your supplies from my budget, *I* feel frustrated. *I* would like you to order from your budget, not mine."

5. **Create Cooperative Power.** Build "power *with*" rather than "power *over*" others involved in the conflict. Explore, and clarify the details. Ask questions to open up options, rather than allowing the conversation to end after statements about *why* proposed solutions will not work.

6. **Manage Emotions.** Eliminate excessive fear, anger, hurt, and frustration. Express emotions appropriately to identify them without allowing destructive emotions to take over the conflict resolution. This may require disengagement from an escalating situation until emotions cool.

7. **Be Willing to Resolve.** Recognize and set aside personal problems that cloud the picture and keep you from wanting to resolve a conflict. Refuse to allow unresolved personal history to get in the way of a conflict resolution.

8. **Map the Conflict.** Identify common needs and concerns, and define the issues in a way that all can agree. Define the issue or problem area, including who is involved, along with their fears and their needs. Remain neutral so that both sides can agree on the mapping of the conflict.

9. **Develop Options.** Come up with more than one "right" solution to an issue. Break the conflict into smaller pieces, research to find more information, and set goals toward the outcome. Generate more potential solutions through brainstorming and consensus-building.

10. **Negotiate.** Compromise, using effective strategies to reach an agreement that is satisfying to all sides. Be hard on the problems and soft on the person. Focus on needs, not positions. Emphasize common ground. Be inventive about options. Make clear agreements.

11. **Mediate.** Help conflicting parties move toward solutions. Be objective and supportive rather than judgmental. Focus on the process, not the content. Reframe. Respond, rather than react. Refocus on the issue and preserve the relationship. Identify and halt unfair tactics.

12. **Broaden Perspectives.** Respect and value differences in viewpoints. Recognize that a long-term time frame may be needed. Assume a global, rather than an individual, perspective. Calm resistance to the broader perspective, recognizing that this perspective may make us feel less secure about our own positions. Remain open to the idea of changing and risk-taking. With one step forward, dynamics can change, and new opportunities open up.

figure 11.3

A CONFLICT RESOLUTION TOOL KIT

Good methods for resolving conflict result in better overall morale, communication, workplace relationships, trust, and commitments. *Can you think of other qualities of effective conflict resolution methods?*

Source: ©2015 Conflict Resolution Network, PO Box 1016, Chatswood NSW 2057, Australia. www.crnhq.org

WINNING ON BOTH SIDES

With win-win situations, companies and individuals grow. Conflicts are resolved with higher morale than before, and communication stays open. *How can people bring more win-win situations to their work environments?*

©stockbroker/123RF

accommodator

Someone who wants to avoid conflict by engaging in positive thinking.

collaborator

Someone who brings both sides together for discussion and not only is most likely to bring about a win-win solution but is actually necessary for it.

low conformers

Individuals who think independently, solve problems creatively, and often cause some conflict in the process.

some real urgency, compromisers tend to see *agreement* as more important than the issue itself. A compromiser generally doesn't feel as much of a need to rush to a solution as a competitor does. If you are a compromiser, watch for the tendency to settle for a lose-lose compromise. Push instead for a win-win solution, following all the steps in that process, so that both sides will feel their main goals have been achieved.

4. An **accommodator** might tell both parties involved in the conflict, "Don't worry; be happy!" Accommodators want to avoid conflict by positive thinking. They tell people to "count their blessings" or "look on the bright side." Keeping the manager happy is also a top priority. The downside to this is that people involved in the conflict may feel they are not being taken seriously, and the accommodator may not be able (or willing) to get others to fully express their reasons for being angry, which may be counterproductive.

5. The fifth type of conflict management style is collaboration. The **collaborator** brings both sides together for discussion. The collaborative approach is not only the most likely to bring about a win-win solution, but is actually necessary for it. The collaborator opens communication channels and learns about what issues each party feels are most important. Collaboration requires more skill than the other styles of conflict management. For example, it is fairly simple to use the competitive method and force your will on others—so it is easy to see why many conflict managers fall back into that style or one of the simpler methods.

» DEALING WITH SPECIAL CONFLICT CASES

Other conflict issues are caused by the specific behaviors of those identified as *problem people*. Such people are those who for one reason or another aren't living up to the expectations of an organization. Some are involved with alcohol or drug abuse. Others are simply people who don't like to do things the way other people do them. What follows is a description of different types of problem behaviors, and strategies for dealing with them.

Low Conformers

High conformers are usually easy to work with. They like to fit in, work well in teams, and are generally friendly toward policies and group norms. **Low conformers** are just the opposite: They think independently, solve problems creatively, and often cause some conflict in the process. Working with and managing this type of personality requires a special capacity for patience and good will.[10]

REAL WORLD EXAMPLE 11.7

Jim frequently traveled for his job in pharmaceutical sales. While the other salespeople followed a strict set of procedures on travel authorization and reporting, Jim, a low conformer, often traveled without checking in or getting preauthorization for his sales calls. His company tolerated it because customers loved his freewheeling spirit, but his supervisors found it very frustrating.

Here are some suggestions that will make working with low conformers less problematic:[11]

- Learn to tolerate their honesty. Low conformers are usually straightforward, using less tact and diplomacy than you might be used to.

- Some low conformers are not straightforward; instead they don't feel the need to communicate much with you about what they are doing. Continue to calmly ask for information.

- Accept the low conformer's firm method of self-expression without labeling it as stubbornness or disloyalty.

- Support low conformers when others are overly critical.

- Accept their independence, and don't be offended if they don't ask for advice.

- Resist the urge to force them to conform. Doing so probably won't work.

- Give relevant positive reinforcement even when they don't seem to need it.

You won't be able to change the low conformer any more than you're likely to change the high conformer. Both personality types are important to an organization, one balancing the other.

Envious People

Envy is wanting what another person has, to the extent of feeling ill will toward the person who has it. Envious co-workers cause conflict that can be damaging to morale and productivity and can spread through a department or division like a virus.

The following are several suggestions for dealing with an envious person at work. Some will be more appropriate for you than others, depending on whether you are a manager or an employee. Some may seem to contradict each other, but just remember that they are simply strategies to try. If one doesn't work, go on to the next.

1. **Avoid destructive conflict with the envious person.** If you keep that goal in mind, your actions will be more focused and purposeful.

2. **Confront the envious co-worker.** Some envious people are dealt with best by calling them on their envy, openly and honestly. Once you have called

REAL WORLD EXAMPLE 11.8

Becca is envious of Matt, whom she sees as having a more impressive work history, and a better education. They make the same salary and have the same title, but she perceives him as being held in higher regard. She envies what she perceives as Matt being treated better and admired by others at work. She talks negatively about Matt behind his back and causes conflict between him and others.

the play, the game usually changes. Because of your approach, you are now perceived as having the power advantage. The envious co-worker will back away and choose someone else as a target (hopefully not another co-worker). One warning: *A vengeful, envious person* often will work even harder behind your back after a confrontation.

3. **Avoid excessive contact with the envious person.** Say hello and good-bye, but avoid making prolonged eye contact or starting a conversation. If the other person wants to chat, politely cut the conversation short. Politeness is very important, for you must avoid making the person feel snubbed. Have short conversations; then, move on.

4. **Discuss the problem with your manager.** This meeting should be a perception check. You're just checking to see if your boss perceives the same attitude that you perceive. Don't turn the discussion into a gripe session; remember that you are trying to avoid open conflict.

5. **Build up the envious person's self-esteem.** People often are envious because of low self-worth. Even when other methods fail, this one often reduces the intensity of the envious behavior.

Whatever course of action you decide to use, don't play into the other person's game: Don't descend to subtle insults and backstabbing. If you wait long enough, the problem will usually pass, and the envy will eventually burn itself out.[12]

Whiners and Complainers

One can readily find people in the workplace who are never happy and who discuss their problems constantly. Whether you are their manager or co-worker, these steps can help you deal with this common source of conflict:

1. **Listen, but not too much.** Whiners and complainers are good at taking advantage of sympathetic listeners. Although you should give honest, relevant complaints an ear when they involve you, learn to pull a rambling gripe session together by asking, "What is your point?" or "What are you going to do to solve this?"

2. **Do frequent reality checks.** You might be able to call the bluff of the chronic whiner by saying something like, "OK, tell me exactly what the

problem is and what you want me to do about it." By forcing the complainer to focus on the purpose for the gripe session, and by stressing the limits of your own power to change things, you can often reduce the complaining.

3. **Challenge the word *unfair*.** *Unfair* is one of the most common words used by whiners and complainers. With them, the word often means "I'm not getting what I want." By demanding specific examples of unfairness, and by demanding facts rather than implications or innuendos, you can force the whiners to focus on what they are really saying.

4. **Be a team leader or player.** As a manager, you can promote a spirit of teamwork and camaraderie in the workplace. You can stress the possibility of transfer for people who aren't team players. As a team member, you can be the kind of team player who won't tolerate the whiners.

Passive, Unresponsive People

Unresponsive people are sometimes the most difficult people to work with because on the surface they often seem agreeable and even easygoing. These personality types react to any confrontation or potential conflict by shutting down.

How can you be sure you are dealing with a passive person? Not all quiet people are passive. Some people don't speak up until they are absolutely sure they have something relevant to say; others are very good at screening out irrelevant material and thus seem somewhat unresponsive.[13] Passive people are different: when you most need a response, they will disappoint you.

Passive people have a variety of different reasons for their behavior. Some people use their absence of response as a way of intimidating—a method of calculated aggression. Others remain quiet because they are afraid of sounding foolish. Still others keep quiet to escape responsibility. Words give a concrete reality to thoughts and feelings. When you speak inner thoughts, you are admitting you have them—a frightening admission for some people. The safer course is to hide them from both others and yourself.[14]

How would you have handled Jim if you had been his manager in Real World Example 11.9?

Once you are convinced that it is a passive person you are dealing with, you can take some positive steps to get meaningful feedback from this type of difficult person:[15]

1. **Ask open-ended questions.** Don't ask passive people any question that can be answered with a *yes* or *no,* or even with a brief phrase. Develop questions that encourage them to open up. Some examples are: "How do you

> ### Complainers and Whiners
>
> This combination is a conflict waiting to start. Learn to recognize the legitimate complaint when you hear it, but don't tolerate this type of chronic behavior. It is counterproductive and causes negative conflict.

> **Passives** are often angry people who express their anger silently and indirectly.

more about...

more about...

REAL WORLD EXAMPLE 11.9

When Joachin was asked to do anything outside of the bare minimum of his tasks at work, his response was always a passive "Will do." The problem was that he seldom completed what he was asked to do. His supervisor was baffled as to how to get him to complete his work. He didn't complain, didn't speak up when she tried to engage him in a conversation, so she usually ended up giving him his task list, and listening to his automatic response, "Will do."

react to that?" "What thoughts on this subject occur to you right now?" or "What would you do if . . . ?"

2. **Develop and use a friendly, silent gaze.** After asking an open-ended question, look directly at the silent person with a quizzical, expectant expression on your face. This expression should not be unduly threatening, but it should urge a hesitant person to talk. If you are to use this technique successfully, you must be willing to maintain the gaze *beyond the limits of your own comfort.* Sometimes, this technique won't work. If it doesn't, move quickly to another method.

3. **Don't fill the space.** A supportive person often is tempted to make enough small talk to fill the uncomfortable empty pauses. If you rescue passive people, you will have enabled them to remain passive.

4. **Make statements to help break the tension.** Call attention to what has been going on. Make a statement such as "I expected you to say something, Ignatio, and you're not. What does that mean?" Then return to the friendly, silent gaze. You might also ask, "Can you talk about what you're thinking?" or "What's on your mind right now?"

5. **Set time limits.** Plan in advance how much time you plan to spend dealing with the passive silent person. Tell the person what the time limit is. Often, a great deal will be said in the last few minutes by the silent person who knows that time is short.

©Pixtal/Age Fotostock

Other types of difficult people produce conflict in the workplace. Dealing with all of them requires patience, good listening skills, and time. Whenever a conflict with a difficult person begins, you must become aware as soon as possible that a difficult person is involved, then plan your strategy accordingly. Once the problem is identified, work toward a solution, attempting to get a commitment from the difficult person.

Because of the nature of difficult people, most of them will never completely stop being difficult. Deal with their difficulties on an event-by-event basis, realizing the limitations of any conflict management procedure.

« # STRATEGIES FOR SUCCESS

Strategy 11.1   Negotiate Win-Win Solutions

1. Get emotions under control.
2. Agree on ground rules.
3. Clarify all positions.
4. Explore multiple needs and issues.
5. Develop alternatives.
6. Choose solutions that are win-win.

The conflict manager should look for underlying reasons, interests, and needs. Once these areas are identified, the leader should get each side to list them in order of importance. The rest of the negotiation process is a series of exchanges, with one side giving up one issue in order to gain another from the other side. At this point in the process, a creative negotiator can bring off concession bargaining moves that would not occur to a less creative mind. **Concession bargaining** is the process of getting each side in a conflict to willingly make concessions in exchange for concessions (compromises) made by the opposing side.

Of course, this process isn't as easy as it sounds. The conflict manager must take the group through a series of steps, following some important guidelines, before the win-win method can work.

1. **Get emotions under control.** If emotions are strong on one or both sides, a conflict manager must put most of the creative effort into calming people down. Leaders should be especially careful that their own emotions are not involved with either side. A good beginning might be "Look, I know you're angry, but if we're going to resolve this, we need to put our feelings aside and try to work on some alternatives. Would you be willing to do that?"[16] The final question is crucial. Press for a commitment to solving the problem, rather than placing the blame.

   People handle their anger in different ways, and the anger itself can become a source of conflict. One side's anger will often feed the anger of the other side until the situation seems hopeless. Both sides may think that the other is not acting in good faith. When you are sitting down to reach a solution, that distrust must be dispelled. Anger *must* be expressed or the other person will not be able to understand the focus of your emotions—yet expressing that anger too strongly (such as with personal insults) can block further communication. If nothing else works, the leader should try getting both sides to explain why they are angry. The focus then becomes the reasons behind the feelings, rather than the feelings alone.

2. **Agree on ground rules.** Once the anger has been dealt with, the conflict manager should establish ground rules. He or she should explain that the rules are meant to keep the process running smoothly, not to force either side to conform. To emphasize this, when establishing ground rules, the conflict manager should encourage both sides to suggest rules. The earlier in the process you can get participation, the better. Some of the basic rules could include:[18]

   - Agree to listen as carefully as possible, without interrupting.
   - Agree to control anger, even if someone disagrees with your position.
   - Agree to treat each other with the respect you would like to receive.
   - Agree on the amount of time you will devote to achieving a solution.
   - Resist the urge to force the participants to conform.

Concession bargaining

The process of getting each side in a conflict to willingly make concessions in exchange for concessions made by the opposing side.

> Concession bargaining is used frequently by union bargaining teams to negotiate flexible issues, such as salaries, benefits, and employee rights.

more about...

REAL WORLD EXAMPLE 11.10

Jeanne was a factory employee who spent virtually all of her free time complaining about her job, personal life, co-workers, or manager. Her favorite word seemed to be "unfair." Everyone was unfair. The job was unfair, espe-cially the pay, and—of course—her manager. Not only did Jeanne cause daily misery for herself, but she made others around her miserable as well.[17]

Once ground rules have been established, they can be used as calming and disciplin-ary devices if the discussion threatens to get out of control. By reminding each side of the rules they agreed to, the leader has a better chance of retaining control.

3. **Clarify all positions.** When emotions are dealt with and the ground rules are set, it is time to get all of the issues, facts, and opinions out for close examination. When both sides have seen what the problems are from the other's perspective, they can move toward an understanding that makes both feel like winners. Both sides will still push for whatever they want most, but they will also be listening to the needs of the other side.

Allow both sides equal time for self-expression. If either one is dominating the discussion, the conflict manager should call for more input from the opposition. Some people become suddenly silent during this phase and need to be encouraged to participate. Stay in the *objective mode* as consistently as possible. Everyone involved should take care not to form value judgments.

more about...

The Objective Mode

The **objective mode** means being "computer-like," not unduly swayed by feelings or emotions. It is calm and does not let emotions interfere with objective decisions.

4. **Explore multiple needs and issues.** Begin this phase by allowing both sides to explain why they chose their position rather than the other one. Then find multiple interests in the issue and look for the ones that both sides share.

5. **Develop alternatives.** Based on the needs and issues you have uncovered, list each possible alternative to be examined carefully later. This can be done much like a brainstorming session: don't allow any value judgments or editorial comments by either side, and strive for *quantity* of ideas, rather than *quality* at this point.

6. **Choose solutions that are win-win.** Explain carefully what a win-win solution is: one that gives something of perceived value to both sides. Then go through each alterna-tive, asking how it can be seen as a win-win solution. Usually a list of acceptable solu-tions will evolve by consensus. When that fails to happen, the conflict manager must make the decisions alone, asking for a consensus of the solutions he or she selects.

For these six steps to work as a conflict management model, several requirements must be met. First, everyone involved in the conflict must be willing to go through the steps, desiring a long-term solution rather than merely fighting to win. Second, all must be willing to take the *time* required to carry out the process to its conclusion; the win-win strategy is often abandoned for lack of time. Third, the conflict manager must be flexible, sensitive, patient, and calm under fire.[19]

REAL WORLD EXAMPLE 11.11

An auto dealer who had been forced to reduce his accounting staff heard constant complaints from the head bookkeeper about working with fewer people. He finally asked, "If you can't manage the job with two fewer people, can you recommend someone who can?" The complaining stopped abruptly.

Strategy 11.2   Make Collaboration Work

1. Identify the problem.
2. Generate a solution.
3. Identify an action plan.
4. Put the action plan to work.

People in collaboration approach conflict resolution as a problem-solving process. This process should include four phases:

1. **Identify the problem.** Make sure that you are dealing with the real issue, not a result of a deeper problem. Otherwise, even a solution that seems to be win-win will be dealing with symptoms, rather than problems.

2. **Generate a solution.** A group can take this step in many different ways, from group discussion to written questionnaires. This method should involve everyone who is directly affected by the conflict.

3. **Identify an action plan.** If possible, get input from both sides in the creation of this plan. Then get an agreement from both sides to follow it.

4. **Put the action plan to work.** Don't forget to follow up on the results. The follow-up is important in preventing future destructive conflict.

Strategy 11.3   Stop Conflicts before They Start

1. Turn the people around you into winners.
2. Work together on common goals.
3. Communicate, communicate, communicate.

The best way to handle negative conflict is by preventing it. Of course, no workplace is totally without negative conflict, but both managers and employees can take steps to prevent many conflicts and soften their impact when they happen.

1. **Turn the people around you into winners.** When people feel they are winners, they are less likely to start harmful conflicts. Self-esteem is a key element in conflict management. Often conflicts are really about self-esteem being undermined. Whatever you can do as either a manager or an employee to bolster the self-esteem of others is likely to prevent harmful conflict. Also, whenever possible, allow for others to be successful at the tasks they perform.

REAL WORLD EXAMPLE 11.12

Renardo, an elderly man, would always shrug and mutter, "Sure, why not?" whenever he was asked to do anything. He showed anger in subtle ways nearly all the time. One reason he was angry was because he had found himself working for a manager who was 20 years younger than he was. The age difference made him feel inferior. His manager found that by asking for his advice, even sometimes when the advice wasn't really needed, the passive anger was reduced.

2. **Work together on common goals.** When a workplace is dedicated to common goals, there is usually little room for harmful conflict. Many times, the goals of the company aren't clearly defined, and employees move blindly in a fog, working more on their own goals and agendas than on the united purpose of the group. If you are a manager, help your staff recognize that the common goals they share are more important than personal status.[20]

3. **Communicate, communicate, communicate.** Listen carefully for hints of discontent. When you need to say something, find the right time and place; then say it clearly but tactfully.

CHAPTER ELEVEN SUMMARY

Chapter Summary by Learning Objectives

LO 11-1 Identify the types of conflict. Although conflict is always present in the workplace, it isn't always negative. Conflict can be seen as either functional or dysfunctional. When classified by the actors in the conflict, five types can be found: inner conflict, person-against-person conflict, intragroup conflict, intergroup conflict, and person-against-group conflict.

LO 11-2 List sources of conflict. Conflict usually springs from one of four sources: content conflict, values conflict, negotiations-of-selves conflict, and institutionalized conflict.

LO 11-3 Define conflict analysis. Analyzing the situation is the first step toward resolving a conflict. Ask such questions as: *Who is involved? What is at stake? How important is time?* and *What are the tie-ins with other issues?* Conflict prevention often involves asking these questions early on.

LO 11-4 Give examples of potential solutions to a conflict. The best solution is nearly always win-win, the solution that makes everyone who is involved feel like a winner. Although they usually don't give permanent solutions to conflicts, win-lose and lose-lose can be used as well.

LO 11-5 **Compare and contrast styles of conflict management.** The Thomas–Kilman Model shows five different types of conflict management styles for use as strategies in conflict resolution: competitor, avoider, compromiser, accommodator, and collaborator. The best one is collaborator, because it can solve most conflicts when allowed enough time and energy.

LO 11-6 **Explain how to deal with special conflict cases.** Problem people produce a different type of conflict. Learning to deal with major problem personality types can be helpful in conflict management. Different strategies must be used for low conformers, envious people, whiners and complainers, and passive people.

key terms

accommodator 288
avoider 288
collaborator 289
competitor 288
compromiser 288
concession
  bargaining 295
conflict 280
content conflict 281

dysfunctional
  conflict 280
functional conflict 280
inner conflict 280
institutionalized
  conflict 285
intergroup
  conflict 281
intragroup conflict 281
lose-lose strategy 287

low conformers 289
negotiation-of-selves
  conflict 283
person-versus-group
  conflict 281
person-versus-person
  conflict 281
values conflict 284
win-lose strategy 286
win-win strategy 287

review questions

1. What are the major causes of conflict in the workplace?

2. What are the four major sources of conflict within organizations? Explain each one, using an example.

3. Explain the Thomas–Kilman Conflict Model. What does this model show as the best method of conflict resolution?

4. Is conflict always negative? If so, what are some effective ways of preventing destructive conflict in the workplace?

5. You are trying to negotiate a workplace conflict through to a win-win solution. What steps would you follow? What pitfalls would you need to avoid?

6. What is negotiation-of-selves conflict, and why is this source of conflict probably the most important in the workplace?

7. What should you do when a person who constantly complains confronts you? Why should you avoid being indifferent or ignoring the person? How would reality checks and being a team leader help?

8. How can a manager or employee tell if he or she is dealing with a passive person? What is the best way to deal with a passive, silent person who is determined not to communicate?

critical thinking questions

1. Try to remember a conflict you have had with someone recently. What were the sources of the conflict? Was the conflict ever resolved? If so, how? Would you resolve it differently if you could replay the event?

2. Have you ever tried to work or study with a difficult person, such as a whiner or envious person? How did you relate to that individual, if at all? Have you ever confronted an envious person? If so, what happened?

working it out 11.1

YOUR CONFLICT MANAGEMENT STYLE

School-to-Work Connection: Interpersonal Skills

This exercise will help you discover the strategies you use, or would be likely to use, in a conflict situation. In the space next to each statement, write "5" if the statement applies often, "3" if the statement applies sometimes, and "1" if it never applies. (This test will not be accurate unless you strive to be completely honest with yourself in answering.) When I differ with someone:

_____ 1. I explore our differences, neither backing down nor forcing my own view.

_____ 2. I disagree openly, then invite some more discussion about our differences.

_____ 3. I look for a mutually satisfactory solution.

_____ 4. Rather than let the other person make a decision without my input, I make sure I am heard and also that I hear the other person out.

_____ 5. I agree to a middle ground rather than look for a completely satisfying solution.

_____ 6. I will admit that I am half-wrong, rather than discuss our differences.

_____ 7. I have a reputation for meeting the other person halfway.

_____ 8. I expect to be able to get out about half of what I really want to say.

_____ 9. I will give in totally rather than try to change the other person's opinion.

_____ 10. I avoid any controversial aspects of an issue.

_____ 11. I agree early on, rather than arguing about a point.

_____ 12. I give in when the other person becomes emotional about an issue.

_____ 13. I try to win the other person over to my side.

_____ 14. I work to come out victorious, no matter what.

_____ 15. I never back away from a good argument.

_____ 16. I would rather win than end up compromising.

To score your responses, add your total score for each of the following sets of statements:

Set A: Statements 1–4 _____
Set B: Statements 5–8 _____
Set C: Statements 9–12 _____
Set D: Statements 13–16 _____

A score of 17 or more on any set is considered high. Scores of 12 to 16 are moderately high. Scores of 8 to 11 are moderately low. Scores of 7 or less are considered low.

Each set represents a different strategy for conflict management:

Set A: Collaboration (I win; you win.)
Set B: Compromise (Both win some; both lose some.)
Set C: Accommodation (I lose; you win.)
Set D: Competition (I win; you lose.)

case study 11.1

Searching for a Win-Win Solution

Scott is executive director and Juanita is fundraising manager at Werner Charities. They are trying to create a more effective donation letter. Their response from the current letter—and the second—have been disappointing to say the least. Both Scott and Juanita are acutely aware of the importance of the success of this mailing. Also, each of them has some definitive ideas about how the letter should look and sound. Scott, the charity's director, believes it is vitally important to address the logical, thoughtful mind of potential donors. He wants the letter to focus on facts, figures, and good works the charity has accomplished. Juanita, the fundraiser, takes the approach that the letter should tug at the heart strings of potential donors. She wants the letter to focus on real life stories of people the charity has helped. Further, Juanita wants to pull in new, younger donors through social media outlets and digital letter delivery who will donate electronically; while Scott wants to retain the older, wealthier, more established donors who prefer a paper letter through the mail with return envelope for sending in checks.

Both Juanita and Scott are known for their expertise in different areas of marketing. Because of company protocol, both of them will need to sign off on this crucial letter and on its delivery method. Also, both have run very successful campaigns in the past.

Right away, tensions started to rise between them. Both of them know that a win-win solution should be their goal. Before anyone could have predicted it, however, they were both raising their voices more than necessary. Both them were sure that the other one's letter design and delivery would ruin the company.

Case Study Questions

1. What steps should Scott and Juanita take to start making some progress toward a win-win solution?

2. What could they have done to prevent the situation from starting out this way? If you were running this donation campaign, how would you set up the campaign so that conflict would not occur?

3. Would a win-lose approach work in this situation? Why or why not?

4. What additional information should you obtain to be effective in settling this difference of opinion?

case study 11.2

Don't Call Him Boss

Lael and Waheid both work for a small software development firm. Both of them have strong résumés and both have about the same number in the "years of experience" column. However, when Waheid was hired, Lael had objected strongly. When she was asked why, she said that Waheid was not qualified for the position. She believed that other applicants who were not hired would have been better in the position.

Six months after Waheid was hired, the manager (Barbara) left to start her own company. As Barbara was leaving, Lael had demanded that it was to be clear that she would not take orders from Waheid. All three agreed.

At first, things seemed calm and workable. After a month had gone by, however, Waheid called a meeting of all seven members of the project team, which included Lael. As Lael saw things, Waheid was usurping power and "trying to run the place." At that meeting, Waheid reviewed everyone's job in detail. He also sent out e-mails, signing himself as project director. The new manager who had taken Barbara's place had not commented on Waheid's signature as project director.

Waheid: Lael, you are all hung up on power issues. Heck, I don't want power. I just want this team to operate efficiently. Just because I sign myself as project director doesn't mean I want to take things over.

Lael: Get real. Just yesterday, two people referred to you as "the boss." And I've heard that from several others.

Waheid: Notice that I didn't ask them to call me that.

Lael: Well, you obviously didn't tell them *not* to, either.

Waheid: I give up.

Case Study Questions

1. These two people seem to be having more than one conflict taking place at the same time. Explain.

2. What could you do to settle the conflict in this case? See if you can come up with more than one solution.

3. What could they have done to avoid this conflict in the first place? What would you have done, as the manager, to set up conditions to avoid a conflict?

CHAPTER TWELVE

12

STRESS AND STRESS MANAGEMENT

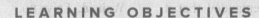

« « LEARNING OBJECTIVES

After studying this chapter, you will be able to:

LO 12-1   Identify the main causes of stress.

LO 12-2   Give examples of external and internal sources of stress.

LO 12-3   Compare and contrast type A and type B personality behaviors.

LO 12-4   Describe the physical effects of stress.

LO 12-5   Explain the cost of stress in the workplace.

« « STRATEGIES FOR SUCCESS

Strategy 12.1   Discard Irrational Beliefs

Strategy 12.2   Change Your Behaviors to Reduce Stress

Strategy 12.3   Take Care of Yourself

In the Workplace: What's Wrong with Me?

SITUATION

Stephanie Williams is a lower-level supervisor at a county agency. At first she enjoyed her job, but lately she just can't seem to concentrate at work. She has also been having trouble sleeping, has lost her appetite, and resumed smoking. To top it off, she seems to be getting every cold and flu that goes around the office.

©Image Source

At home, things have not been easy financially since her divorce last year. Her three children are pretty easygoing kids, but over the summer Stephanie missed two weeks of work when her daughter had chicken pox, and several more days this fall when her son fell off the playground equipment at school and broke his arm. Now she has used up all her vacation time and sick leave, and she has even had to take some unpaid leave days. Meanwhile, her ex-husband has fallen behind in his child support payments, and she is feeling overwhelmed.

Stephanie's supervisor, Donna Clark, has called her in several times in the past month to talk about Stephanie's performance. She has told Stephanie that the office is getting complaints from clients about poor service in the office, and she wants to know why Stephanie is not handling routine things in her usual efficient manner.

Over lunch, Stephanie tells her friend and co-worker Lakeesha Jones, "I just don't know what's the matter with me. I can't seem to get anything done, I lose my train of thought all the time, I don't feel well half the time, I'm always tired, and I keep snapping at the kids for no reason. Am I going crazy? What's wrong with me?"

DISCOVERY

Lakeesha answers, "I don't know what your problem is, but you'd better snap out of it or you're going to lose your job. I heard that Donna has been looking over files in personnel, and you know what that means! Somebody is going to get the ax!"

"Oh, no!" Stephanie wailed. "Lakeesha, I just *can't* lose my job! What am I going to do?"

THINK ABOUT IT

What seems to be wrong with Stephanie? What kinds of actions could Stephanie take on her own to help herself? If you were Lakeesha, what would you identify as Stephanie's problem? What would you suggest Stephanie do to help her situation? Have you had friends or co-workers in similar situations, or have you yourself experienced them? How were they resolved?

» CAUSES OF STRESS

Which of these two situations do you believe would be more stressful?

- During the past year, you were fired or laid off from your job, and a close friend died.
- During the past year, you got married, added a healthy baby to your family, received a big promotion at work, and moved into a new and bigger house.

The answer may surprise you: stress researchers would say that the second situation is more stressful. This is because the more major life changes you are experiencing, the more stress you are likely to feel. This reasoning will be explored in more detail in this chapter. First, though, is an explanation of what is meant by *stress* and *stressors.*

According to psychologists, **stress** can be defined as *the nonspecific response of the body to any demand made on it.*[1] In other words, any reaction or response your body makes to a new situation is stress. Ongoing situations that seem to be too much for us to handle will also cause stress. The *reaction* is both emotional and physical.

Hans Selye, a Canadian physiologist who researched stress and its effects for 50 years, believed that human bodies are nearly always in some kind of stress. He maintained that some stress is necessary for life, and he distinguished between two kinds of stress. The first is **eustress,** or good stress—the kind of pleasant, desirable stress you might feel when playing tennis or attending a party. The second is **distress,** or bad stress—the kind of stress you might feel during an illness or when going through a divorce.[2] Even though there are positive effects of stress, and some kinds of stressful events are pleasurable, this discussion of stress will actually refer to *distress,* which fits the everyday definition of stress.

Stress is your *body's reaction* to a new situation, or an ongoing situation that seems overwhelming. A **stressor** is the situation or event itself that caused your body to react. Stress can be caused by major life changes and everyday hassles, as well as many other sources. Stressors can be caused by internal factors, such as a negative or suspicious thinking style, or the kind of worry about ongoing life problems that Stephanie was experiencing in our opening vignette. Stressors can also come from external sources, such as "red tape" or bureaucracy at work or school that is outside your control.

Life Changes and Daily Hassles

Any change can be stressful, especially **major life changes.** However, according to some stress researchers, the **daily hassles** that everyone experiences can be very stressful as well, possibly even more so because they happen more frequently and seem to pile up on top of one another.[3]

One day you might be rushing out the door for work and you spill coffee on yourself. You set your keys down, run and change your clothes, only to forget where you put your keys. You finally find them, but by now you are late

stress

Any reaction or response made by the body to a new situation.

eustress

Positive stress, the kind felt when doing something one enjoys, such as playing tennis or attending a party.

distress

Negative stress, the kind felt during an illness or when going through a divorce.

stressor

A situation or an event that causes the body to react (causes stress).

major life changes

Changes in your life, such as divorce, that increase daily hassles, leaving you stressed and worn out.

daily hassles

The daily annoyances, such as getting stuck in traffic or misplacing your keys, that can cause stress in your life.

for work. You drive too fast, get pulled over, and receive a speeding ticket. You make it to work and find there is no place left to park. You finally find a space, grab your belongings from the car and run for the office, but in your haste you drop a set of important papers into a nearby mud puddle—and your workday has not even started yet!

Major life changes and daily hassles can go hand in hand—especially when major life changes *cause* daily hassles.

Imagine that you have just gotten a divorce. This is a major life change that can lead to many daily hassles you may not have had before. You may have to move, set up a new child care arrangement, take over a larger share of the housework or yard work, open a new bank account, find a new grocery store, explain your situation repeatedly to friends or acquaintances, and so on. These daily hassles can leave you feeling stressed and worn out.

Even if your stress is due to a pleasant change, such as starting college, daily hassles can occur. You may be very excited to begin your new adventure in college, but the little hassles such as finding parking, finding the bookstore, figuring out which books to buy, finding the library, getting your picture taken for your student identification card, and standing in line for registration and admissions or figuring out the online application and registration system can leave you feeling drained and stressed—and you haven't even found your classrooms or started classes yet!

MANY SOURCES OF STRESS

Stress can be caused by many different factors: both positive and negative major life changes, as well as smaller everyday problems. *Do you have different ways of dealing with different kinds of stress, whether in the workplace or in your personal life?*

©Ragnar Schmuck/Getty Images

Chronic Stressors

Chronic stressors are inescapable, day-to-day situations or conditions that cause stress. They are more stressful than daily hassles, but not as stressful as a major life change. Things like poverty, ongoing abuse, and long-term health problems are examples of chronic stressors. Being discriminated against because of issues such as race or ethnicity, gender, age, or religion is also a chronic stressor.

In the past few years, researchers have focused attention on the chronic stress of being a member of a minority group. Even when there is no outright evidence of racism, simply being the only member (or one of the few members) of a particular race in a variety of settings such as work or school can cause stress.[4] Similar stressful experiences occur when you are a female in a male-dominant career, or vice versa; when you speak a different first language from your co-workers; when you have a different religious background; and other factors. Diversity issues will be discussed in more detail in Chapter 14.

Chronic Stress

"We know that chronic stress can take a toll on a person's health. It can make existing health problems worse, and even cause disease, either because of changes in the body or bad habits people develop to cope with stress. The bottom line is that stress can lead to real physical and emotional health consequences," says the executive director for professional practice for the American Psychological Association.

—Katherine C. Nordal, PhD

American Psychological Association, Stress in America: Coping with Change, http://www.apa.org/news/press/releases/stress/2016/coping-with-change.PDF (retrieved June 20, 2017).

more about...

Stress in College

"Living a stress-free life is not a reasonable goal. The goal is to deal with it actively and effectively."

—Stanford psychiatrist David Spiegel

Stress in College

College is easily one of life's ultimate stressors. The demands placed upon students to constantly perform at a high academic level, to work constructively with peers from different backgrounds in the classroom and on group projects, and to manage the constant barrage of work assignments and tests—all while trying to balance a healthy lifestyle outside of academics—can be daunting.

But without some stress, people would not get as much done. The extra burst of adrenaline that helps you finish your final paper, or put the finishing touches on a big project assignment, or prepare for an important exam, is positive stress. In this case, the stress is a short-term physiological tension that promotes mental alertness. Researchers at the University of California, Berkeley, have found that short bursts of stress lasting a few minutes to a few hours can actually be good for you. According to Professor Daniela Kaufer, "Some amounts of stress are good to push you just to your level of optimal alertness, behavioral and cognitive performance." Short bursts of stress push your creativity and productivity. "You always think about stress as a really bad thing, but it's not," says Kaufer.[6]

If you are unable to return to a relaxed state, however, the stress can become negative. Over time, the cumulative changes in your body that stress can cause (such as increased heart rate and blood pressure, and muscle tension) may take their toll on your health and cause you mental and physical exhaustion, and short-term or chronic illness. It is unrealistic to think that we can do away with stress, but identifying it and managing it actively and effectively is key!

» SOURCES OF STRESS

In addition to studying major life changes, daily hassles, and chronic stress, psychologists studying causes of stress have identified specific internal and external sources of it in people's lives.

External Stressors

According to psychologists, **external stressors** can include anything and everything from outside sources that causes you pain or discomfort, frustration, or conflict.[5]

1. *Pain or discomfort.* Chronic or even temporary pain can make you feel stressed and lower your job performance. Think of the last time you had a bad toothache or headache and how much that interfered with your concentration. Discomfort (even something as minor as the workroom being too hot or too cold) can have a negative effect on you as well.

2. *Frustration.* The feeling you get when a goal you are trying to attain is blocked defines **frustration.** For example, you might feel frustrated when a co-worker takes credit for your creative ideas.

3. *Inner conflict.* The previous chapter introduced you to several ways of thinking about conflict. In this chapter, we will examine one of those in more detail, as a source of stress: **inner conflict.** Inner conflict is the kind of pressure you feel when you are forced to make a choice. Even though you feel it internally, it is considered an external stressor because the *source* of this conflict comes from outside. This type of conflict is the feeling you get when you are torn in two or more directions.

We all experience several kinds of inner conflict. These include approach-approach, approach-avoid, and avoid-avoid conflict. The first of these, approach-approach, is the feeling of conflict you get when torn between two desirable goals. For example, you may really like your job and enjoy your co-workers, but when offered a promotion, you are also excited about the prospect of making more money. You want to stay in your current job and spend time with your friends at work, but you also want the promotion that would give you more money. You can't have both at the same time.

An approach-avoid conflict occurs when you are drawn toward and away from something at the same time. For example, you may really want that promotion, but it would mean transferring to another state, and you are reluctant to pull up stakes and start over again somewhere else. If you stay, you make less money; if you go, you have the enormous task of moving to another state. Deciding either way causes a push-pull of the approach-avoid conflict.

An avoid-avoid conflict occurs when you are torn between two *undesirable* options. For example, you may not get along with your supervisor and you may dread going to work each day, but at the same time you hate the idea of pounding the pavement looking for a new job. Or you may not want to tackle the huge project assigned in a class, but you do not want the "F" that would result from not turning it in.

Internal Stressors

According to psychologists, **internal stressors** can include your own perceptions or interpretations of a stressor, as well as personality factors.[7]

External	Internal
Bureaucracy, deadlines	Suspicious outlook, over-analyzing situations
Financial problems	Negative thinking and negative self-talk
Unemployment	Chronic worry, dread, depression
Poor health	Poor social skills, poor health habits
Relationship issues	Shy or unassertive personality
School pressures	Aggressive or bossy personality
Problems in the workplace	Hostile, impatient, time-urgent
Loss (grief, bereavement)	Overly competitive, perfectionist
Daily hassles	Calm outside, agitated inside
Unexpected bad news	Poor time management
Organizational rules, policies, red tape	Poor lifestyle choices (lack of sleep, smoking, overeating, etc.)
Physical environment (heat, noise, etc.)	Self-critical, take things personally
Behavior of others (rude, bossy, etc.)	Unrealistic expectations, all-or-nothing thinking, rigid thinking
Major life changes	

chronic stressors

Inescapable, day-to-day situations or conditions that cause stress.

external stressors

Stressors that include anything from outside sources that causes you pain and discomfort.

frustration

The feeling people get when goals they are trying to attain are blocked.

inner conflict

Conflict within an individual; it might involve values, loyalties, or priorities; the pressure you feel when you are forced to make a choice.

internal stressors

Your perceptions of stressors, which may vary depending on personality.

EXTERNAL AND INTERNAL SOURCES OF STRESS (EXAMPLES)

Sources: "What Are the Sources of Stress?" Woodbridge Hospital, Singapore; Institute of Mental Health Online (retrieved June 1, 2008), www.imh.com.sg/patient _education/overcm_stress .htm. See also The Stress Clinic, TheStressClinic.com, www .thestressclinic.com/ (retrieved June 1, 2008).

DAILY HASSLES

When daily hassles start to pile up, especially early in the day, they can have a strong effect on you. Even though the stress is short term, it can be as intense as some types of long-term stress. *How do you deal with those days when nothing seems to go right?*

©Stefka Pavlova/Moment Open/Getty Images

cognitive appraisal

The thinking evaluation of an event or situation that varies from person to person and, for an individual, from day to day.

figure 12.1

SOURCE OF STRESS

Which of these sources of stress seem to apply most directly to you?

Source: American Psychological Association, *Stress in America*™ http://www.apa.org/news/press/releases/stress/2016/coping-with-change.PDF (posted Feb. 23, 2017).

Every person has a different perception of the same situation or stressor. A major problem to one person may be an exciting challenge to another. Let's take the example of a common event in the business world since the 1980s: downsizing. Two middle managers who are laid off may see their situations quite differently: One sees the layoff as a chance for a new start in another work situation, whereas the other sees it as a terrible personal and professional disaster. What makes each of them perceive the same events differently? Two basic internal factors are their cognitive appraisal of each situation, and their individual personality factors.

1. *Cognitive appraisal.* Cognitive appraisal can be thought of as your "thinking evaluation" of an event or a situation. In the process of making a **cognitive appraisal,** you unconsciously ask yourself two questions. The first one is: *Is this stressor harmful to me in any way?* If the answer to that question is yes, then you also ask yourself: *Do I have the resources (time, energy, and so on) to handle this stressor?* If the answer to that question is no, then you feel stress. These questions and responses are processed in a fraction of a second, usually faster than you are aware.

Cognitive appraisal varies not only from person to person, but from day to day with the same person or the same situation. What makes you spend some mornings in rush-hour traffic cursing and shaking your fist at other drivers, while you spend other mornings during the same traffic-filled commute singing along with the radio, smiling with empathy at other drivers? Part of the answer lies in the number of daily hassles you experience: The more stressors you encounter, the more annoyed you feel at new stressors and the more difficulty you have adapting to them. (See Figure 12.1.) Sometimes you may feel a

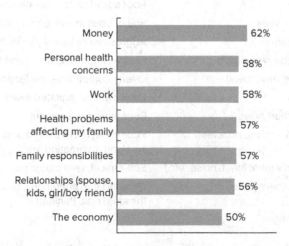

Percent Somewhat/Very Significant in 2016

Source	Percent
Money	62%
Personal health concerns	58%
Work	58%
Health problems affecting my family	57%
Family responsibilities	57%
Relationships (spouse, kids, girl/boy friend)	56%
The economy	50%

BASE: All respondents 2016 ($n = 3511$)

particular situation is potentially harmful; at other times you may not. Sometimes you *do* feel you have the energy (a resource) to handle a particular situation, but at other times you just *don't* have the energy.

Another part of the answer to why cognitive appraisal varies so much lies in the individual internal factors that make each person unique. Here is a closer look at another specific type of internal factor, the irrational belief system.

2. *The unnecessary stress of irrational beliefs.* Albert Ellis, a well-known psychologist, argued that one of the internal causes of stress (i.e., stress that you put on yourself) is an **irrational belief system.**[8] These irrational beliefs include such things as believing that everyone must like you, or that you must never make mistakes. At worst, some people **catastrophize,** or turn an irrational belief into an imagined catastrophe. For example, let's say that in Zena's weekly department meeting, her co-worker made a remark that sounded innocent enough, but which made her look very industrious, while it made Zena look a little incompetent: "I noticed that Zena wasn't able to finish the accounts receivable forms in time to ship out yesterday, so I went ahead and finished those up last night. You can thank me by buying me lunch, Zena!" Other people in the meeting just smile or chuckle, but Zena is thinking, "I will never make a good impression with these people. I am never going to get ahead in this company. I'll probably just get demoted for the rest of my life. And I can't work anywhere else, because no one here will give me a good recommendation. I might even get fired. They'll probably turn my friends and family against me too, because they won't want to be around me after I get fired. Why can't I ever do anything right?" Zena turned one event into a catastrophe with her irrational beliefs.

According to Ellis, it can be understandable to believe things should turn out better than they actually do. However, it is irrational to *expect* that they will, and irrational to believe that you cannot survive unless they do. Ellis believed that not just stressors themselves, but also people's *beliefs* about stressors, are sources of stress. Using an example in which your

Stress in the United States

A 2017 survey on stress in the United States found that stress levels have risen over the past decade. Findings include:

- The number of Americans reporting extreme stress continues to be high— 20% said their stress is an 8, 9, or 10 on a 10-point scale.
- 31% reported their stress level had increased in the past year.
- Top sources of stress include money (62%), work (58%), the economy (50%), family health problems (57%), and personal health concerns (58%).
- Eight in 10 Americans in the beginning of 2017 reported experiencing at least one symptom of stress, including headache (34%), feeling overwhelmed (33%), feeling anxious or nervous (33%), or feeling sad or depressed (32%).
- For the first time in this annual survey, Americans reported increased stress due to the safety issues of threat of terrorism, gun violence, or mass violence; as well as the political climate and future of the economy.
- Women report more stress than men, and minorities are more likely to report higher stress levels related to finances. Younger adults are more likely to report increased stress levels. Adults with lower income feel higher stress.
- On a more positive note, four in 10 Americans report they are doing better at managing stress compared with 10 years ago.

Source: American Psychological Association, *Stress in America*™ http://www.apa.org/news/press/releases /stress/2016/coping-with-change.PDF (posted February 23, 2017; retrieved June 22, 2017).

irrational belief system

A way of thinking that causes internal stress by substituting a realistic belief with one that is destructive, illogical, and largely false.

catastrophize

To turn an irrational belief into an imagined disaster.

REAL WORLD EXAMPLE 12.1

A working mother was having a rough morning, full of hassles and feeling overwhelmed. Rushing to finish breakfast with her son, she spilled her coffee on her black sweater. Her young son said to her, "Mommy, you should always wear black clothes, because then no one can see the coffee you spill on yourself and you don't have to change your clothes." Children have a way of putting stressors into perspective!

figure 12.2

ELLIS'S ABC APPROACH TO STRESS

This ABC formula illustrates how stress develops inside of people. An *activating event* triggers people to form a *belief* about it, which in turn shapes the *consequences. How much can your beliefs affect the outcome of stressful situations?*

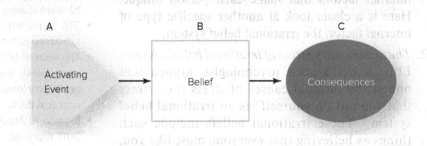

A — Activating Event

B — Belief

C — Consequences

DEALING WITH EXTERNAL STRESSORS

Stress can be caused by external factors that are both ordinary and out of your control, ranging from an uncomfortable environment to frustration and conflict. *How do you manage the stress caused by factors beyond your control?*

©Ingram Publishing RF

supervisor asks you to redo some work, take a closer look at Ellis's ABC approach to stress in Figure 12.2. In this idea, the A stands for an *activating event*—in this case, being asked to do the work over again. The B stands for your *belief* about the activating event—in this case, the irrational beliefs that arise from having to redo the work. The C stands for the *consequences* of the eventual outcome caused by the activating event and your beliefs about it—in this case, the anxiety and misery you feel, and the behavior resulting from those feelings.

Irrational beliefs, then, can lead to catastrophizing an event—a stressor—or blowing it out of proportion. This makes you less able to cope with it, which in turn makes you less able to solve the problem and adds more stress. The biggest culprit in your emotional stress and anxiety, according to Ellis, is the B (or belief) part of the ABC. It is not the event itself that is responsible for your emotional response; it is your belief about it. Unfortunately, irrational beliefs can become a vicious cycle and repeat themselves endlessly as negative emotions turn into negative behaviors. (See Figure 12.3.) Using the earlier example of the remarks made in the department meeting, we can see that Zena's irrational beliefs can lead to depression and anxiety, and these lead to low motivation and low energy, which can make her less likely to finish other projects in the future. This just repeats the cycle until she says, "I was right; I can't do this job at all. What's the point of even trying?" And the eventual outcome is that she quits trying.

Is there any hope for reducing the stress of irrational beliefs? Yes, according to Ellis. You can try to reduce the stress of irrational beliefs by changing them yourself, using his principles of "rational-emotive therapy" to improve

Ten Irrational Beliefs

Although everyone has irrational beliefs, according to Albert Ellis (1913–2007), each person has a different set of them. Ten of the most common ones can be summarized as follows. As you read this list, ask yourself (honestly!) how many of them you believe or have you believed.

Irrational belief #1:   I must have love or approval from all of the people who are important to me.

Irrational belief #2:   I must prove myself to be thoroughly competent, adequate, and achieving at something important.

Irrational belief #3:   When people act obnoxiously or unfairly, they should be blamed for being bad, rotten, or wicked individuals.

Irrational belief #4:   When I am seriously frustrated, treated unfairly, or rejected, I must view the situation as awful, terrible, horrible, and catastrophic.

Irrational belief #5:   Emotional misery comes from external pressures and I have little ability to control or change my feelings.

Irrational belief #6:   If something seems dangerous or fearsome, I must preoccupy myself with it and make myself anxious about it.

Irrational belief #7:   It is better to avoid facing my difficulties and responsibilities than it is to use self-discipline to obtain rewarding things.

Irrational belief #8:   My past experiences remain all-important. Since something once strongly influenced my life, it has to keep determining my feelings and behavior today.

Irrational belief #9:   It is awful and horrible if I do not find good solutions to life's grim realities.

Irrational belief #10:   I can achieve maximum happiness by inertia or inaction or by passively and uncommittedly "enjoying myself."[9]

figure 12.3

IRRATIONAL BELIEFS AND STRESS

Irrational beliefs can cripple people facing stress because they make them fear outcomes that do not actually exist. Most of these irrational beliefs take situations to extremes—even though that can create more problems and stress. *What are your irrational beliefs, and what do they do to your stress level?*

type A and type B personalities

Two standard personality-related sets of behaviors. Type A behaviors are characterized by impatience, hostility, perfectionism, and a sense of time urgency. Type B behaviors are characterized by flexibility, the ability to relax and delegate work, and a minimal sense of time urgency.

your own belief system and replace irrational beliefs with more rational ones. In a nutshell, this means changing the B of the ABC. Strategy for Success 12.1 explains this in more detail.

» TYPE A AND TYPE B PERSONALITY BEHAVIOR

So far in this discussion of the internal stressors, you have examined cognitive appraisal and irrational belief systems. Turn your attention now to the third type of internal stressor, personality factors—also known as **type A and type B personalities.**

Survivor Guilt

Research on the *survivors* of mass layoffs and downsizing (i.e., those who kept their jobs) has found that these employees can suffer more stress effects than the *victims* of layoffs. Survivors have reported feeling more stress, less control on the job, lower job satisfaction, and "survivor guilt," along with poorer health and quality of life than victims of layoffs who later found jobs. Survivors also missed work more often and reported more drug use.[10]

more about...

REAL WORLD EXAMPLE 12.2

Marco has a type A personality. He walks and eats quickly and combines two or more tasks to save time. He finishes other people's sentences for them, finishes other people's work if he feels they are too slow, and feels guilty when he is not busy. He also becomes extremely irritated when having to wait for anything such as a dentist appointment or a meeting.

more about...

Time Urgency

In the final words of Queen Elizabeth I (1533–1603), "All my possessions for a moment of time."

HOLDING ON TO SELF-DEFEATING BELIEFS

An important step in getting rid of irrational beliefs is to dispute, or argue against, beliefs that sabotage your ability to stay calm in stressful situations. Think about your beliefs; if any are self-defeating, eliminate them. *How can you get rid of self-defeating beliefs?*

©Syda Productions/Shutterstock

This personality theory has become so popular that most people are already familiar with it. According to this theory, people can be categorized into either of these two personality types on the basis of their behaviors and personality styles. Type A people are seen as impatient, hostile perfectionists with a sense of time urgency. Type B people are more relaxed.

The danger of being like Marco in Real World Example 12.2 is that type A people seem more likely to have cardiovascular problems such as heart attacks and strokes. Type B people, on the other hand, are more flexible, more relaxed, better able to delegate work, and less time-urgent.[11] Two bits of folk wisdom are sometimes heard about type A and type B people in the workplace. The first is that top-level executives are likely to be type Bs, with type A assistants frantically running around doing their work for them. This is because type Bs can delegate responsibility, whereas type As are such perfectionists that they have to do all the work themselves and will never get to the top because of this. The second thing heard about types A and B is that the road to becoming a CEO is paved with the dead bodies of type As (presumably dead from heart attacks), with type Bs stepping over the bodies on their way to the top.

Although the type A and type B personality idea has been very popular in recent years, psychologists now say it may not be as useful as originally thought. People are not so simply categorized. They may act like a type A one day and a type B the next, or with some issues they act like one type and with other issues the other type. In addition, they may act like one type on the outside but feel completely different inside. The best point to learn from the type A/type B personality theory and stress debate is that it is most important for people to examine their *behaviors*. The truth seems to be that the behaviors of constant anger (sometimes called *toxic hostility*) and, to a lesser extent, time urgency (sometimes called *hurry sickness*) probably have worse health effects than does an overall personality type.[12]

If you recognized yourself in the risky type A behavior profile above, relax! These behaviors are just habits; they don't have to be permanent. Later in this chapter you will examine ways to change behavior, or cope with stress in a healthy way. If your behaviors are more relaxed than hostile, don't gloat! Too much of a good thing is a problem, as well: People who are overly relaxed, to the point of having depressive personalities, also have an increased risk of disease.

To find out if you fit into a type A or a type B personality behavior profile, take the test at the end of the chapter (see Working It Out 12.1). Remember, these are just *behaviors,* which can be changed. Behaviors are not some unchangeable aspect of personality that has been set in stone.

You may know someone with a different kind of personality than type A or type B, someone who just seems to be a *survivor.* This type of person, in spite of stressors and problems that seem impossible to overcome, manages just fine. Why are some people in stressful situations able to come out smiling, while others fail? Suzanne Kobasa and others in the past three decades have been studying what they call the **hardy personality,** or resilient personality.[13]

Regardless of the situation, these people seem to have three things in common—the "three Cs" of a hardy personality: challenge, commitment, and control. Where others see terrible problems to overcome, they see *challenges* to meet. People with a hardy personality also have a sense of *commitment.* It doesn't matter to what; it could be to their jobs, education, a religion, a political cause, to raising their children, or to a healthier lifestyle for themselves. They just feel a sense of purpose or a mission in life. Finally, they feel that they are in *control* of their lives and in charge of what happens to them, instead of seeing themselves as passive beings with no say in the course of their own lives. This is the idea of the "internal locus of control" introduced in Chapter 2.

LEARNING FROM THE OTHER SIDE

Neither a type A nor a type B personality is free from stress. They both deal with stress in different ways, with benefits and risks to each method. *Why is it important to learn from the opposite type if you classify yourself according to this personality theory? What can you learn by observing others who act differently under stress than you do?*

©RuslanDashinsky/Getty Images

》 THE PHYSICAL EFFECTS OF STRESS

You can see that stress can have more than just emotional and psychological effects. It can also have serious, even life-threatening, physical effects. To reduce the harmful effects of stress, you need to understand how this process works.

How Our Bodies Adapt to Stress

In his book *The Stress of Life,* Hans Selye developed and tested a theory about what stress does to people physically. He called it the *general adaptation syndrome,* or GAS. According to this theory, when you are first

hardy personality

A resilient personality type, characterized by the ability to meet challenges, a sense of commitment, and a feeling of being in control of life.

figure 12.4

SEYLE'S GENERAL ADAPTATION SYNDROME

Source: John W. Santrock, *Adolescence,* 7e (New York: The McGraw-Hill Companies, Inc., 1996).

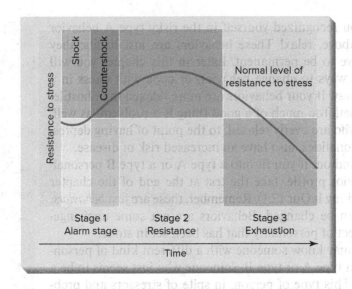

HANS SELYE

©Bettmann/Contributor/Getty Images

confronted with a stressor, your body responds with an activation of the sympathetic nervous system. This has come to be known as the *fight-or-flight response.* During the fight-or-flight response, your body quickly (in a matter of seconds) gets ready to confront or to escape the stressor by specific physical and chemical reactions. These include increased heart rate, blood pressure, respiration, stomach acid, tensed muscles, and a sudden release of adrenaline. When the fight-or-flight response is activated, according to Selye, you have entered the first stage of GAS, the *alarm stage.*[14] (See Figure 12.4.)

Once the alarm is sounded, you enter the second stage of GAS, the *stage of adaptation.* You adapt to the stressor and can usually return to normal. As you try to restore lost energy and repair any damage done to your body, your sympathetic nervous system is still activated, but not at the high level it was during the alarm stage. As you successfully cope with the stressor, you activate your parasympathetic nervous system. Heart rate, blood pressure, respiration, and muscles then relax. Most of the time, people at this stage are able to cope with the stressor and soon return to normal.

In some cases, though, you are not able to adapt to a stressor and can end up using up (or exhausting) all of your physical resources. You then enter the third stage of GAS, the *stage of exhaustion.* During this stage, the parasympathetic nervous system is still activated, so you appear relaxed, but the stressor is still present. In this stage, you are unable to cope with the prolonged stressor, and you can become vulnerable to other stressors.

As the school term nears an end, for example, stress increases so that during final exams week many students are using up all their stored energy and physical resources. By the end of the term, students have completely used up their energy and resources, and they enter the stage of exhaustion. Then, instead of enjoying the break between terms, they may wind up catching a cold or the flu, or becoming accident-prone. The same thing can happen at work when employees exhaust themselves trying to get everything finished and out of the way before they go on vacation. Instead of enjoying their vacation time, they get sick!

Selye would say these students and employees have succumbed to a *disease of adaptation*. In the most extreme cases, people exposed to prolonged stress may even die. You may know of a case where an elderly friend or relative fell and broke a hip (because balance declines and bones get more brittle with age), entered the hospital for treatment of the broken hip, and died soon thereafter of pneumonia or heart failure. According to Selye's theory of GAS, if the stress of healing the broken hip was prolonged, then the patient entered the stage of exhaustion and fell victim to a disease of adaptation (pneumonia or heart failure).

According to Selye, extreme responses to stress may have been essential in early times when people were facing attacks by wild animals. Today, however, these reactions are harmful if they persist. Think about the physical symptoms present during the fight-or-flight response. What happens in the long run, say, when you are stuck in traffic every day during your commute to work and your heart rate, blood pressure, respiration rate, and stomach acids increase? The muscle tension in your neck, head, and back that appeared because the traffic (a stressor) triggered the alarm stage may, over time, turn into a headache, stiff neck, or backache. The increased heart rate may eventually turn into cardiovascular disease. The increase in blood pressure may turn into hypertension, eventually resulting in a stroke or heart attack. The increase in stomach acid may turn into heartburn, indigestion, or ulcers.

Remember that in Selye's theory, eustress (stress from positive events) and distress (stress from negative events) both produce the physical and chemical

Hans Selye (1907–1982) was a Canadian doctor and medical educator who pioneered research on different types of stress. He began his studies on stress in 1926, during his second year in medical school. He co-founded the Canadian Institute of Stress in 1979, which is still active today, offering training programs and consultations for workplaces and individuals, and reporting findings on stress research. His classic book, *The Stress of Life*, was originally published in 1956 and has been revised over the years.

Taking Charge

An anonymous quote says, "Yesterday is a canceled check, tomorrow is a promissory note, today is ready cash: Use it!"

Stressors . . . or Situations?

As one woman said during her treatment for cancer, "Stop feeling sorry for me! I'm not *dying* of cancer, I'm just *living with* cancer!" This rethinking of her diagnosis, she says, helped her fight the disease and eventually recover.

Adding Fuel to the Fire

Researchers found that one reason people with type A behaviors are more susceptible to coronary artery disease is that they are also more likely to smoke and to eat high-cholesterol fast foods. Reducing stress and learning to relax may reduce the "need" to smoke, and the "need" to buy prepared food rather than cooking nutritious meals, both of which then reduce the risk of heart disease.

Source: From *The Harvard Heart Letter*, President and Fellows of Harvard College, January 1992, p. 104.

more about...

more about...

more about...

more about...

INCREASE HEALTH BY DECREASING STRESS

By paying attention to factors such as nutrition, exercise, and proper sleep, you can avoid the debilitating long-term effects of most types of stress. *What do you do to strengthen your body against stress?*

©Samuel Borges Photography/Shutterstock

changes of the fight-or-flight response because your body cannot tell the difference between the two. Imagine a friend telling you, for example, that he wasn't able to sleep, had no appetite, felt dizzy and lightheaded, and couldn't concentrate. Without any more information, would you guess that he was coming down with the flu or falling in love? Events that you interpret as good or bad can produce the same physical reactions. They are both stressors because they make demands on your body to adapt or to change. As you have learned, it is adapting to change that is stressful.

Although Selye's original book is more than 60 years old, its theories are supported even more today by the work of health psychologists and medical researchers who study long-term effects of stress and the relationship of stress to the immune system.

In a "meta-analysis" (a study of studies) made public in 2004, researchers examined the results of almost 300 studies that took place over a 40-year span (1960–2000) and included almost 20,000 people. What they found supported Selye's ideas about the GAS's stages of alarm, resistance, and exhaustion. In the short term, stress gets the immune system "revved up" and ready to fight the stressor. In the long term, though, chronic stress wears down the immune system, and immunity begins to break down. This long-term wear and tear makes the immune system much less able to fight new stressors as they come along, or handle continuing stressors. Not surprisingly, these researchers also found that people who were at risk—for example, who were elderly or already ill—had the worst outcomes. This research reminds us of the importance of keeping stressors in check, and finding ways to manage the possible damage of long-term, chronic stress.[15]

Stress and the Immune System

The immune system serves three basic functions. Briefly, these include:

1. Recognizing foreign cells and attacking them.
2. Developing antibodies to recognize foreign invaders in the future.
3. Sending white blood cells and other helper cells to the location of an injury or infection to speed healing.

Just by having chronic stress, you can actually weaken your immune system and fall victim to an illness that you would normally fight off with ease.

more about...

Are You a "Constant Checker?"

An annual survey conducted by the American Psychological Association found that more than four out of five American adults say they check their e-mail, texts, and social media accounts often or constantly. These "constant checkers" also are more likely to experience higher levels of stress. Regarding these "constant checkers," researcher Lynn Bufka says that ". . . while technology helps us in many ways, being constantly connected can have a negative impact on both their physical and mental health." Her recommendation? Take time to unplug. Taking a periodic "digital detox" can reduce the stress of the ever-present technology in our lives.

American Psychological Association: APA's Survey Finds Constantly Checking Electronic Devices Linked to Significant Stress for Most Americans (February 23, 2017), http://www.apa.org/news/press/releases/2017/02/checking-devices.aspx (retrieved June 20, 2017).

Medical research is finding evidence that even serious chronic illnesses such as cancer are linked to stress as well. Because your immune system is weakened by stress, anything from the common cold to an uncommon cancer is more likely to invade when you are under stress for long periods of time. Other stress-related illnesses can include asthma, ulcers, colitis, skin disorders such as eczema or hives, allergies, strokes, and heart attacks. Medical research suggests that the effects of stress can strike back as long as 20 years later or even longer. Men who were highly anxious in middle age, studies show, are much more likely 20 years later to have high blood pressure than men who had a calmer outlook on life.[16]

You can probably recognize the fight-or-flight feelings of immediate stressors, but how can you know when you are overstressed? Take the stress self-test at the end of this chapter to find out how much stress you are under. How can you recognize excessive stress in other people? Researchers have found that people under stress may act restless, impatient, competitive, and pressured. They may have had recent changes in work or personal lives that would help explain the excessive stress.[17] See Figure 12.5 for ways managers can reduce workplace stress.

The Connection between Chronic Stress and Mental Illness

Researchers at the University of California, Berkeley, have found that chronic stress produces long-term changes in the brain that make people more likely to develop anxiety and mood disorders later in their lives, including PTSD (post-traumatic stress disorder). Researchers are still investigating exactly what these changes are, and how these stress levels result in mental illness. Researcher Daniela Kaufman believes one possible explanation is that the connections in the brain that lead to an "alarm" response are strengthened over time with stress, unintentionally strengthening these pathways and making the stress response more likely to occur. The link between chronic stress and physical illness is well documented, and the new direction of research into the link between chronic stress and mental illness will bring an even greater understanding of the damage caused by stress.

Source: Robert Sanders, "New Evidence That Chronic Stress Predisposes the Brain to Mental Illness," *Berkeley News,* http://news.berkeley.edu/2014/02/11/chronic-stress-predisposes-brain-to-mental-illness/ (posted February 11, 2014).

more about...

» THE COST OF STRESS IN THE WORKPLACE

In this chapter we have focused on the effects of stress at the individual level. However, there are enormous costs to business and to society because of stress, as well. According to the American Institute of Stress, stress-related problems cost the American economy more than $300 billion every year![18] These costs are an estimate based on lower productivity due to stress, lost days of work, worker's compensation claims, health insurance and health-care costs, stress management programs, and lawsuits that are a result of stress-related illness or injuries.

Employees increasingly report stress-related headaches, back pain, exhaustion, anxiety, anger, insomnia, and digestive upsets from their jobs. Close to 90 percent of visits to the doctor are for stress-related symptoms. Up to 80 percent of industrial accidents are blamed on stress. In a survey of employees' stress-related symptoms, most employees reported feeling at least three symptoms. About one-fifth of those surveyed had missed work because of stress, and one-third had thought about quitting as a way of relieving stress. Specific

figure 12.5

REDUCING WORKPLACE STRESS

Managers can do a lot to reduce stress in their work environments. The key elements are clear, positive communication and "leading by example" by handling stressful situations with calmness and fairness. *What can your current (or most recent) manager do to reduce stress at his or her workplace?*

Source: Sigmund Ginsberg, "Reducing the Stress You Cause Others," *Supervisory Management* 35 (December 1990), p. 5. See also: Christina Maslach and Michael P. Leiter, "Take This Job and Love It," *Psychology Today,* September/October 1999.

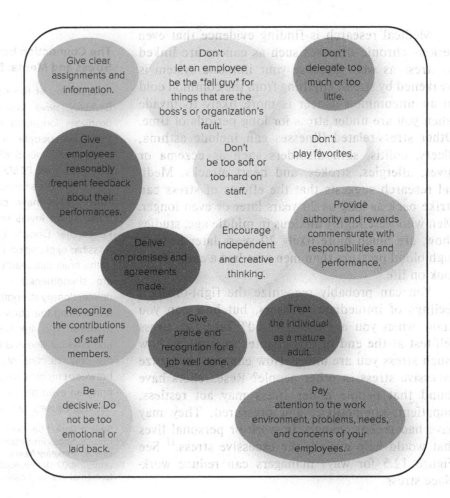

Give clear assignments and information.

Don't let an employee be the "fall guy" for things that are the boss's or organization's fault.

Don't delegate too much or too little.

Give employees reasonably frequent feedback about their performances.

Don't play favorites.

Don't be too soft or too hard on staff.

Provide authority and rewards commensurate with responsibilities and performance.

Deliver on promises and agreements made.

Encourage independent and creative thinking.

Recognize the contributions of staff members.

Give praise and recognition for a job well done.

Treat the individual as a mature adult.

Be decisive: Do not be too emotional or laid back.

Pay attention to the work environment, problems, needs, and concerns of your employees.

conditions on the job that employees reported as stressful included crowding, noise, air pollution, poor lighting, and uncomfortable temperatures.

Employees also reported stress from management, including having no say in decisions, too much or too little structure, racism, sexism, frustrating company policies, and low pay. They also reported stressful relationships with supervisors, peers, and other staff members, as well as individual stressors, such as boredom, work overload, too much responsibility, no promotions, and disagreements with management. Psychologically stressed employees reported feeling depressed, anxious, frustrated, fatigued, and bored, with lowered self-esteem. Stressed employees were more likely than non-stressed employees to have accidents on the job, eat or smoke too much, have outbursts of anger, and abuse alcohol or other drugs.[19]

Increasing numbers of employees are seeking help for stress through employee programs, and they are also increasing stress-related worker's compensation claims and lawsuits. There is no reason to think that stress and the costs of dealing with stress are going to decrease any time soon. It is up to the organizations to research and implement programs and resources to help reduce workplace stress.

Considering the physical and psychological problems associated with stress, it is not hard to imagine that stress also affects self-esteem. Stress makes you feel overwhelmed, unable to do what you have to do. Stress makes people less productive and less successful, which lowers self-esteem. These become part of a vicious cycle in which effectiveness and self-esteem both sink lower. Stress can also make people turn to poor coping substitutions such as substance abuse. Being caught in a web of substance abuse can lower self-esteem still further. Therefore, stress impacts all areas of people's lives: physical health, mental health, social life, and job performance. Learning to change the things you can change to reduce stress in your life is certainly worth the time and effort! (See Figure 12.6 for ways to alleviate the stress that leads to **job burnout**.)

job burnout

Physical and emotional exhaustion resulting from long-term stress or frustration in one's workplace.

figure 12.6

AVOIDING JOB BURNOUT

Managers can beat burnout in themselves and their employees by adhering to these simple principles. *Which of these principles seems most important to you?*

Source: Christina Maslach and Michael P. Leiter, "Take This Job and Love It," *Psychology Today,* September/October 1999. See also: Michael P. Leiter and Christina Maslach, *Banishing Burnout: Six Strategies for Improving Your Relationship with Work* (San Francisco, CA: Jossey-Bass, 2005).

Beating Burnout

Employee stress can lead to **job burnout.** Employees who feel insecure, misunderstood, frustrated, overloaded, overwhelmed, undervalued, and alienated often do the bare minimum at work or leave their jobs. Burnout is bad for employees and employers alike. Can job burnout be beaten? Experts Christina Maslach and Michael P. Leiter have interviewed thousands of people about job burnout. They list six key areas for employee happiness and reduced job burnout.

1. **Workload** must be manageable. Employees who feel that they have too much work to do in too little time with too few resources feel burned out. When workload is manageable, employees can meet demands and seek out new challenges.

2. Employees need a sense of **control.** Rigid office policies or chaos in the work environment can prevent employees from finishing work and feeling productive. Employees who are allowed to make decisions, solve problems, and determine the outcomes of their projects are more productive.

3. Employees must have an opportunity for **rewards.** Low pay, little praise, and no recognition leave employees feeling undervalued, unhappy, and resentful. When the work seems valuable to others, employees take pride in their work and work harder at tasks.

4. A feeling of **community** buoys employees. Conflict or tension among co-workers leaves everyone feeling angry, anxious, suspicious, and fearful. Being physically or socially isolated also leaves employees without a sense of community. Being able to share ideas, praise, and humor with co-workers leads to greater cohesiveness, respect, support, and team spirit.

5. Trusting the workplace to be **fair** keeps employees loyal. When some employees feel they do the lion's share of the work while others get the praise, a feeling of fairness is lost. Favoritism isn't fair. Employees are left feeling distrustful, cynical, and disloyal. Respect and justice, along with mutual respect between co-workers, form the basis for fairness in the workplace.

6. Shared **values** promote ethical behavior. Employees who don't share the company's values may do something unethical, or may do something that clashes with their personal values. This leads to employees feeling bad about themselves and their work. Meaningful work that doesn't cause a clash between the organizational norms and personal principles is more satisfying to employees.

STRATEGIES FOR SUCCESS

Strategy 12.1   Discard Irrational Beliefs

1. Evaluate the consequences of the belief.
2. Identify your belief system.
3. Dispute the self-defeating belief.
4. Practice effective ways of thinking.

Since one of the internal sources of stress is an irrational belief system, to reduce stress you must change your irrational beliefs by replacing them with rational beliefs. Whenever you start thinking along the lines of "I've failed the midterm exam! I'm going to flunk this class and get kicked out of school!" you must stop that irrational thought. Replace it with something more rational, such as "I've failed the midterm exam. If I get a tutor and spend more time studying, I can do better on the next exam and still pass the class."

Albert Ellis believes that for any irrational belief, you can follow these four steps to replace it with a more rational belief:

1. **Evaluate the consequences of the belief.** (Part C of the ABC) Negative emotions as a result of a stressor may seem to be natural, but they aren't inevitable. Ask yourself if these reactions are helping you live effectively, and helping you solve your problems.

2. **Identify your belief system.** (Part B of the ABC) Ask yourself why you are feeling the specific emotions aroused by the irrational belief. Ellis believes that by examining the irrational belief, you can figure out what is causing the negative consequences (negative emotions).

3. **Dispute the self-defeating belief.** After you have identified an irrational belief, you can argue against it.

4. **Practice effective ways of thinking.** Continue to examine your reactions to activating events. Try substituting more real beliefs and imagining more successful outcomes.

Strategy 12.2   Change Your Behaviors to Reduce Stress

1. Take charge of your life.
2. Use humor.
3. Compare yourself with others.
4. Take advantage of stress.
5. Learn to live with unavoidable stress.

Remember that one of the internal sources of stress is your personality style or behavior. Changing your personality involves both cognitive (thought-related) and behavioral strategies. You may assume that you cannot change your personality, but you can change your behaviors to more healthy and less stress-producing ones. Learn to recognize and monitor the toxic hostility behaviors and the hurry sickness, which cause you more stress. Use the following strategies to reduce these behaviors:

1. **Take charge of your life.** Think of the three Cs of the hardy personality—challenge, commitment, and control. Tell yourself to think positive thoughts—that the stressor you are facing is a challenge, not a problem, that you are in control of your own life.

Take charge! Confront stressors when you can in a thoughtful and assertive way. Stay committed to your goal instead of giving up. Remind yourself to take charge when stress rises.

2. **Use humor.** Learn to see the humor in situations, and increase the amount of humor in your life. An increase of humor reduces stress, because you physically can't feel both at the same time. Humor also makes you feel better, distracts you temporarily from the stressor, and lets you relax.

3. **Compare yourself with others.** Another cognitive strategy is social comparison. By comparing yourself with others who are in a similar situation but worse off, you may feel better about your situation. This does not mean you should listen to the horror stories that well-meaning friends or co-workers delight in telling! You will cope better when you hear encouraging stories about people in situations like yours.[20]

4. **Take advantage of stress.** Pay attention to your stress levels and learn what your optimal level is in order to be productive. Remember, with too little stress or challenge, you may become bored, unmotivated, and unproductive. With too much stress, you will be overwhelmed. Find out how much is right for you.

5. **Learn to live with unavoidable stress.** Finally, as a cognitive strategy for coping with stress, learn to live with the stressors you cannot avoid. This does not mean giving in to stress; it means accepting the fact that some stressors are unavoidable. Learn to think about these stressors in different ways than before.

Strategy 12.3   Take Care of Yourself

1. Use relaxation techniques.
2. Increase your fitness: exercise, eat well, and reduce/quit smoking and drinking.
3. Make time for rest and leisure.
4. Get social support.
5. Try to reduce stress in the workplace.
6. Manage your time.
7. Stop procrastinating!

According to stress research, some amount of stress is inevitable and even good for you (it keeps you motivated and alive!), so you don't want to eliminate all stress. Your goal should be to reduce or minimize the negative effects of stress by coping with or managing stress.

1. **Use relaxation techniques.** In addition to changing your thoughts, you can use specific relaxation strategies as a way of reducing or managing stress. Since relaxing and feeling stress are not physically compatible, you can't do both at the same time. Forcing yourself to relax means you are getting rid of stress (at least temporarily!). Some simple relaxation techniques include deep breathing, progressive relaxation, meditation, and biofeedback.

   To use *progressive relaxation*, you would close your eyes and imagine your entire body becoming relaxed, slowly, one muscle group at a time. *Meditation* is a relaxation technique that teaches you to focus outward, becoming aware of sensory input around you; or inward, becoming more self-aware.

REAL WORLD EXAMPLE 12.3

C. W. Metcalf, a business consultant and entrepreneur, makes his living by teaching ways of adding humor to the workplace. He says that he has more requests than he can handle because companies across the country are beginning to recognize the value of humor. Metcalf set up workshops for Owens-Corning Fiberglass during its downsizing that he says were successful in preventing possible problems such as sabotage, threats to management, and suicide attempts.[21]

Biofeedback requires the use of a machine that gives you information (feedback) about specific biological (bio) processes. By learning to recognize what a change in heart rate and skin temperature feel like, you can actually learn to control such processes as heart rate, respiration, skin temperature, and perspiration. Many people have successfully used biofeedback to treat such stress-related illnesses as asthma, migraine headaches, epilepsy, and high blood pressure, as well as to control other physical processes that were once thought to be out of their control.[22]

2. **Increase your fitness: Exercise, eat well, and reduce/quit smoking and drinking.** Relaxation is one behavioral strategy used to manage stress and increase wellness. Another strategy is to increase general overall fitness. The more physically fit you are, the less negative the effects of stress will be, and the stronger your immune system will be to fight stress-related illnesses. Stay healthy by eating a nutritionally sound diet that is low in fats and sugars and high in fibers. Follow an exercise plan. If you are overweight, lose weight. If you smoke or drink alcohol a great deal, cut down or stop. Avoid long exposure to the sun or to harmful chemicals. If your workplace is excessively noisy, ask for earplugs and use them.

3. **Make time for rest and leisure.** Getting enough sleep at regular times and building leisure activities into your schedule will help you manage stress better. You need sleep to stay healthy. You may be thinking, "I can't add leisure activities to my schedule! I have too much to do already!" If so, you are just the person this suggestion is aimed at. Stop and think about the stress that your behaviors are creating for yourself.

4. **Get social support.** Friends, family, or even a support group can help in relieving stress. Examples of social support may include things such as receiving a tuna casserole when you are sick or personal loans when you are low on cash. It also includes emotional support, such as sympathy and understanding, when you are unhappy or stressed. But remember: Whatever your support network gives you, you will probably be asked to return at some time when others are stressed. Be clear on whether some family members or friends cause more stress than they relieve.

5. **Try to reduce stress in the workplace.** Organizations can help reduce stressors in the workplace, too. One source of stress that employees often mention is rigid work schedules that don't allow for family obligations or emergencies. Companies are increasingly offering flextime, job sharing, telecommuting, and compressed workweeks. Scheduling that allows employees to meet their needs means less absenteeism and higher productivity. Helping employees cope with stress on the job means lower turnover rates, more commitment and loyalty from employees, higher productivity, and better relationships with co-workers.[23]

   Nationwide, companies are offering services to reduce workplace stress. Services range from counseling (e.g., psychological, nutritional, weight control, and substance abuse counseling) to onsite health and fitness centers and day-care facilities. What, you might ask, does day care have to do with workplace stress? Businesses are realizing that stress at home spills over into stress at work (and vice versa), so the best way to combat workplace stress is to reduce overall stress.

Many companies take this subject seriously enough to catch the attention of outside agencies: Johnson & Johnson, for example, has won several awards for their employee health programs.

6. **Manage your time.** One of the easiest and most productive ways to combat stress behaviorally is to learn to manage time better. This will help you know what to expect and how to feel some control over your schedule and your life. Time management can be a problem when you waste time (underutilization), or schedule too many things into one time slot (overload).

   Whether your problem is overload or underutilization, you can take specific steps to learn to manage your time better. Start by making a list of all the regular activities you carry out in a day for work, school, family activities, and even leisure time. Make another list of upcoming events and deadlines. Put together a master time schedule with daily activities as well as dates to remember, filling in each time block with activities scheduled. Keep a daily time plan (an index card will fit neatly into a pocket), but also a monthly calendar for those upcoming events. Plan ahead, but set realistic timetables for getting work done. Allow an extra cushion of time for emergencies or unforeseen events. Reward yourself along the way (but not until *after* you have completed your work!) with activities you like, such as talking to friends, going out to eat, watching television, and so on. Modify the schedule until it is workable. Then stick to it!

7. **Stop procrastinating!** *Procrastination*, or putting things off until later, allows you to avoid things you don't really want to do. Procrastination ultimately increases your stress level! To reduce procrastination, make a specific plan about what you need to do, break large tasks into small chunks, reward yourself for work done along the way, and give yourself credit for a job well done.[24] Reread the material on procrastination in Chapter 2.

Everyone will have different approaches that work, as well as different types and levels of stress; therefore, you will want to choose what applies to you to suit your needs. Perhaps you plan too much work in too short a time frame. Then, to make matters worse, you procrastinate and fail to meet all of your deadlines. At the same time, your fitness level is high, and you have a large social support network. In a case like this, you would probably want to focus on preceding steps 6 and 7. You probably would not need to focus on steps 2 and 4. You might also want to incorporate the remaining steps in your life to increase overall well-being.

CHAPTER TWELVE SUMMARY

Chapter Summary by Learning Objectives

LO 12-1 **Identify the main causes of stress.** Stress is a part of everyone's life. Stress is the body's reaction to a stressor, which can be caused by life changes and daily hassles; by chronic stressors; by external circumstances; or by internal cognitions, belief systems, and personality-related behaviors.

LO 12-2 **Give examples of external and internal sources of stress.** External stressors can include anything from outside sources that cause pain, discomfort, frustration, or conflict. Examples are deadlines, poor health, work or school pressures, or financial problems. Internal stressors can include your own reactions of a stressor, as well as personality factors. They include irrational beliefs, poor social skills, unrealistic expectations, and poor time management, just to name a few.

LO 12-3 **Compare and contrast type A and type B personality behaviors.** Type A and type B personalities are two standard personality-related behaviors. Type A behaviors include impatience, excessive time-consciousness, and perfectionism. Type B behaviors include a more relaxed and flexible outlook, with less focus on time and deadlines.

LO 12-4 **Describe the physical effects of stress.** Stress occurs in three stages as your body sounds the alarm that a stressor is occurring, tries to cope with the stressor, and if coping fails, exhausts its resources and becomes vulnerable to illness due to a weakened immune system.

LO 12-5 **Explain the cost of stress in the workplace.** Stress-related problems cost the American economy more than $300 million per year. These costs include lost work, insurance claims and costs, stress management programs, and stress-related lawsuits.

key terms

catastrophize 311	external stressors 309	job burnout 321
chronic stressors 309	frustration 309	major life changes 306
cognitive appraisal 310	hardy personality 316	stress 306
daily hassles 306	inner conflict 309	stressor 306
distress 306	internal stressors 309	type A and type B
eustress 306	irrational belief system 311	personalities 313

review questions

1. What is meant by stress and stressors? Identify two sources of eustress, and two sources of distress, in your own life.

2. How are major life changes different from daily hassles? How can a major life change lead to daily hassles? Discuss examples of these in your own life.

3. Suppose that you were really looking forward to going to work one day, but when you left for work you realized your tire was flat. Your stress level increased. Discuss how this situation leads to internal and/or external sources of stress.

4. Are there any chronic stressors in your own life, or the life of someone you know? Describe the stressor, and possible coping strategies.

5. Do you hold any of the irrational beliefs described by Ellis? How do they affect your perception of events?

6. According to Ellis, what is catastrophizing? Do you ever find yourself catastrophizing? In what situations? How can you minimize it?

7. What is the difference between meditation and biofeedback? How can each be used to reduce stress? What other specific suggestions for coping with stress can you incorporate into your own life?

8. Suppose you are driving to work one day on your usual route past the City Zoo, when a giant grizzly bear escapes, runs out of the entrance, growling and roaring, and heads straight for your car. Describe the physical and chemical changes that you would experience, according to the general adaptation syndrome (GAS).

critical thinking questions

1. A life without stress seems like a pleasant and desirable goal. Do you agree with Selye that stress is necessary in order to motivate you and keep you alive? Why or why not? What do you think would happen if you didn't have any stress in your life?

2. Some people say that since everyone is going to die anyway, it would be better to enjoy life without worrying about diet, exercise, and other behaviors that may prolong life while reducing the enjoyment of life. Why do you think these people feel this way? What do you think?

working it out 12.1

Behavior Activity Profile—Type A Measure

Each of us displays certain kinds of behaviors, thought patterns, and personal characteristics. For each of the 21 sets of descriptions below, circle the number that you feel best describes where you are between each pair. The best answer for each set of descriptions is the response that most nearly describes the way you feel, behave, or think. Answer these in terms of your regular or typical behavior, thoughts, or characteristics.

1. I'm always on time for appointments. 7 6 5 4 3 2 1 I'm never quite on time.

2. When someone is talking to me, chances are I'll anticipate what they are going to say by nodding, interrupting, or finishing sentences for them. 7 6 5 4 3 2 1 I listen quietly without showing any impatience.

3. I frequently try to do several things at once. 7 6 5 4 3 2 1 I tend to take things one at a time.

4. When it comes to waiting in line (at banks, theaters, etc.), I really get impatient and frustrated. 7 6 5 4 3 2 1 Waiting in line simply doesn't bother me.

5. I always feel rushed. 7 6 5 4 3 2 1 I never feel rushed.

6. When it comes to my temper, I find it hard to control at times. 7 6 5 4 3 2 1 I just don't seem to have a temper.

7. I tend to do most things like eating, walking, and talking rapidly. 7 6 5 4 3 2 1 I tend to eat, walk, and talk slowly.

TOTAL SCORE 1–7 _____ = S

8. Quite honestly, the things I enjoy most are job-related activities. 7 6 5 4 3 2 1 I enjoy leisure-time activities more than job-related activities.

9. At the end of a typical workday, I usually feel like I needed to get more done than I did. 7 6 5 4 3 2 1 In a typical workday, I feel I accomplished everything I needed to.

10. Someone who knows me very well would say that I would rather work than play. 7 6 5 4 3 2 1 Someone who knows me well would say that I would rather play than work.

11. When it comes to getting ahead at work, nothing is more important. 7 6 5 4 3 2 1 Many things are more important than getting ahead at work.

12. My primary source of satisfaction comes from my job. 7 6 5 4 3 2 1 I regularly find satisfaction in non-job pursuits, such as hobbies, friends, and family.

13. Most of my friends and social acquaintances are people I know from work. 7 6 5 4 3 2 1 Most of my friends and social acquaintances are not connected with my work.

14. I'd rather stay at work than take a vacation. 7 6 5 4 3 2 1 Nothing at work is important enough to interfere with my vacation.

TOTAL SCORE 8–14 _____ = J

15. People who know me well would describe me as hard driving and competitive. 7 6 5 4 3 2 1 People who know me well would describe me as relaxed and easygoing.

16. In general, my behavior is governed by a desire for recognition and achievement. 7 6 5 4 3 2 1 My behavior is governed by what I want to do—not by trying to satisfy others.

17. In trying to complete a project or solve a problem, I tend to wear myself out before I'll give up on it. 7 6 5 4 3 2 1 I tend to take a break or quit if I'm feeling fatigued by a project or problem.

18. When I play a game (tennis, cards, etc.) my enjoyment comes from winning. 7 6 5 4 3 2 1 My enjoyment in playing games comes from the social interaction.

19. I like to associate with people who are dedicated to getting ahead. 7 6 5 4 3 2 1 I like to associate with people who are easygoing and take life as it comes.

20. I'm not happy unless I'm always doing something. 7 6 5 4 3 2 1 Frequently, "doing nothing" can be quite enjoyable to me.

21. What I enjoy doing most are competitive activities. 7 6 5 4 3 2 1 What I enjoy doing most are non-competitive pursuits.

TOTAL SCORE 15–21 _____ = H

Source: John M. Ivancevich and Michael T. Matteson, *Organizational Behavior & Management,* 11e (The McGraw-Hill Companies, Inc.) pp. 240–242.

Impatience	(S)	Job Involvement	(J)	Hard Driving and Competitive	(H)	Total Score	(A) S + J + H

The Behavior Activity Profile attempts to assess the three type A coronary-prone behavior patterns, as well as provide a total score. The three a priori types of type A coronary-prone behavior patterns are shown:

Items	Behavior Pattern	Characteristics
1–7	Impatience (S)	Is anxious to interrupt
		Fails to listen attentively
		Gets frustrated by waiting (e.g., in line, for others to complete a job)
8–14	Job Involvement (J)	Focal point of attention is the job
		Lives for the job
		Relishes being on the job
		Gets immersed in job activities
15–21	Hard Driving/Competitive (H)	Is hardworking, highly competitive
		Is competitive in most aspects of life, sports, work, etc.
		Races against the clock
1–21	Total score (A)	Total of S + J + H represents your global type A behavior

Score ranges for total score are:

Score	Behavior Type
122 and above	Hard-core type A
99–121	Moderate type A
90–98	Low type A
80–89	Type X
70–79	Low type B
50–69	Moderate type B
40 and below	Hard-core type B

Percentile Scores

Now you can compare your score to a sample of more than 1,200 respondents.

Percentile Score		Raw Score
Percent of Individuals Scoring Lower	**Males**	**Females**
99%	140	132
95%	135	126
90%	130	120
85%	124	112
80%	118	106
75%	113	101
70%	108	95
65%	102	90
60%	97	85
55%	92	80
50%	87	74
45%	81	69
40%	75	63
35%	70	58
30%	63	53
25%	58	48
20%	51	42
15%	45	36
10%	38	31
5%	29	26
1%	21	21

working it out 12.2

STRESS SELF-TEST

School-to-Work Connection: Personal Qualities Skills

How much stress are you under? To measure the degree of stress you suffer, take this stress test. Circle the appropriate number for each question and tally your total score. A score of 12 or lower indicates a low degree of personal stress reactions; between 13 and 24 reflects a moderate degree; higher than 24 indicates that you're experiencing a high degree of stress. Although your score might not altogether surprise you, it would be wise to consult your doctor to determine whether you have a health problem that requires medical attention, one that might be contributing to your stress level and your ability to withstand it.

How Often Do You Suffer From	Never	Hardly Ever	Sometimes	Often
1. Aches in back, head, or neck	0	1	2	3
2. Too many issues on your mind at once	0	1	2	3
3. Chest pains	0	1	2	3
4. Low interest in physical intimacy	0	1	2	3
5. An urge to drink a lot of alcohol	0	1	2	3
6. Feelings of anxiety and being uptight	0	1	2	3
7. Difficulty falling or staying asleep	0	1	2	3
8. A feeling of depression	0	1	2	3
9. A feeling of being overwhelmed	0	1	2	3
10. An inability to think clearly	0	1	2	3

"Vital Signs," *Sales and Marketing Management*, Novemeber 1992, p. 93. Reprinted with permission of Sales and Marketing Management.

case study 12.1

Bonnie the Bumblebee

James rested his head in his hand and mused as he watched his supervisor, Bonnie, buzz around the office at high speed. He liked to think of her as a giant bumblebee: always moving and often stinging. Bonnie was always in a hurry because she felt she had to do her own work and then redo everyone else's. The stinging came often in the form of criticizing her employees, upper management, her family, and everything else. James, in contrast, preferred a slower, more steady but thorough pace of work. He didn't see any advantage to constantly being so critical and rushed all the time.

"James, you're going to have to do this spreadsheet all over again. I just don't have time to fix it for you, and the Finance Department will never accept it in this form."

Suddenly, she stopped and looked thoughtful. "You know, James, I'm going to be eligible for early retirement in only eight years. I'll probably be promoted to upper management soon. You're a lot younger than I am, but you should be thinking about your future with this company. I think you're probably capable, yet you just don't seem to have the drive, the aggression, that I had at your age. You're just too *nice* or something. Don't you want to make anything of yourself?"

James only smiled and said, "Well, Bonnie, I'll have to think about that." In fact, James had thought quite a lot about the differences between the two of them. He was quite certain that of the two of them, he'd be more likely to be promoted to upper management.

Case Study Questions

1. Is James correct—will he more likely make it to upper management, or will Bonnie? Why? Which style do you see more often in management? Explain why this might be the case.

2. Thinking of the personality behaviors discussed in this chapter, what characteristics would lead you to categorize Bonnie and James as either type A, type B, or hardy?

3. Does Bonnie seem stressed? If so, from what sources (major life changes, daily hassles, chronic stressors, internal stress, or external stress)? If not, why?

4. Does one of the work behavior styles above describe you? After reading this chapter, are you inclined to make any changes? Explain.

case study 12.2

Overworked, or Just Overstressed?

Rick Russell and Arturo Garcia were friends in high school. Last year they both graduated with above-average grades. Now, both are attending their local community college, studying business and hoping for successful lives. They have talked a lot about transferring to a four-year college in the future, maybe before finishing the two years where they are. Although both did well in high school, Rick seems to be really struggling to keep up with both school and a part-time job.

"Art, how do you handle all the stuff you're doing in your life and still stay so calm? How do you manage to get all those good grades? I can barely keep my C average and keep from getting on academic warning. All these instructors want way too much work from us. They act like we don't have a life outside of school. In fact, they seem to think that their classes are the only things we're doing at all!"

Art looked dubious. "You're always exaggerating, Rick. If you really look at it, we don't have that many more assignments than we had last year, and you seemed to do fine then. What's going on that's so radically different from high school? You played baseball and ran track in high school and you still graduated with a B average. What's changed, anyway?"

"This isn't high school, Art, in case you haven't noticed! The work is a lot harder here, and the instructors never remind us when stuff is due or when exams are going to be. I'm always getting my work in late, and I never feel ready for tests when they come. At least in high school my mom or my teachers would pester me about getting things done. Here, it doesn't seem like anybody cares! A lot of my teachers act like they don't care whether I come to class or not."

"Why are you blaming everybody else?" Art replied. "I saw you hanging out in the student lounge all morning yesterday, and you knew that we had a project due in English comp. You need to learn how to manage your time better. Why can't you get it together?"

Case Study Questions

1. Do you think Rick will ever "get it together"? What are the real causes of his frustration? Why isn't Arturo having the same kinds of problems?

2. Sketch out a rough time management plan for Rick, one that includes a 20-hours-per-week job and 12 credits of coursework, along with some personal time and study sessions.

3. What kinds of specific items would a long-term calendar for Rick need to include?

CHAPTER THIRTEEN

YOUR EXTERNAL AND INTERNAL CUSTOMERS

In the Workplace: Good Service: The Other Half of Success

SITUATION

Home Fridays is more than just a simple property management business. It is a company that is built almost totally on selling peace of mind to people who are out of town or who own second homes.

The idea came to Shannon Bassett when she was having problems with her own second home. One winter night she and her husband arrived rather late during a snowstorm. The company that had been contracted to clean the leaves and pine needles out of the gutters had not done their job. With a heavy snowfall on the way, the gutters promised to be a mess unless something was done right away. Both weary from a long road trip, the couple had to get out their stepladders and clean the gutters themselves.

©Ingram Publishing/SuperStock

DISCOVERY

Later that evening, Shannon started thinking, "What if someone owned a company that would make certain that things like this never happened?" A few months later, Shannon owned that company. Its name, Home Fridays, was a take-off on weekend travelers and the peace of mind they can now have knowing that someone who cares is there on weekends, or any other day of the week help is needed. This company takes care of any detail the owner wants, including yard maintenance, house cleaning, minor repairs—whatever needs attention. They've even been known to stock the refrigerator with selected goodies just before the customer's arrival.

At least once a week, someone from Home Fridays visits the customer's house, checking for everything from break-ins to frozen pipes. The company then sends regular reports to clients, along with photographs to reassure them that the place still looks great. They even start and drive cars regularly, to keep them in running condition. When a security alarm system rings, they are the first to be called.

Years have gone by; the company survived the recession of 2007 and even did some growing during both bad times and good. In 2017, the company was sold but continued to be the life-saver for customers with problems. Even more importantly, Home Fridays continued to predict and to prepare for problems.

THINK ABOUT IT

Home Fridays sells peace of mind, responding to a need that nobody else had thought of fulfilling. The entire operation is built on top-notch customer service, service you can always depend on. In other words, Home Fridays sells customer satisfaction.

What makes the Home Fridays company so successful? Are their policies applicable to other businesses?

What other businesses can you think of that provide better customer service than similar businesses provide? What makes them better in this regard?

» WHAT DO CUSTOMERS REALLY WANT?

In business circles it is often said that any company's scarcest resource is capital; that is, money to invest. Rather than capital, an increasing number of people running businesses today are realizing that *satisfied and happy customers* are the most crucial resource. Without a good base of customers, any business will fail. Without customers, you simply don't have a business— or a future.[1]

good feelings and solutions

The only two things customers really buy.

In *How to Win Customers and Keep Them for Life,* Michael LeBoeuf points out that customers buy only two things: **good feelings and solutions** to problems.[2] Everything that a customer wants from you will fall into one of those two categories. For example:

- You don't sell clothes. You sell a sharp appearance, style, attractiveness, comfort, and warmth.
- You don't sell insurance. You sell financial security for people and their families.
- You don't sell toys. You sell happy moments for children.
- You don't sell a house. You sell comfort, contentment, a good investment, pride of ownership, privacy, and space.

Home Fridays doesn't sell home maintenance or property management as much as they sell a pleasant experience and relief from worry. Every moment you are on the job, think about feelings and solutions. Make those two goals your most important activities. If you do, your relationship with customers should improve as you keep your goals in mind.[3]

What feelings does your customer show when he or she first approaches you? What nonverbal signals can you use as clues to the customer's real feelings? Be sure your own feelings are not getting in the way of understanding— or reacting correctly to—the customer.

The importance of leaving customers with good feelings cannot be overemphasized. High-quality customer service has never been more important than it is today. The most obvious reason for this increased importance is greater competition. The competition from European and Asian countries with a high customer service emphasis has caused American businesses to look more closely at how they treat those who buy from them. A second reason for this emphasis is the growth of services in the United States over the past few decades. Today there are many new services available that did not exist several years ago. They might include going to a debt counselor, hiring a webmaster, receiving online health care services, or consulting with an aromatherapist.

more about...

The Transition to a Service Economy

Watch an animated gif of the American economy's shift from the dominant economic sector of manufacturing in 1990, to a predominantly service economy in 2013. Open the website linked here:

https://www.washingtonpost.com/blogs/govbeat /wp/2014/09/03/watch-the-u-s-transition-from-a -manufacturing-economy-to-a-service-economy-in -one-gif/?utm_term=.707d5814a87c

Reid Wilson, *The Washington Post,* "Watch the U.S. Transition From a Manufacturing Economy To a Service Economy, in One Gif" (posted September 3, 2014, retrieved June 20, 2017).

These are just a few examples of the thousands of new services offered to Americans today. While the manufacturing economy was the dominant sector in 1990, today the American economy is based on delivery of services.

This final reason for high-quality customer service is the most important one: Keeping customers happy and loyal simply makes good economic sense. Maintaining an ever-growing group of satisfied customers is essential to staying in business and making a profit. Without loyal customers, businesses fail—and, sadly, many do fail every day.

≫ CUSTOMER SERVICE: A DEFINITION

What is good customer service? Customer service guru John Tschohl says, "You have good service only when customers think you do."[6] He also says that customer service is part of successful selling because satisfied customers come back to be customers again. According to the American Management Association, 65 percent of a typical company's business comes from repeat business by *current* customers.

Good service, which nearly always includes good human relations, is the main reason for repeat business. The cost of finding a new customer is considerably greater than the cost of keeping one you already have.[7] Unhappy customers have a high cost, too: The average disgruntled customer tells at least 8 to 10 people about the unpleasant experience.[8] Clearly, treating your customers as the most important part of the organization will pay off in the long run, in terms of both growth and added profits.[9]

Working on improving customer relations is also excellent for your own self-development. Learning what works in the process of satisfying customers can aid you in cultivating your own skills in problem solving for other areas of life. Dealing successfully with customers is a learning process that is ongoing and can always be improved.

Customer relations skills can be transferred to almost any other occupation or profession. If you are an employee who has a vested interest in the success of the company you are working for, the development of customer service skills is worthwhile for you. Also, customer relations presents one of the most challenging aspects of human relations skill development. You will never be wasting your time by learning how customers think, respond, and perceive reality. Any other business you might enter later in life will involve customers in some way. This includes internal customers.

Repeat Customers

Surveys over the past several years find that 65% of a typical company's business comes from the repeat business of existing customers.[4] Conversely, 90% of dissatisfied customers will not return for repeat business.[5]

SATISFYING THE CUSTOMER

When customers pay for products and services, they buy good feelings or the solution to a problem, too. *Why is it important to recognize the real needs of customers?*

©Ariel Skelley/Blend Images

» THE INTERNAL CUSTOMER

internal customer

The person who depends on the other people in the company to provide the services and products for the external customer.

For the past several years, the term "internal customer" has been used more and more often to describe an important relationship among managers, employees, and external customers. When the person who is connected long term to a company is treated the way an external customer should be, the results are predictably positive. One definition of the **internal customer** is the person who depends on the other people in the company to provide the services and products for the external customer.[10]

Internal customers usually don't walk away when the service is bad. Unlike their external counterparts, they are tied to the company more directly than that. However, this is exactly why treating them right is really important to the overall success of the business.

Management expert Shep Hyken provides an example of an internal customer. In the example, she is a clerk in the payroll department. She depends on the managers throughout the company to give her the information she needs to produce an accurate payroll each week. One manager doesn't get that information to her on time, and when the e-mail does arrive, it contains several errors. This manager has failed an internal customer. The manager's responsibility to that payroll clerk is just as important as the responsibility of the company to any single external customer.[11]

As Hyken puts it, "A company that has an excellent service reputation didn't get it without everyone in the company being a part of the service strategy. Someone once said that if you aren't working directly with the outside customer, you are probably working with someone who is."[12]

What is your responsibility to the internal customer? If you are a manager, it's your role to be sure the needs of every person in your area are being met, just as should be the case with the external customer. If you are a worker, do your best to be the kind of loyal fan you would be of, let's say, a favorite restaurant or some other business where you are a contented repeat customer. The internal customer concept is helpful in creating a company with memorable customer service.

Think about how a business or company functions. Every employee is accountable to someone, whether to outside customers or internal customers. In his article on improving internal customer relations, business consultant Lane Baldwin says, "Make no mistake. Your teammates are as important to your success as the people walking through your door. And the better you serve your teammates, the more they will help you succeed."[13] For the remainder of the chapter, then, when you read the word *customer*, think about customers as those who buy products and services from you, and those who are connected in some way that makes the company's existence possible.

» THE TWO SIMPLEST PRINCIPLES OF CUSTOMER SERVICE

two simplest principles

Finding out what the customer needs, and doing whatever is necessary to satisfy it.

When you are dealing with any type of customer, the **two simplest principles** help greatly:

REAL WORLD EXAMPLE 13.1

Luis Alvarez was a department store clerk in a small town. One day an elderly lady came in to look at the bicycles on display. "My, my," she said. "The bikes seem a lot different than they used to be—more gears, more colors, less chrome. The last time I looked at bicycles was almost 20 years ago."

Luis had no idea what this customer really wanted. In fact, he wasn't even sure that she was a customer at all. She spent several minutes reliving the past when her three children had ridden bicycles on the vacant lot where the department store now stood. After asking questions about her interest in the bikes, Luis determined that this lady

simply needed to chat. She was lonely. Luis fulfilled that need by remaining friendly and sympathetic.

Two months later, Luis was surprised when the same elderly lady returned to the store and purchased three new bicycles as Christmas presents for her grandchildren. By finding out her real need—to be listened to—he had made a good impression, which later resulted in three major sales. Luis had followed the two simplest principles. He realized the customer needed to talk to him, and he responded to her needs by listening to her. In return, she came back as his paying customer.

1. Find out what the customer needs.
2. Do whatever is possible to satisfy those needs.

By listening carefully to the customer's stated needs, you might discover unspoken needs. In some cases, the customer doesn't have a thorough understanding of what his or her own needs are. Your task in that case becomes one of probing and asking a series of questions to find out what is behind the surface statements.[14]

Although these two principles are very simple, you must remember that besides the immediate needs of the purchase, each customer has basic human needs that all people share. (See Figure 13.1.) Often customers simply want to be noticed, listened to, and taken seriously. Remembering their basic needs could be the only difference between your business and a competitor's. Having quality products alone, without the positive treatment of customers, is simply not enough for a business to succeed.

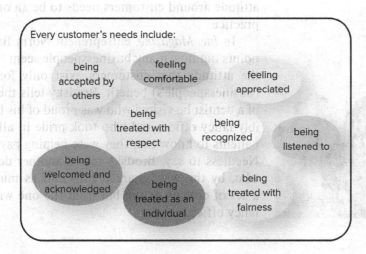

Every customer's needs include:

- being accepted by others
- feeling comfortable
- feeling appreciated
- being treated with respect
- being recognized
- being listened to
- being welcomed and acknowledged
- being treated as an individual
- being treated with fairness

figure 13.1

THE CUSTOMER'S NEEDS— BASIC HUMAN NEEDS

Understanding the customer as a person just like yourself will make it easier to anticipate his or her needs and help to find solutions. *How many of these needs do you feel when you are making a purchase?*

You are a cashier in a retail store. Someone who is apparently not a customer presents a five dollar bill and asks for change. In fact, it looks like she just walked in from the bus stop outside and needed change for the bus. What do you do?

The wise choice in answer to the question in Real World 13.2 is to treat the person with the same cordiality you would treat a paying customer. After all, that person's opinion of your establishment might bring him or her back again. The customer's positive experience might even influence a friend or family member to shop there. The same type of policy is also wise to follow when a nonpaying customer wants to use the restroom facilities in your business, or even one who asks for directions to the location of your competitor. Treating others well is not only good business; it is the right thing to do.

» ISSUES IN CUSTOMER SERVICE

WHEN YOUR CUSTOMERS ARE OTHER BUSINESSES

When your customers are other businesses, you must not only maintain the same high-level service you would give to individuals, but you must also get to know the business. *How can you learn more about the businesses with which you work?*

©Hero Images/Getty Images

Knowing the *issues* involved in customer service is important for anyone wanting to develop the *skills* of effective customer service. These issues should help in that process.

Your Customers and Your Attitude

What kind of attitude do you show toward customers? If you are having a bad day, do you let your customers know with your attitude? When your day is not going your way, do you come off as smug and arrogant, irritated and annoyed, distracted and down, or too humble? Or can you set those feelings aside and bring a winning attitude to your customers? Checking your attitude around customers needs to be an ongoing practice.

In *Inc. Magazine,* entrepreneur Norm Brodsky points out how many businesspeople seem to have the attitude that customers exist only for their (businesspeople's) benefit. Brodsky tells the story of a dentist he visited who was proud of his incredibly fancy office, and who took pride in allowing patients to know that they were helping pay for it. Needless to say, Brodsky found another dentist—who, by the way, charged him half as much for a set of crowns as the bid from the one with the fancy office.[15]

REAL WORLD EXAMPLE 13.3

At a popular second-hand clothing store, the owners had decided that they were going to become an all-cash business, and would no longer accept credit or debit cards. The issue was totally out of the control of anyone at the store, even the manager. Most of the employees who worked at the boutique found that an argument would start as soon as they told the customer, "Sorry, we can't accept your card because we only accept cash now." However, Eric, one of the employees on the busy weekend shift, was always able to work smoothly through the day with no customer problems. Soon the others started asking Eric for help every time a customer became agitated by the new policy. After Eric spoke to the customer, he or she would always leave satisfied. What did Eric do that was so effective?

Many people who have contact with customers seem to feel that once they have "landed" a customer, they can start taking the customer for granted. Whenever you deal with customers, remember to treat them the same way later on as you treated them when you were trying to win them over the first time. Nobody likes to be taken for granted, and customers are no exception.

Delivering Bad News

One of the touchiest human relations issues is the tough task of giving customers unwelcome news—especially when they expect nothing but good news. Obviously, some businesses must do this more than others. For example, a loan officer in a bank will have to refuse a certain number of applicants every month. A reservations clerk may have to break the "no vacancy" news quite often. A manager may have to tell a salesperson that a major buyer canceled an order, and the salesperson's commission will be much smaller than expected. No matter how often you have to do it, though, you may never get used to saying no to customers. Developing sound **bad news skills** is essential, and it will make the job less unpleasant.

In the Real World Example above, what did Eric do that was so effective? In a very polite voice, he would say, "I'm really sorry, ma'am (or sir), but our owners have decided that because of the high fees that the credit card companies are charging us, we will become a cash-only business and stop accepting credit and debit cards. I'm sorry for the change, but this will actually help us pass on savings to you, and keep our prices low. And for your convenience, we've recently installed a new low-fee ATM near the dressing rooms." A few customers would express dismay, but most would actually say thanks to Eric before taking out cash, or heading to the ATM.

Notice the steps that Eric took in delivering the bad news to customers. First, he used a polite tone of voice. Second, he didn't dwell on long apologies. Although he said "I'm sorry" twice, his message wasn't an apology: It was an explanation. Third, he dealt specifically with why the problem existed. Fourth, he closed his remarks with a positive statement as to what could be done to make the situation better for both the business and the customer. Those four rules (as shown in Figure 13.2) can help when giving customers messages that they would rather not hear.

bad news skills

The skills necessary to deliver bad news to customers but still retain their business and goodwill.

figure 13.2

GIVING A CUSTOMER BAD NEWS

When giving a customer bad news, focus on explanations and solutions rather than apologies and excuses. A brief apology is almost always necessary, but do not dwell on it; rather, look for a win-win solution. *How can you help customers understand the options available?*

Four Rules for Giving a Customer Bad News

1. **Use a polite tone of voice.** Make it a point to check on this. For many people, vocal tone is mostly unconscious, unless they try specifically to take notice of it.
2. **Don't spend too much time and energy on apologies.** Apologizing is fine, but most customers want *reasons* and *action*.
3. **Deal with why the problem exists.** If you don't know, let the customer know that you will find out; then do it. If the problem's cause is impossible to discover, go to step 4.
4. **Talk about what can be done to solve the problem.** If possible, this includes alternatives and suggestions from which the customer can choose. When only one possible course of action is available, *sell* the customer on why that action is the best.

Most customers would rather not hear the word *policy*. "We can't do that because it's against company policy" is one of the weakest refusals anyone can use. If you work for a manager who tells you that you must use that line, at least find out the reasoning *behind* the policy so that you can explain it clearly to the customer.

Encouraging Complaints

In some way, every customer has a problem. If nothing else, the problem is that the customer is in need of the goods or services your company provides. Perhaps the problem is dissatisfaction with some part of your operation—or your competitor's. Learn to focus on the problem. Ask yourself: "What can I do to solve the problem *as this person sees it?*"

Don't rely on being told what the problem is. Later in this chapter you will read about an angry customer who yells and screams. Learning how to deal with that type of person is certainly necessary. However, yellers and screamers are in the minority. Most customers are like the **"nice" customer** (see Figure 13.3). These customers would actually be more helpful if they were a bit less nice, because then they would provide better feedback. Many companies today realize that customer complaints are necessary and should be encouraged in every way possible.[16]

Bill Gates, founder of Microsoft, saw unpleasant news about the way his business was performing as evidence of a need to change. "Unhappy customers are always a concern," he muses. "They're also your greatest opportunity." Gates says that adopting a learning attitude toward your customers rather than a defensive position can make customer complaints the most important part of your road to improving the quality of whatever you are doing.[17]

Try to influence everyone in your company to think of complaining customers in a positive way. Without them, you would have only a vague idea of what

"nice" customer

The customer who never complains, but responds to bad service by taking his or her business elsewhere.

figure 13.3

The Nice Customer Statement

Some people in businesses make the incorrect assumption that if anything is wrong, the customer will say so. Here's a little statement that is posted on the walls of businesses all across the country:

> I'm a nice customer. You all know me. I'm the one who never complains, no matter what kind of service I get. I'll go into a restaurant and sit quietly while the waiters and waitresses gossip and never bother to ask if anyone has taken my order. Sometimes someone who came in after I did gets my order, but I don't complain. I just wait.
>
> And when I go to a store to buy something, I don't throw my weight around. I try to be thoughtful of the other person. If a snooty salesperson gets upset because I want to look at several things before making up my mind, I'm just as polite as can be. I don't believe rudeness in return is the answer.
>
> The other day I waited in line for almost 15 minutes for a cup of coffee while the barista chatted with his old friend. And when he did finally serve my coffee, he spilled some on my sleeve. But did I complain about the service? Of course not.
>
> I never kick. I never nag. I never criticize. And I wouldn't dream of making a scene, as I've seen some people do in public places. I think that's uncalled for. No, I'm the nice customer. And I'll tell you who else I am.
>
> I'm the customer who never comes back!

Author Unknown (but nice)

THE NICE CUSTOMER
The nice customer may not complain or make a scene, but he or she won't come back, either. You can lose loyal customers without knowing it if you wait for the nice customer to let you know about a problem. The nice customer may also tell many others about his or her bad experience in your establishment, losing you many potential customers. *What is a good way to help the nice customer let you know his or her true feelings?*

changes need to be made. Also, how about giving them another name? Instead of calling them "complainers," consider calling them consultants or critics.

To encourage complaints, you must understand what a customer complaint is. It is not a personal attack, nor is it a signal that your relationship with the customer is broken forever—or even temporarily, in most cases. A complaint is *an opportunity to improve.* Customer complaints inspire improvements to service that would otherwise have gone unnoticed to people in many businesses.

An emphasis on careful listening to complaints sends the signal to customers that yours is a customer-focused business. It says, "We view our

Customer Self-Esteem

"Help them to like themselves better, and they'll love you."

—Michael LeBoeuf

Source: Michael LeBoeuf, *How to Win Customers and Keep Them for Life* (New York: G. P. Putnam's Sons, 1988), p. 46.

more about...

customers as partners; we want to build relationships with them."[18] When customers perceive that you are willing to listen, and that you are encouraging their response, they will be much more likely to respond honestly and openly.

When people in a business solicit complaints, they often phrase questions in a way that will encourage a neutral or positive response. For example, you might ask a restaurant customer, "How was your meal?" or even, "Was everything okay?" and you are likely to get the response, "Yes, it was fine," whether it was really fine or not. However, if you ask, "What one thing could we have done to improve your dining experience?" an honest and helpful complaint is much more likely to result. If you are in management, do all that you can to make complaining easy for the customer. Offer a complaint phone line where the customer won't be put on hold for a long time. Use various methods of rewarding customers who complain. Many large retail companies now offer a chance to win a shopping spree or a cash prize in return for answering a customer service survey. You don't need to give away thousands of dollars to get customer feedback, however. Thank-you notes, phone calls, gifts, "consultant of the month" awards—all of these are ways to reward customers who offer helpful complaints.

Most important of all, make sure that you do all you can to correct the problems customers are complaining about. Without that step, most of the rest is meaningless. Once you get this new attitude toward complaints, you'll probably develop new attitudes toward all of your customers. After that, your human relations with them will improve.

Figure 13.4 shows one company's way of expressing attitudes of value toward customers.

figure 13.4

THE TEN COMMANDMENTS OF GOOD BUSINESS

As you can see, remembering the customer is the key to every one of these "Ten Commandments." *How can these ideas help you keep the customer in perspective?*

Source: Minit Lube Corporate Policy Statement. Used with permission.

1. **A CUSTOMER** is the most important person in any business.
2. **A CUSTOMER** is not dependent on us—we are dependent on the customer.
3. **A CUSTOMER** is not an interruption of our work—the customer is the purpose of it.
4. **A CUSTOMER** does us a favor when he calls—we are not doing the customer a favor by serving him or her.
5. **A CUSTOMER** is part of our business—not an outsider.
6. **A CUSTOMER** is not a cold statistic—the customer is a flesh-and-blood human being with feelings and emotions like our own.
7. **A CUSTOMER** is not someone to argue or match wits with.
8. **A CUSTOMER** is a person who brings us his or her wants—it is our job to fill those wants.
9. **A CUSTOMER** is deserving of the most courteous and attentive treatment we can give.
10. **A CUSTOMER** is the life-blood of this and every other business.

» HANDLING THE DIFFICULT CUSTOMER

"The customer is always right." Everyone has heard this, but is it true? It's true only in terms of the attitude it expresses. Although the customer may be very wrong, you may still be called upon to treat that customer as though everything seen through his or her eyes is correct. Carrying out such an attitude requires more than a little self-discipline. It also requires some courage.

Remember two things when dealing with an unreasonable, angry, or overly demanding customer. First, stay focused. The success of the company depends on satisfying your customers, no matter how unreasonable they might seem. If you can remain focused on those long-term needs, rather than on a short-term need to express your own anger or frustration, you will be the winner. When dealing with the general public, many people begin to feel that a large percentage of those they deal with are nasty and unreasonable. Actually, in most businesses, difficult customers make up less than 3 percent of the total. Because of the impact of the negative people, we often generalize carelessly. Part of staying focused is remembering how most customers are reasonable and easy to deal with.

Second, avoid the **self-esteem trap.** The customer is probably upset about something that has little to do with you directly. Even if the problem is the result of one of your own mistakes, don't take the attack personally, and especially don't let it affect your own self-esteem. Don't allow anyone's emotional outbursts to make you have negative feelings about yourself.

Sometimes, the only way to get a customer to communicate with you is to help him or her calm down and cool off. Instead of using your energy to show that you are right and that the customer is wrong, put your energy into getting the customer calmed down. Some obvious exceptions to this rule would be customers who are sexually harassing or physically assaulting employees, as well as customers who are involved in other illegal activities.

self-esteem trap
The circumstance that comes from taking a customer's attack personally and letting it affect your self-esteem.

Maintaining Your Self-Esteem

When dealing with an angry customer, remember this important self-talk: "This is just business; it's not personal."

Source: Steven A. Eggland and John W. Williams, *Human Relations at Work* (Mason, OH: South-Western, 1981), p. 155.

Arguing with Customers

"However right an action or reaction might appear, if it winds up angering the customer, it's wrong."

Source: R. S. Dreyer, "Cool Hand Lucas," *Supervision,* July 1990, pp. 17–18.

more about...

more about...

» GOING THE EXTRA MILE

"Giving the customer the pickle" or not charging extra for small requests is simply good business. If this has ever happened to you, you will remember how it feels when you ask for change at a retail store only to hear the cashier say, "Sorry, we don't make change unless you're buying something." When you do need to make a purchase, will you come back to that store? Won't you be likely to tell some of your friends and family about the incident? By refusing you the small extra, the store may have lost a dozen future sales.

REAL WORLD EXAMPLE 13.4

Bob Farrell (1927–2005), motivational speaker and restaurant entrepreneur, often repeated the story of a new waitress he hired. A customer who had been coming to this same restaurant for a few years asked the new waitress why the customary pickle wasn't in his hamburger. The waitress replied, "A pickle will cost you extra." As you might expect, this answer irritated the customer greatly. When Farrell heard the story, he coined a phrase that he used often when he spoke in public: "Give them the pickle!" Farrell urged all companies to figure out what their "pickle" is, and give it to customers.

figure 13.5

BUSINESSES GOING THE EXTRA MILE

Many successful businesses go the extra mile by offering customers free services to ensure goodwill. Going the extra mile can include anything from free coffee and donuts to supervised child care or running personal errands. *When did a company "going the extra mile" make you want to stay their customer?*

Source: Barbara A. Glantz, *Building Customer Loyalty* (Burr Ridge, IL: Richard Irwin Co., 1994), p. 26.

going the extra mile

When a company gives customers small extra products or services as a way of showing appreciation for their business.

Ways to Go the Extra Mile

- A cleaning establishment keeps careful business records. When their computer software alerts them that the customer has spent a total of $500 with that cleaner, the order they are picking up is free.
- A suburban Illinois bank serves coffee and donut holes at all times in its lobby. They also have a play area for customers' children and provide child care while the customer is doing business.
- An auto parts store posts free online tutorials for its customers that explain how to do various car repairs.

None of the examples discussed in Figure 13.5 would cost a company much money, and the payback is well worth it. When a company gives customers small "extras" as a way of showing appreciation, it is called **going the extra mile**—and it nearly always pays for itself.

» CUSTOMER SERVICE ETHICS

Acting ethically is essential in all dealings with customers and would-be customers. When deciding on the ethical approach to a situation, ask yourself, "Would I want all of my procedures to be made public knowledge?"

Customer service is a critical aspect of successful business development, and of maintaining lucrative business relationships. The customer service ethics of a company or organization define the quality of the services the customer will receive. With this in mind, a strong, well-trained customer service staff is the "face" of the business, but the culture of the business is dictated by managers' support for their staff (and their adherence to strong ethical standards in delivering customer service). Sometimes, working under stress can bring out the best—and worst—in an organization's employees' delivery of customer service.

Christopher MacDonald, a business ethics consultant and professor at Duke University and Ryerson University, suggests that workplace ethics are a crucial dimension of customer service, noting several ways that customer service can become *unethical*. Dr. MacDonald has found that:

> Front-line service representatives can do unethical things like lose orders, lie to customers, or even sabotage their own work;

> Managers may say they commit to providing "post-sale" quality service, but then provide fewer resources than needed for this important customer service function;

> Senior management may make policy decisions that result in unethical customer treatment, such as making it difficult for customers to request warranty service, or limiting the amount of time and attention devoted to each customer's needs.

Unethical customer service can result in victimized customers, or may create a frustrating gap between the service that the customer expects and actually receives, and can negatively affect a business' reputation through negative online reviews and plain old word-of-mouth.[19] So how does a company ensure the highest standards of professionalism and ethics in its delivery of customer service? Most simply, by promoting its desired values (ethics), and making sure frontline workers follow the rules (compliance). This takes the form of being truthful to customers, safeguarding sensitive information, and displaying empathy and concern to customers with problems.[20] By making sure that customers know that their satisfaction is guaranteed, and by following the philosophy that the customer's needs are of the greatest importance, much of the ethics issue will take care of itself. Both employees and managers, though, must bear in mind the ethical issues when considering overall needs of their company. You will learn more about ethics in Chapter 15.

Many organizations and companies, especially those that deal extensively with the public, have adopted formal, written "Customer Service Code of Ethics" (see example below). Have you noticed this kind of formal policy at places you do business, or where you've worked?

Customer Service Code of Ethics

"We promise to provide value-added customer service through:

1. Polite and courteous service.
2. Handling requests in a timely manner with consistent follow through and communication.
3. Mastering knowledge of Human Resources laws, rules, policies, and concepts and on-going issues within the organization.
4. Proactive problem solving and guidance.
5. Offering confidentiality and an open door policy.
6. Facilitating positive change through employee relations programs, services, and consultation.
7. Encouragement of a high level of employee morale through recognition and effective communication.
8. Promoting learning and personal growth to increase individual success and the overall value of the organization.
9. Operating with integrity and promoting accountability.
10. Providing a safe and healthy working environment."

Source: State of Oregon, Department of Public Safety Standards and Training, Human Resource Division, 2013.

》 POOR GEORGE STORY

Who is the running the business? As this chapter ends, one final point must be emphasized: You must set limits as to the extent to which you will allow a customer to run your business. Regardless of how important

REAL WORLD EXAMPLE 13.5

Junko Kawaguchi is a receptionist at an insurance company. On Friday afternoon her boss says, "I'll be out the rest of the day. Hold my calls." Thirty minutes later, an irate customer asks to see Junko's boss and tells her, "I have a 3:00 appointment, and this claim has to be handled today, or I'll lose everything!" What should Junko do? What would you do?

YOUR CUSTOMER'S SELF-ESTEEM

To succeed with customers, you must learn to bolster their self-esteem. When customers are uneasy about purchases, your ability to comfort them will help them trust you and your product or service. *How can you tell if a customer's self-esteem is interfering in his or her interaction with you? What are ways to support a customer's self-esteem in that case?*

©Floresco Productions/Age Fotostock

more about...

An excellent guideline for **ethical customer service** is the Golden Rule: Are you treating the customer the way you would like to be treated in a similar situation?

the customer is, he or she must never be allowed to undermine company decisions. Les Schwab, Inc. is a successful tire store chain in the western United States. When the founder, Mr. Schwab, was still alive, he used the following story at training sessions for tire store managers. He called it the "Poor George Story."

George was a very likable, hardworking owner of a small tire store. One day John, a trucker, came into George's store and asked, "George, I need four tires for my pickup. How much?" George glanced quickly at his price sheet and replied, "The tires are $60 each. Do you want 'em balanced?"

"Of course, I want 'em balanced" was the answer.

"Well, $240 for the tires and $20 for the balancing—that's a total of $260."

"Oh, man! That's too much," countered John.

At this point George thought to himself, "I would hate to lose this sale; and, besides, business hasn't been very good lately." So without even doing the math, he said to John, "Tell you what, I'll throw in the wheel balance for nothing." George had made his first big mistake: He gave in, letting his customer know that his prices were variable.

Seeing that he could bargain, John came back with, "Make it $225, and you have yourself a deal."

George did some quick arithmetic and noticed that by selling the tires for $225, he would still have a profit margin of $33. Since business was so slow, he replied, "Okay, John, we'll put them on."

To run a tire store, the cost is 25 to 26 percent of sales, but George lowered himself to 14.7 percent. He wouldn't have to make this mistake many times before going broke.

Once the tires had been mounted and balanced, John asked if he could charge the tires. George said yes, but he had always assumed that since his operation was so small, he didn't need a policy on charging interest or to construct a formal collection policy.

Thirty days later, John received his bill for $225. John thought to himself, "Good old George, he won't mind if I skip him this month." When he received a second bill, John figured that he should at least pay part of the bill. He gave George $50 and acted as if he were doing George a big favor. Five months later, the purchase was finally paid off.

After a few years, George went into bankruptcy. Hearing about the sad occurrence, John told his friends, "I sure do miss old George; he was a great guy. I guess he just wasn't a very good businessman." The next time John needed tires, he went to a chain store. There, the clerk quoted him the price, charged him $10 per tire for the wheel balance, and required a credit check and a long credit application form to fill out and sign. Although they charged him 18 percent interest, John didn't argue at all. And he didn't even think of trying to bargain them down to a lower price.

At the end of the story, George is broke. He goes to work for the same chain store that sold John his new tires. He sells tires at listed prices; he doesn't bargain; he charges interest; and he gives credit only to customers who qualify and will pay promptly. The moral of the story is: Respect your customers and give them only the highest-quality service, but *never let your customers run your business.*

FINDING A BALANCE

Although keeping your customers satisfied is an essential part of good business, attention to customer service needs to be balanced with firm leadership—including ethics and perspective—in order for a business to succeed. *How can customer service sometimes conflict with ethics, or let a customer run your business?*

©Juice Images/Glow Images

STRATEGIES FOR SUCCESS

Strategy 13.1   **Establish a Bond with the Customer**

1. Understand the customer's real needs.
2. If your customer is another business, learn about that business.
3. Provide exceptional service.
4. Avoid taking your special relationship for granted.

Few factors will create more impact on overall and repeat sales than *bonding* with the customer. If you form meaningful relationships with your customers, they are much more likely to return and buy from you again. This practice is also known as **relationship selling.** When you have established a relationship with a customer, service is usually perceived more positively. For example, an attorney or real estate agent's services will be seen in a better light if they establish trust with their clients.[21]

Here are four principles that will help you form a bond of trust with your customers:

1. **Understand the customer's real needs.** Careful listening to the customer can compensate for a great number of drawbacks in a company. Think about your relationship with someone who is trying to sell you a product or service, or an internal customer on your work team you'll be working with on future projects. Wouldn't you rather deal with someone who is sensitive to your needs and desires?

2. **If your customer is another business, learn about that business.** Customers will be more likely to bond with you if you show a genuine understanding of their business

relationship selling

Forming meaningful relationships with your customers, which makes them much more likely to return and buy from you again.

and what it means to them both personally and professionally. Read annual reports, trade journals, and newspaper and magazine articles to acquaint yourself with the business you are dealing with, including knowledge of their competitors. Learning about the "business" of a customer includes learning about the functions and processes of other departments in your own company, who may be internal customers.

3. **Provide exceptional service.** Exceptional service yields the strongest bond of all. Providing exceptional service isn't always totally up to you, and even as a manager you might not have as much control over the quality of service as you would like. You can be creative, and it is usually possible to innovate.

4. **Avoid taking your special relationship for granted.** Don't ever misuse the bond you have created. As mentioned earlier in the chapter, avoid ever getting to the point where you take the customer for granted. Remember, the customer includes your co-workers and other internal customers as well. The bond you have worked hard to create is a precious commodity; treat it—and your customers—accordingly.

Strategy 13.2   Support the Customer's Self-Esteem

1. Put the customer at ease.
2. Put yourself in the customer's place.
3. Make the customer feel understood.
4. Make the customer feel important.
5. Praise the customer appropriately.

As with all parts of the human relations process, the customer relations issue has a great deal to do with self-esteem—in this case, the self-esteem of the customer. Almost all customers need to have their self-esteem bolstered.

You probably have a favorite store, bar, or restaurant where you feel welcome, where you feel comfortable and at ease. That feeling of ease cannot be packaged and sold as a commodity. Yet it is very real—and extremely important to customers of any business, in any place.

When you deal with customers, you need to be always aware that their self-esteem is a big issue, if not the most important one. However, many people in business ignore their customers' needs. Instead, they get wrapped up in trying to impress customers with the things they are selling, or with their own part of the company's tasks—and with themselves. Focusing on the customer's self-esteem will make the customer interested in your products and more likely to want to continue a positive working relationship.

Here are some steps you can take to build up your customers' self-esteem:

1. **Put the customer at ease.** Getting your customer to relax, and to feel comfortable with you and your company, is the most important first step. Smile with a genuine smile, not a phony one. Use the customer's name—but be careful about using it too soon, because certain customers do not like being called by their first name by people they don't know very well. Stand just close enough to the customer so as not to invade personal space. (See **Chapter 6.**) Try to use a similar tone of voice, rate of speaking, and body language as the customer. These details are subtle, but customers tend to identify with people who have mannerisms like their own.[22]

2. **Put yourself in the customer's place.** *Empathy* is the ability to imagine yourself in the other person's place. Develop empathy by asking yourself, "If I were this customer, with the needs she has, how would I feel?" This habit can be difficult to form and cultivate. But if you begin thinking this way, it will improve all areas of your human relations, not only customer relations.

3. **Make the customer feel understood.** Like all other people, customers need to feel they are communicating successfully. Be sure to interpret what they say correctly. Asking a question that starts out with "Do you mean . . . ?" can go a long way toward letting the customer know that you care enough to listen and understand what he or she is saying. If you are at all unclear about what the customer means, ask questions until you are sure.[23]

4. **Make the customer feel important.** One of the worst things you can do is to allow distractions (such as phone calls or other interruptions) to pull your concentration away from the customer. While you are dealing with a customer, act as though nothing else is as important. Let people know you are absorbed in being with them. To the customer, you are the whole company—so do all you can to make that feeling go both ways.

5. **Praise the customer appropriately.** You don't have to try too hard when praising a customer. Has the customer accomplished something special recently? Congratulate him or her specifically. But do so in the framework of authentic caring. This is another habit that will likely help in relationships outside of work, too. Praise is a powerful human relations tool, but use it wisely. Insincere praise can be much worse than none at all.

   Be sure to make the praise specific. A generalized compliment can leave the customer wondering, "What did that really mean?"[24] Don't just say that Mr. Johnson asks good questions that show he knows the product; tell him sincerely that you admire that quality in a customer! If your only knowledge of the quality you want to praise is general, ask a specific question in a nonthreatening way. A specific question shows real interest and often leads to a point where you can offer sincere praise.

Strategy 13.3   Handle the Difficult Customer Professionally

1. Let the customer vent.
2. Get the facts.
3. Be sure you understand the customer's feelings.
4. Suggest a solution.
5. End positively.
6. Don't expect to win them all.

Here are some easy-to-follow guidelines for dealing with a customer who is already angry.[25]

1. **Let the customer vent.** You should allow an angry customer to speak his or her mind. This approach might be difficult, but being a good listener (even to an angry, perhaps ranting customer) is still the best approach. Cutting the customer off usually does more harm than good. Let the customer know that you sympathize and care enough to hear everything. Have you ever noticed your anger disappearing after you have gotten somebody to listen to you? Quite possibly, the customer mainly needs the chance to express some strong emotions on the issue; all you need to be is the sounding board.

2. **Get the facts.** If possible, have all available information on the case right in front of you. If the customer is wrong, be sure that your sources are correct. Ask questions to verify what the customer is telling you. If two or more versions seem to contradict each other, ask questions until you are satisfied that you have found the truth. If the customer is wrong, don't say so directly. In all cases, focus on what can be done to solve the problem, rather than to place blame.

3. **Be sure you understand the customer's feelings.** A great deal of expressed anger can confuse you when you are trying to listen. Are you sure you understand the main issue in the mind of the customer? What you see as the main issue might not be what the customer thinks it is. Only when you have completed this step and know what the customer thinks is wrong can you find out how to make it right. Remember also that one of the most popular emotions you will encounter from customers will be *fear*. Identifying the source of that fear is an important step in solving a clash with an upset customer.

4. **Suggest a solution.** Be specific and clear. Be careful not to make promises that the company might not let you keep. If the solution you can offer isn't what your customer wanted, clearly explain why you have to offer this solution instead. Avoiding using "company policy" as an excuse. If you must use that phrase, explain the reasons for the policy as best you can.

5. **End positively.** Once you have agreed to a solution, thank the customer for his or her patience and for bringing the problem to your attention. Don't apologize too much. Instead, focus your attention on the future. Mention steps that can be taken on both sides to prevent such problems from happening again. Don't hesitate to include things you will do personally to prevent future occurrences. Your main purpose now is to keep the customer's future business.[26]

6. **Don't expect to win them all.** You can be as patient, empathic, helpful, and efficient as possible, and still have a percentage of customers who will remain angry and/or fearful. Some customers simply are difficult people, and they will stay that way no matter what anyone does. Again, don't take their words or actions personally. If possible, ask your manager for help.[27]

When the time arises to use these six steps in the workplace, do the best you can. If you don't remember all of them, at least remember to do everything you can to keep an angry customer's complaint from turning into an argument. It takes two people to make an argument. As the representative of the company, you must refuse to become that second person. You may have to suppress the desire to answer back defensively. In the end, though, your self-control will pay off because you'll have kept your cool—and demonstrated to everyone around you that you can handle stressful situations.

Strategy 13.4   Keep Customers Satisfied

1. Personalize the customer's experience.
2. Utilize technology.
3. Provide seamless access.
4. Talk to customers.
5. Use social media.

To reduce the loss of unhappy customers—both internal and external—to competitors, keep current customers happy. Considering that our largest economic sector is the service sector, and that online shopping for both goods and services is on the rise, remember technology in your customer service. Keeping up with social media and modernizing applications will help retain satisfied customers.

1. **Personalize the customer's experience.** Address the customer by name. Find out what the customer wants and expects in the way of service. Personalize and customize the customer's experience.

2. **Utilize technology.** Go mobile where possible. Use mobile applications for convenient access and services for customers.

3. **Provide seamless access.** Create easy access for customers to move between sales channels. Provide sales and services that make the customer experience easy.

4. **Talk to customers.** Ask customers what types of technology they use and invest in the services and applications that will support those technologies.

5. **Use social media.** Use technology to gather immediate data for decision making for your business. Find customer preferences for sales and services through social media channels. Advertise up to the minutes with social media.

Source: Ira Sager, *Bloomberg*, "Angry Customers Cost Companies $5.9 Trillion," https://www.bloomberg.com/news/articles/2013-10-22/angry-customers-cost-companies-5-dot-9-trillion (posted October 22, 2013; retrieved June 20, 2017).

CHAPTER THIRTEEN SUMMARY

Chapter Summary by Learning Objectives

LO 13-1 **Explain how to determine what customers really want.** No matter what business you are in, customers really want only two things: good feelings and solutions to problems. By listening to the customer, you can discover the customer's needs in these two categories.

LO 13-2 **Define customer service.** You have good service only when the customer thinks you do. Good customer service always includes good human relations.

LO 13-3 **Describe the internal customer.** The internal customer is the person who depends on the other people in the company to provide services and products for the external customer.

LO 13-4 **List the two simplest principles of customer service.** (1) Find out what the customer needs. (2) Do whatever is possible to satisfy those needs.

LO 13-5 **Give examples of issues in customer service.** Major issues in customer service include: (1) your customers and your attitude, (2) delivering bad news to customers, and (3) encouraging complaints. All three are very important in creating a customer-friendly business.

LO 13-6 **Compare and contrast ways to handle a difficult customer.** When dealing with an unreasonable, angry, or overly demanding customer, stay focused and avoid the self-esteem trap. When customers are already angry, let them vent. Find out the facts, making sure that you also understand the customer's *feelings;* then suggest a solution. End as positively as possible. Don't expect success in all cases; some difficult customers will remain difficult no matter what you say or do.

LO 13-7   **Explain the significance of going the extra mile.** Going the extra mile means giving customers those little extras to show your appreciation of their business. These little "perks" are inexpensive and have a tremendous potential payoff in customer satisfaction.

LO 13-8   **List ways to use strong ethics in customer service.** Good ethics in treatment of customers nearly always comes back as customer satisfaction.

LO 13-9   **Explain the moral of the Poor George story and how it relates to customer service.** The Poor George story illustrates how someone in business can keep the customer from running the business. Treat your customers well, with great respect and deference, but never let the customer make business decisions for you. That is, don't let the customer run your business.

key terms

bad news skills 341	internal customer 338	self-esteem trap 345
going the extra mile 346	"nice" customer 342	two simplest
good feelings and solutions 336	relationship selling 349	principles 338

review questions

1. Explain what it means to say that customers really want *feelings* and *solutions,* rather than products and services. When you are a customer, what does that mean to you?

2. Define the term "internal customer." Why is the concept of *internal* customer service important to an overall understanding of customer service?

3. Why is an understanding of the "nice" customer of great importance in improving customer service? Have you ever known or been someone like this "nice" customer, who is unhappy but only leaves and never returns rather than voicing concerns to the business?

4. What are the "two simplest principles" of customer service? What importance does listening play in the use of those principles? Have you ever seen them violated?

5. Explain the importance of forming a bond with the customer. How does one go about establishing such a bond?

6. What are the four steps in giving the customer bad news? Explain each step.

7. What are some steps one can take to build the customer's self-esteem? Which step, in your opinion, is the most important? Explain.

8. What is meant by "going the extra mile"? Provide an example from your life of either serving customers or being a customer. How did your experience affect you? Was there ever a time when someone didn't go the extra mile?

critical thinking questions

1. Try to recall if you can identify a businessperson who was able to establish a bond with you or one of your family members. How was this accomplished?

2. Have you ever been the victim of a company's poor customer service policy, as either an external or internal customer? What specifically occurred? How did this treatment make you feel? What would you have changed in that situation if you had the power to do so?

working it out 13.1

THE DIFFICULT CUSTOMER

School-to-Work Connection: Interpersonal Skills

A woman approaches the ticket counter at a large airport where you work as a ticketing agent and demands to see the manager. You ask if you can be of any assistance since the manager is not available. She immediately challenges the airline's in-cabin kennel policy as unfair and discriminatory. She explains that she has to travel 1,000 miles to take care of a sick sister. Her toy poodle, from which she has never been separated, is completely housebroken and "never barks or bites." She can't stand the thought of her "little baby" cramped up in a small in-cabin pet kennel under the seat in front of her. After all, "dogs are very social animals, and my little baby might get depressed if I put her in a cage." She is holding the dog tightly in her arms. The pooch is clothed in a designer jacket made for small dogs and has her nails polished bright red. The woman loudly demands that she be allowed to bring the pet on board with her and sit the dog in her lap during the flight.

What should you do? Place an X on the line next to the actions that are the most appropriate responses to this difficult situation.

_____ 1. Show slight disgust on your face, so she will know you consider her to be the problem.

_____ 2. Laugh and make light of the situation.

_____ 3. Remain calm, cool, and patient.

_____ 4. Sympathize with her feelings of fear and frustration. Tell her that you don't like to leave your pets alone, either.

_____ 5. Walk away and find your manager.

_____ 6. Become distant and less cooperative.

_____ 7. Disarm her by asking, "Are you serious?"

_____ 8. Explain carefully about the relative comfort of the soft in-cabin kennel, and how many pets fly your airline each day.

_____ 9. Ask her to understand the airline's need to consider all of the passengers.

_____ 10. Thank her for her understanding and cooperation.

Answers: 3, 4, 8, and 10 are the most appropriate choices. All of the other choices would probably do more harm than good.[28]

working it out 13.2

ROLE-PLAYING THE CUSTOMER

School-to-Work Connection: Interpersonal Skills

Purpose: To experience the difficulties in dealing directly with customer problems.

Procedure: Two students should volunteer to play the parts of a customer and an employee, role-playing the following situation:

Ron (or Rhonda) works in the men's fashions department in Bernstein's, a large department store. Delmar Wiggins, a customer, places three shirts and a sweater on the counter. In a friendly voice, he jokes, "I guess this is all I can afford." When Mr. Wiggins offers his Bernstein's charge card, Ron quickly runs a computerized check for the approval. The card is denied. Ron excuses himself for a moment and reaches for a phone out of earshot from the customer. His call to the office confirms that Mr. Wiggins hasn't paid a cent on his already-large bill for over four months.

Instructions: The student who plays Ron (or Rhonda) should proceed with the plan for fair treatment of Mr. Wiggins. Remember that Ron needs to keep Mr. Wiggins as a cash customer in the future, and hopefully, for this sale as well. Mr. Wiggins should act innocent, as though he has no knowledge of a bad account, but he also should be willing to comply with whatever reasonable suggestions Ron comes up with.

The student who plays Mr. Wiggins may decide to deny the fact that payments are overdue. In this case, Ron (or Rhonda) needs to find other ways of dealing with the customer. He or she could say something like, "It appears that they have not received your most recent payments. I am sure that there is some misunderstanding. Would you like me to put you on the line with them so that you can confirm your most recent payments?" Mr. Wiggins, knowing that no such payments have been sent, will probably back down and agree to another method of payment.

working it out 13.3

School-to-Work Connection: Interpersonal Skills

Will you change careers during your lifetime or keep the same job for your entire career? Most of us will change jobs 7 to 10 times during our careers. How successful such job changes will be depends on how much planning and preparation you have done. Career planning should focus on both short-term and long-term transitions. Each of these has different tasks. Both should be done with some careful thought and honest reflection.

Short-term planning: Short-term planning is aimed at just the next few years. Barriers that can be overcome sometimes stand in the way of this planning. For some people, personal traits such as procrastination and lack of motivation are career barriers. Family pressures and peer pressure to work in a certain occupation, or to avoid some occupations, can also stand in the way of a successful job change. Following are some suggestions to get you started with short-term planning.

1. Think about your lifestyle now and in the future. Are you happy with it? Do you want to change it, or keep it the same? Does your current job allow you to have the lifestyle you want?

2. Think about your likes and dislikes. What tasks do you enjoy, both at work and away from work? What do you avoid? How does your job fit with these likes and dislikes?

3. Define what you are most passionate about: What gives you energy and "flow"? Do these activities happen at work in your current job?

4. List your strengths and weaknesses from the perspective of an employer. What skills and abilities, work experience and training, knowledge and experiences, do you have? What do you lack?

5. How do you define success? Are you able to achieve your vision of success in your current career path?

6. How would you describe your personality? Does your personality fit with your current job?

7. What is your dream job? Has this class revealed anything to you about careers and occupations that might interest you?

8. Examine your current situation. Identify a starting point for career advancement or job change. Be realistic, but define some goals to work toward. Finally, with the information you have gathered in answering these questions, you can work toward those goals. Narrow down your career choices. Identify additional training you will need. Develop a timeline and an action plan for meeting your short-term career planning goals.

Long-term planning: Long-term career planning requires that you think 5 years, 10 years, or longer into the future. Your guidelines for this planning are broader and more general.

1. Because the workforce and technology are changing so fast, you may have job skills that won't be needed in the future. Identify core skills that will always be in demand. Communication skills, creativity, teamwork, problem solving, and many of the skills discussed in this textbook are core skills.

2. Examine employment trends. The "Occupational Outlook Handbook" published annually by the Bureau of Labor Statistics (BLS) is a good place to start (the updated handbook is readily available online through a quick keyword search).

3. Stay current in your short-term career planning. Keep up on newly emerging industries, technologies, and occupations. Keep an open mind (stay in the "open mode") while you creatively explore new ideas. Don't get locked into one idea; you can always change your mind as new information comes along.

Whether you love your job and want to keep it forever, or can't wait to find the next one, short-term and long-term career planning can help. You can put yourself in a better position to advance in your career, or begin a completely new occupation, with some strategic planning. Think of career planning as an interesting journey. Take your time, and be willing to head to a new adventure in a different direction if one should arise.

Source: Randall S. Hansen, "Developing a Strategic Vision for Your Career Plan," *Quintessential Careers,* www.quintcareers.com.

case study 13.1

The Car Salesman Who Lost the Sale

Jody Schneider had been out of high school for two years when she landed a good office job with opportunities for advancement. This week was the one-year anniversary of getting that job. As she had promised herself, she was taking some time off work to fulfill her long-held dream of buying a brand-new car.

She had done some research. Not only had she spent weeks poring over brochures that her older brother had given her, she also had read *Consumer Report* articles on all of the cars within her price range. At the first dealership, she was snubbed by three salespersons before she finally found one who was willing to take her seriously. Her second try was about the same. Still, she did not find the car she wanted at the first dealership or the second. By the time she had approached the third car lot, she had begun to lose some of her initial enthusiasm.

But that was where she found the car of her dreams. It was exactly what she had been looking for. After the test drive the salesman, Joe, asked her to make him an offer. "Any offer; just whatever you think is reasonable," he said. Jody knew that she could bargain. She started with a very low figure—about $3,000 below the price on the sticker. "Well, I'll see what I can do," Joe replied. "I'll have to ask the boss; I hope he's in a good mood."

Twenty minutes later, Jody walked to the back of the showroom to the candy machine. She had heard a familiar voice ask someone: "Well, d'ya think I've stalled this one long enough?" It was now clear that Joe was not busy discussing this offer with the boss. Jody asked one of the customer people the whereabouts of the sales manager. "He's gone for the day" was the reply.

Quickly, Jody returned to Joe's office. When Joe walked in a minute later, he said without pausing, "Well, I'm sorry; the boss just won't go for it, but let's see if we can work out a deal that will be almost as good." Joe was startled when Jody answered, "I refuse to play any more of your silly, time-wasting games!"

With that, Jody walked out.

Case Study Questions

1. What procedures and attitudes covered in this chapter could have helped Joe make the sale to this would-be customer? (Remember, this was to be the car of her dreams.)

2. Several years ago, a number of car dealerships tried to change the traditional methods of selling cars in the U.S. (most notably, the Saturn Corporation). As a potential customer, what advice would you give them to aid in their attempts?

3. Specifically, what suggestions would you give car dealers who use Joe's tactics, if they want to boost return business?

4. What suggestions would you make to Joe in terms of the internal customers at the car dealership?

case study 13.2

The Battle of the Bedroom Set

John and Jeanne Casey had just moved into their dream home. It was spacious and comfortable—the house they had been hoping for. The spacious master bedroom definitely called for a bedroom set that was larger than the one they had been using for the past 15 years.

After searching the entire area, they found the perfect set. The only problem was that they wanted it in king size not queen; that meant ordering it from an out of town warehouse. At first, Jasper Furniture seemed very accommodating. They promised the set would arrive in 60 days at the most. After nearly 70 days had passed, Jeanne called the store to see why it was taking so long. The sales clerk she spoke with acted as if she was bothering him. "After all," he replied impatiently, "we're talking about a shipment that is only 10 days late."

A full month went by after that phone call. Twice during that month, John dropped by the store to inquire about the shipment. The first time, the staff member they spoke with blamed the sales clerk for submitting an incomplete order. The second time, the people he talked to blamed the supplier. Both times, they promised to call when the furniture arrived. Another two months later, no one had called. Together John and Jeanne went down and demanded their money back.

This time they spoke with the manager, who immediately blamed the supplier. The store had done its best to get the order completed, according to the manager.

"No," John replied. "No matter what deficiencies your suppliers have, we're not angry with them, but with you. You have been of no help through this entire ordeal, and you have left us waiting for months! Our whole house is full of furniture that we have bought here over the years, but we will not buy from you again. You could have prevented this problem. You—not your supplier—could have salvaged the situation."

Case Study Questions

1. What specific actions could Jasper Furniture have taken to prevent losing a long-term return customer like the Caseys?

2. Pretend you are a new manager just hired by Jasper a few days before the final scene in the case. What steps would you take to restore the Caseys' positive attitude about Jasper Furniture?

3. Do issues exist here related to internal customers? Explain.

4. Discuss the principles in this chapter illustrated by this case.

CHAPTER FOURTEEN

HUMAN RELATIONS IN A WORLD OF DIVERSITY

LEARNING OBJECTIVES

After studying this chapter, you will be able to:

- Describe how human relations are affected when they are part of a diverse society.
- Explain how prejudiced attitudes pose a challenge to human relations
- Identify the origins of prejudice.
- List types of discrimination.
- Define sexual harassment
- Describe the connections among prejudice, discrimination, and self-esteem.
- Give examples of how to decrease prejudice.

STRATEGIES FOR SUCCESS

Assess Your Knowledge

Reducing Sexual Harassment

CHAPTER FOURTEEN

14

HUMAN RELATIONS IN A WORLD OF DIVERSITY

 LEARNING OBJECTIVES

After studying this chapter, you will be able to:

LO 14-1   Describe how human relations are affected when they are part of a diverse society.

LO 14-2   Explain how prejudiced attitudes pose a challenge to human relations.

LO 14-3   Identify the origins of prejudice.

LO 14-4   List types of discrimination.

LO 14-5   Define sexual harassment.

LO 14-6   Describe the connections among prejudice, discrimination, and self-esteem.

LO 14-7   Give examples of how to decrease prejudice.

 STRATEGIES FOR SUCCESS

Strategy 14.1   **Assess Your Knowledge**

Strategy 14.2   **Reducing Sexual Harassment**

In the Workplace: In the Minority

SITUATION

"This way please, Miss Ong." Jane chuckled at being called "Miss" and looked around with amazement as her new boss, Mr. Singh, led her through a quick tour of the office. This new job would be her first professional job since graduating from college earlier that year. Jane had grown up as a third-generation Chinese American in Seattle, and had technically been considered a minority group member, but she'd always felt right at home among other Asian Americans, as well as the Hispanics, African Americans, and Caucasians in her classes and neighborhood. But this new office in downtown Oakland, California, was a whole different experience! As she walked toward her new office, she passed dozens of her new co-workers already busy at work. Even though this was a large financial organization with offices around the world, Jane had not expected the diversity she saw on her first day. She saw her new colleagues dressed in clothing she had never even seen back in Seattle, and she heard languages and accents she couldn't quite identify. She recognized Mandarin

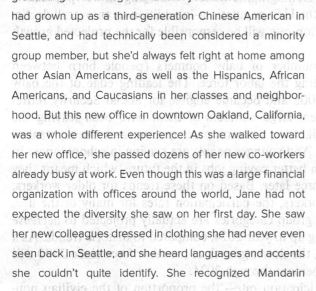
©moodboard/SuperStock

Chinese and Spanish, and would later learn that there were at least 10 other languages spoken among her co-workers, including Korean, Tagalog, Armenian, German, Cambodian, Hindi, Malay, Vietnamese, Finnish, Ibo, and others. She instantly recognized a Canadian accent as she reached to shake the hand of the inhabitant of the next desk over. "Hi, I'm Jane," she said, trying not to sound too eager. . . .

DISCOVERY

As Jane continued to walk through the maze of offices, smiling and shaking hands or greeting new people, she thought, "This is amazing! I've got so much to learn about my new colleagues!" She looked forward to getting started.

THINK ABOUT IT

How might the diversity in Jane's new environment affect her on a day-to-day basis? What might she need to know in order to work successfully with such a diverse population of co-workers? How can finding yourself in a new role or environment help you better understand yourself and others?

» A DIVERSE SOCIETY

American society has grown more diverse in recent decades, and Americans like Jane will find that the workforce reflects this growing participation of older employees, women, minorities, and immigrants across a wide spectrum of job sectors. (See Figure 14.1.)

Labor Force Diversity

The U.S. Bureau of Labor Statistics (BLS) has projected that the labor force will grow at an average annual rate of 0.5 percent through 2024, a slower rate than in recent decades. Demographic factors—including slower population growth and the aging of the U.S. population—in addition to an overall declining labor force participation rate will be responsible for the projected growth of the labor force.

Currently, a large number of baby boomers (people born between 1946 and 1964) are exiting the labor force. The leading edge of the baby boomers turned 62 in 2008 and became eligible for Social Security retirement benefits. Since then, large numbers of them have been leaving the labor force every year. Likewise, women's participation rates already peaked more than a decade ago. And younger people are staying in school longer in order to be able to obtain better paying jobs in the future, which means they are entering the labor force later. Based on these trends for older workers, women, and younger workers, the participation rates for many of the age, gender, race, and ethnic group categories are actually projected to *decrease* during the decade leading up to year 2024, compared to historic trends. As a result of all these factors, the slower growth of the labor force since 2000 will continue, at around 0.5 percent through 2024.

The labor force participation rate—"the proportion of the civilian non-institutional population that is in the labor force"—is one of the key measures of labor market activity. Each age, gender, race, and ethnic group exhibits a different socioeconomic trend and thus a different labor force participation rate. It is critical to note that while the size of the overall labor force is contracting:

- Women will continue to enter the labor force at a faster pace than men.
- The proportion of older employees may increase, in part because baby boomers may increasingly choose to remain in the workforce past the traditional retirement age.
- Racial and ethnic minorities have assumed an increasing presence in the labor force, and the result can be seen in the growing diversity of the workforce.
- Hispanics will continue to expand their workforce participation; the Hispanic share of the labor force is projected to double from 15 percent in 2010 to 30 percent in 2050.

Human Relations in a World of Diversity   «   CHAPTER 14   **365**

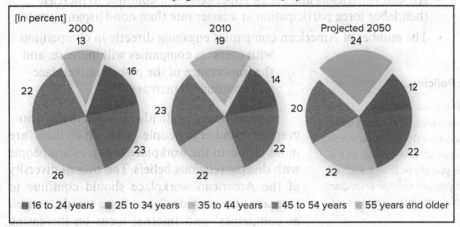

Labor force by age, 2000, 2010, and projected 2050

[In percent]

2000   2010   Projected 2050

■ 16 to 24 years   ■ 25 to 34 years   ■ 35 to 44 years   ■ 45 to 54 years   ■ 55 years and older

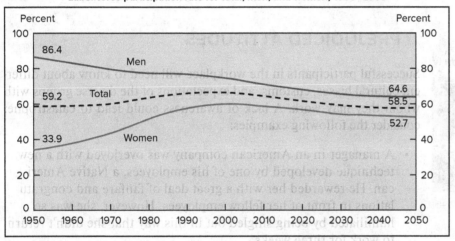

Labor force participation rate for total, men, and women, 1950–2050

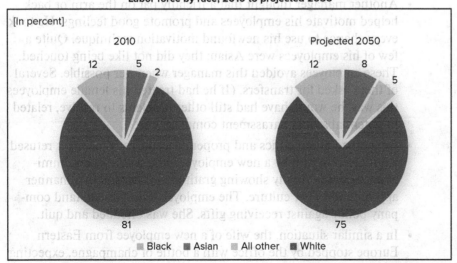

Labor force by race, 2010 to projected 2050

[In percent]

2010   Projected 2050

■ Black   ■ Asian   ■ All other   ■ White

figure 14.1

THE FUTURE OF
WORKPLACE DIVERSITY

Source: Mitra Toosi,
"Projections of the Labor
Force to 2050: A Visual Essay,"
Monthly Labor Review, October
2012, www.bls.gov.

- African Americans and Asian Americans will continue to increase their labor force participation at a faster rate than non-Hispanic whites.
- The number of American companies engaging directly in competition with overseas companies will increase, and the importance of the global marketplace will continue to increase.

And while not explicitly included in the demographic numbers, people with disabilities are more visible in the workplace today, as are people with diverse religious beliefs. The overall diversity of the American workplace should continue to increase, due to wider labor force trends, as well as companies' own internal focus on increasing the diversity among their employee ranks.

more about...

Corporate Diversity Policies

Companies often publish their diversity policies in statements on their websites under links titled "Corporate Social Responsibility" or "Corporate Ethics" or "Company Values." Take a look at the websites for companies you do business with, or any large organizations you are familiar with. Can you find such a link? What information does each company include?

HANDLING PREJUDICE

Everyone needs to know how to handle prejudice when it's encountered, and everyone needs to know how to eliminate prejudice within himself or herself. This applies especially to people whose jobs involve working with the public. *How can someone's prejudiced attitude affect others when working with the public?*

©Terry Vine/Blend Images/Getty Images

» PREJUDICED ATTITUDES

Successful participants in the workplace will need to know about different cultural biases, customs, and expectations of the diverse groups with whom they may work. A lack of awareness could lead to catastrophe; consider the following examples:

- A manager in an American company was overjoyed with a new technique developed by one of his employees, a Native American. He rewarded her with a great deal of fanfare and congratulations in front of her fellow employees. However, she was so humiliated by being singled out in this way that she didn't return to work for three weeks.
- Another manager thought that a friendly pat on the arm or back helped motivate his employees and promote good feelings. He took every chance to use his newfound motivation technique. Quite a few of his employees were Asian; they did not like being touched. These employees avoided this manager whenever possible. Several of them asked for transfers. (If he had treated his female employees this way, he would have had still other problems to resolve, related to potential sexual harassment complaints.)
- Concerned about ethics and proper procedures, a manager refused a gift given to him by a new employee, who was a recent immigrant. She was simply showing gratitude for her job in a manner appropriate to her culture. The employee didn't understand company policy against receiving gifts. She was offended and quit.
- In a similar situation, the wife of a new employee from Eastern Europe stopped by the office with a bottle of champagne, expecting that her husband's fellow employees would stop and help celebrate

the new job. Instead, people just said hello and returned to work. The woman was mortified. Her husband quit a few days later.[1]

It is not unusual now to find companies that have regular diversity training programs, workshops, and other resources for their employees. Many companies have made a commitment to improving the workplace climate of their organizations by hiring diversity officers as part of the administrative team, and by establishing policies of working only with suppliers who have similar policies.

All of these stories are about misunderstandings of the other person's cultural expectations. No conscious prejudice was involved, nor hatred or viciousness of any kind. Problems in the diverse workplace happen because of honest mistakes, as well as because of stereotyping and prejudice. Since stereotyping and prejudice do occur on the job, an in-depth look at them is important.

Prejudice is one type of attitude. All attitudes have three parts: what you *think*, *feel*, and *do*. These three parts of an attitude exist whether you are talking about the NBA playoffs, state politics, or creamed spinach. For example, you may *think* to yourself, "Creamed spinach is green," then *feel* a negative reaction to that particular color of green: "That color reminds me of slime. Gross!" As a consequence, you *do* something (or in this case choose to *not* do something) by not eating the creamed spinach.

In talking about diversity in the workplace, you can think of prejudice against other people as part of a specific, often harmful attitude. Like other attitudes, this one is composed of three parts. **Stereotypes** are your *thoughts or beliefs* about specific groups of people. **Prejudice** is how you *feel* as a result of those thoughts or beliefs. **Discrimination** is your *behavior*, or what you do (or intend to do, or are inclined to do) as a result of your stereotypes and prejudice. A closer look at these components follows.

Stereotypes

A stereotype is a thought or belief about members of a given group. That belief may be positive, negative, or neutral; and it is usually oversimplified, exaggerated, and/or overgeneralized. Whether it is a positive belief ("Asians are good students and employees") or a negative one ("senior citizens are too old to be good employees"), it is potentially damaging because it lumps everyone into one group without recognizing their individual characteristics.

People also stereotype tasks and jobs: a manager's job has often been stereotyped as "a man's job," whereas clerical or secretarial duties are labeled "women's work." Stereotypes hurt minorities, women, men, and members of other groups. Hiring, promotions, and job evaluations are areas where stereotypes can affect who is accepted or passed over.

A study of stereotyping and prejudice on the job uncovered these examples:

---

stereotypes

Your thoughts or beliefs about specific groups of people.

prejudice

The outcome of prejudging a person. Prejudice in communication is the unwillingness to listen to members of groups the listener believes are inferior, such as other ethnic groups or women; it can also take more subtle forms; how you feel as a result of the stereotypes you believe in.

discrimination

Your behavior, or what you do (or intend to do, or are inclined to do) as a result of your stereotypes and prejudice.

- "My supervisor follows me to the restroom, lunchroom, telephone, or whenever I am away from my work area. I think it's because I'm the only minority there."
- "She scrutinizes my work closer than she does the white employees. She gives me orders in a derogatory way."
- "He constantly makes vulgar remarks about me, such as calling me the 'entertainment and recreation committee.' "
- "She always shakes her finger in our faces when she doesn't like something we did."[2]

In each of these cases, the stereotyping has resulted in feelings of prejudice and discriminatory behavior against an employee.

Prejudice

Prejudice means "to prejudge" or make a judgment without knowing a person beforehand. It sums up the negative feelings or evaluations about people and groups that are stereotyped. Prejudice causes **bias,** which is a tendency to judge people before you know them, basing the judgment only on their membership in some group or category of people. Bias can be negative or positive; that is, we may lean *toward* or favor a person or group, or lean *away from* or disfavor a person or a group.

Everyone has certain prejudices, whether conscious or otherwise, and whether you believe it or not. Even people who consider themselves unprejudiced often have certain *strong* likes and dislikes based on categories of people. Prejudice undermines human relations, and it is hard on productivity. It is disruptive and causes low morale in the workplace or in any other place where it occurs unquestioned.

bias

A tendency to judge people before knowing them, basing the judgment only on their membership in some group or category of people.

institutional prejudice

Prejudice that is caused by policies in the workplace that are not intentionally set to exclude members of specific groups or to treat them differently, but which have that effect anyway.

Discrimination

Discrimination is acting or intending to act, or being inclined to act, on a prejudicial attitude. Prejudice is a feeling; discrimination is an act. Not all feelings of prejudice result in acts of discrimination, but individual acts of discrimination usually come from prejudiced feelings.

Discriminatory acts that are not caused by prejudice include discriminatory policies in the workplace that are not intentionally set to exclude members of specific groups or to treat them differently, but which have that effect anyway. These policies are referred to as **institutional prejudice,** or exclusionary policies.

A step toward eliminating discrimination in the workplace came with the passing of the Civil Rights Act of 1964. This law makes it illegal to discriminate against anyone because of race, color, religion, sex, or national origin.

The Beginning of Civil Rights

more about...

The civil rights movement's first major victory came 10 years earlier than the Civil Rights Act of 1964 with *Brown v. the Board of Education*, a 1954 U.S. Supreme Court case that outlawed school segregation.

Title VII of this law covers any employer who does business between states and who employs at least 15 people for at least 20 weeks per year. This definition of *employer* also includes governments and other public institutions, schools and colleges, unions, and employment agencies. The Civil Rights Act was amended in 1972. In that year, the **Equal Employment Opportunity Commission (EEOC)** was established to monitor these laws.

» ORIGINS OF PREJUDICE

For American society to eliminate prejudice, it needs to know where prejudice comes from. For decades, psychologists and sociologists have been very interested in studying what causes prejudice. Although they do not agree on any one cause, there are a few theories that can be summarized. In general, the origins of prejudice can be divided into three broad categories: social causes, cognitive (thinking) causes, and emotional causes.[3] (See Figure 14.2.)

Social Causes of Prejudice

Many theories have been put forth about how social factors cause prejudice. One theory is that people form prejudices to try to raise their own self-esteem, such as when climbing the career or social ladder. It's easier for people to feel superior when they are able to identify other groups of people as inferior. This unequal status leads to prejudice. It also becomes a vicious cycle when people then use the fact that they are higher up on the status pole to justify their prejudice and discrimination toward people they view as lower status.

Another social theory is that prejudice helps people define themselves and feel socially accepted. When people belong to a group and feel accepted, they tend to rate other groups as inferior. Conforming to a group's standards also helps people feel more accepted, and many groups encourage *us-versus-them*

Equal Employment Opportunity Commission (EEOC)

A federal agency established to monitor the laws set in place by the amended Civil Rights Act of 1964, as amended in 1972.

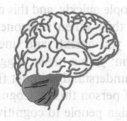

Social	Cognitive	Emotional
• Status	• Thinking	• The "right way"
• Self-esteem	• Reasoning	• Habit
• Us vs. them	• Categorization	• Ethnocentrism
• In group/out group	• Boxes	• Competition

figure 14.2

THE ORIGINS OF PREJUDICE

The three origins of prejudice are social ones (the need to feel higher in status than others), cognitive (the need to categorize and stereotype people), and emotional (such as habit, or ethnocentrism). *Which type of prejudice can be most damaging?*

feelings and behaviors. For example, a new university student in a strange city may join a fraternity or sorority to make friends, but this could mean missed opportunities to form friendships outside of the group. In this example, prejudice may be used to reduce the student's anxiety, insecurity, and inner conflict. These same feelings are also social causes of prejudice.

A final social theory of prejudice looks at institutional support systems, or the way organizations and society itself unintentionally create institutional racism, sexism, or exclusionary policies. For example, men and women make up about equal proportions of the population, but men are still highly overrepresented in films and television shows as main characters, narrators for commercials, and authority figures.[4] This has the effect of promoting the idea that men really are authority figures who know much more about kitchen floor wax or dog food than women know about such things.

> **more about...**
>
> **Scapegoating** is *the practice of unfairly blaming others (such as ethnic groups) when something goes wrong.* The term originated from an ancient biblical custom of sending a goat into the wilderness after the sins of the community were placed upon its head.

All it takes to create prejudice is for people to identify themselves as part of a group (the in-group) while they see others as part of a different group (the out-group). If that seems too simple to be true, try this easy experiment on your own: go to any high school football or basketball game and actively cheer for the visiting team while sitting with the home team spectators. Note how you feel—and how the home team spectators behave toward you.

scapegoating

The practice of unfairly blaming others (such as ethnic groups) when something goes wrong.

Cognitive Causes of Prejudice

Cognitive causes have to do with thinking and reasoning processes. Some psychologists believe that prejudice originates with a process called **cognitive categorization,** in which the mind quickly sorts information into categories to function efficiently. Cognitive categorization is generally a necessary skill; for instance, if every time you walked into a classroom you had to take the time to figure out all over again which objects to sit on and which objects to write with, you would fail in school and in life. The problem is that cognitive categorization also allows you to categorize people quickly, and this can lead to prejudice.

cognitive categorization

A process in which the mind quickly sorts information into categories to function efficiently.

Think about how you do this. When someone is walking toward you on the sidewalk, for example, you quickly and unconsciously notice some characteristics about the person: young, male, sagging pants, and carrying a skateboard. You feel able to understand, without figuring out each characteristic separately, what *type* of person this is. Cognitive categorization goes too far, however, when you assign people to cognitive *boxes,* then negatively evaluate them based on the boxes you've put them in.[5]

Emotional Causes of Prejudice

ethnocentrism

The belief that one's ethnic group is more normal than others; an emotional source of prejudice because of people's gut-level feelings about how right their group is—and, in turn, how wrong they think other groups are.

Ethnocentrism is the cause of a great deal of prejudice that people experience. Human beings tend to see their own ethnic groups as the most normal,

REAL WORLD EXAMPLE 14.1

The employees at the distribution center had begun to kick it into high gear as the first truck of the night rumbled up to the loading dock. This was an experienced team, equal numbers men and women, and they were essentially interchangeable in their roles. With all the pallet jacks in use, several on the team had begun to hand-carry items off the truck. When Ivan saw Jessica transferring a heavy load onto the conveyor belt, he called out, "Hey Jessica, don't worry about that! It's heavy, and besides, I don't want you to mess up your outfit—let me get it for you!" Jessica, a high school wrestling champion who could deadlift more than most men her size, laughed off the suggestion. She had seen this subtle form of gender bias before, but refused to buy into the notion that she should have diminished responsibilities because of her gender.

and they believe their way of seeing and doing things is *the* right way. Ethnocentrism is an emotional source of prejudice because of people's gut-level feelings about how right *their* group is—and, in turn, how wrong they think other groups are.

Ethnocentrism exists everywhere, not just in the United States. Most societies are ethnocentric. This phenomenon is not intentional; the familiar way of doing things just seems right to most of us. If what is familiar is right, then by extension, many people feel that what is unfamiliar must be wrong. People are creatures of habit, and if it is their habit to live a certain way, doing otherwise may be strange or unusual.

Another theory about the emotional causes of prejudice is that people look for a target to blame when they are frustrated. When members of two groups are competing for scarce resources (such as jobs in an area with high unemployment), this competition can lead to frustration, followed by aggression, prejudice, and discrimination.[6]

» TYPES OF DISCRIMINATION

Discrimination comes from any number of different sources, and can be aimed at a variety of different targets. Here we explore some major types of discrimination that may be targeted at certain groups.

Racism

Racism, which is prejudice and discrimination based on race, is one of today's most important social topics. This topic is filled with emotion and controversy and has been at the heart of many conflicts throughout history. Many people who lived through World War II or through the 1950s and 1960s expected that by the 21st century, racism in America would be a thing of the past. Sadly, they were wrong. Minorities in the United States still experience widespread discrimination and prejudice.

racism
Prejudice and discrimination based on race.

HOW THE MEDIA CREATES PREJUDICE

Advertisements often portray men as authority figures and women as sex objects for no reason other than prejudice. *Are these images meant to portray reality, or are these models given roles by misguided advertisers? How can you identify institutional prejudice?*

©Lars A. Niki

more about...

Black Girls Code

Black Girls Code (BGC) is a nonprofit organization created in 2011 in San Francisco, California, to help African-American youth, mainly girls, learn computer programming and coding, as well as website, robot, and mobile application building. The goals of this organization are to provide African-American youth "with the skills to occupy some of the 1.4 million computing job openings expected to be available in the U.S. in 2020" and to create community leaders and STEM (science, technology, engineering, math) teachers. BGC has now grown to several states and at least one other country, South Africa. Thousands of youth have now learned coding skills through BGC. Other organizations with similar goals include Girls Who Code, Native Girls Code, and I Look Like an Engineer. Within one organization, Black Girls Code is addressing three of the major types of discrimination addressed in this chapter: racism, sexism, and economic discrimination.

See http://www.blackgirlscode.com/

Indications can be seen worldwide that the issue is at least as serious as it was in the days of Adolf Hitler. *Genocide,* which is the systematic murder of an entire racial, ethnic, or national group, continues around the world. In the 1990s, genocide occurred in Rwanda and the former Yugoslavia. In the 2000s, the location was Darfur when in 2004 the U.S. government declared genocide to be occurring in this area of the Sudan.[7] In 2017, horrific actions in Myanmar against the Rohingya minority have been labeled "ethnic cleansing" by the United States and by the United Nations.[8] Unfortunately, these are just a few of the examples we can find of widescale racism that has had serious impacts on large groups of people.

Racial prejudice is proving to be extremely difficult to overcome, and many people in the United States still have not been accepted as part of mainstream society. Ethnocentrism is one of the factors in this problem, but certainly not the only one. Prejudice is another major reason. Racial and ethnic groups such as African Americans, Asians, Hispanics, Native Americans, Jews, and other groups still strive for equal status in American society.

For example, America's history of racial inequality has created large gaps in education and employment that are still very real today. Look at unemployment rate statistics and you will find significant differences by race or ethnicity in recent years. Data for mid-2017 (as an example) reveal such differences:

- Total U.S. unemployment rate: 4.9 percent
- Unemployment rate for white Americans: 4.3 percent
- Unemployment rate for African Americans: 8.1 percent
- Unemployment rate for Asian Americans: 3.5 percent
- Unemployment rate for Americans of Hispanic origin: 5.9 percent [9]

If these percentages don't seem drastically different to you, remember that they represent thousands of people who are all actively looking for work (*seeking work* is required in order to be counted in this statistic). Recall that once a person *feels* his or her chances at securing a job are severely diminished, he or she may remove themselves from the workforce. Thus, unemployment figures are always certainly higher than reported.[10]

Research has shown that African-American employees tend to be recommended for promotions less often and are less satisfied with their careers than white employees, in large part because of the

REAL WORLD EXAMPLE 14.2

SooMei and Tracey are American businesswomen who often work in Argentina. They respect those who stick to schedules because punctuality is a shared value in their culture. However, when they work in Argentina, where an appointment might take hours—or days—to be kept, SooMei sees such practices as inefficient, and is annoyed; to her, the American way makes the most sense. Tracey has taught herself to think without ethnocentrism and sees the difference as just that: a difference.

stigma that arises when employees belong to a minority group.[11] What many employers fail to realize is that by discriminating against employees because of their racial prejudices, these employers are damaging their own productivity (by reducing morale) and not capturing the skills and talents of these employees. With the historic two-term presidency of Barack Obama, Americans have shown a willingness to set aside racism and select an African American to lead our nation. But many of Obama's struggles to pass legislation that would benefit a majority of Americans were stymied by resistance to him as an outsider, largely because of lingering perceptions about his his ethnicity and Arabic name. Thus, Obama's historic election to the highest political office in our country may have signaled that the national discourse on race continues to evolve, but persistent national struggles about race during, and after, his time in office indicate that we are by no means at the crossroads of a new, "post-racial" society.

Economic Prejudice

Economic prejudice, which can be defined as the struggle and resentment between the *haves* and the *have-nots,* is an ancient and often ugly battle. The American Revolution in 1776, the Russian Revolution in 1917, and India's independence from Britain in 1947 are a few historical examples. In these situations, the have-nots—who were at first powerless—joined together against their oppressors and won.

One of the theories of prejudice is that competition leads to frustration and aggression. In the United States, when economic times are hard, prejudice can focus on groups—often ethnic groups—that are seen as taking something away from "ordinary Americans," even if members of these ethnic groups *are* Americans. When the economy sagged in Michigan several decades ago, Japanese Americans were singled out because of auto employees' anger at Japanese auto manufacturers for hurting the American car market. In some cases, even people of other Asian national origins, such as Chinese, were mistaken for Japanese and discriminated against, with at least one attacked in the street.

economic prejudice

Prejudice and discrimination toward people who are poorer or wealthier than you are.

History Repeats Itself

Just as Japanese Americans were unfairly blamed for the slump in American auto manufacturing, they were also blamed decades earlier for Japan's involvement in World War II. They were deprived of their belongings and sent to internment camps until the war ended. It was not until 1989 that the U.S. government repaid them for their losses.

more about...

figure 14.3

PRIMARY FORMS OF DISCRIMINATION

Although there are many forms of discrimination, the three primary ones are racism, economic discrimination, and sexism. *How can employers fight each of these?*

DISCRIMINATION: THREE PROBLEM ISSUES	
Type	**Issues to Consider**
Racist	Acceptance of minorities
	Assimilation versus separation
	Educational opportunities
	Cultural biases
	Hiring and recruitment policies
Economic	Power struggles
	Resources
	Resentment
	Competition for limited opportunities
Sexist	Male chauvinism and male advantage
	Gender roles
	Wage discrepancies
	Educational opportunities
	Tradition versus innovation

As with all prejudice, economic prejudice goes both ways. Not only do the poor resent the rich and stereotype them as selfish and uncaring, but the rich often look down on the poor and stereotype them as lazy or worthless. Many of those who live a middle-class or above existence are fond of reminding others that the United States is still a land of opportunity, where "you just have to work hard enough." They may believe that the have-nots simply refused the golden opportunity that was there for them. However, such an oversimplification is another example of how cognitive categorization leads to prejudice. (See Figure 14.3.)

Sexism

sexism

Prejudice and discrimination based on gender.

The term *male chauvinism* was coined during the 1960s to describe a feeling of male superiority over females that is quite similar to ethnocentrism. This is also known as **sexism.** Because a man may have attitudes and stereotypes of women in society, he may choose to see them as being of less worth—in other words, he may devalue women's contributions, or may even objectify or dehumanize women. This can happen in different ways. For example, one type of man sees females as inferior, not really worth listening to, and needing a man to be complete. Another type puts women on a pedestal. This sounds better, but it can be at least as frustrating to women as the first behavior. If a woman is placed on a pedestal, she is still not being seen as a fellow human being, and this distortion easily translates into numerous forms of inequality because she is expected to fulfill unrealistic expectations that the man has determined for her. This less direct form of male chauvinism is

Gender Prejudice in the Business World

Man	Woman
A businessman is aggressive.	A businesswoman is pushy.
He is careful about details.	She's picky.
He loses his temper because he is so involved in his job.	She's bitchy.
He's depressed (or hung over) so everyone tiptoes past his office.	She's moody, so it must be her time of month.
He follows through.	She doesn't know when to quit.
He's firm.	She's stubborn.
He makes wise judgments.	She reveals her prejudices.
He's a man of the world.	She's been around.
He isn't afraid to say what he thinks.	She's outspoken and opinionated.
He exercises authority.	She's a tyrant.
He's discreet.	She's secretive.
He's a stern taskmaster.	She's difficult to work for.

figure 14.4

HOW TO TELL A BUSINESSMAN FROM A BUSINESSWOMAN

Although men and women bring the same traits into the business world, many prejudiced employers and co-workers continue to perceive these traits as positive in men and negative in women. *Why do these prejudices persist?*

Robert Fulmer, *Practical Human Relations* (Homewood, IL: Richard D. Irwin, Inc., 1983), p. 360.
©McGraw-Hill Education

difficult to deal with because this man may honestly think he is treating women very fairly and kindly. Think of Jessica at the distribution center from the previous example in this chapter.

Women in most societies are expected to be feminine, a term associated with disempowering behaviors such as dependence, instability, emotional insecurity, a willingness to take orders but not give them, and passivity. When these expectations toward women exist in a workplace, so does prejudice; an obvious paradox occurs when a woman in such an organization becomes a manager or assumes another role of authority. (See Figure 14.4.)

Women have made significant strides since the 1950s in promoting inclusion and equality with their male counterparts. Despite these gains, American society still contains a number of areas where very little progress has been made. For example, consider the highest levels of the United States government. Since 1789, of the more than 2,000 senators in the history of United States Congress, only 50 have been female. And with more than 10,000 members of the House of Representatives since its inception, just 288 members have been female. During the 1992 election year, jubilantly dubbed "The Year of the Woman," only 2 women were elected to the Senate (out of 100 senators), and just 28 women (out of 435 members) to the House of Representatives.[12]

Girls on the Run

Girls on the Run is a nonprofit organization found in all 50 states with the goal of teaching girls aged 8–18 confidence and life skills. "Running is used to inspire and motivate girls, encourage lifelong health and fitness, and build confidence through accomplishment." The program began in 1996 in Charlotte, North Carolina, and has now served more than one million youth.

See: Girls on the Run, https://www.girlsontherun.org/.

more about...

**MORE COMPLICATED
THAN IT LOOKS**

Although economic
prejudice is rooted in the
hardships that spring from
economic competition, it
can sometimes blend with
ethnic prejudices and have
a doubly powerful impact
on the groups against
which it is prejudiced. *What
are some ways to get at the
real causes of prejudice, in
order to stop it?*

©Image Source

Workplace Conditions for Women

Although women find it possible to be promoted to the supervisory
level (the lowest level of management), many report great difficulty
in getting into middle- and upper-level management, where the major
decisions are made. In the 1990s, very few chief executive officers
(CEOs) of publicly held corporations were women, and not much has
changed in the decades that have followed. One reason may be that
women are perceived by men as not being able to handle power when
they get it.[13] In fact, many women who are promoted to upper management positions succeed, and some feel this is because they had to
work harder to be accepted. Some who fail in higher positions may
do so because of indifference, scapegoating, or hostility from their male
colleagues.

Women's average income has been rising in recent years, but women still
do not make as much as men do, even in the same occupations. Compared
to non-Hispanic white men, white non-Hispanic women are paid 81 cents
on the dollar and Asian women are paid 88 cents on the dollar. By contrast,
the penalty is much larger for black and Hispanic women, who are paid only
65 cents and 59 cents on the white male dollar, respectively. In terms of the
impact on women's paychecks, this means that relative to the typical white
man, black women take home $7.63 less per hour and Hispanic women take
home $8.90 less per hour.[14]

The Fast Track versus the Mommy Track

Another problem women often face in the workplace is being expected
to choose between the *fast track* and the *mommy track* when climbing
the career ladder. Since women still shoulder most of the housework
and child rearing in traditional American homes, if they choose the fast
track they will have to forego at least some of these domestic responsibilities. In the fast track, employees are expected to work extra hours,
ask for extra work, and work nights and weekends. The fast track seems
to ask women to forget that they have families, or place families second
in importance after jobs, rather than helping families balance home and
work responsibilities.

What happens in the mommy track is just the opposite. When women
try to balance family responsibilities with work responsibilities, they
receive fewer promotions or raises, and are often stuck in low-wage jobs.
What most women want (and what many employers are slow to give) is a
compromise: a job that offers satisfying work and a chance for advancement, with enough flexibility to allow for raising a family, too. This can be
offered through flextime, manageable workloads, the option to telecom-
mute all or part of the week, setting up onsite child care, and through
other ways that reflect an employer's understanding of employees' personal needs.

By not allowing this kind of flexibility, many employers are restrict-
ing women with families from certain jobs, which is another type of

discrimination. Not only are these employers short-changing women who would like to have had such jobs, but they are also shortchanging their own businesses by not employing (or by underemploying) a large pool of potential employees with a high degree of talent and skills.

The three categories of discrimination just discussed (racism, sexism, and economic inequality) easily come to mind when considering prejudice and discrimination in the workplace, but there are other types of prejudice that don't fall neatly into one of those categories.

Overweight People

Court cases over the past decade have repeatedly ruled against prejudice against overweight people, at least where hiring and firing are the issues. In a landmark 1989 case, flight attendant Sherry Cappello, a 25-year veteran of American Airlines, was fired for being 11 pounds overweight. Because of a lawsuit Cappello filed, American Airlines was forced to change its weight-requirement policies.[15]

Although one might see Cappello's victory as a small one, prejudice against overweight people is still an issue today. In the words of Dr. Albert Stunkard, a physician who specializes in obesity, "The extent to which overweight people have difficulty in obtaining work goes far beyond what can be justified by medical data and must be due to discrimination."[16] This issue will be critical in years to come: as the nation struggles with increasing obesity rates, will the stigma of obesity recede?

The LGBT Workforce

A topic once thought of as controversial or taboo—homosexuals in the workplace—has now become widely accepted, and the emphasis seems to have shifted from accommodating the individual worker, to creating an inclusive, inviting work environment for people of all backgrounds, including individuals who identify as lesbian, gay, bisexual, transsexual, or anyone who is non-heterosexual or non-cisgender (where personal identity and gender do not correspond with birth sex).

According to the Centers for Disease Control (CDC), 38% of Americans are obese—a trend that continues to escalate into one of America's most serious ongoing crises. The health consequences of obesity can affect an organization if workers must take time from work to address health issues, and resources and workplace dynamics can be strained. Across the wider economy, absenteeism due to obesity or other health issues can impact national health-care spending and the economy as a whole.

Source: Centers for Disease Control, https://www.cdc.gov/nchs/fastats/obesity-overweight.htm. Visited July 2017.

PREJUDICE AGAINST HOMOSEXUALS

Does a person's appearance reveal sexual orientation? You cannot tell a person's sexual orientation by appearance alone. Nonetheless, prejudice, hostility, and general misunderstanding of homosexuality continue. *How can you deal with homophobia in the workplace?*

©JupiterImages/Comstock Images/Alamy Stock Photo

more about...

Anti-Discrimination Complaints

In states that have anti-discrimination policies in place, LGBT (Lesbian, Gay, Bisexual, Transgender) complaints are equivalent to the number of complaints filed based on sex, and fewer than the number of complaints filed based on race.

Source: "The State of the Workplace: for Lesbian, Gay, Bisexual, and Transgender Americans" (PDF). Human Rights Campaign. Retrieved July 2017.

more about...

LGBT and EEOC

The U.S. Equal Employment Opportunity Commission (EEOC) is responsible for enforcing federal laws that make it illegal to discriminate against a job applicant or an employee because of the person's race, color, religion, sex (including pregnancy), national origin, age (40 or older), disability, or genetic information. While Title VII does not include gender identity and sexual orientation as components of protection from sex discrimination, the EEOC and federal circuit courts have taken the position that they should be included. The EEOC resolved 1,650 charges and recovered $4.4 million for LGBT individuals who filed sex discrimination charges with EEOC in fiscal year 2016, with the data showing a steady increase in the four years the agency began collecting LGBT charge data. From fiscal year 2013 through fiscal year 2016, nearly 4,000 charges were filed with EEOC by LGBT individuals alleging sex discrimination, and EEOC recovered $10.8 million for victims of discrimination.

Source: EEOP, https://www.eeoc.gov/eeoc/statistics /enforcement/lgbt_sex_based.cfm.

Many current employment policies forbid discrimination on the basis of sexual orientation or sexual preference. And a growing number of states, counties, and cities have passed laws to make discrimination against gays and lesbians illegal.[17] And while there is a growing national consensus on protecting LGBT workers from discrimination, in 2017 it was still true that:

- There is no federal law protecting the rights of LGBT employees in the United States. Title VII of the Civil Rights Act of 1964 does not include sexual orientation in its protections. Although every Congress since 1974 has introduced legislation to include sexual orientation, it has never passed.

- There is no state-level protection for sexual orientation in 28 of the 50 U.S. states. This means employees can be fired for identifying as LGBT.

- There is no state-level gender identity protection in 30 of the 50 U.S. states. Employees can be fired for being transgender.[18]

While individual states and the national government wrestle with policies protecting LGBT workers, they will continue to debate quality of life issues, such as on-the-job harassment, whether or not unmarried life partners of homosexuals should receive the same employment benefits as legally married spouses, and other issues. Discussions around the issue will continue to evolve. For example, the U.S. military's so-called "Don't Ask Don't Tell" policy (the official U.S. policy that prohibited military personnel from discriminating against or harassing "closeted" homosexual or bisexual service members or applicants, while barring openly gay, lesbian, or bisexual persons from military service) was instituted in 1993, then overturned in 2011. In 2017, a ban was imposed on transgendered people serving in the military, but this ban was immediately challenged in court and has not yet been implemented. Attitudes about equal protection for same-sex couples have stirred debate even at the highest levels of government, including the U.S. Supreme Court.

The Elderly

Until 1967 no law protected older people from discrimination. Many employers justified such discrimination on the grounds that older people are slower and less healthy, and therefore don't perform as well as younger employees. In 1986, President Reagan signed an amendment to the 1967 law, making it illegal to discriminate against anyone over 40.[19] Specifically, the Age Discrimination in Employment Act (ADEA) protects employees and job applicants from being discriminated against because of their age in hiring, promotions, discharge, pay, terms or conditions of employment, and privileges given by the employer. It also abolishes mandatory retirement for some employees (including federal employees) and raises the mandatory retirement age for others from age 55 to 70. Because of the ADEA, setting a mandatory retirement age is allowed now only when it is necessary to maintain normal business operations; for example, firefighters and law enforcement officers can still be forced to retire at a certain age.

Recent studies show that **ageism,** or negative attitudes toward older people, is still very much alive.[20] More than most other groups, though, the elderly are fighting back. Consider this startling statistic: in 1989, employers paid around $9 million in damages and compensation in cases brought under Title VII (discrimination on the basis of race, color, religion, sex, or national origin) of the Civil Rights Act. In that same year, employers paid $25 million on lawsuits involving the ADEA.[21] That's a ratio of almost 3 to 1.

These same trends continued into the 1990s and beyond: in one discrimination lawsuit, four restaurant employees, age 44–50, were awarded $6.7 million.[22] In another age bias case, Thomson Consumer Electronics, Inc., and the International Brotherhood of Electrical Workers settled with 800 employees who shared an award of $7.1 million.[23] In a third age bias case, Lockheed Martin settled a complaint for $13 million in back pay and jobs for 450 older employees who had been dismissed. The amounts in these three cases *alone* exceeded the total amount awarded in 1989! And this same trend has not yet slowed down: for the years 2003–2007, the total amount paid by employers who lost age bias lawsuits for each of those years totaled $313.9 million, climbing to $435.5 million for the years 2008–2012. According to its published reporting, by 2016, the EEOC recorded 20,857 charges of discrimination based on age (22.8 percent of total EEOC charges).[24]

Currently, employees age 40 and older are covered under ADEA. This is a huge group of employees, and as the baby boomers (those born between 1946 and 1964) age, it will grow even more. As you can see, this is an important law, not to be ignored. We all should also remember that *this is the one group everyone will belong to some day.*

---

more about...

"Shooting" Down Stereotypes: The San Diego Splash

It should not surprise anyone that women have their own basketball teams, but not many teams are made up only of women in their 80s and 90s. The San Diego Splash plays 3-on-3, half-court games. They stay fit, both mentally and physically, and have fun doing so. "We play to win," says one team member. These athletes challenge our stereotypes about the abilities of aging adults.

Enjoli Francis, *ABC News*, "For This Group of Seniors, it's Basketball over Bingo Any Day," http://abcnews.go.com/Sports/group-seniors-basketball-bingo-day/story?id=48379676 (posted June 30, 2017; retrieved July 1, 2017).

ageism

Prejudice and discrimination toward older people.

People with Disabilities

About 18 percent of the U.S. population in the 18–64 age group is physically or developmentally disabled. A surprising 85 percent of this number who could be working, are not. This waste of talent is overwhelming.[25] The greatest barrier to the hiring of these would-be employees is prejudiced attitudes that, like most others, are based on largely inaccurate information. Think of this misinformation as myths; then read the information in Figure 14.5 to determine whether you are harboring any of these myths.

Employees who are disabled are also protected by law from discrimination, originally under the Rehabilitation Act of 1973. That law was never greatly effective because the courts kept struggling with the definitions of *handicapped* and *disabled*.[26] The remedy to this issue came in July 1990, when the Americans with Disabilities Act (ADA) became law. The overall purpose of this law is to allow people with disabilities to enjoy most of the benefits that everyone else enjoys.

The ADA prohibits discrimination by companies in any of the following areas: employment, public transportation, telecommunication, and other privately owned services to the public (hotels and motels, restaurants and bars,

figure 14.5

MYTHS ABOUT HIRING PEOPLE WITH DISABILITIES

Many people still hold on to myths about the reliability and talents of people who have disabilities. The unfortunate result is that as many as 85% of all working-age people with disabilities are unemployed. *How are people with disabilities better employees than most people think?*

Source: George E. Stevens, "Exploding the Myths About Hiring the Handicapped," *Personnel,* December 1986.

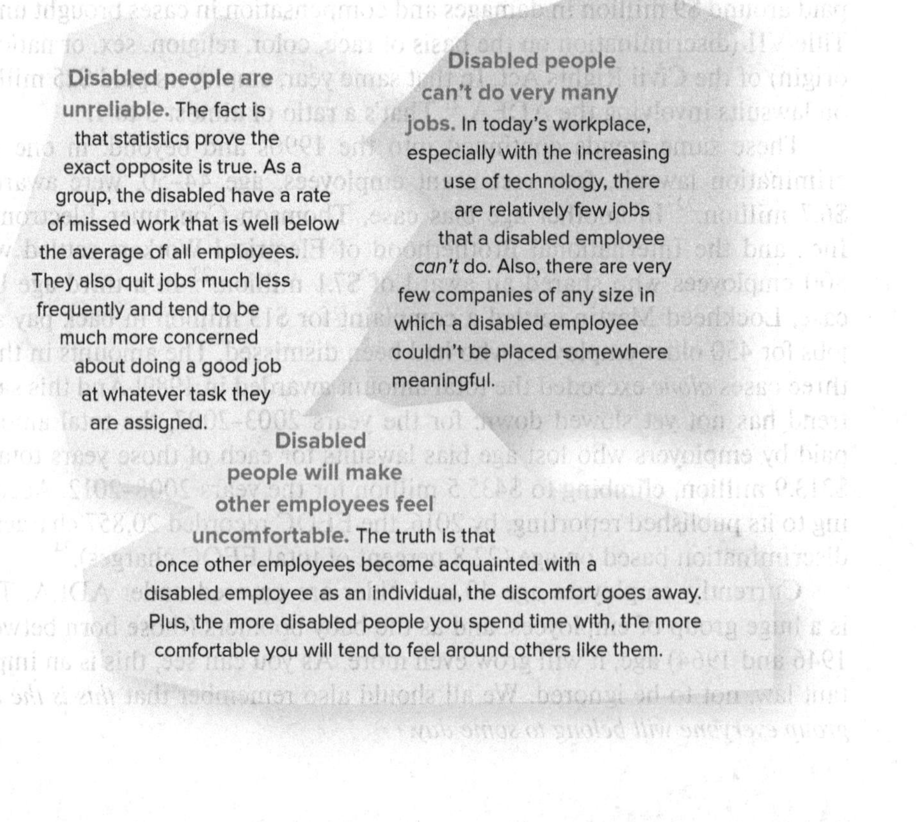

Disabled people are unreliable. The fact is that statistics prove the exact opposite is true. As a group, the disabled have a rate of missed work that is well below the average of all employees. They also quit jobs much less frequently and tend to be much more concerned about doing a good job at whatever task they are assigned.

Disabled people can't do very many jobs. In today's workplace, especially with the increasing use of technology, there are relatively few jobs that a disabled employee *can't* do. Also, there are very few companies of any size in which a disabled employee couldn't be placed somewhere meaningful.

Disabled people will make other employees feel uncomfortable. The truth is that once other employees become acquainted with a disabled employee as an individual, the discomfort goes away. Plus, the more disabled people you spend time with, the more comfortable you will tend to feel around others like them.

public gathering places). Also, the law requires that benefits and opportunities for people with disabilities must be of the same quality as those offered to everyone else, if possible. This law continues to be modified and refined, but because of it, access has improved for those with disabilities.[27]

Religious Groups

The experience of prejudice and discrimination based on religion goes back millennia, and a shared history of religious persecution goes back to the very founding of our country. Many of the Pilgrims who arrived in the New World came to escape religious intolerance, and were followed by hundreds of thousands of others who came for the same reason. Based on its unique history, of all the people of the world, Americans should be the least prejudiced when religious differences are involved—but are they?

The EEOC reports a steady increase in complaints based on religion over the past 20 years. In fiscal year 2007, the EEOC reported 2,880 charges of religious discrimination and had recovered $6.4 million in monetary benefits for people bringing the charges. By 2011, the number of charges of religious discrimination had climbed to 4,151, the highest number during the 20-year period from 1997 to 2016, with $12.6 million in monetary benefits recovered. The total number of charges was down slightly in 2016, with 3,825 reports and $10.1 million in settlements.[28]

In the past several years, members of Muslim groups have found themselves increasingly discriminated against in the United States and elsewhere. The facts show that members of religious groups often find themselves the objects of discrimination both at work and in social circles. Title VII of the Civil Rights Act of 1964 forbids discrimination against members of any religion. Employers are generally required to accommodate employees who express a need to practice religious beliefs at work, but they do have some flexibility in how these accommodations will be made.[29]

more about...

Faith Communities Extend a Hand

In early 2017, arson fires in two different parts of the country destroyed mosques and threatened to divide communities, but local faith communities offered assistance. When the Islamic Center of the Eastside in Bellevue, Washington, was destroyed by arson, the Bellevue Stake of the Church of Jesus Christ of Latter-Day Saints opened their doors to the displaced mosque members. The LDS church has sat next door to the Islamic Center for decades, but with shared space the two faith communities have drawn closer together. In Victoria, Texas, after the Victoria Islamic Center was burned down, members of the B'Nai Israel temple opened their synagogue for mosque members to gather and pray. In both cases, several local churches also offered assistance. Concern and compassion across religions can change social norms, in concert with legislation to change behaviors.

Gabe Cohen, KOMO News, "Church Takes in Bellevue Muslim Community After Arson," http://komonews.com/news/local/church-takes-in-bellevue-muslim-community-after-arson (posted January 20, 2017, retrieved July 2, 2017).

Madeline Farber, "How Jews and Christians in This Texas Town Are Helping Muslims Whose Mosque Burned Down," *Time*, http://time.com/4657876/texas-mosque-fire-jewish-christian-communities-help/ (posted February 2, 2017; retrieved July 2, 2017).

Pregnant Women

The issue of pregnancy has been reexamined numerous times as women's roles have grown in an increasing number of workplaces. Through the 1970s a female job applicant was routinely asked if she was pregnant or planning to become pregnant, and what her employment, child care, and other plans

382   PART IV   »   Thriving in a Changing World

would be if she were to have children. These types of questions are now illegal because they have been shown to severely affect hiring decisions and hurt women's chances for employment and advancement. Even today, a visibly pregnant woman runs such risks of discrimination—although it will probably be left unsaid by her employer.

» SEXUAL HARASSMENT

sexual harassment

Behavior that is defined by the EEOC as "Unwelcome sexual advances, requests for sexual favors, and other verbal or physical conduct of a sexual nature."

The phrase **sexual harassment** was coined by Lin Farley, author of *Sexual Shakedown,* in the late 1970s. What is sexual harassment? The answer is spelled out clearly by EEOC guidelines: "Unwelcome sexual advances, requests for sexual favors, and other verbal or physical conduct of a sexual nature. . . ." Sexually harassing behaviors include forced fondling, sexual slurs, and unwelcome flirting; it also includes sexually suggestive pictures or other material posted where others can see it.[30] (See Figure 14.6.)

The problem of sexual harassment in the workplace goes back to the time when men and women first started working together, but people such as Farley have called attention to this long-ignored problem. You have already seen in this chapter how much the workforce is changing. Record numbers of sexual harassment (and sexual assault) reports now being made public remind us of the seriousness and the enormous extent of this

more about...

Hostile Environments

When sexual harassment relates to indirect actions like posting pornography or talking about sex in a manner that makes others uncomfortable, this is called creating a **hostile environment.** It is considered equally as serious as direct harassment.

figure 14.6

EMPLOYER'S SEXUAL HARASSMENT POLICY STATEMENT

Every employer needs to have a policy on how to deal with this issue, then inform each employee about it. Such an action will help prevent occurrences, as well as give employers guidance on how to act on complaints. *What are the components of an effective sexual harassment policy?*

Source: Robert K. McCalla, "Stopping Sexual Harassment Before It Begins," *Management Review,* April 1991, p. 46.

Sample Sexual Harassment Policy Statement

Sexual harassment of employees or applicants for employment will not be tolerated in this company. Any employee who feels that he or she is a victim of sexual harassment by a supervisor, co-worker, or customer should bring the matter to the immediate attention of (name and title of person). An employee who is uncomfortable for any reason about bringing the matter to the attention of his or her supervisor should report the matter to the human resources department.

Complaints of sexual harassment will receive prompt attention and will be handled in as confidential a manner as possible. Prompt disciplinary action will be taken against persons who engage in sexual harassment.

unacceptable behavior. As women and men work together more and more, this problem of sexual harassment will need to continue to be examined, addressed, and resolved to prevent it from getting worse.[31]

The EEOC reports that the most common type of harassment consists of unwanted sexual teasing, jokes, remarks, and questions.[32] A survey by the AFL-CIO found that among top workplace concerns, 78 percent of women cited sexual harassment. In fact, the only concern expressed more often was regarding economic discrimination: 94 percent rated equal pay for equal work as their top concern.[33]

Sexual harassment is not limited to male supervisors harassing female employees; anyone can become a victim of sexual harassment. In college settings, female professors have been harassed by male students and male professors, as well by female students and colleagues. While fewer reports are filed by men, sexual harassment can occur between people of either—or the same—sex. (See Figure 14.7.)

Stopping Sexual Harassment

Telling the harasser to stop is the best way to make sure the person knows the behavior is *unwanted*. Failing to let the person know the behavior is unwanted makes it more difficult to convince the supervisor or a trial judge that harassment occurred. Keep a dated notebook of occurrences and your responses. Tell a supervisor what is going on. If the harasser *is* your supervisor, report the situation to the next higher manager.

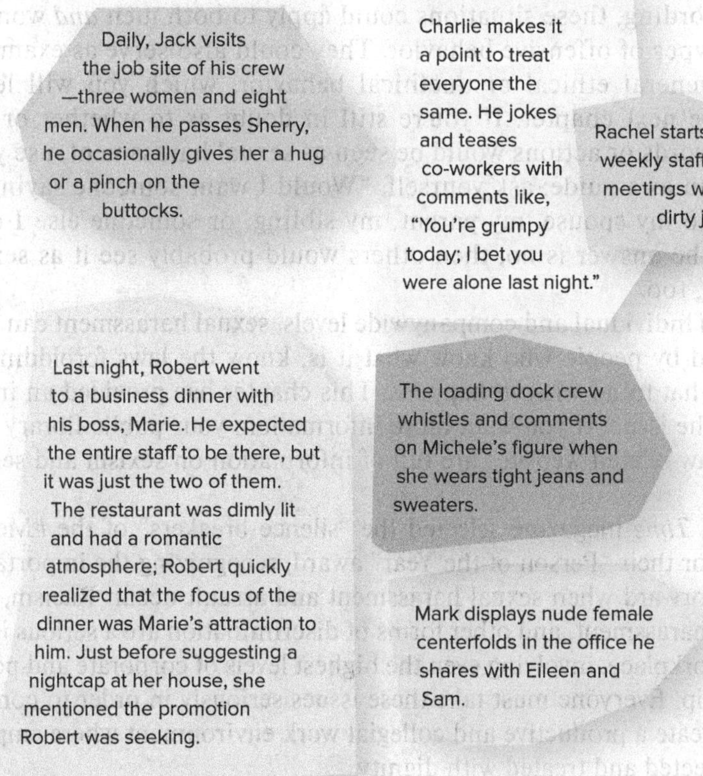

more about...

figure 14.7

IS THIS SEXUAL HARASSMENT?

While reading these instances, make sure that you ask yourself if all of the key elements to sexual harassment are present. *Are any elements missing in any of these?*

Daily, Jack visits the job site of his crew—three women and eight men. When he passes Sherry, he occasionally gives her a hug or a pinch on the buttocks.

Charlie makes it a point to treat everyone the same. He jokes and teases co-workers with comments like, "You're grumpy today; I bet you were alone last night."

Rachel starts weekly staff meetings with a dirty joke.

Last night, Robert went to a business dinner with his boss, Marie. He expected the entire staff to be there, but it was just the two of them. The restaurant was dimly lit and had a romantic atmosphere; Robert quickly realized that the focus of the dinner was Marie's attraction to him. Just before suggesting a nightcap at her house, she mentioned the promotion Robert was seeking.

The loading dock crew whistles and comments on Michele's figure when she wears tight jeans and sweaters.

Mark displays nude female centerfolds in the office he shares with Eileen and Sam.

What can you do as an ordinary employee when someone sexually harasses you? The simplest and most effective method is just to ask or tell the person to stop. According to one survey by the U.S. Merit System Protection Board, this simple tactic worked for 61 percent of the women who tried it. Telling fellow employees about the problem, or threatening to do so, proved in the same study to be second best. This was effective about 55 percent of the time. Just remember that *the worst response is no response:* ignoring the problem and hoping it will go away hardly ever works, and will only cause you a higher level of stress.[34]

Some critics claim that the spotlight on sexual harassment over the past few decades has changed the workplace into a sterile environment. Is this true? Is today's workplace one in which no one feels relaxed, feels free to chat or exchange jokes with co-workers, or can compliment a co-worker? Some people claim so, and report feeling stifled, uncertain, timid, and resentful of the new rules. These claims, though, are usually greatly exaggerated—usually by people resentful of women entering the workforce or of women's rights in general.

Good advice for both men and women is to adopt the new slogan, "Don't Be a Jerk at Work." That is, use common sense: those who are thin-skinned should be less so; those who are obnoxious should stop being so.[35] Follow the commonsense guide in Figure 14.7 to recognize what types of behaviors will lead to sexual harassment complaints. With modified wording, these situations could apply to both men *and* women, and to all types of offensive behavior. They could also serve as examples regarding general ethical or unethical behavior, which you will learn about in the next chapter. If you're still in doubt as to whether or not particular words or actions would be seen as sexual harassment, use your own reaction as a guide: ask yourself, "Would I want someone saying or doing this to my spouse, my parent, my sibling, or someone else I care about?" If the answer is no, then others would probably see it as sexual harassment, too.

On both individual and companywide levels, sexual harassment can best be prevented by people who know what it is, know the laws forbidding it, and know what to do when it happens. This chapter has provided an introduction to the issue. If you want more information, your public library and numerous law-related websites are full of information on sexism and sexual harassment.

In 2017, *Time* magazine selected the "silence breakers" of the #MeToo movement for their "Person of the Year" award, recognizing the importance of coming forward when sexual harassment and assault occur. Racism, sexism, sexual harassment, and other forms of discrimination are a serious issue in today's workplace, involving even the highest levels of corporate and political leadership. Everyone must take these issues seriously in order to combat them and create a productive and collegial work environment where employees are respected and treated with dignity.

» PREJUDICE, DISCRIMINATION, AND SELF-ESTEEM

Recall that positive self-esteem is critical in so many aspects of life, including professional success. And note that we may all harbor certain prejudices. A general observation about *extremely* prejudiced people is that they may suffer from low levels of self-esteem. In contrast, tolerant people may tend to feel more comfortable with who they are and have little trouble accepting the basic humanity of others. As a person's self-esteem improves, prejudices may become shaky and eventually disappear.

What about the victims of discrimination? If you have ever felt prejudice from any person or group, you know just how distressing these feelings are. Unless you are a person with a firmly grounded, high self-esteem level, discrimination can lower your self-esteem temporarily or permanently. Victims of violent hatred have been known to even side with those who oppress them, once their self-esteem has been thoroughly broken down.

In his classic 1954 book *The Nature of Prejudice,* Gordon Allport stated that the effects of being victimized by discrimination fall into two basic categories. The first category is blaming oneself, which can be seen in withdrawal, self-hatred, or aggression against one's own group. The second category is blaming external causes, which is seen in fighting back against the discrimination, becoming suspicious of outsiders, or having increased or exaggerated pride in one's own group.[36] One of the saddest dangers of discrimination is its tendency to become a **self-fulfilling prophecy,** which occurs when a victim believes that prejudice against him or her is deserved and then becomes what the stereotype states. As Allport said, "One's reputation cannot be hammered, hammered, hammered into one's head without doing something to one's character."[37] In other words, a lifetime of discrimination can have devastating effects for individuals and their families.

> **When Prejudice Turns Inward**
>
> **Internalized prejudice** is when a person believes prejudicial remarks and assumptions, and in turn accepts being treated in a discriminatory manner—which may include falling for the self-fulfilling prophecy.

more about...

self-fulfilling prophecy

The tendency for a prediction to actually occur once it is believed; for example, when a victim believes that prejudice against him or her is true, then fulfills these negative expectations.

» LOOKING AHEAD

What can be done to reduce feelings of prejudice and acts of discrimination in the workplace? Consider from what we know about cognitive categorization (introduced earlier in this chapter) that prejudging others seems to be a natural human trait. So when a member of a group acts in a way we expect, our stereotype is confirmed. When the person acts differently from the way we expect, we may decide that he or she is the exception to the rule. These negative ideas are hard to get rid of! Does this mean there is no hope for reducing prejudice and discrimination? The good news is that some negative feelings and behaviors can be permanently eliminated. The bad news is that there is no simple cure.

Although the federal government has taken solid steps to define and forbid discrimination in the workplace, there are still steps you can take individually and in your organization as well. A key ingredient for people to begin to understand and appreciate members of other groups is contact; communication as a result of contact is crucial to understanding others. Employees need the opportunity to interact and communicate with each other, because **proximity** (physical closeness) and exposure to other people generally increase the chance that they will come to better know, understand, and like each other.[38] It will also reduce any tendency to stereotype groups of people; after all, you wouldn't be likely to prejudge the group your best friend and her family belong to.

Contact by itself is not enough. Recall that one of the causes of prejudice and discrimination is unequal status. If this is the case, prejudice will not diminish. Businesses can take steps to hire employees who are frequent targets of discrimination into all levels within the company. So the second necessary ingredient in reducing prejudice and discrimination is ensuring **equal status** for everyone.

A third important ingredient in reducing prejudice and discrimination is *cooperation* instead of competition among members of "different" groups. Psychologists have discovered that when members of different groups not only must cooperate but also must depend on each other to reach common goals—also known as **interdependence**—conflict is greatly reduced. Working together works!

proximity

Physical closeness; here, it refers to contact between members of a diverse workplace.

equal status

The condition that occurs when companies hire employees who are frequent targets of discrimination into all levels within the company.

interdependence

A relationship in which members of different groups not only must cooperate but also must depend on each other to reach common goals.

« STRATEGIES FOR SUCCESS

Strategy 14.1   Assess Your Knowledge

1. True-False Test for Employees
2. True-False Test for Managers

Here are two brief tests you can take that will help you evaluate your own acquaintance (and comfort) with the subject of sexual harassment. The first test is for employees; the second, for managers. You may find it useful to take both tests, whether you are a manager or not.

1. **True–False Test for Employees**

T F   1. If I just ignore unwanted sexual attention, it will usually stop.

T F   2. If I don't mean to sexually harass another employee, there's no way my behavior can be perceived by him or her as sexually harassing.

T F   3. Some employees don't complain about unwanted sexual attention from another employee because they don't want to get that person in trouble.

T F   4. If I make sexual comments to someone and that person doesn't ask me to stop, then I guess my behavior is welcome.

T   F   5.   To avoid sexually harassing a woman who comes to work in a tradition-ally male workplace, the men simply should not try to humiliate her.

T   F   6.   A sexual harasser may be told by a court to pay part of the judgment to the employee he or she harassed.

T   F   7.   A sexually harassed man does not have the same legal rights as a woman who is sexually harassed.

T   F   8.   About 90 percent of all sexual harassment in today's workplace is done by males to females.

T   F   9.   Sexually suggestive pictures or objects in a workplace don't create a liability unless someone complains.

T   F   10. Telling someone to stop his or her unwanted sexual behavior usually doesn't do any good.

Answers: 1—False,   2—False,   3—True,   4—False,   5—False,   6—True,   7—False, 8—True, 9—False, 10—False

2. **True-False Test for Managers**

T   F   1.   Men in male-dominated workplaces usually must change behavior when women work there.

T   F   2.   An employer is not liable for the sexual harassment of one of its employ-ees unless that employee loses specific job benefits or is fired.

T   F   3.   A sexual harasser may have to pay part of a judgment to the employee he or she has harassed.

T   F   4.   A supervisor can be liable for sexual harassment committed by one of his or her employees against another.

T   F   5.   A supervisor can be liable for the sexually harassing behavior of man-agement personnel even if he or she is unaware of that behavior and has a policy forbidding it.

T   F   6.   It is appropriate for a supervisor, when initially receiving a sexual harass-ment complaint, to determine if the alleged recipient overreacted or misunderstood the alleged harasser.

T   F   7.   When a supervisor talks with an employee about an allegation of sexual harassment, it is best to ease into the allegation.

T   F   8.   Sexually suggestive visuals or objects in a workplace don't create a liability unless an employee complains about them and management allows them to remain.

T   F   9.   The lack of sexual harassment complaints is a good indication that sex-ual harassment is not occurring.

T   F   10. It is appropriate for a supervisor to tell an employee to handle unwel-come sexual behavior if the employee is misunderstanding the behavior.

Answers: 1—False,   2—False,   3—True,   4—True,   5—True,   6—False,   7—False, 8—False, 9—False, 10—False.[39]

How do you prevent sexual harassment? Understand that the problem is serious, and that related cases are costing U.S. corporations, governments, and small companies millions of dollars per year.

Strategy 14.2   Reducing Sexual Harassment

1. Write a policy statement.
2. Post the policy statement in a public place.
3. Talk about the policy.

These are the most important steps a manager can take to prevent—or at least to reduce—incidents of sexual harassment in the workplace.

1. **Write a policy statement.** If you are a supervisor or manager, you should have a fairly brief but well-written policy concerning sexual harassment.

2. **Post the policy statement in a public place.** This policy should be printed in fairly large print and posted in central locations where all employees can see it.

3. **Talk about the policy.** Besides writing and posting the policy, refer to the policy in meetings and memos, so it won't become just another poster the boss put up. Hold regular training sessions and workshops to keep communication open, and create a culture where harassment is not tolerated.

If a sexual harassment case from your company gets to court (or even to the attorneys for an out-of-court settlement), a central question will be whether or not your company had a clear, well-defined policy against sexual harassment.[40]

CHAPTER FOURTEEN SUMMARY

Chapter Summary by Learning Objectives

LO 14-1   Describe how human relations are affected when they are part of a diverse society. Diversity in the workplace is increased when people of different races, national origins, religions, and ages—as well as both men and women—work together. Diversity is also found in differing lifestyles and personal attributes. The challenge to human relations is to make this mixture of people an asset, rather than a liability.

LO 14-2   Explain how prejudiced attitudes pose a challenge to human relations. Prejudiced attitudes, nearly always based on stereotypes, interfere with work and cause morale and productivity issues. Prejudiced attitudes have components of thinking, feeling, and doing.

LO 14-3   Identify the origins of prejudice. Prejudice can come from social causes, including those that are media-created, cognitive causes as part of belief systems, and emotional causes including ethnocentrism.

LO 14-4   List types of discrimination. The major types of discrimination in today's world include racism, sexism, religious prejudice, economic prejudice (one of the oldest prejudices in the world), and ageism. Prejudice against others based on sexual and gender orientation, weight, and disabilities are also too common.

LO 14-5 **Define sexual harassment.** Sexual harassment is defined by the Equal Employment Opportunity Commission as "Unwelcome sexual advances, requests for sexual favors, and other verbal or physical conduct of a sexual nature."

LO 14-6 **Describe the connections among prejudice, discrimination, and self-esteem.** Prejudice can be defined as the way one feels as the result of the stereotypes one believes. It can also be seen as the unwillingness to give credibility to others of different backgrounds, and seeing them as inferior. Discrimination is one's behavior based on that person's stereotypes and prejudices. Both prejudice and discrimination are tied in with self-esteem issues involving the perceived self-worth of people, based on the way they are treated by others.

LO 14-7 **Give examples of how to decrease prejudice.** Prejudice can be reduced individually and in the workplace by increasing contact and communication with members of diverse groups, by placing people in equal-status positions, and by encouraging cooperation and interdependence, rather than competition.

key terms

ageism 379
bias 368
cognitive
  categorization 370
discrimination 367
economic
  prejudice 373

Equal Employment
  Opportunity Commission
  (EEOC) 369
equal status 386
ethnocentrism 370
institutional prejudice 368
interdependence 386
prejudice 367

proximity 386
racism 371
scapegoating 370
self-fulfilling
  prophecy 385
sexism 374
sexual harassment 382
stereotypes 367

review questions

1. What are the three components of an attitude? Describe the three components of a prejudiced attitude.

2. What individuals and groups can you think of who are likely targets of prejudice and discrimination? Do you fit into any of these groups that are likely targets? Have you ever found yourself a target of prejudice or discrimination as a member of this group? Explain.

3. Discuss some of the sources of prejudice. Within these sources, can you think of a particular prejudice that you have and how it arose? Explain your personal example.

4. Discuss the negative effects of discrimination in the workplace, both on the individual and on the business organization. Have you seen any discriminatory acts occurring in your workplace? Explain.

5. Describe steps that can be taken in the workplace to reduce or prevent sexual harassment.

6. How is institutional racism or institutional sexism different from open racism or sexism?

7. What is meant by the term *self-fulfilling prophecy?* Think of an example in your life or someone else's where a self-fulfilling prophecy (either positive or negative) arose. Explain your personal example.

8. What are some of the common myths about people with disabilities in the workplace? What is being done to protect employment for this group?

critical thinking questions

1. Under what circumstances is it acceptable to treat co-workers or employees differently because of their differences? Should you be blind to differences between co-workers or employees, or recognize them openly?

2. People today talk a lot about "tolerance." Is there a difference between *tolerance* and *acceptance* of differences, whether they are cultural, gender-related, religious, or other? Explain the differences.

working it out 14.1

IMPRESSION FORMATION: ARE PERCEPTIONS INFLUENCED BY ETHNICITY?

School-to-Work Connection: Interpersonal Skills

Do people hold generalized perceptions of others just because of their ethnicity? This project will help you discover that for yourself.

First, decide on two ethnic groups or nationalities you would like to study (as a class or as an individual project). They may include African Americans, Native Americans, Japanese, French, Italians, Swedes, Costa Ricans, or any other ethnic or national group. Next, each student should approach at least two people and ask them to take part in a study on impression formation. If this is a class project, decide with your classmates what two groups you want to study. Those who agree to participate should be asked to conjure up an image of members of a particular ethnic or national group and then describe their characteristics on the rating scale that follows. Half the participants should be asked to describe a member of the second ethnic or national group chosen for the study. The data collected from all the students will allow you to compare the participant's perceptions as influenced by awareness of a person's ethnicity or nationality.

Part One. The person you have in mind is (ethnic or national group).

Describe this person using the rating scale in the table at the end of these instructions.

1. When you think about people in this group, what is the first thing that comes to mind?
2. What is most characteristic of members of this group?
3. What is most definitely not characteristic of them? (What would be surprising or unexpected to see?)
4. What characteristic do you think most people assign to members of this group?

Part Two. Now do the same for the second person and ethnic or national group. Examine your results. Are you surprised by any of these results? Do you hold certain perceptions about people just by being aware that they belong to a specific group? If so, what can you do about it? How can you reduce your stereotypic beliefs about members of certain ethnic groups?

Part Three. Try this exercise again, substituting male and female for the two ethnic or national groups, or young person and elderly person, or physically able and physically challenged, and so on.

RATING SCALE

Dominant	1	2	3	4	5	6	Submissive
Warm	1	2	3	4	5	6	Cold
Unambitious	1	2	3	4	5	6	Ambitious
Stupid	1	2	3	4	5	6	Smart
Clean	1	2	3	4	5	6	Dirty
Disliked	1	2	3	4	5	6	Liked
Poised	1	2	3	4	5	6	Unpoised
Unaggressive	1	2	3	4	5	6	Aggressive
Insensitive	1	2	3	4	5	6	Sensitive
Active	1	2	3	4	5	6	Passive

Source: Adapted from Ayala Pines and Christina Maslach, *Experiencing Social Psychology: Readings and Projects,* 3rd ed. (New York: McGraw-Hill, Inc., 1993), pp. 203–205.

working it out 14.2

GENDER STEREOTYPES IN THE MEDIA

School-to-Work Connection: Interpersonal Skills

Much of what people learn about men and women comes from the way they are portrayed on television and in movies, online, and in magazines. How are men and women portrayed differently in the media? This is the question you will try to answer in this project.

Pick one type of medium: your favorite online news source, magazine, TV program (a news program, a soap opera, cartoons, music videos, situation comedy, etc.), or radio programs (news format, rock music, sports, etc.). Decide on your research sample gathering (a week, seven issues, ten hours, etc.) and the particular material you are going to observe. Record your results.

1. What was your source (what type of medium)?
2. What were you looking at (advertisements, cartoons, music lyrics, or other)?
3. How did you collect your data (at what times, how often, and so on)? What exactly did you observe (what programs and how many hours, or what magazine and how many issues)?
4. What themes around gender did you discover? Were there any surprises in what you found? Is the media's portrayal of men and women accurate? How powerful are the media's messages on gender?

Source: Adapted from Ayala Pines and Christina Maslach, *Experiencing Social Psychology: Readings and Projects,* 3rd ed. (New York: McGraw-Hill, Inc., 1993), pp. 203–205.

case study 14.1

It's None of Your Business

More than 25 years ago, well after the Civil Rights Act made discrimination in hiring illegal, a professor with a Ph.D. was interviewing for a research job at a university in California. Although many of the questions asked by the interviewer were clearly not allowable, the interviewer persisted. Some of those questions were:

- How old are you?
- Are you married?
- Do you have any children?
- How old are they?
- What type of day-care arrangement do you have?
- What type of backup day-care arrangements have you made?
- Are you planning on having more children?
- What kind of car do you drive?
- Is it reliable?
- How will you get to work if you have car trouble?

Case Study Questions

1. Thinking about the questions, if you were considering hiring someone and wanted to be sure that you were hiring a reliable employee, these are things you might want to know as well. So why can't you ask these questions? What is inherently wrong with wanting to know these things about a potential employee—why is it illegal, when not directly related to job tasks?

2. Using the skills you have learned in previous chapters and the information you have learned in this chapter, what would you have said to this interviewer during the interview, in order to end these personal questions?

3. Let's say the interviewer continued this line of personal questions, even after you said something. The interview ended, and you were not hired. Would you have felt bias had occurred in this hiring? Would you have taken further action? Explain.

case study 14.2

Two Against One

Elena Aguilar-Trujillo was the department director in a medium-sized interior design company. Although the start-up company seemed to be getting new business in all the time, it was still struggling financially, and salaries were low.

Elena supervised eight employees. They all seemed to get along well, with the exception of Julia and Ava, two employees who were very good friends and seemed to form an alliance against the department secretary, Miranda. In fact, they seemed to sabotage and undercut her whenever they could. Elena couldn't understand it. They had all grown up in the same area of the state, were all women, were the same age, and had similar interests. If anything, they should be closer than anyone else.

Events finally came to a head when Miranda asked for six weeks off without pay in order to go on a long sailing trip with her husband in their new boat. "That does it!" exclaimed Julia. "We *have* to get rid of her! She's always prancing around here, showing off her new clothes and jewelry, bragging about all the stuff her husband buys her. I've had it with her!" Then Ava chimed in, "Me too! If we don't fire her, I might just have to go get a job somewhere else!"

Elena was shocked and tried to remember any situations in which Miranda was boastful, but couldn't remember any. Then it dawned on Elena: the real problem these two employees had with the secretary had nothing to do with her work or behavior at all. They were just resentful that their secretary was more financially successful than they were. They were just getting their careers started, but Miranda's husband had his own successful business, and Miranda didn't have to work if she didn't want to.

"Ava and Julia, meet me in my office in 10 minutes," said Elena. "We need to talk."

Case Study Questions

1. What type of prejudice is being illustrated here? What is it based on?

2. If Elena did decide to fire Miranda in order to keep the peace within the department, what legal recourse would Miranda have, if any? Explain.

3. Let's say you have been called in as a mediator to settle this interdepartmental conflict. What steps will you take? What will these steps be based on?

BUSINESS ETHICS AND SOCIAL RESPONSIBILITY

LEARNING OBJECTIVES

After studying this chapter, you will be able to:

LO 15-1   Define ethics.

LO 15-2   Explain the importance of a code of ethics.

LO 15-3   Describe the process of rationalizing unethical behavior.

LO 15-4   Explain ethics in the context of the U.S. workplace.

LO 15-5   Describe the influence of group goals on ethics.

LO 15-6   Give examples of global ethics issues.

LO 15-7   Define social responsibility.

LO 15-8   Describe the process of whistleblowing.

STRATEGIES FOR SUCCESS

Strategy 15.1   Making Ethical Decisions: A Quick Ethics Test from Texas Instruments

Strategy 15.2   Becoming Culturally Aware of Ethical Conduct

In the Workplace: An Unethical Pile-Up

SITUATION

Chloe loved her job running the small business start-up section of a large multinational firm. She had been with the company for three years. During the past year, however, things had begun to change. It had started when the marketing director resigned to go back to college. Chloe's supervisor told her that since there was some overlap in their positions, it would be great if Chloe helped manage the marketing division. Then a half-time research analyst resigned to take a full-time job at another company. Chloe's supervisor told her that since she was really good at understanding data, it would be great if Chloe could take on that job for a while.

When yet another employee in the research department left the company to retire, Chloe was prepared. Her supervisor stopped by her office and began the conversation:

"So I guess you heard J.J. has retired. I think it would be great if . . ."

"Hold on," said Chloe, "if you are going to ask me to take J.J.'s job too, you're going to have to find me an assistant or maybe two, give me a raise, and a new title. I cannot take on another full-time job on top of the extra work you have already given me."

©Somos Images/Alamy Stock Photo

Her supervisor, Chuck, was surprised. "But I thought you loved this company and wanted to help it succeed! Why would you turn down a chance to help us out? Besides, you're so good at what you do, I'm sure this extra work won't be too much of a burden. You're efficient, you can handle it. And don't forget, your job description does say 'other duties as assigned.'"

DISCOVERY

Chloe held firm. "I cannot take on another person's full-time job in addition to my own and the other jobs you have given me. I can't be good at all these jobs when I'm stretched so thin."

Chuck held firm, too. "The company cannot hire extra people right now; you know how the budget looks. If you are refusing a job assignment, then that is insubordination. I will have to write you up, and begin a discipline process."

THINK ABOUT IT

What are Chloe's options now? What would you do if you were in her place? Do you believe an ethical standard has been violated here? Explain.

» WHAT IS ETHICS?

ethics

The expression of the standards of right and wrong based on conduct and morals in a particular society.

morality

A system of conduct that covers all broadly based, mostly unwritten standards of how people should behave and generally conform to cultural ideals of right and wrong.

Ethics refers to the standards of conduct and morals in a particular society; in short, ethics expresses the standards of right and wrong. However, ethics and morality are not identical concepts. **Morality** is how behavior should generally conform to cultural ideals of right and wrong. It represents broadly based, mostly unwritten standards of how people should behave. Ethics is more precise and is often based on written guidelines. Ethics also often addresses deeper issues of fairness, equity, and compromise.[1]

In this chapter, you will examine the complex issue of ethics in the workplace. You will learn about the many ways ethics plays a part in your relationships with others on the job. You will also learn about specific actions that both managers and employees can take to develop stronger ethical conduct on the job.

The practice of business brings many benefits to society. The business world has provided jobs for millions, created a high standard of living, and given many people an opportunity to achieve the dream of business ownership. However, businesses do not always uphold the highest ethical standards. Highly publicized scandals damage the public image of many businesses, and because of the alarming number of scandals in the global financial sector in recent years, a new awakening to the issues of business ethics has emerged. So many new courses in ethics are being taught in high schools and colleges that ethics education has been called "a major growth industry in academia."[2] (See Figure 15.1.)

In addition to being different from morality, ethical standards are also different from *law,* which is another code of conduct. Although both ethical standards and laws are generally agreed upon within specific cultures, laws are different because they are always set down in writing, and descriptions of them are available to the public. Ethics violations are not always punishable, but violating the law carries specific penalties: in other words, laws have *teeth.* In contrast, it is difficult to pin down when ethics violations have occurred and what, if anything, the penalties for such violations should be. This is because although ethics are often in writing, there are usually no written guidelines on how to act when these same ethics are violated. Some organizations have addressed this issue, though, by creating guidelines on punishing and terminating employees who violate established ethical guidelines.

One common public perception is that *business* and *ethics* are terms that can hardly be used in the same sentence. That perception is based on the misunderstanding that profit and morality simply do not mix, and that one can't make money without becoming corrupt.

more about...

Ethical Policies in Organizations

Few professions have strict and enforceable **ethical policies.** The medical profession and the legal profession are two exceptions: both have procedures to discipline members who behave unethically.

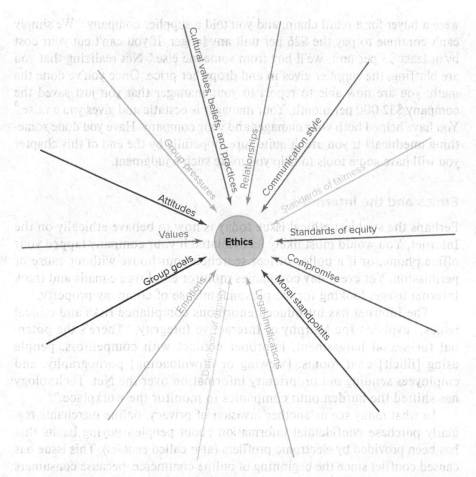

figure 15.1

FACTORS INFLUENCING WORKPLACE ETHICS

Several personal and professional factors influence a person's ethics on the job. Furthermore, personal ethics can be greatly reshaped by the ethical standards already in place at a company, and counteracting forces may simultaneously push a person toward unethical conduct and pull him or her away from it. For instance, a salesperson may be tempted by financial incentives to lie to a customer about services or products, but a fear of getting caught or being punished in some way may change that person's mind. *Do your personal ethics stay the same at your job, or do they change somewhat from home to work? Why?*

The following are other misconceptions that affect people's understanding about ethics:

1. *All ethical problems have simple solutions in which right and wrong are always obvious.* This statement ignores the fact that gray areas exist and that often a great deal of soul-searching might be essential to make a truly ethical decision. These gray areas also sometimes create a need to compromise, which can be misunderstood as indecisiveness to someone expecting a cut-and-dried answer.

2. *Ethics is simply a matter of complying with a set of rules or regulations.* In reality, a legal issue is often not the same as an ethical issue, and vice versa.[3] An example is the legal versus ethical issues seen in a hostile take-over of a corporation. Those in charge of the takeover may be following legal rules and corporate practice, but the overall ethics of their actions might be questionable.

Even the most ethical person should be willing to admit that all of us are sometimes faced with ethical and moral dilemmas. The most ethical course of action isn't always clear-cut and obvious. For example, suppose that you were a buyer for a retail chain, and you told a supplier company, "We simply can't continue to pay the $26 per unit any longer. If you can't cut your cost by at least $3 per unit, we'll buy from someone else." Not realizing that you are bluffing, the supplier gives in and drops her price. Once you've done the math, you are now able to report to your manager that you just saved the company $32,000 per month. Your manager is ecstatic and gives you a raise.[4] You have helped both your manager and your company. Have you done something unethical? If you aren't quite sure, hopefully by the end of this chapter you will have some tools to help you make such a judgment.

Ethics and the Internet

Perhaps the stickiest ethical issue today is how to behave ethically on the Internet. You would most likely feel violated if your company tapped your office phone, or if a police officer searched your house without cause or permission. Yet every day companies monitor employee e-mails and track Internet usage, looking for the personal misuse of company property.

"The Internet has introduced enormous compliance risks and ethical issues," explains Joe Murphy of Interactive Integrity. "There's the potential for sexual harassment, improper contact with competitors, people using [illicit] chat rooms, [viewing or downloading] pornography, and employees sending out proprietary information over the Net. Technology has shifted the burden onto companies to monitor the workplace."[5]

In what many see as another invasion of privacy, online merchants regularly purchase confidential information about people's buying habits that has been provided by electronic profilers (also called *cookies*). This issue has caused conflict since the beginning of online commerce, because consumers often resent having their personal information sold without their consent. Many people also see this as a threat to their privacy. Companies will need to start writing policies and guidelines to address these issues before lawsuits and bad publicity create irreversible damage.

According to Jo Ann Barefoot of KPMG Consulting, "Technology is putting people into terrain where they don't know what the ethics issues are. Regarding customers and privacy issues, the rules, regulations, and laws are going to lag. In the meantime, there is a lot of risk, like costly litigation or bad publicity; and companies should have some guidelines."[6]

Another Internet ethics issue is copyright infringement, where online businesses have been caught using, distributing, and even selling copyrighted materials such as text, images, and music. A lawsuit against an early music file-sharing site, Napster.com, which offered free MP3 downloads of copyrighted music, stopped their distribution of copyrighted materials. However, in the wake of Napster's shutdown, peer-to-peer file sharing, including use of various "bit-torrent" sites and streaming sites, has been much harder to control.

All of these examples illustrate the countless ways in which the Internet challenges the ethics of employees and businesses, creating new debates and asking new questions about ethics.

ETHICS AND TECHNOLOGY

How has widespread use of the Internet created new kinds of ethical dilemmas? What strategies would you suggest for making ethical decisions in Internet-related ethical issues?

©Getty Images

REAL WORLD EXAMPLE 15.1

In March 2013, Internet users across the globe faced an unprecedented slowing of the Internet resulting from the biggest cyber attack in history. Surprisingly, computer systems around the world had slowed or become disabled by collateral damage from the deliberate actions of just one group of hackers set on dismantling the website of The Spamhaus Project, a European spam-fighting group that had blacklisted a major spam-hosting site called CyberBunker. Spamhaus serves as a clearinghouse of information on illegal spamming, and may be responsible for up to 80% of all spam that gets blocked. For its part, CyberBunker maintained that Spamhaus continually overstepped its bounds, and had unfairly targeted its data-storage company in its spam-fighting efforts. As a result of the feud, the cyber attack slowed Internet traffic to a crawl for several days. This event raised a number of alarming ethics questions, including: Is it ethical to send spam? And what are the ethics of slowing or disabling the entire Internet in order to attack your business rival and make your point? While many serious and damaging cyber attacks have happened since then, the later attacks were clearly illegal, while the Spamhaus/CyberBunker incident focused on ethics.

» CODES OF ETHICS

If ethical issues aren't the same as moral or legal issues, how can you judge them? Some companies have developed specific **ethical codes** that are accepted and abided by in all levels of the firm.

Texas Instruments (TI) has published a manual for managers called *Ethics in the Business of TI*. The company's philosophy of business, contained in this booklet, is that ". . . good ethics and good business are synonymous when viewed from moral, legal, and practical standpoints."[7] The entire book sets forth ethical guidelines for nearly every area of business the company could be involved in. It even covers some common gray areas such as political contributions, conflicts of interest, and corporate spying. Texas Instruments has over 30,000 employees in more than 30 countries. Their code of ethics also includes information on ethics guidelines for employees in the global market.

Texas Instruments and the TI Ethics Office are well known as active leaders among ethics professionals. In addition, TI has received several awards from the business community for excellence in business ethics. However, as an individual in the average workplace, one that does not provide such well-known guidelines, how do you know whether you are on the right track regarding your ethical decisions? The ethics test in Strategy for Success 15.1 at the end of this chapter, which was developed by Texas Instruments, can be helpful.

Codes of ethics like that of Texas Instruments are usually based on one of the following ethical approaches: *principles of justice, individual rights,*

ethical codes

Formalized sets of ethical guidelines developed by some companies for use at all levels of an organization.

Another Well-Known Ethical Code

Johnson & Johnson has published a well-known ethical code directed to their consumers, employees, communities, and stockholders. This multinational medical and pharmaceutical manufacturing company is more than 130 years old and employs more than 127,000 people today. Link to https://www.jnj.com/about-jnj/jnj-credo to read their full credo.

more about...

principle of justice

An ethical philosophy that holds that all decisions should be consistent, unbiased, and based on fact.

principle of individual rights

An ethical philosophy that holds that all decisions should respect basic human rights and the dignity of the individual.

principle of utilitarianism

An ethical philosophy that holds that all decisions should do the greatest good for the largest number of people.

principle of individualism

An ethical philosophy that holds that all primary goals should achieve long-term self-interests, with the emphasis on long-term; self-interest should not justify short-sighted actions.

categorical imperative

A principle developed by philosopher Immanuel Kant, which asks the question, "What would the world—or my company—be like if everyone were to do this?"

utilitarianism, individualism, or the *categorical imperative.*[8] These are the most common ethical philosophies, and they can be summarized as follows:

1. The **principle of justice** focuses on making sure that all decisions are consistent, unbiased, and based on fact. For example, a manager using this principle would want to be certain that he or she had all of the facts in a given case before making a decision. The judicial systems of most countries are based on the principle of justice, including that of the United States.

2. The **principle of individual rights** focuses on basic human rights and the dignity of the individual. Using this principle, a manager would never expect an employee to act in a way that would deny the employee's religious beliefs. Someone adhering to this principle would refuse to steal from anyone simply because such an action would reduce the *dignity* of the victim.

3. The **principle of utilitarianism** means making decisions that promise to do the greatest good for the largest number of people.[9] Using utilitarianism, a manager would lay off 50 employees now to provide several hundred new jobs in the future. Someone who lives by this principle would have little problem sacrificing hundreds of soldiers in a war effort to help the overall good of the country, especially if the country were populated with tens of millions of citizens.

4. The **principle of individualism** holds that a person's primary goal is to achieve long-term self-interests, with the emphasis on *long-term;* self-interest would not justify shortsighted actions.[10] Under this principle, a corporate director would not engage in price-fixing. Although

STAYING ETHICAL ON THE JOB

Some jobs present strong temptations to be unethical, such as by cheating customers. An employee must avoid unethical shortcuts. *How have you responded to pressures to behave unethically on the job?*

©James Lauritz/Getty Images

profitable in the short term, this would hurt the company in the long run. Notice that most people who adhere to the principle of individualism would likely seem as honest, ethical, and unselfish as anyone else.

5. The **categorical imperative** is an ethical principle that results from the question, *What would the world—or my company—be like if everyone were to do this?* This ethical idea was developed years ago by philosopher Immanuel Kant.[11] Think of yourself as the ruler of a country who could legislate the ethical choice you are thinking about into a national law. Would that law be fair? Would it be one you would like and respect?[12] What would be its far-reaching effects? A person following the categorical imperative would keep himself or herself from committing a crime by visualizing a world (or even a neighborhood) where everyone commits that same crime regularly. The individual would ask, "Would that be a world, or neighborhood, in which I would want to live?"

Does one of the principles listed above—justice, individual rights, utilitarianism, individualism, or the categorical imperative—seem the most appropriate to you? Additional principles are listed in Figure 15.2. Some choices are better and more popular than others. Which choice or combination of choices seems most appropriate to your values? Which choices are the most useful for the workplace?

more about...

"Don't Be Evil"

The ethical credo for Alphabet, the parent company for Google, is summarized very simply: Don't be evil. To explain, the preface of their longer document begins with:

"'Don't be evil.' Googlers generally apply those words to how we serve our users. But 'Don't be evil' is much more than that. Yes, it's about providing our users unbiased access to information, focusing on their needs and giving them the best products and services that we can. But it's also about doing the right thing more generally—following the law, acting honorably, and treating co-workers with courtesy and respect."

The ending sentence of Alphabet's ethical credo sums up the full credo with: "And remember . . . don't be evil, and if you see something that you think isn't right—speak up!"

Alphabet, Inc., Google Code of Conduct, https://abc .xyz/investor/other/google-code-of-conduct.html last updated April 28, 2017 (retrieved June 20, 2017).

figure 15.2

What Does Ethical Mean?
Possible answers include:
• What most people around me consider appropriate behavior.
• Whatever reflects the Golden Rule.
• Whatever is not against the law.
• What my feelings tell me to do.
• Whatever is in line with my religious beliefs.
• Whatever is customary in my society.
• Whatever would be approved of by a neutral panel of people in my line of work.
• Whatever doesn't hurt other people.
• What does the most good for the most people.

WHAT IS YOUR DEFINITION OF ETHICAL?
Ethics can be hard to define because many people's personal ethics are summed up by their feelings and gut instinct, which are hard to quantify. Also, answers like "What my feelings tell me to do" may be acceptable for an ethical person, but completely unacceptable for someone with little or no ethical concerns. *What is your definition of the word ethical?*

REAL WORLD EXAMPLE 15.2

Luis, a maintenance manager, offers a day off with pay to his employee Monica to thank Monica for not reporting an accident on the job. Luis tells himself that he never *saw* any written code saying that this was not allowed—but he never looked for one, either.

» RATIONALIZING UNETHICAL BEHAVIOR

rationalize

To justify unethical behavior with excuses.

Even people with a good knowledge of ethical principles can fall prey to the temptation to **rationalize** unethical behavior. Management expert Saul Gellerman warns that unethical behavior in the workplace often starts with one or more of four basic rationalizations:[13]

1. A belief that the unethical behavior is within ethical and legal limits—because it is more convenient to believe that it is.

2. A belief that because the chosen behavior will work for the best interest of either the individual or the company, the company would *expect* that it be carried out.

3. A belief that nobody will notice. The theft of a few cents from each depositor at a savings bank, for example, would most likely go unnoticed—or would it? Several cases are on record of just such a crime being discovered and prosecuted—even when the theft per depositor was as small as *a fraction of a penny per month.*

4. A belief that because the chosen behavior helps the company, the company will go along with it and protect the person if he or she is caught.

more about...

Rationalizing

Rationalizing is a term that means finding an excuse for behavior that causes embarrassment, shame, anxiety, or pain. It is one of the defense mechanisms described by the late psychoanalyst Sigmund Freud.

Whenever you are expected to make a work-related decision, be aware of these four rationalizations. When you are justifying a decision that seems unethical, ask yourself whether you are being honest with yourself in your rationalizing. Since rationalization is often done without conscious thought, you must be alert to the use of this mental manipulation of the facts.[14]

As with almost all of the topics presented in this book, self-esteem plays a part in this discussion. People with high self-esteem are more likely to feel good about themselves, which allows them to not seek the short-term gains of unethical behavior and not engage in rationalization to justify it. People with high self-esteem are also more likely to feel a healthy connection with others around them, and so are more likely to act in a socially responsible way.

REAL WORLD EXAMPLE 15.3

At Matco Plastics, the head of the production department is being promoted to vice president. Hoping to be her replacement, the eight supervisors employed under her spend the three months before she leaves both massaging the boss and undercutting one another. They now work in an environment that is negative for all of them.

» ETHICS IN CONTEXT

In Chapter 3, you learned about the importance of using self-disclosure and being honest in your relationships with others. This can become an ethical issue when people act insincerely in their relationships with other people in order to achieve their own ends. Loss of trust is the result, and, as you learned in Chapter 1, trust is the basic element of relationships.[15] Politics exists in any company, and gaining political power isn't in itself an unethical behavior. However, when people compromise their own integrity to succeed at getting ahead in the company, an important ethical line has been crossed.

In the United States there is a widespread belief that if you are agreeable and easy to get along with, your job will remain secure. The idea seems to be that, although unpleasant and dishonest, the practice of "sucking up," "kissing up," or **boss massaging**, is a necessary price one must pay for success. Most people do not judge those who play this game because it is so common.[16] Many times, this game includes competition among co-workers.

The employee wishing to rise above this disharmony can have trouble remaining detached from it. If you find yourself in such a position, remember that *no one can force you to act unethically.*

If you are the boss who is being massaged, an honest look at the power realities should show that you are free to take many actions to discourage such behavior. Be a manager who makes it clear that your employees' performance is based on merit, and be consistent in the application of that philosophy.

boss massaging

The practice of currying favor, or kissing up, with a manager to achieve your own goals.

» THE INFLUENCE OF GROUP GOALS

The biblical story of the Good Samaritan tells of a Samaritan in ancient times who came upon a man who had been beaten and robbed by criminals. Though a stranger, the unnamed Samaritan bandaged the victim's wounds and paid for food and lodging until the man had healed.[17] This parable has served for centuries as an example of how an individual should act when finding a helpless person in great need. However, often, the exact opposite occurs: when encountering someone in need, many people look the other way because other people's goals or a group's pressures override the need. This creates an ethical conflict: even when people have learned helping behavior in their families and communities, they sometimes find themselves unable

REAL WORLD EXAMPLE 15.4

Tina will retire in a few months. The company wants to hire an internal replacement. Josh and Denise both report to Tina, they are the only internal candidates, and they both want the position. Josh begins to spend a lot of time helping people in the division finish their work, taking people to lunch, and especially, volunteering for anything Tina needs to have done. Denise spends her time working hard on her own projects, and expects to be judged on her own merits. She feels that Josh is acting unfairly to gain an advantage. When she calls him on it, he acts surprised and says he thought they both just wanted the same thing: for the company to be successful. Tina tells others that Josh is really "stepping up" and should get the position. *Is anything unethical going on? Would you be more like Josh, or like Denise, in this scenario? Why?*

to transfer those behaviors to the workplace. Research by social scientists shows that many people change their ethical standards between home and work. Researchers discovered that two-thirds of the respondents in a survey of 200 marketing managers used different sets of moral decision-making standards at home and work.[18]

Perhaps someday you will work for a company that encourages you to leave your ethics at the door when you come to work. Such companies do exist; however, the perception that management wants you to behave unethically is often more imagined than real. Make sure that you are interpreting your company and its management fairly, and that you do not assume that unethical actions are required of you that actually are not.[19]

Whatever the company attitude, everyone who works for a company should closely examine how his or her personal ethics fit into the ethics of the firm. If compromise is necessary to continue as an employee, make sure that the compromise does not force you into areas of ethical choice where you would be opposing your own values. Few situations cause more stress than compromises with your own conscience.

WORKING IN THE GLOBAL MARKET

Even everyday events such as buying dinner can be very different in other countries, and American businesspeople who want to succeed internationally have to be flexible and open-minded to such differences. *How might a different cultural situation cause problems for someone used to American ethics?*

©SetsukoN/Getty Images

» GLOBAL ETHICS ISSUES

As trade expands, people need to recognize differing ethical views among the nations of the world and acknowledge these differences with an attitude of acceptance. American values, beliefs, and practices are not the only ones in this world. American values have their roots in the ancient cultures of Greece and Rome, as well as that of the British Empire. Judeo-Christian religious influences have also been a large factor, as are the U.S. Constitution and Bill of Rights. Other nations have value systems that may come from very different—though equally valid—sources.[20]

REAL WORLD EXAMPLE 15.5

Mara, an electronics engineer in a computer company, stole an innovative idea for software from a competing company. She assumed that she would be expected to take any steps that could help the company compete in the software market. After all, her manager, her department, and the whole company would benefit. Instead, she was reprimanded.

A Historical Perspective

The values and customs of other countries are not inferior, primitive, or degraded. They have different origins, evolutions, and applications through history. They are based on differing histories and cultural memories. Practices that might seem unethical to Americans often have cultural histories that go back thousands of years. (See Figure 15.3.)

Take a look at the acceptance of bribery and kickbacks as an example of the differences among countries and cultures. Most governments have laws concerning bribes and payoffs. Any law, however, is only as effective as its enforcement. In some countries in Africa and other parts of the world, age-old traditions that *require* payoffs are rooted in a communal heritage, and an entire tribe or village benefits from such payoffs. If the community is the enforcer of law, one can easily see why tradition would overcome any written law in most cases.

If you do business with foreign companies, especially in developing countries, you need to understand three concepts, discussed in the following sections, that seem to be widely believed and practiced.[21]

The Inner Circle

Most communal societies make a strong distinction between insiders and outsiders. Those who are in the **inner circle** are, depending on the culture, family members, tribal members, or trusted friends. In China an inner circle might include people who speak the same dialect. In India members of an inner circle would likely be from the same historical caste or social class. In many cases, a skillful American or other Westerner can become sufficiently trusted to break into the inner circle, but such acceptance can require

inner circle

A clique of trusted family members, tribal members, or friends (depending on the culture) who are at the center of power or influence.

figure 15.3

ETHICAL STANDARDS

Although many basic ethical standards are practiced throughout humanity, their application varies from culture to culture. What is considered politeness, hospitality, and punctuality can vary greatly, even within regions of the same country. *Which of these propositions do you agree with most?*

Source: Adapted from Gene R. Lacznick and Jacob Naor, "Global Ethics: Wrestling with the Corporate Conscience," *Business,* Summer 1985, pp. 8–9.

Ethical Propositions for the Global Business Climate

- There are diverse standards of ethical behavior around the world.
- Enforcement of law, not existence of law, often determines behavior.
- You cannot be too ethical.
- Multinational corporations have high ethical responsibility and accountability.
- The likelihood of ethical misjudgments is relatively high.
- A country's concern with ethics increases with its economic well-being.

REAL WORLD EXAMPLE 15.6

By paying a cash bribe and gaining a million-dollar customer, sales manager Ron thought that even if he were caught, the company would thank him for landing the account. Instead, he was fired for this unethical behavior that resulted in leaving the company legally vulnerable and damaging its reputation as a company with integrity.

great skill and patience. The possibility of unjust treatment toward outsiders is always a consideration, and outsiders should watch carefully for this. In some inner circles, fairness and kindness to those outside the circle are not considered to be necessary.

Future Favors

future favors

A practice commonly seen in developing countries based upon mutual obligation and resulting in the exchange of favors over years and even generations; also used in some industrialized countries such as Japan and South Korea.

Within these inner circles, one will find the assumption of **future favors**. Traditional Japanese call it *inner duty;* in Kenya, it is known as *inner relationship,* and for traditional Filipinos is it known as *inner debt.* The practice can be found in nearly any culture that respects the inner circle concept. It translates into *I owe you; I pay you off. Now you owe me.* The trading back of favors can go on for years, even generations. When a typical American says, "I owe you one," the seriousness with which such an expression is both meant and understood is much less than in most developing countries.

Gift Exchange

gift exchange

A strong tradition in many cultures, in which giving gifts creates a future obligation to the receiver; it can also be a rite of passage into an inner circle.

Americans who witness a **gift exchange** in another country may suspect bribery, but such an accusation would horrify most people who practice this custom. In some cultures, this tradition of exchanging gifts goes back to ancient times. In today's global marketplace, the tradition often becomes a standard tool of business. Although gift exchange does exist in the Western world, the sense of obligation related to it (based on future favors) is not nearly as strong. This tradition is related to the concept of the inner circle, too, as the gift exchange is often the rite of passage into that circle.

≫ SOCIAL RESPONSIBILITY

Social responsibility

The practice of acting ethically while understanding your actions are part of the larger, interactive picture of your workplace, community, and world.

Social responsibility means putting ethical standards to work in all areas of the global community in which you live. Being socially responsible is acting ethically while understanding that your actions are part of the larger, interactive picture of the workplace, the community, and the world. Social responsibility includes acting ethically with customers, co-workers, suppliers, competitors, and the community in which you live.

REAL WORLD EXAMPLE 15.7

Harley-Davidson Company has an ethical code based on the company's definition of "healthy working relationships." It contains five points: being truthful, practicing fairness, keeping promises, respecting others, and encouraging intellectual curiosity.[22] The company also has a 12-point philosophy of "financial ethics" that all employees and managers have to read and sign.[23]

What types of social responsibilities does a typical workplace have? Every workplace has an obligation to make choices or decisions about issues such as environmental pollution, discrimination, employee safety and health, dishonesty, and community commitments such as volunteerism. The growing awareness over the past few decades of such obligations has prompted many companies to become more socially responsible. (See Figure 15.4.)

One of the difficulties in deciding whether or not a company is socially responsible is that there is disagreement about just *whom* the company should be responsible *to*. Three views of social responsibility that are commonly accepted are traditional (or classical), stakeholder (or accountability), and affirmative (or public) social responsibility.[24]

1. *Traditional social responsibility* says that a company or organization is responsible only to itself and to making a profit. In this view, the government and general public, not companies, are responsible for solving social problems. In an organization, though, any decision that does not directly benefit shareholders is considered irresponsible. This view of social responsibility is based mostly on materialistic ideals that emerged with the Industrial Revolution in the late 1880s when large corporations were first formed. Today it is still practiced worldwide but is often criticized as selfish and destructive.

2. *Stakeholder social responsibility* holds that companies are responsible to **stakeholders**—that is, to any group they interact with as a business. In this view, a company is responsible not just to make a profit, but also to answer to customers, competitors, unions, suppliers, consumer groups, government agencies, and so on. This view emerged in the 1930s during the Great Depression, when views on employee rights and human relations underwent significant progress. This perspective goes beyond what is good for the company and commits a company to having ethical responsibilities.

3. *Affirmative (or public) social responsibility* is the most broadly based of the three perspectives. In this view, companies are not just responsible to their profit margin and their stakeholders, but they are also responsible to the general public and society at large. Companies in this view would

ETHICAL OR PERSONAL CONFLICT?

Sometimes in intercultural business settings, you will be asked to agree to things that make you feel ethically uncomfortable. You need to determine if these requests reflect genuine cultural traditions of the people with which you are working, or if an ethical conflict is occurring. *How can you determine whether a situation is truly unethical, or if it is just your personal discomfort with the issue?*

©alvarez/Vetta/Getty Images

stakeholders

Any group that a business interacts with, such as customers, competitors, unions, suppliers, consumer groups, and government agencies.

REAL WORLD EXAMPLE 15.8

The rapidly growing trade relationship with China has already taught other countries some hard lessons on differing attitudes about what is ethical. Marketers at Toyota discovered the Chinese proverb that says "When you get to the foot of the mountain, a road will appear." The Japanese company decided to use a clever spin-off from that proverb: "Wherever there is a road, there is a Toyota." Most of us would admit that the statement isn't literally true, but most other cultures—including the United States—are used to that sort of come-on to get the customer's attention. Not the Chinese. Chinese government authorities saw the slogan as highly unethical and accused Toyota of false advertising.[25]

be expected to avoid creating social problems such as pollution and poverty, and to work toward goals that improve conditions for everyone. This view came about in the 1960s, when social unrest escalated and disapproval of business practices became more publicized. It is based most heavily on ethical principles, in particular those of moral rights, justice, and the categorical imperative.

figure 15.4

COMPANIES THAT CARE

Thousands of companies give back to their communities in different ways every year. The key to effective social responsibility is to consider the entire community when business decisions are made, and to give back things that the community wants and will appreciate. *What is your favorite example of corporate social responsibility? (It doesn't have to be from this list.)*

Source: www.starbucks.com /aboutus/csr.asp; www .att.com/about/community/; www.gapinc.com/public/ SocialResponsibility/socialres .shtml; www.levistrauss.com/ responsibility/; www.benjerry .com; wwwmerrillynch.com /index.asp?id7695_8149 _8688_8170.

Here are just a few of the thousands of examples of corporate social responsibility:

Starbucks, the Seattle-based coffee company, has been working to improve local communities since 1997, when it launched a literacy program. Today, the company provides matching grants to help nonprofit agencies, to improve youth job skills training, and to provide clean water access to people in developing countries.

AT&T has developed technology that reduces pollution and shares this technology with other companies.

GAP, Inc. (which also includes Old Navy, Intermix, Athleta, and Banana Republic) works to improve factory conditions worldwide, to help provide access to clean water, and to meet sustainability goals in manufacturing sites. They also support job training in local communities, and provide incentives for their employees to volunteer for local area efforts.

Levi-Strauss, one of the world's largest clothing companies and a global employer, donates millions of dollars and incentivizes employee volunteer efforts to improve living conditions for refugees, to reduce stigma to members of the LGBT community, and to help reduce climate degradation and provide clean water access.

Ben and Jerry's Homemade, Inc., though taken over by corporate giant Unilever, has remained socially responsible. In 2004, the company supported research on sustainable dairy farming practices and on new eco-friendly refrigeration technology that could have great environmental impact in the future. Their mantra "business has a responsibility to the community and environment" has not changed as they continue to support local and global communities, and their own employees, in efforts to be socially responsible.

Bank of America Merrill Lynch launched has made a $2 billion pledge to support charities that address critical issues, including education and employability, cultural understanding, and environmental sustainability. They support and provide incentives for employees to volunteer for local efforts.

REAL WORLD EXAMPLE 15.9

The administrative board of a nonprofit organization started a mentoring program for at-risk children in a semi-rural community. Shortly afterward, another organization opened an after-school program for at-risk children. These two organizations had the same goals and served similar populations, and so began competing for grants and contributions from the same sources. Hard feelings and conflict arose until both organizations were able to secure enough funding to continue without financial worries. Might there have been a more optimal path for the two nonprofits?

A Few Cautions About Social Responsibility

Just as there are many difficult questions regarding ethics, there are also many difficult questions regarding social responsibility. For example, what happens when a company can no longer afford to support charities or organizations that have become dependent on them? A move to protect the company's economic health by cutting charitable funding may seem selfish to outside observers.

How does a company choose to support specific organizations while not helping others? Choosing among equally important organizations can create hard feelings among nonprofit organizations or charities, although this may not be obvious to corporate donors.

Companies or individuals may also find that their acts of social responsibility are misunderstood and resented by the community. As well, differences in political views among the general public mean that some corporate social responsibility activities are seen as desirable and valuable by some people, while being viewed as undesirable and inappropriate by others.

These examples are not meant to discourage you from becoming socially responsible. They are only meant to show you that social responsibility—just like the larger issue of ethics in general—often contains a lot of gray areas and difficult choices.

❯❯ BLOWING THE WHISTLE

What do you do when you have found unethical conduct taking place in your company? Most strategies involve **whistleblowing**—turning in the offending person or people and exposing the truth.

more about...

Social responsibility is also demonstrated at the individual level. People who volunteer for coastal clean-up activities, recycling centers, adopt-a-highway programs, child mentoring activities, hospice care facilities, and so on are acting in a socially responsible manner.

more about...

Corporate Social Responsibility

Forbes magazine reported findings from a survey conducted in 2017 by Reputation Institute, a global company based in New York. About 47,000 people participated in the survey across 15 markets to name the corporations they believe to have the best reputations for international corporate social responsibility. Here are the top 10:

1. Microsoft
2. Google
3. The Walt Disney Company
4. BMW (British Motor Works)
5. Apple
6. Daimler (Mercedes Benz)
7. Volkswagen
8. Sony
9. Colgate-Palmolive
10. LEGO Group

Forbes, "The Top 10 Companies with the Best Corporate Social Responsibility Reputation," https://www.forbes.com/pictures/efkk45mmlm/the-10-companies-with-the-best-csr-reputations/#11c7a0cc6626 (retrieved June 20, 2017).

whistleblowing

Turning in or otherwise exposing people who behave unethically in your company.

REAL WORLD EXAMPLE 15.10

Several years ago, a small-town physician announced publicly that he would offer an incentive of $40 a month to all the teenagers in his community who did *not* get pregnant while in high school. This offer on his part was meant to help curb the spiraling rate of pregnancies among young teens in his particular community. His offer was subsequently interpreted by some members of his community as promoting contraception with a pro-abortion hidden agenda. He became the target of criticism and controversy.

more about...

Protection for Whistleblowers

The Government Accountability Project was established in 1977 to help employees who blow the whistle on unethical corporate practices. They provide legal help and advocacy for such employees.

THE NEED FOR WHISTLEBLOWING

When companies behave unethically, the answer might be to "blow the whistle." Companies such as this can cause severe environmental or financial damage that affects human health and lives. *What are the possible costs of not blowing the whistle on unethical corporate behavior?*

©ColorBlind Images/Blend Images

EXECUTIVE OFFICES

The first law passed to protect whistleblowers was the Lloyd–La Follette Act of 1912, which protected federal employees who gave information to Congress.[26] Wider protection for those who blow the whistle on dangerous, fraudulent, or unethical practices in their workplace has been in existence since the 1970s. Although free speech rights are guaranteed under the First and Fourteenth Amendments to the Constitution, retaliation against whistleblowers was so widespread that enacting specific laws became necessary. The Whistleblower Protection Act was passed in 1989 and strengthened in 1994. In addition to federal laws, many individual states also have their own whistleblower protection laws. Nevertheless, the Government Accountability Project states that "Every year, thousands of Americans witness wrongdoing on the job . . . [that] may jeopardize the health, safety, or lives of others . . . [and] most employees remain silent in the face of such misconduct" for various reasons, such as fears of retaliation and the belief that there is nothing they can do to stop the misconduct.[27]

In 2006, the U.S. Supreme Court ruled against whistleblowers when the court voted *not* to protect government employees from retaliation after they have blown the whistle on employers. In May 2007, the first "Whistleblowers Week" event was held in Washington, D.C., to encourage the U.S. Congress to pass stronger protective laws for whistleblowers in both the private sector and the government. The Whistleblower Protection Enhancement Act of 2007 was introduced into Congress but wasn't signed into law for another five years until November 2012, likely due to the complexity of the issue of whistleblowing.

Some of the strategies available to the person who faces the moral choices of the whistleblower include:

- Secretly threatening the offender with blowing the whistle unless the unethical action is stopped or corrected.
- Anonymously blowing the whistle within the company, keeping your identity a secret.

REAL WORLD EXAMPLE 15.11

In 1997, at the Hanford nuclear plant in Richland, Washington, seven pipefitters became vocally concerned about tank farm pipes that didn't meet safety standards. These "tank farms" hold millions of gallons of nuclear waste and had been leaking into the surrounding community. When asked to attach a valve to the system that they felt was unsafe, they refused. All seven were fired. Two months later, by court order, they were all rehired. However, in 1998 five of the seven were fired again. Years of legal struggling went by. Finally, in 2005, they had their day in court, along with four others who became involved later, and won the lawsuit. A Department of Energy contractor was ordered to pay damages.[29] The 11 have sworn that they blew the whistle only because they were afraid of potential physical harm to themselves and the rest of the community.[30] The federal government has since taken the Hanford danger seriously, by authorizing the Government Accountability Project in early 2008 to set up a nonprofit organization, Hanford Challenge, to oversee cleanup of the site. By 2013, the Department of Energy, which oversees Hanford (regarded as the nation's most contaminated nuclear site), confirmed that eight tanks have been leaking an estimated 1,150–1,300 gallons of toxic, radioactive waste a year, and that an additional 14 more tanks may also be leaking nuclear waste into the ground.

- Secretly threatening a responsible manager that you will blow the whistle outside of the company unless a change is made in the conduct.
- Sabotaging the results of the unethical behavior in some way.
- Publicly blowing the whistle within the organization.
- Quietly refusing to carry out an unethical plan.
- Secretly or publicly blowing the whistle outside of the company.[28]

For reasons that remain unclear, people have traditionally looked down on the person who "tells on" someone else, especially in some areas of life. In grade school, for example, being a tattletale is not respected. As adults, most people don't like busybodies who seem to be prying into other people's business. For these reasons and others, even many otherwise moral and ethical people are afraid of blowing the whistle. After all, one's job might be at risk, or the whistleblower might be excluded from the informal work group. Other, less rational fears include losing one's nerve at the last minute, not having the courage to follow through once the accusations have been made, or worrying that the purity of one's intentions might be mistaken for backstabbing.

These types of fear are not unfounded. "There is very little protection in industry for employees

Hacktivism

"Hacktivism" (hack + activism) is a newer form of whistleblowing that uses computers and computer networks to promote political rights, free speech, human rights, and freedom of information ethics. Considering their actions a form of civil disobedience, hacktivists have targeted foreign governments with spotty human rights records, religious organizations, multinational corporations, and even the United States government. In a notable case of "hacktivism," Army soldier Bradley Manning allegedly provided whistleblowing website WikiLeaks with sensitive U.S. military data that has embroiled the soldier and the founder of WikiLeaks Julian Assange in scandal for years. In another example, the hacktivist group called Anonymous has brought attention to global issues in several hacktivist acts. Dozens of hacktivist acts have caught international attention in recent years, and more are sure to come.

more about...

REAL WORLD EXAMPLE 15.12

Sonia is the president of a mid-sized firm. When one of her friends, William, asked her about an open vice-president position, she encouraged him to apply. The company had strict rules about hiring in order to prevent nepotism or other ethical dilemmas: a screening committee would send forward finalists for Sonia to interview, and she would select the final candidate from among those sent up from the committee. In this case, Sonia's friend William did not make the semi-finalist list. She directed the committee to keep sending more semi-finalists, until William's name appeared. Then she hired him.

Was this a breach of ethics? If you agree that it was, what would you do? Would you be a whistleblower?

who object to carrying out immoral, unethical, or illegal orders from their superiors," says David Ewing, former executive editor of the *Harvard Business Review.* "If the employee doesn't like what he or she is asked to do, the remedy is to pack up and leave. This remedy seems to presuppose an ideal economy, where there is another company down the street with openings for jobs just like the one the employee left."[31]

The list on the previous pages (the list breaks across 2 pages) includes some of the more secretive choices available to a potential whistleblower. The reason some of the more secretive of these choices might be necessary is that many companies punish whistleblowers in various ways for their honesty.[32] A new movement encourages whistleblowing in a few U.S. companies by providing rewards. Such a system, though, may only create distrust among employees if it leads to increased spying.

The best solution is the kind of leadership that makes whistleblowing unnecessary. The ethical tone of an organization nearly always originates in top management and moves downward. Thus, top management is in an ideal position to create an ethical environment for everyone who works in the company.

Several years ago a marketing company in Boston (which was a subsidiary of a larger firm in Los Angeles) was run by a group of young managers who always bragged about how they were "fooling the big shots in California." When these managers discovered that many of their own salespeople were faking their appointment schedules during training, they were surprised. However, they should have known that their unethical attitude would set the tone for their employees.

Management can also create low ethical standards by any of the following managerial mistakes:

- Favoritism occurs when one employee is given extra privileges and allowances. This creates resentment among other employees and the impression that they, too, are entitled to these same extra privileges—even if they are unethical.

- "Fudging" with the expense budget is a managerial mistake. Managers who allow employees to use company expense budgets for items of

Business Ethics and Social Responsibility   «   CHAPTER 15   **415**

doubtful use to the company, or for obvious personal use, are allowing unethical treatment and encouraging it to continue. Managers should also be careful not to do the same, thus setting a bad example. This behavior may also be illegal, setting employees and their managers up for possible legal ramifications.

- Lying to or otherwise manipulating other departments or offices within one's company creates an atmosphere of distrust, which erodes team spirit.

Most people will face ethical dilemmas during their lives. Knowing one's own values and standards (as covered in Chapter 4) is essential; but some situations, such as the one about the unethical treatment of an experienced employee in this chapter's opening story, are still difficult to navigate. There are no easy answers to offer here. Hopefully, though, you now have a heightened awareness of the issues surrounding ethics in the workplace after studying this chapter.

STRATEGIES FOR SUCCESS

Strategy 15.1   **Making Ethical Decisions: A Quick Ethics Test from Texas Instruments**

1. Is it legal?
2. Is it consistent with the company's stated values?
3. If you do it, will you feel bad?
4. How would it look in the newspapers?
5. Do you think it's wrong?
6. If you're not sure—ask.
7. If you don't get a clear answer, keep asking until you do.

Texas Instruments, a giant manufacturer of electronics and computer chips, teaches its employees to run through these seven steps whenever they have a question about whether a business action is ethical.

1. **Is it legal?** If not, then don't do it, even if it's borderline.
2. **Is it consistent with the company's stated values?** Texas Instruments has a clearly stated set of corporate values. Actions that don't fit with them shouldn't be undertaken.
3. **If you do it, will you feel bad?** If so, there's probably something wrong.
4. **How would it look in the newspapers?** If having people "find out" through public sources—including social media—will be embarrassing, there's a problem.
5. **Do *you* think it's wrong?** If so, don't do it.
6. **If you're not sure—ask.** Never feel you have to make a decision on ethics by yourself. Get help from others.
7. **If you don't get a clear answer, keep asking until you do.** Don't fudge an ethical problem by saying you "tried" to get help but couldn't. Keep asking—the boss, the company's lawyers, and human resources personnel—until you get a clear answer.[33]

Strategy 15.2   Becoming Culturally Aware of Ethical Conduct

1. Look closely at the situation.
2. Evaluate the intentions.
3. Explore your options.

Asking the following questions in some detail should be helpful in ethics clarification for anyone who is dealing with an unfamiliar culture.

1 **Look closely at the situation.** Be sure you understand the traditions and customs of the culture you are dealing with. Be sure you are listening carefully to the issues of the situation, remaining as open-minded as possible.

2 **Evaluate the intentions.** What are the principles behind the desires of the foreigner you are dealing with? Are you making the mistake of evaluating intentions only through your own traditions and value system? Do you understand the other person's true intentions clearly? Most importantly, once you have established the issues, you need to ask yourself whether you are being asked to take an action that would violate your personal ethics or those of your company—regardless of the cultural context.

3 **Explore your options.** Do you have several options to choose from? Do you know what they are? Which option is the most ethical for you, your company, and your own safety?

Often, these three steps can be taken only after considerable dialogue. Learn to listen carefully both to fellow foreigners who understand the culture better than you do, and to the nationals themselves. Because of the influence of American culture worldwide, many foreigners have a much greater knowledge of the West than Americans may have of the foreign culture. This knowledge gives them a decided advantage; however, it also gives them an opportunity to translate their cultural norms into a common language that makes their intentions easier to understand.

By all means, do not *sell out* your values to those of another culture. Americans simply need to be more sensitive to the cultural differences involving ethical choices among countries and cultures—not just for humanitarian reasons. However, they need to better understand ethical issues as they come up and also to develop overall business success when working with people from other countries and cultures.[34]

CHAPTER FIFTEEN SUMMARY

Chapter Summary by Learning Objectives

LO 15-1 Define ethics. Ethics refers to the standards of conduct and morals in a particular society. In short, it expresses the standards of right and wrong as accepted among a specific group of people.

LO 15-2 Explain the importance of a code of ethics. Codes of ethics vary from person to person and from company to company. Codes of ethics provide agreement and documentation for the manner in which the company sees itself ethically operating. The major ethical codes mentioned in this chapter are: the principles of justice, individual rights, utilitarianism, and individualism. Also, Immanueal Kant's categorical imperative is often used in company decision making.

LO 15-3 Describe the process of rationalizing unethical behavior. Rationalization is the use of reasonable-sounding excuses to explain unethical conduct. The four most common rationalizations are: (1) a belief in the legality of the behavior because of the convenience of doing so, (2) a belief that the company would expect that the behavior be carried out, (3) the belief that nobody will notice, and (4) the belief that since the behavior will help the company, the company will protect the employee.

LO 15-4 Explain ethics in the context of the U.S. workplace. A major ethical issue in the United States is the issue of "boss massaging." Anyone working here, or in some other countries, must look carefully at this practice and decide on its integrity, or lack of it.

LO 15-5 Describe the influence of group goals on ethics. Many people with strong personal ethics find themselves unable to carry their values into the workplace; this can be from the pressure of the larger group. The Parable of the Good Samaritan and the Parable of the Sadhu (in the end-of-chapter Working It Out) are used in this chapter to explore that issue.

LO 15-6 Give examples of global ethics issues. When doing business in other countries and cultures, you must become sensitive to the differences in ethical definitions and attitudes. Be certain that you understand the thinking of the other culture before acting or jumping to conclusions. Especially remember these three concepts: the inner circle, future favors, and gift exchange.

LO 15-7 Define social responsibility. Social responsibility means putting ethical standards to work in all areas of work and life. Three common views of social responsibility are traditional (or classical), stakeholder (or accountability), and affirmative (or public) social responsibility.

LO 15-8 Describe the process of whistleblowing. If you discover unethical behavior in your own organization, you will likely consider whistleblowing. At least seven approaches to whistleblowing are available. Knowledge of your own ethical standards will help greatly in any decision involving ethical choices.

key terms

boss massaging 405
categorical
  imperative 403
ethical codes 401
ethics 398
future favors 408
gift exchange 408

inner circle 407
morality 398
principle of individual
  rights 402
principle of
  individualism 402
principle of justice 402

principle of
  utilitarianism 402
rationalize 404
social
  responsibility 408
stakeholders 409
whistleblowing 410

review questions

1. Briefly define *ethics*. Give your own definition of ethics as the term applies to your own values. Do you think it is a good idea to base your decisions on what "feels" right? Are there any outside forces that influence your behavior?

2. What is a code of ethics? In your opinion, how effective are such codes?

3. Evaluate Texas Instruments' and Alphabet's Codes of Ethics in the "Codes of Ethics" section in this chapter. What is the key to their popular appeal?

4. Define the term *rationalizing*. What role does rationalization play in making bad ethical decisions? Thinking back, have you ever rationalized a bad ethical decision? Explain.

5. Explain the ethical problems involved in boss massaging. When is this practice a good idea? When is this practice a bad idea? Explain what may occur when employees are involved in boss massaging.

6. What major ethical issues are likely to confront someone who is doing business in a foreign country? Give some specific examples. What are some strategies for becoming culturally aware of ethical conduct in foreign countries?

7. How does the Internet create new ethical issues? Do you believe it is unethical for an employee to use the Internet on a company computer for personal use during company time? Is it unethical for the employer to monitor that usage? Explain.

8. What is your attitude toward whistleblowing? Would you ever be a whistleblower if the situation merited such action? Why or why not?

critical thinking questions

1. There are times when people feel they must act unethically in the short term in order to benefit the greater good in the long term. Can you think of a time or a situation that you are familiar with in which this has happened? Is it *ever* acceptable to act unethically?

2. Ethical standards often are made into laws over time. In many states, children under age 16 must wear helmets when riding bicycles. Several years ago, this was only an ethical standard that some parents chose and others did not. Do you think that all ethical standards should have "teeth" in the way that laws do? Who would govern codes of ethics? Or should some or all codes of ethics be made into laws so that they carry more weight?

3. Consider the ethics of "hacktivism." Is former Army soldier Chelsea Manning a hero for trying to promote open, transparent government, or a traitor who gave military secrets to a whistleblowing website? With regard to the Internet battle between CyberBunker and Spamhaus—who was right or wrong in this case? And finally, who is in charge of the Internet; that is, who is in charge of its content and for policing unethical behavior?

working it out 15.1

ETHICAL OR NOT?

School-to-Work Connection: Interpersonal Skills

Objective: This exercise will help you clarify differences in a group's opinions of what *ethical* means.

Procedure: Divide into groups of four or five. Using the criteria listed below, arrive at a group consensus as to what is meant by the term *ethical.* These suggestions can be combined, changed, or ignored by group consent. Avoid democratic voting if possible, and instead seek consensus agreement. Next, as a group, create a story illustration—either factual or made up—that illustrates the group definition of ethics you have created.

As the last step, all groups will share both definitions and story illustrations with the rest of the class. Discuss the differences and the reasons for them.

Ethical is:

_____ what most people around me consider appropriate behavior.

_____ whatever does the most good for the greatest number of people (the *utilitarian principle*).

_____ whatever action reflects the Golden Rule.

_____ whatever is not against the law.

_____ what my feelings tell me to do.

_____ whatever action is in line with my religious beliefs.

_____ whatever is customary in the society I am in.

_____ whatever action would be approved of by a neutral panel of people in my line of work.

_____ whatever doesn't hurt other people.

working it out 15.2

THE PARABLE OF THE SADHU

School-to-Work Connection: Interpersonal Skills

Objective: This parable will help you better understand the conflict between individual and corporate ethics.

Procedure: Break into groups of four or five. Read the following parable: The biblical story of the Good Samaritan is well known in Western culture. A parable of another kind comes from the article "The Parable of the Sadhu," written by Bowen McCoy of *Harvard Business Review.* McCoy tells of a trip to Nepal in which he walked 600 miles through 200 villages in the Himalayas. At a high elevation, one of the members of a party of New Zealanders who had joined him discovered an Indian holy man—called a *sadhu*—nearly naked and unable to walk. No one wanted to step forward from the group and help him, at least not to the point of helping him down the slope to warmth and safety. He was given some clothing, but since he was unable to walk, his likelihood of surviving without help was very small. In the end, the group left him, presumably to die.

The arguments for and against this lack of action were debated afterward at length. McCoy's friend Stephen summarized the dilemma by saying, "I feel that what happened with the sadhu is a good example of the breakdown between the individual ethic and the corporate ethic. No one person was willing to assume ultimate responsibility for the sadhu. Each was willing to do his bit just so long as it was not too inconvenient. . . ."

All of the travelers who ignored the sadhu were intent on the goal of reaching an 18,000-foot mountain pass to get to a village on the other side. Partly because of the importance of this goal in everyone's mind, the suffering individual was all but forgotten. In other words, an unethical action that an individual in other circumstances would not have taken became possible because of group pressures and group goals. These same forces of goals and the pressures to reach them exist in business. The parable thus asks this question: to what extent can an employee or manager of a company ignore the intense needs of a suffering individual in order to achieve the goals of the larger group?[35]

Most importantly, the parable of the sadhu illustrates the conflict of the individual's personal ethics versus the ethics of the group. Most people learn their moral and ethical values from their families or communities, but for various reasons, they don't always transfer those same values to the other groups (such as the workplace).

Discussion: After you have read the parable of the Sadhu in your small group, begin discussing this topic. In your group, come to consensus on the relevance of this parable to ethics in the workplace. How could your workplace be improved with an awareness of the lesson in this story?

What do you think *you* would have done if you had been the one to come across the sadhu? Have you experienced any situations in which you have been faced with helping—or not helping—someone in distress? What did you do? What did others around you do? Why do you think these people chose the actions they did?

case study 15.1

Life Over Profit

The following scenario is adapted from a classic ethics test developed by psychologist Lawrence Kohlberg more than 50 years ago. Read the ethical dilemma presented and then answer the Case Questions that follow.

A woman living in Europe was near death from a rare kind of cancer. The doctors knew of only one drug that might save her, a type of radium that a druggist in her town had recently developed. The drug was expensive to make, but the druggist was charging patients 10 times the cost of producing it. He paid $200 for the radium but charged $2,000 for a small dose of the drug.

The sick woman's husband, Heinz, went to everyone he knew in an attempt to borrow the money, but he could only get about half of the $2,000 he needed. He told the druggist that his wife was dying and begged him to sell the drug cheaper, or to extend some credit. But the druggist insisted, "No! I discovered the drug, and I'm going to make money from it." Heinz became desperate and broke into the store to steal the drug to save his wife.[36]

Case Study Questions

1. Was the husband's behavior excusable under the circumstances? Was it ethical?

2. If you were a police officer in the town, would you have arrested the husband for theft?

3. Should the druggist who made the drug face any penalty? Were his actions ethical?

4. If you were Heinz, would you have stolen the drug? If not, why not? What would you have done instead?

case study 15.2

No Sense of Humor?

Cecilia is the CEO of a mid-sized company. One of Cecilia's favorite expressions is "If people don't like working here, we'll help them leave." She has been at the company only a year, and people are not sure how seriously to take her. But in the past year, Cecilia has identified several top managers she thought were "not a good fit" with the company, and she "helped them leave." Many of the managers are now nervous about losing their jobs, and are careful not to say or do anything to confront her.

Cecilia meets weekly with her 10 top-level managers. During these meetings, she often makes fun of other staff who are not present, or the members of the Board of Directors, mocking them and imitating them in an unflattering way.

During these times, some of the managers laugh at her antics, while others look down at their notes, sneaking looks at the other managers at the table to try to gauge their reactions. Early on, when she had just joined the company, one of the managers asked a pointed question about the ethical boundaries of the company. She became angry and accused him of having no sense of humor. He was demoted soon thereafter. Since then, no one at the company has felt comfortable speaking up, or calling her out on her mockery of staff and board members. No one wants to go over her head and tell the Board of Directors what is going on. So Cecilia just continues this behavior, and now people expect it of her.

Case Study Questions

1. How does this situation present an ethics issue?

2. How is it tied to self-esteem?

3. How does it tie to the concept in an earlier chapter of the internal customer?

4. If you were one of the managers at the table, what would you do?

glossary

accommodator Someone who wants to avoid conflict by engaging in positive thinking.

achievement needs Occur in people who are goal oriented and take personal responsibility for achievements.

active listening Listening with greater concentration, less tolerance for distractions, and more feedback to the speaker.

affiliation needs Occur in people who want to be accepted and liked by others.

ageism Prejudice and discrimination toward older people.

aggression Hurting others and putting them on the defensive.

Asian phenomenon A circumstance that exists when people make rules, then follow them even after the situations to which they originally applied no longer exist.

assertiveness Standing up for your rights without threatening the self-esteem of the other person.

attitude An evaluation of people, ideas, issues, situations, or objects.

authority The vested power to influence or command within an organization.

autocratic leaders Leaders who make all the decisions and use authority and material rewards to motivate followers.

autonomy Independence, the ability to act and make decisions on one's own without undue interference from management.

avoider Someone who would rather not be around conflict at all and values neutrality highly.

bad news skills The skills necessary to deliver bad news to customers but still retain their business and goodwill.

beginning The *last* of three general steps in the acceptance of personal loss. This is where "experimenting" and "completion" take place. (See **ending** and **neutral zone.**)

behavior modification The process of changing behavior because of a reward or lack of a reward.

bias A tendency to judge people before knowing them, basing the judgment only on their membership in some group or category of people.

blind pane The pane in the Johari Window that contains everything other people can see about you, but you can't see yourself.

boss massaging The practice of currying favor, or kissing up, with a manager to achieve your own goals.

brainstorming A type of spontaneous group discussion to help find multiple solutions to problems.

bureaucracy A formal organization in which each person has specific duties and responsibilities and is assigned to only one supervisor.

catastrophize To turn an irrational belief into an imagined disaster.

categorical imperative A principle developed by philosopher Immanuel Kant, which asks the question, "What would the world—or my company—be like if everyone were to do this?"

change agent The person responsible for an organizational change effort.

charismatic power Power that is based on the attractiveness a person has to others.

chronic stressors Inescapable, day-to-day situations or conditions that cause stress.

cliché conversation The level of communication with the least amount of self-disclosure, including niceties such as, "Have a nice day."

coercive power Power that depends on the threat of possible punishment.

cognitive appraisal   The thinking evaluation of an event or situation that varies from person to person and, for an individual, from day to day.

cognitive categorization   A process in which the mind quickly sorts information into categories to function efficiently.

cognitive dissonance   The emotional state that results from acting in ways that contradict one's beliefs or other actions.

collaborator   Someone who brings both sides together for discussion and not only is most likely to bring about a win-win solution but is actually necessary for it.

collective habits of thought   Ways of thinking that occur when groups have own beliefs about *what* should be done and *how* it should be done.

communication   The giving and receiving of ideas, feelings, and information among people.

compensating   The use of a strength to make up for a real or perceived weakness.

competitor   Someone who is most likely to try a win-lose approach to conflict resolution, especially if he or she is personally involved in the conflict.

compromiser   Someone who uses his or her skills to blend differences and form a workable alternative.

compulsive gambling   The inability to control one's betting habit.

concession bargaining   The process of getting each side in a conflict to willingly make concessions in exchange for concessions made by the opposing side.

conditional positive regard   Acceptance of individuals as worthy only when they behave in a certain way.

conflict   A process that begins when one person sees that another person has damaged—or is about to damage—something that the other person cares about.

conformity   Behaving in a way that meets a specified standard, in coordination with a group.

consultative leaders   Leaders who tend to delegate authority and confer with others in making decisions, but who makes the actual decisions independently.

content conflict   Conflict that tends to focus on disagreements over what a statement or concept means.

context   A point of reference (or a place from which to begin) when communicating.

creative process   The way in which creativity helps you develop ideas and solve problems.

creativity   The ability to produce ideas or solutions to problems that are unique, appropriate, and valuable.

culture stories   Stories that illustrate the values of the people who make an organization work.

daily hassles   The daily annoyances, such as getting stuck in traffic or misplacing your keys, that can cause stress in your life.

defensiveness   The inappropriate reaction to another's behavior as though it were an attack.

denial   Failure to confront your problem; characteristic response by an alcoholic.

discrimination   Your behavior, or what you do (or intend to do, or are inclined to do) as a result of your stereotypes and prejudice.

displays   Gestures that are used like nonverbal punctuation marks, such as pounding your fist on the table.

distancing   The distance of physical space you maintain between other people and yourself.

distress   Negative stress, the kind felt during an illness or when going through a divorce.

dysfunctional conflict   Destructive conflict.

economic prejudice   Prejudice and discrimination toward people who are poorer or wealthier than you are.

eight intelligences   Eight separate areas in which people put their perceptiveness and abilities to work.

either/or fallacy   When you see only one of two extremes as a possible solution, while ignoring the endless number of creative choices that might exist between the extremes.

emblems   Gestures that are used in a specific manner because they have a specific meaning, usually one understood by both sender and receiver; the peace sign is an example.

emotional competence   A learned capability based on emotional intelligence; results in outstanding performance at work.

emotional intelligence (EI)   The ability to see and control your own emotions and to understand the emotional states of other people.

emotional mind A powerful, impulsive, sometimes illogical awareness; an ability to perceive emotions.

employee appraisal Feedback to an employee from supervisors on how he or she has performed over a given period.

employee assistance programs (EAPs) Company-sponsored programs that treat employees with substance abuse problems, marriage and family conflicts, and financial difficulties.

ending The *first* of three general steps in the acceptance of personal loss. This is where "emotional standstill," "denial," and "anger" take place. (See **neutral zone** and **beginning**.)

entrepreneurship The risk-taking entrance into your own enterprise.

Equal Employment Opportunity Commission (EEOC) A federal agency established to monitor the laws set in place by the amended Civil Rights Act of 1964, as amended in 1972.

equal status The condition that occurs when companies hire employees who are frequent targets of discrimination into all levels within the company.

ERG theory A refinement of Maslow's hierarchy that includes only three needs areas: existence (mostly physical needs); relatedness (needs linked to relationships); and growth (internal esteem needs and self-actualization).

esteem needs In Maslow's hierarchy, include recognition from peers and colleagues.

ethical codes Formalized sets of ethical guidelines developed by some companies for use at all levels of an organization.

ethics The expression of the standards of right and wrong based on conduct and morals in a particular society.

ethnocentrism The belief that one's ethnic group is more normal than others; an emotional source of prejudice because of people's gut-level feelings about how right their group is—and, in turn, how wrong they think other groups are.

eustress Positive stress, the kind felt when doing something one enjoys, such as playing tennis or attending a party.

expectancy In *expectancy theory,* the likelihood that if a person tried, the result would be better performance.

expectancy theory Developed by Victor Vroom to explain human behavior in terms of people's goals, choices, and the expectation that goals will be reached.

expert power Power that comes from a person's knowledge or skill in areas that are critical to the success of the firm.

external locus of control This occurs in people who feel they have no control over the events in their lives.

external stressors Stressors that include anything from outside sources that causes you pain and discomfort.

extraversion Characteristic of a happy attitude in which a person's behavior is directed outward, toward others.

extrinsic motivators Those motivators that come from outside sources, such as money and fame.

extrinsic rewards or motivators External factors intended to provide motivational incentives, including salary, bonuses, promotions, praise, or high grades in classes.

family violence Violence that can be defined as physical, emotional, verbal, or sexual violence against another family member.

fear of failure The fear that occurs when people are afraid of looking bad in front of others.

fear of success The fear that occurs when people who have not experienced much success in their lives feel they do not deserve it.

feedback Information given to people either on how well they are performing a task, or on how clearly they are being understood.

filtering A method listeners use to *hear only what they want to hear,* which may result in failing to receive messages correctly.

finding your niche Finding the place where you thrive and are most content; includes finding the type of job or career where you will be most satisfied.

first-, second-, and third-degree games In transactional analysis, categories of games based on intensity of play. First-degree games are relatively harmless; second-degree games are moderately harmful; third-degree games are extremely damaging.

flow The feeling of oneness with an activity that allows an individual to uniquely experience an event or activity by becoming totally engaged in the process; term was coined by Mihalyi Csikszentmihalyi.

force field analysis A model in which the status quo is like a battlefield being fought for by two armies: the driving force and the restraining force.

formal group A group that is usually governed by the formal structure of the organization.

free-rein leaders Leaders who set performance standards, then allow followers to work creatively to meet standards.

frustration regression principles A principle that says that someone who fails to reach a higher need level will sometimes become frustrated and regress (go back) to a lower need level, and stay there for some time—perhaps forever.

frustration The feeling people get when goals they are trying to attain are blocked.

functional conflict Constructive conflict.

future favors A practice commonly seen in developing countries based upon mutual obligation and resulting in the exchange of favors over years and even generations; also used in some industrialized countries such as Japan and South Korea.

game An encounter between two people that produces a "payoff" for the one who starts the game, at the expense of the other player.

gift exchange A strong tradition in many cultures, in which giving gifts creates a future obligation to the receiver; it can also be a rite of passage into an inner circle.

goal setting Allows employees to set their own goals.

going the extra mile When a company gives customers small extra products or services as a way of showing appreciation for their business.

good feelings and solutions The only two things customers really buy.

grapevine A network within the informal organization that communicates incomplete, but usually somewhat accurate information.

group Two or more people who interact, share common goals, have unspoken or formal rules or norms, maintain stable role relationships, and form subgroups.

group dynamics The set of interpersonal relationships within a group that determine how group members relate to one another and that influence task performance.

group process The way group members deal with one another while working on a task.

groupthink A problematic type of thinking that results from group members who are overly willing to agree with one another because of time pressure, stress, and low collective self-esteem.

gut level communication Level of communication in which feelings are expressed honestly.

hardy personality A resilient personality type, characterized by the ability to meet challenges, a sense of commitment, and a feeling of being in control of life.

Hawthorne Experiment A five-year study conducted at the Western Electric plant in Hawthorne, Illinois, that showed that workers performed better when someone was paying attention to them.

hidden agendas The secret wishes, hopes, desires, and assumptions hidden from the group. People often try to accomplish hidden agendas while pretending to care about the group goals.

hidden pane The pane in the Johari Window that contains information and feelings that you are hiding from other people.

high-context culture A culture in which the *social context* surrounding a written document is far more important than the document itself. One must be very careful about cultural norms, nonverbal behaviors on both sides, and anything else involving the overall atmosphere of the communication.

higher self-esteem When people have healthy feelings about themselves and are therefore more likely to succeed in personal and career goals.

Holmes–Rahe Readjustment Scale A listing of many kinds of changes, rated from 100 to 0 on the basis of their intensity and the adjustment problems they can create.

horizontal communication Messages that are communicated between you and your equals in the formal organization.

human relations The skill or ability to work effectively through and with other people.

hygienes   (also called "dissatisfiers") The qualities in the workplace that are outside the job itself (examples: company benefits, policies, job security). When these factors are weak or missing, motivation will fall; however, when they are high, motivation will not be strong or long term.

ideal self   The way you would like to be or plan to become.

ideas and judgments   Expressed through conscious thoughts, opinions, and theories in this level of communication.

illustrators   Gestures that are used to clarify a point, such as pointing when giving directions.

impostor phenomenon   A feeling successful people experience when they are afraid that they did not really succeed because of their own talents and hard work.

informal group   A group that tends to form around common interests, habits, and personality traits.

informal organization   The ever-changing set of relationships and interactions that are not formally put together; they form naturally in the workplace.

information overload   The type of listening that happens when a listener is overwhelmed with incoming information and has to decide which information will be processed and remembered; this is a common cause of poor listening skills.

inner circle   A clique of trusted family members, tribal members, or friends (depending on the culture) who are at the center of power or influence.

inner conflict   Conflict within an individual; it might involve values, loyalties, or priorities; the pressure you feel when you are forced to make a choice.

inner critic   An inner voice that attacks people and negatively judges their worth.

inner saboteur   Negative inner voices that form mental habits that sabotage our actions, keeping us from reaching our full potential.

institutional prejudice   Prejudice that is caused by policies in the workplace that are not intentionally set to exclude members of specific groups or to treat them differently, but which have that effect anyway.

institutionalized conflict   Conflict that occurs when a conflict factor is built into the structure of the organization.

instrumental values   Values that reflect the ways you prefer to behave leading toward larger life goals.

instrumentality   The likelihood that something good (or bad) will come from an increase in effort.

intelligence   Traditionally seen as reasoning ability, as measured by standardized tests.

intensity   The degree to which an individual shows serious concentration or emotion; another dimension of nonverbal communication.

interdependence   A relationship in which members of different groups not only must cooperate but also must depend on each other to reach common goals.

intergenerational care   Day care not only for children but also for elderly family members.

intergroup conflict   Takes place when already-formed groups have conflicts with each other.

internal customer   The person who depends on the other people in the company to provide the services and products for the external customer.

internal locus of control   Occurs in people who feel they are in control of the events in their own lives.

internal stressors   Your perceptions of stressors, which may vary depending on personality.

intragroup conflict   Conflict that occurs when two groups form and take sides.

intrinsic motivators   Factors that motivate a person from within, such as the joy and excitement of the discovery process.

intrinsic rewards   In *expectancy theory,* the internal factors related to the value of work, including the amount of creativity allowed, the degree of responsibility, and the satisfaction of helping others.

intuition   Direct perception or insight.

irrational belief system   A way of thinking that causes internal stress by substituting a realistic belief with one that is destructive, illogical, and largely false.

job burnout   Physical and emotional exhaustion resulting from long-term stress or frustration in one's workplace.

job enrichment   The upgrading of a job that makes it more interesting, meaningful, or rewarding and provides long-term motivation.

Johari Window   A composite of four panes that shows you ways of relating to others: the open, blind, hidden, and unknown panes.

kaizen   Literally, "to become good through change." The concept of *kaizen* is one of restructuring and organizing every aspect of a system to ensure optimal efficiency.

leadership   The ability to influence others to work toward the goals of an organization.

legitimate power   Power based on the position a person holds in an organization that is effective only when followers believe in the structure that produces this power.

Lewin change model   A workplace change model with three steps; unfreezing the status quo, making changes, then refreezing to the previous work mode.

locus of control   The name given to the perceived location of the control you feel you have over events that happen to you; this control is perceived to be located within the individual (internal locus of control) or is attributed to external factors (external locus of control).

logical incrementalism   A model that acknowledges that bringing about changes in a large organization is usually time-consuming and complicated, and presents a method of simplifying the process.

long-term goals   Those things you decide to work for after developing a life plan for the future.

looking-glass self   The self you assume others see when they look at you.

lose-lose strategy   A strategy in which everyone gives up something, and the focus is on compromise.

love and belongingness needs   Include complete acceptance from family and friends. The third level of Maslow's hierarchy.

low conformers   Individuals who think independently, solve problems creatively, and often cause some conflict in the process.

low-context culture   A culture in which a written agreement, such as a contract, can be taken at face value.

lower self-esteem   Occurs when individuals are unable to see themselves as capable, sufficient, or worthy.

lower self-worth   Occurs when an individual believes himself or herself to have little of value to offer the world.

major life changes   Changes in your life, such as divorce, that increase daily hassles, leaving you stressed and worn out.

manifest needs theory   Developed by David McClelland to show that all people have needs that motivate them in life and on the job. These three needs include power needs, affiliation needs, and achievement needs.

Maslow's hierarchy of needs   Shows that people tend to satisfy their needs in a certain order: first, physiological needs, then safety and security, belongingness and love, esteem, and finally, self-actualization.

mentor   A person who acts as a guide or teacher for another, leading that person through experiences.

morale   Overall mood of an individual or group, based on attitudes and satisfaction.

morality   A system of conduct that covers all broadly based, mostly unwritten standards of how people should behave and generally conform to cultural ideals of right and wrong.

motivation   The force of the need or desire to act.

motivators   (also called "satisfiers") The factors in Herzberg's theory that cause real, long-term motivation, usually containing *intrinsic* motivation factors (examples: interesting and challenging tasks, advancement, achievement, growth).

mutual respect   The positive consideration or regard that two people have for each other.

negotiation-of-selves   Conflict that is involved in the process of defining yourself to others and responding to their implied definitions of themselves.

networking power   Power that is attained by gaining contact and knowing the right people.

neutral zone   The *second* of three general steps in the acceptance of personal loss. The neutral zone is the area where "helplessness" and "bottoming out" take place. (See **ending** and **beginning**.)

"nice" customer   The customer who never complains, but responds to bad service by taking his or her business elsewhere.

nine-dot puzzle   A puzzle that is used to show people's respect for rules that don't exist. Participants are asked to connect nine dots using only four straight lines, without lifting the pen off the paper. Most fail because they feel the need to stay "inside the box" formed by the nine dots.

nominal group method   An exercise that encourages creativity within a group framework by allowing everyone to offer ideas individually.

nonconversation   A way to describe the amount of actual conversation in cliché conversation.

nonverbals   Ways of communicating without speaking, such as gestures, body language, and facial expressions.

norm   A standard of behavior expected of group members.

OD change agent   A company's formal change agent; often an outside consultant who specializes in planned change or organizational development (OD).

OD intervention   Training tools that teach members of the organization how to solve problems they face or make needed changes to organizational development (OD).

open mode   A state of mind where you are relaxed, expansive, less purposeful, and more fun than in the everyday closed mode.

open pane   The pane in the Johari Window that contains information that you know about yourself and that you have no reason to hide.

optimal experience   The pleasure in performing the process of an activity itself, rather than achieving the goal.

organizational change   Change that a group of people must learn to accept and implement.

organizational citizenship behavior   An attitude of willingness to go above and beyond the behaviors that are generally associated with life in the workplace.

organizational climate   The emotional weather within an organization that reflects the norms and attitudes of the organization's culture and affects worker morale, attitudes, stress levels, and communication.

organizational communication   Oral and written communication in an organization. It has formal and informal dimensions and travels vertically and horizontally.

organizational development (OD)   A planned, companywide, systematic method of achieving change in an organization.

organizational or corporate culture   An organization's network that includes the shared values and assumptions within it.

overloading time   Planning too many activities into one time slot.

participative leaders   Leaders who encourage the group to work together toward shared goals.

peak communication   Communication characterized by complete openness and honest self-disclosure. It happens rarely.

perception   The way in which a person views the world.

personal competence   The ability to be self-aware, motivated, and self-regulated.

personal control   The power people perceive they have over their destinies.

person-versus-group conflict   Conflict that occurs most often when a member of a group breaks its rules, or norms.

person-versus-person conflict   Conflict that involves two people who are at odds over personality differences, values conflicts, loyalties, or any number of issues.

physiological needs   The most basic of Maslow's hierarchy of needs having to do with the satisfaction of physical needs, including food and shelter.

positive attitude   A position resulting from healthy self-esteem, optimism, extraversion, and personal control.

Positive Intelligence Quotient, or Positivity Quotient (PQ)   Defeating self-sabotage to create healthy responses to life's challenges.

positive psychology   A subfield within psychology that focuses on experiences, individual traits, and institutions that create happiness and hope, rather than focusing on mental illness.

positive self-talk   A popular method of building self-esteem by thinking and speaking positively about yourself.

power needs Desired by individuals who want to control and influence other people.

power The ability of one person to influence another.

prejudice The outcome of prejudging a person. Prejudice in communication is the unwillingness to listen to members of groups the listener believes are inferior, such as other ethnic groups or women; it can also take more subtle forms; how you feel as a result of the stereotypes you believe in.

principle of individual rights An ethical philosophy that holds that all decisions should respect basic human rights and the dignity of the individual.

principle of individualism An ethical philosophy that holds that all primary goals should achieve long-term self-interests, with the emphasis on long-term; self-interest should not justify short-sighted actions.

principle of justice An ethical philosophy that holds that all decisions should be consistent, unbiased, and based on fact.

principle of utilitarianism An ethical philosophy that holds that all decisions should do the greatest good for the largest number of people.

procrastination Putting off until later the things a person should be doing now.

productivity The ratio of an organization's inputs, or its resources, to its outputs, or the goods and services it produces.

proximity Physical closeness; here, it refers to contact between members of a diverse workplace.

psychological contract An agreement that is not written or spoken but is understood between people.

quality circles Bring employees and managers together to brainstorm and find ways to improve quality and performance.

racism Prejudice and discrimination based on race.

Rath Test Finds out if the values you think you have are the ones you truly have.

rational mind An awareness of reality, which allows you to ponder and reflect.

rationalize To justify unethical behavior with excuses.

real self The way you really are when nobody is around to approve or disapprove.

red flag words Words that bring an immediate emotional response (usually negative) from the listener, generally because of strong beliefs on the subject.

regression Slipping backward to an earlier stage of growth; it can be either temporary or permanent.

regulators Gestures that are used to control the flow of communication; eye contact is a common type of regulator.

reinforcement theory Explains human behavior in terms of repetition. Behavior that is rewarded enough times will be repeated, whereas behavior that repeatedly receives no reward will probably discontinue.

reinforcers Incentives such as awards, bonuses, promotions, gifts, and even compliments.

relationship selling Forming meaningful relationships with your customers, which makes them much more likely to return and buy from you again.

repress To block off memories that may cause pain, embarrassment, or guilt.

reward power Power that comes from the user's ability to control or influence others with something of value to them.

role model A person to whom an individual can look for guidance by example, but who isn't necessarily actively interacting with the individual.

rumor mill A gossip network that produces mostly false information.

safety and security needs In Maslow's hierarchy, include physical safety from harm and the elements as well as financial security.

sandwich generation Middle-aged adults who are taking responsibility for both dependent children and parents at the same time, and being sandwiched by these obligations.

SCAMPER A strategy, created by Bob Eberle, to release your creative mind.

scapegoating The practice of unfairly blaming others (such as ethnic groups) when something goes wrong.

scientific management A system based upon scientific and engineering principles.

script In relationship transactions, a psychological script like a movie or theater script, with characters, dialogue, etc., that most people heard as children.

second right answer Refers to a method of decision making in which people get rid of the stumbling block that prevents them from looking for more than one solution.

selective listening The type of listening that happens when a listener deliberately chooses what he or she wants to pay attention to.

self-actualization Highest level of Maslow's hierarchy of needs; occurs when one has fulfilled his or her potential.

self-awareness The knowledge of how you are being perceived by others.

self-concept The way you picture yourself to be.

self-direction The ability to set short-term and long-term goals for yourself.

self-discipline The ability to teach or guide yourself to set up and carry out your goals and plans.

self-disclosure The process of letting other people know what you are really thinking and feeling.

self-efficacy The confidence an individual has in his or her ability to deal with problems when they occur and to achieve goals.

self-esteem The regard in which an individual holds himself or herself.

self-esteem trap The circumstance that comes from taking a customer's attack personally and letting it affect your self-esteem.

self-fulfilling prophecy The tendency for a prediction to actually occur once it is believed; for example, when a victim believes that prejudice against him or her is true, then fulfills these negative expectations.

self-image The way you honestly see yourself.

self-justification Explaining your behavior so that you feel it is correct.

self-perception What and how you believe yourself to be.

self-respect Positive self-image with high self-esteem.

self-sabotage Damaging your own credibility or competence.

setting priorities Deciding ahead of time which tasks are the most, and least, important.

seven major life changes Loss, separation, relocation, a change in relationship, a change in direction, a change in health, and personal growth.

seven stages of personal change Emotional standstill, denial, anger, helplessness, bottoming out, experimenting, and completion.

sexism Prejudice and discrimination based on gender.

sexual harassment Behavior that is defined by the EEOC as "unwelcome sexual advances, requests for sexual favors, and other verbal or physical conduct of a sexual nature."

short-term goals The specific plans of action for the things you would like to accomplish right now or in the immediate future.

skill variety The opportunity and ability to use numerous different skills in one's position at work.

social competence Empathy for others combined with sensitivity and effective social skills.

social responsibility The practice of acting ethically while understanding your actions are part of the larger, interactive picture of your workplace, community, and world.

stakeholders Any group that a business interacts with, such as customers, competitors, unions, suppliers, consumer groups, and government agencies.

status The rank an individual holds within a group.

stereotypes Your thoughts or beliefs about specific groups of people.

stress Any reaction or response made by the body to a new situation.

stressor A situation or an event that causes the body to react (causes stress).

substance abuse The continued use of a psychoactive substance even though it is causing or increasing problems in a person's life.

task activity The assignment of tasks to get a job done.

task identity The worker's perception of the meaningfulness of a job, often based upon the worker's permission to start a job and see it through to completion.

task maturity Having the skill set necessary to complete a job, as well as the ability to set and meet realistic goals and the ability to take on responsibility for the task.

task significance A worker's perception that the task directly affects other people's work or lives.

team building The process of creating and encouraging a group of employees to work together toward achieving group goals and increased productivity.

ten "mental locks" Rules or beliefs that keep people from being as creative as they otherwise could be.

terminal values Values likely to maintain a high priority throughout your life.

Theories X and Y Theory X managers see workers as lacking ambition, disliking work, and wanting security above all else. Theory Y managers see workers as enjoying work, able to assume responsibility, and being creative.

time analysis Tools available to help with analyzing your use of time so that you can see where to become more efficient in time management.

time management Making effective use of available time.

to-do list A list of what you need to do, when, and where.

Total Quality Management (TQM) A management organizational philosophy that was very influential in the 1980s and 1990s, which stated that quality must be present in the product or the service produced, and in the process itself of producing the goods or service. (See **quality movement.**)

trust Firm belief in the reliability, truth, ability, or strength of someone or something.

two simplest principles Finding out what the customer needs, and doing whatever is necessary to satisfy it.

type A and type B personalities Two standard personality-related sets of behaviors. Type A behaviors are characterized by impatience, hostility, perfectionism, and a sense of time urgency. Type B behaviors are characterized by flexibility, the ability to relax and delegate work, and a minimal sense of time urgency.

unconditional positive regard The acceptance of individuals as worthy and valuable regardless of their behavior, usually applied to parental acceptance of children.

underutilizing time Making poor use of available time.

unknown pane The pane in the Johari Window that contains unknown talents, abilities, and attitudes, as well as forgotten and repressed experiences, emotions, and possibilities.

valence The value a person places on a reward.

value systems Frameworks people use in developing beliefs about themselves, others, and how they should be treated.

values The worth or importance you attach to different factors in your life.

values conflict Conflict that occurs when one set of values clashes with another, and a decision has to be made.

vertical communication Messages that are communicated according to an organization's chain of command by flowing both upward and downward.

whistleblowing Turning in or otherwise exposing people who behave unethically in your company.

win-lose strategy A strategy that allows one side of a conflict to win at the expense of another.

win-win strategy A strategy that leads to a solution in which both sides feel they have come out on top.

work team A group of employees with shared goals who join forces on a work project.

references

Chapter 1

[1] Richard Baran, "Interpersonal Relationship Skills or How to Get Along for Productivity and Profit," *Personnel Administrator,* April 1986, p. 12.

[2] Janette Moody et al., "Showcasing the Skilled Business Graduate: Expanding the Tool Kit." *Business Communication Quarterly,* March 2002, p. 23.

[3] U.S. Census, Population, Projections of Size and Composition of the U.S. Population, https://www.census.gov/content/dam/Census/library/publications/2015/demo/p25-1143.pdf (retrieved May 11, 2017).

[4] Mihalyi Csikszentmihalyi, published on July 1, 1996, last reviewed on June 9, 2016, "The Creative Personality," *Psychology Today,* https://www.psychologytoday.com/articles/199607/the-creative-personality (retrieved June 20, 2017).

[5] http://reports.weforum.org/global-gender-gap-report-2015/report-highlights/ (retrieved May 13, 2017).

[6] Mitra Toosi, "Projections of the Labor Force to 2050: A Visual Essay," *Monthly Labor Review,* October 2012, pp. 3–14.

[7] W. Richard Plunket, *Supervision: The Direction of People at Work* (Dubuque, IA: W. C. Brown, 1983), p. 161.

[8] M. R. Hansen, "Better Supervision for A to W," *Supervisory Management,* August 1985, p. 35.

[9] https://venturebeat.com/2011/12/27/ocean-marketing-how-to-self-destruct-your-company-with-just-a-few-measly-emails/ (retrieved May 13, 2017).

[10] Fyodor Dostoevsky, *The House of the Dead.* (London: JM Dent & Sons Ltd., 1933).

[11] Nancy E. Roberts, "Most Managers Fail; Here's Five Reasons Why." http://EzineArticles.com/?expert=Nancy_E_Roberts (retrieved March 27, 2013).

[12] Anon., The Importance of Human Relations in the Workplace." http://avaha1978.hubpages.com/hub/The-importance-of-human-relations-in-the-workplace (retrieved May 28, 2013).

[13] Suneel Ratan, "Why Busters Hate Boomers," *Fortune,* October 4, 1993, pp. 57–70.

[14] Philip Bump, "Here Is When Each Generation Begins and Ends, According to Facts." March 25, 2014, *The Atlantic.* https://www.theatlantic.com/national/archive/2014/03/here-is-when-each-generation-begins-and-ends-according-to-facts/359589/ (retrieved May 13, 2017).

[15] "China GDP Annual Growth Rate," *Trading Economics,* https://tradingeconomics.com/china/gdp-growth-annual (retrieved October 20, 2017).

[16] Robert Kaplan, "How We Would Fight China," *Atlantic,* June 2005, pp. 49–64. http://www.bloomberg.com/apps/news?pid =20601013&sid=av1phRnqSgCM&refer=emergingmarkets (retrieved March 27, 2013).

[17] Jeff Poor, "Life Expectancy Increasing or Decreasing, Depending on What Day It Is." Business and Media Institute. http://www.businessandmedia.org/printer/2007/20070913152112.aspx (retrieved March 27, 2013).

[18] Caleb Hannan, "Management Secrets from the Meanest Company in America," *Bloomberg Businessweek* January 7, 2013, pp. 46–51.

[19] Eriq Gardner, "Dish Network's Charlie Ergen Is the Most Hated Man in Hollywood." *The Hollywood Reporter,* April 2, 2013 (accessed April 4, 2013 at http://www.hollywoodreporter.com/news/dish-networks-charlie-ergen-is-432288).

[20] Paul R. Timm and Brent D. Peterson, *People at Work: Human Relations in Organizations* (Minneapolis/St. Paul, MN: West Publishing, 1993), pp. 122–123. See also "William Ouchi on Trust," *Training and Development Journal,* December 1982, p. 71.

[21] Stephen R. Covey, *The Seven Habits of Highly Effective People* (New York: Simon and Schuster, 1989), pp. 66–67.

[22] Mary Ellen Guffey and Dana Loewy, *Essentials of Business Communication* (Mason, OH: Cengage Learning, 2013), p. 7.

[23] John R. Dickman, *Human Connections* (Englewood Cliffs, NJ: Prentice Hall, 1982), pp. xi–xii.

[24] Michael Drafke, *The Human Side of Organizations* (Upper Saddle River, NJ: Pearson Prentice-Hall, 2006), pp. 211–214.

[25] David Krech, Richard Crutchfield, and Egerton Ballachey, *Individual in Society* (New York: McGraw-Hill, 1962), pp. 527–529.

[26] Peter F. Drucker, *The New Realities* (New York: HarperCollins, 1990).

[27] James R. Lowry, B. W. Weinrich, and R. D. Steade, *Business in Today's World* (Cincinnati, OH: South Western Publishing, 1990), p. 243.

[28] L. K. Frankel and Alexander Fleisher, *The Human Factor in Industry* (New York: Macmillan, 1920), p. 8.

[29] Ibid., pp. 10–28.

[30] Max Weber, *The Protestant Ethic and the Spirit of Capitalism,* trans. Talcott Parsons (New York: Scribner, 1930), pp. 121–156.

[31] Max Weber, *The Theory of Social and Economic Organization,* ed. and trans. A. M. Henderson and T. Parsons (Oxford University Press, 1947), pp. 22–57.

[32] Frederick W. Taylor, *The Principles of Scientific Management* (New York: Harper and Brothers, 1923), pp. 35–38.

[33] Daniel Nelson, *Frederick W. Taylor and the Rise of Scientific Management* (Madison, WI: University of Wisconsin Press, 1980).

[34] Daniel A. Wren, *The Evolution of Management Thought* (New York: Ronald Press, 1972), pp. 158–168.

[35] Henry C. Metcalf and L. Urwick, eds., *Dynamic Administration: The Collected Papers of Mary Parker Follett* (New York: Harper and Row, 1942), pp. 20–38.

[36] Elton Mayo, *The Human Problems of an Industrial Civilization* (New York: Macmillan, 1933).

[37] John G. Adair, "The Hawthorne Effect: A Reconsideration of the Methodological Artifact," *Journal of Applied Psychology,* May 1984, pp. 334–345. See also Mitchell Cohen, "The Hawthorne Studies, Another Look." http://nyc.indymedia.org/en/2010/10 /112886.html (retrieved March 30, 2013).

[38] George T. and John W. Boudreau, *Human Resource Management* (Homewood, IL: Richard Irwin, 1991), pp. 605–609.

[39] Mary Walton, *The Deming Management Method* (New York: Putnam, 1986), pp. 3–21. Also, John Hunter, "Eliminate Sales Commissions: Reject Theory X and Embrace Systems Thinking," *The W. Edwards Deming Institute Blog,* http:// blog.deming.org/2012/11/eliminate-sales-commissions -reject-theory-x-management-and-embrace-systems -thinking/ (entered November 1, 2012; retrieved March 28, 2013).

Chapter 2

[1] Joseph L. Massie and John Douglas, *Managing: A Contemporary Introduction,* 5th ed. (Englewood Cliffs, NJ: Prentice-Hall, 1992).

[2] Samuel E. Wood and Ellen Green Wood, *The World of Psychology* (Boston, MA: Allyn & Bacon, 1999). See also Kimberly Fulcher, "Envisioning Your Ideal Self," SelfGrowth.com, www.self growth.com/articles/Fulcer2html (retrieved March 16, 2008).

[3] Samuel E. Wood and Ellen Green Wood, *The World of Psychology* (Boston, MA: Allyn & Bacon, 1999). See also "How Do You Talk to Yourself?" Norwich University Online, www.leadersdirect .com/talkself.html (retrieved March 15, 2008).

[4] Mary Pipher, *Reviving Ophelia: Saving the Selves of Adolescent Girls* (New York: Ballantine Books, 1994).

[5] Carolyn M. Ball, *Claiming Your Self-Esteem* (Berkeley, CA: Celestial Arts, 1990), p. 138.

[6] Stanley Coppersmith, *The Antecedents of Self-Esteem* (San Francisco: Freeman, 1967).

[7] Amy L. Gonzales and Jeffrey T. Hancock. "Mirror, Mirror on my Facebook Wall: Effects of Exposure to Facebook on Self-Esteem" Cyberpsychology, Behavior, and Social Networking, Volume: 14, Issue: 1–2, 2011, pp. 79–83.

[8] Wayne Weiten and Margaret Lloyd, *Psychology Applied to Modern Life: Adjustment at the Turn of the Century,* 6th ed. (Belmont, CA: Wadsworth, 1999).

[9] Spencer Rathus, *Psychology,* 6th ed. (Fort Worth, TX: Harcourt Brace Jovanovich, College Division, 1998).

[10] Ibid.

[11] Alfred Adler, *The Individual Psychology of Alfred Adler* (New York: Basic Books, 1956), p. 48.

[12] Hertha Orgler, *Alfred Adler: The Man and His Work* (New York: New American Library, 1963).

[13] Julian Rotter, "External Control and Internal Control," *Psychology Today,* June 1971, pp. 37–42, 58–59 [13]. See also Samuel

E. Wood and Ellen Green Wood, *The World of Psychology* (Boston, MA: Allyn & Bacon, 2006), pp. 339–340.

[14] Matthew McKay and Patrick Fanning, *Self-Esteem* (Oakland, CA: New Harbinger, 1987), p. 181.

[15] Adapted from Matthew McKay and Patrick Fanning, *Self-Esteem* (Oakland, CA: New Harbinger, 1987).

[16] Stephen R. Covey, *The Seven Habits of Highly Effective People* (New York: Simon & Schuster, 1989).

[17] Ibid. See also Neil A. Fiore, *The Now Habit* (Los Angeles, CA: Jeremy P. Tarcher, 1989), pp. 6–26.

[18] Denis Waitley, *Psychology of Success: Developing Your Self-Esteem* (Homewood, IL: Richard D. Irwin, 1993), p. 76. See also B. David Brooks and Rex K. Dalby, *The Self-Esteem Repair and Maintenance Manual* (Newport Beach, CA: Kincaid House, 1990), p. 55.

[19] Robert Rosenthal and Lenore Jacobson, *Pygmalion in the Classroom: Teacher Expectations and Pupils' Intellectual Development* (Norwalk, CT: Irvington Publishing Co., 1992). See also Cecilia Elena Rouse, and Lisa Barrow, "U.S. Elementary and Secondary Schools: Equalizing Opportunity or Replicating the Status Quo?" Opportunity in America, Volume 16, Number 2, Fall 2006. Future of Children: A Collaboration of The Woodrow Wilson School of Public and International Affairs at Princeton University and The Brookings Institution, www.futureofchildren.org /information2826/information_show.htm?doc_id=392628 (retrieved March 14, 2008).

[20] Victoria Clayton, "Are We Raising a Nation of Little Egomaniacs? Debate Erupts Over Whether Kids Get Too Much Praise or Not Enough," MSNBC, 2008 MSNBC Interactive, Mon., April 2, 2007, /www.msnbc.msn.com/id/17821247/ (retrieved March 14, 2008).

[21] Lilian Katz, "How Can We Strengthen Children's Self-Esteem?" KidSource Online, www.kidsource.com/kidsource/content2/ Strengthen_Children_Self.html (retrieved July 30, 2005). See also Robert W. Reasoner, "Review of Self-Esteem Research," National Association for Self-Esteem, posted 2004, www.self -esteem-nase.org/research.php (retrieved March 15, 2008).

[22] Lisa Firestone, PhD, in "How to Tame Your Inner Critics," *Psychology Today,* posted April 11, 2016 (https://www .psychologytoday.com/blog/compassion-matters/201604 /how-tame-your-inner-critic). See also Robert Firestone, Lisa Firestone, Joyce Catlett, and Pat Love (2002) *Conquer Your Critical Inner Voice: A Revolutionary Program to Counter Negative Thoughts and Live Free from Imagined Limitations* (Oakland, CA: New Harbinger Publications).

[23] Ibid.

[24] Ibid.

[25] Ibid.

[26] References with further characteristics of the scale: Rich Crandal, "The Measurement of Self-Esteem and Related Constructs," in J. P. Robinson and P. R. Shaver, eds., *Measures of Social Psychological Attitudes,* rev. ed. (Ann Arbor: ISR, 1973), pp. 80–82; M. Rosenberg, *Society and the Adolescent Self-Image* (Princeton, NJ: Princeton University Press, 1965) (Chapter 2 discusses construct validity); E. Silber and Jean Tippett, "Self-Esteem: Clinical Assessment and Measurement Validation," 16 *Psychological Reports,* pp. 1017–1071 (discusses multitrait-multimethod

470 REFERENCES

investigation using RSE), 1965; Ruth C. Wylie, *The Self-Concept*, rev. ed. (Lincoln, NE: University of Nebraska Press, 1974), especially pp. 180–189.

Chapter 3

[1] Carl Rogers, "What It Means to Become a Person," in Clark E. Moustakas, ed., *The Self: Explorations in Personal Growth* (New York: Harper & Row, 1956), pp. 195–211.

[2] Marie Lundquist, *Holding Back: Why We Hide the Truth About Ourselves* (New York: Harper & Row, 1988), p. 5.

[3] Ibid.

[4] Joseph Luft, *Group Process: Introduction to Group Dynamics* (Palo Alto, CA: National Press, 1970). See also Phillip C. Hanson, "The Johari Window: A Model for Soliciting and Giving Feedback," in *The 1973 Annual Handbook of Group Facilitators* (San Diego, CA: University Associates, 1973), pp. 114–119.

[5] Sam Keen and Anne V. Fox, *Telling Your Story: A Guide to Who You Are and Who You Can Be* (New York: Signet, 1973), pp. 22–24.

[6] This list is based on Marie Lindquist, *Holding Back*, p. 26.

[7] Maxwell Maltz, *Psycho-Cybernetics* (New York: Simon & Schuster, 1960), pp. 165–167.

[8] Roy F. Baumeister and Dianne M. Tice, "Four Selves, Two Motives and a Substitute Process Self-Regulation Model," in Roy F. Baumeister, ed., *Public Self and Private Self* (New York: Sprinter-Verlag, 1986), p. 63.

[9] Lisa Rosh and Lynn Offerman, "Be Yourself, but Carefully," *Harvard Business Review*, October 2013.

[10] Michal Kosinski, David Stillwell, and Thore Graepel "Private traits and Attributes are Predictable from Digital Records of Human Behavior," from the *Proceedings of the National Academy of Sciences in the United States of America*. Edited by Kenneth Wachter, University of California, Berkeley, CA, and approved February 12, 2013 (received for review October 29, 2012).

[11] This list of disadvantages is based on Marie Lindquist, *Holding Back*, pp. 27–33. Also see John Powell, *Why Am I Afraid to Tell You Who I Am?* (Allen, TX: Argus Communications, 1969), pp. 77–83.

[12] The following five levels come from John Powell, *Why Am I Afraid to Tell You Who I Am?* (Allen, TX: Argus Communications, 1969, pp. 50–62; republished by Thomas More Association, 1990).

[13] John Powell, (1969, 1999), *Why Am I Afraid to Tell You Who I Am?* p. 58.

[14] This is a terrific oversimplification of Maslow's point. For further reading, see Abraham Maslow, "Lessons from the Peak Experiences," *Journal of Humanistic Psychology*, February 1962, Vol. 2, pp. 9–18. Also see Abraham Maslow, *Religions, Values, and Peak Experiences* (Columbus: Ohio State University Press, 1964).

[15] John Powell, *Why Am I Afraid to Tell You Who I Am?*, p. 62.

[16] Ibid., p. 77.

[17] Ibid., p. 80.

[18] These three advantages of "gut level" communications are based on John Powell, *Why Am I Afraid to Tell You Who I Am?*, pp. 79–85.

[19] R. D. Laing, *Knots* (New York: Perennial Press, 1972). See also R. D. Laing, H. Phillipson, and A. R. Lee, *Interpersonal Perception* (New York: Perennial Press, 1972).

[20] This list of fears is based in part on Susan Jeffers, *Feel the Fear and Do It Anyway* (New York: Ballantine, 1987), pp. 11–18, and on Marie Lindquist, *Holding Back*, p. 155.

[21] Dale Carnegie, *How to Stop Worrying and Start Living* (New York: Pocket Books, 1953).

[22] Virginia Satir, *Peoplemaking* (Palo Alto, CA: Science and Behavior Books, 1972), pp. 75–79.

[23] L. Miller, R. Archer, and J. Berg, "Eliciting Self-Disclosure," *Journal of Personality and Social Psychology*, vol. 44, 1983, pp. 1234–1244.

[24] Ibid.

Chapter 4

[1] Lucian Ghinda, "54 Sources of Happiness" Ghinda.com/blog/2010/54-Sources-of-Happiness/ (retrieved February 8, 2013).

[2] David G. Myers, "The Secret of Happiness," *Psychology Today*, 25 (July/August 1992), p. 38–45.

[3] Martin Seligman, *Learned Optimism: How to Change Your Mind and Your Life* (New York: Simon and Schuster, 1990).

[4] O'Connor Anahad, "Really? Optimism Reduces the Risk of Heart Disease," *New York Times*, www.nytimes.com (posted April 23, 2012).

[5] C. S. Carver, C. Pozo, S. D. Harris, V. Noriega, M. F. Scheier, D. S. Robinson, A. S. Ketcham, F. L. Moffat, Jr., and K. C. Clark, "How Coping Mediates the Effect of Optimism on Distress: A Study of Women with Early Stage Breast Cancer," *Journal of Personality and Social Psychology*, 65 (1993), pp. 375–390.

[6] William J. Chopik and Ed O'Brien, "Happy You, Healthy Me? Having a Happy Partner Is Independently Associated With Better Health in Oneself," in *Health Psychology*, 2017, Vol. 36, No. 1, 21–30.

[7] M. F. Scheier, J. K. Weintraub, C. S. Carver, "Coping with Stress: Divergent Strategies of Optimists and Pessimists," *Journal of Personality and Social Psychology*, 51 (1986), pp. 1258–1264.

[8] Andrew Steptoe, Samantha Dockray, and Jane Wardle (2009), Positive Affect and Psychobiological Processes Relevant to Health. *Journal of Personality*, 77: 1747–1776 .

[9] Diener, E., & Chan, M. Y. (2011). "Happy People Live Longer: Subjective Well-Being Contributes to Health and Longevity," *Applied Psychology: Health and Well-Being*, 3, 1–43.

[10] S. A. Everson, D. E. Goldberg, G. A. Kaplan, R. D. Cohen, E. Pukkala, J. Tuomilehto, and J. T. Salonen, "Hopelessness and Risk of Mortality and Incidence of Myocardial Infarction and Cancer," *Psychosomatic Medicine* 58 (1996), pp. 113–121.

[11] Carl Jung, *Psychological Types* (Princeton, NJ: Princeton University Press, 1971).

[12] Amanda Enayati, "Workplace happiness: What's the Secret?" CNN, Living. www.cnn.com (posted July 10, 2012).

[13] Huffington Post, "Happiness: Study Suggests Large Circle of Friends Is Key to Well-Being in Midlife." www.huffingtonpost.com (posted August 22, 2012, retrieved March 4, 2013).

[14] CIFAR Knowledge Circle, "Real-Life Friends Make You Happier." http://knowledgecircle.cifar.ca/exchange (Issue No. 3, February 13, 2013).

[15] Judith Rodin, "Aging and Health: Effects of the Sense of Control," *Science* 233 (1986), pp. 1271–1276.

[16] David G. Myers, "The Secret of Happiness," pp. 38–45.

[17] Michael W. Kraus, "The Happiness Chronicles I: The Dark Side to Happiness?" *Psychology Today.* Posted March 23, 2012. (https://www.psychologytoday.com/blog/under-the-influence/201203/the-happiness-chronicles-i-the-dark-side-happiness).

[18] Webster's New World Dictionary, (World Publishing Co., 1972), p. 513.

[19] Frances Merrit Stern, "Getting Good Feedback—and Giving Back in Kind," *Training/Human Resource Development,* April 1982, p. 34.

[20] Dow Scott and Stephen Taylor, "An Examination of Conflicting Findings on the Relationships between Job Satisfaction and Absenteeism: A Meta-Analysis," *Academy of Management Journal,* 28 (1985), pp. 599–612.

[21] Edwin A. Locke, "The Nature and Causes of Job Satisfaction," in *Handbook of Industrial and Organizational Psychology,* Marvin D. Dunnette, ed. (New York: John Wiley & Sons, 1983), pp. 1332–1334.

[22] Edward E. Lawler and Lyman W. Porter, "The Effect of Performance on Job Satisfaction," *Industrial Relations,* October 1967, pp. 20–28.

[23] Mark Ehrrant and Stephanie Nauman, "Organizational Citizenship Behavior in Work Groups: A Group Norms Approach," *Journal of Applied Psychology,* December 2004, pp. 960–972.

[24] *The Wall Street Journal,* January 12, 1988, p. 1, and Tom W. Smith, *Job Satisfaction in the United States* (April 2007) NORC/University of Chicago (retrieved March 2013 from www.news.uchicago.edu).

[25] Marcia A. Finkelstein, "Individualism/ Collectivism and Organizational Citizenship Behavior: An Integrative Framework," *Social Behavior and Personality,* Vol. 40 (October 2012).

[26] Paul Thagard Ph.D., "What Are Values?" *Psychology Today,* https://www.psychologytoday.com/blog/hot-thought/201304/what-are-values (retrieved May 21, 2017).

[27] Daniel Yankelovich, "The New Psychological Contracts at Work," *Psychology Today,* 11 (May 1978), pp. 46–50.

[28] Daniel Yankelovich and John Immerwahr, *Work in the 21st Century* (Alexandria, VA: American Society for Personnel Administration, 1984), pp. 16–17.

[29] Best College Reviews, "Cheating in College: The Numbers and Research" http://www.bestcollegereviews.org/cheating/ (retrieved May 20, 2017).

[30] Schroeder, Peter, "Harvard Students Withdraw after Cheating in 'Intro to Congress' Course." The Hill. www.thehill.com (posted February 2, 2013).

[31] David Callahan, *The Cheating Culture: Why Americans Are Doing Wrong to Get Ahead* (Orlando, FL: Harcourt, 2004), pp. 44–107.

[32] Milton Rokeach, *The Nature of Human Values* (New York: Free Press, 1973), pp. 3–12.

[33] Leon Festinger, *A Theory of Cognitive Dissonance* (Stanford, CA: Stanford University Press, 1957). See also: Robert Levine, *The Power of Persuasion: How We're Bought and Sold* (New York: Wiley, 2003).

[34] Ibid. See also: E. Aronson, "Dissonance, Hypocrisy, and the Self-Concept" in E. Harmon-Jones and J. S. Mills, *Cognitive Dissonance Theory: Revival with Revisions and Controversies* (Washington, DC: American Psychological Association, 1998).

[35] John Tierney, "Go Ahead, Rationalize. Monkeys Do It, Too," *New York Times,* Science. http://www.nytimes.com/2007/11/06/science/06tier.html?_r=1&oref=slogin (posted November 6, 2007).

[36] Martin Seligman, *The Optimistic Child* (Boston, MA: Houghton Mifflin, 1995), pp. 219–223.

[37] Ibid.

[38] From *Time,* October 2, 1995, pp. 60–68. These suggestions are thoroughly revised but generally inspired by: Elwood N. Chapman, *Your Attitude Is Showing* (New York: MacMillan, 1991), pp. 23–25.

[39] Harry Levinson, "What Killed Bob Lyons?" *Harvard Business Review: On Human Relations* (New York: Harper & Row, 1979), pp. 332–333.

[40] Source: Maxwell Maltz, *Psycho-Cybernetics: A New Way to Get More Out of Life* (New York: Simon & Schuster, 1960), pp. 91–93.

[41] Louis Rath, Merrill Haron, and Sidney Simon, *Values and Teaching* (Columbus, OH: Charles Merrill Publishers, 1976).

Chapter 5

[1] Peter Drucker, *Management: Tasks, Responsibilities, Practices* (New York: Harper & Row, 1974), p. 455.

[2] C. H. Deutsch, "Why Women Walk Out on Jobs," *The New York Times,* April 29, 1990, p. F27.

[3] Spencer Rathus and Jeffrey Nevid, *Adjustment and Growth: The Challenges of Life,* 7th ed. (New York: Harcourt Brace College Publishers, 1999).

[4] Edward Hoffman, *The Right to Be Human: A Biography of Abraham Maslow* (Los Angeles: Jeremy P. Tarcher, 1988), p. 154. See also Laurie Pawlik-Kienlen, "Self-Actualization in Action: How to Apply Maslow's Hierarchy of Needs to Your Life," *Suite101.com,* posted March 21, 2007, http://psychology.suite101.com/article.cfm/fulfill_your_potential (retrieved May 1, 2008).

[5] Abraham Maslow, *Motivation and Personality* (New York: Harper & Row, 1970), pp. 46–65.

[6] Robert Tanner, "Motivation—Applying Maslow's Hierarchy of Needs Theory," https://managementisajourney.com/motivation-applying-maslows-hierarchy-of-needs-theory/ (posted January 2, 2017; retrieved May 25, 2017).

[7] Richard M. Steers and Lyman Porter, *Motivation and Work Behavior,* 3rd ed. (New York: McGraw-Hill, 1983), pp. 3–5.

[8] Clayton Alderfer, *Existence, Relatedness, & Growth* (New York: Free Press, 1972), pp. 12–26.

[9] See www.netmba.com/mgmt/ob/motivation/erg. Accessed May 1, 2008.

472   REFERENCES

[10] David C. McClelland, *Human Motivation* (Glenview, IL: Scott, Foresman, 1985).

[11] David C. McClelland and David Burnham, "Power Is the Great Motivator," *Harvard Business Review* 54 (March–April 1976), pp. 100–110.

[12] Ibid., pp. 102–110.

[13] S. M. Klein and R. R. Ritti, *Understanding Organizational Behavior* (Boston, MA: Kent Publishing, 1984), pp. 256–258.

[14] A. Kukla, "Foundations of an Attributional Theory of Performance," *Psychological Review,* 79 (1972), pp. 454–470.

[15] David C. McClelland, *Human Motivation.* See also R. B. McCall, "Academic Underachievers," *Current Directions in Psychological Science* 3 (1994), pp. 15–19.

[16] Sibin Wu and Grace K. Dagher, Management Research News, "Need for Achievement, Business Goals, and Entrepreneurial Persistence," *Management Research News* 30(12): 928–941. November 2007 (https://www.researchgate.net /publication/241674423_Need_for_achievement_business_goals _and_entrepreneurial_persistence, retrieved May 25, 2017).

[17] Frederick Herzberg, "One More Time: How Do You Motivate Employees?" *Harvard Business Review,* Winter 1979, pp. 101–121. See also Frederick Herzberg, *Work and the Nature of Man* (New York: Harper & Row, 1966).

[18] Frederick Herzberg, "Workers' Needs: The Same Around the World," *Industry Week,* September 21, 1987, pp. 29–31.

[19] J. R. Hackman and Gene Oldman, *Work Redesign* (Reading, MA: Addison-Wesley, 1980).

[20] Ibid.

[21] Andrzej Marczewski, (April 2012). *Gamification: A Simple Introduction* (1st ed.). p. 3. ISBN 978-1-4717-9866-5. https://trends. google.com/trends/explore?date=all&q=gamification, retrieved May 28, 2017.

[22] Jane McGonigal, *Reality Is Broken: Why Games Make Us Better and How They Can Change the World* (New York: Penguin Books, 2011).

[23] Brian Burke, "How Gamification Motivates the Masses," *Forbes,* https://www.forbes.com/sites/gartnergroup/2014/04/10/how-gami fication-motivates-the-masses/#7bf7beb25c04, retrieved May 28, 2017. http://www.chicagotribune.com/lifestyles/ct-tribu-play-at-work -story-20111010-story.html, retrieved May 28, 2017.

[24] http://www.enterprise-gamification.com/mediawiki/index .php?title=Target_-_Checkout_Process_at_the_Cashier, retrieved June 4, 2017.

[25] Jane McGonigal, *Reality Is Broken: Why Games Make Us Better and How They Can Change the World* (New York: Penguin Books, 2011).

[26] http://www.gartner.com/technology/research/gamification/, retrieved May 28, 2017.

[27] Victor H. Vroom, *Work and Motivation* (New York: John Wiley & Sons, 1964), pp. 170–174.

[28] Hina Raheel, "Leadership and Motivation: The Effective Application of Expectancy Theory," *Journal of Pioneering Medical Sciences Blog,* August 17, 2013. http://blogs.jpmsonline.com/2013/08/17/leader ship-and-motivation-the-effective-application-of-expectancy-theory/.

[29] Barry M. Staw, *Intrinsic and Extrinsic Motivation* (New York: John Wiley & Sons, 1976). See also Uco J. Wiersma, "The Effects of Extrinsic Rewards in Intrinsic Motivation," *Journal of Occupational and Organizational Psychology* 65 (1992), pp. 101–114.

[30] B. F. Skinner, *Beyond Freedom and Dignity* (New York: Alfred A. Knopf, 1971).

[31] Eric Berne, *Games People Play* (New York: Grove Press, 1964), pp. 34–37.

[32] Michael LeBoeuf, *The Greatest Management Principle in the World* (New York: Berkeley Publishing, 1987), pp. 12–27.

[33] B. F. Skinner, *Beyond Freedom and Dignity,* pp. 17–48.

[34] R. A. Katzell and D. E. Thompson, "Work Motivation: Theory and Practice," *American Psychologist* 45 (1990), pp. 144–153.

[35] Leong Teen Wei and Rashad Yazdanifard, "The impact of Positive Reinforcement on Employees' Performance in Organizations," *American Journal of Industrial and Business Management,* 2014, 4, 9–12 Published Online January 2014 (http://www.scirp .org/journal/ajibm) http://dx.doi.org/10.4236/ajibm.2014.41002 (retrieved May 25, 2017).

[36] Jack Falvey, "To Raise Productivity, Try Saying Thank You," *The Wall Street Journal,* December 6, 1982, p. 26.

[37] Joel Brockner, *Self-Esteem at Work: Research, Theory, and Practice* (Lexington, MA: Lexington Books, 1988), pp. 159–161, 192. See also Matthew McKay and Patrick Fanning, *Self-Esteem* (Oakland, CA: New Harbinger Publication, 1987), pp. 159–189.

Chapter 6

[1] Frank K. Sonnenberg, "Barriers to Communication," *Journal of Business Strategy* 11 (July/August 1990), pp. 56–58.

[2] Sandra Hagevik, "Just Listening," *Journal of Environmental Health* 62 (July 1999), pp. 26–32.

[3] Sonnenberg (1990), "Barriers to Communication," p. 56.

[4] Lyle Sussman and Paul D. Krivonos, *Communication for Supervisors and Managers* (Easton, PA: Alfred Publishing Company, 1979), pp. 66–68.

[5] Anthony Allesandra, quoted in *The Power of Listening,* Revised Edition (firm) (CRM Films, 1987).

[6] John Stewart and Carole Logan, *Together: Communicating Interpersonally* (New York: McGraw-Hill, 1993), pp. 246–247.

[7] Edward T. Hall, *The Silent Language* (Greenwich, CT: Fawcett Books, 1959), pp. 51–53.

[8] Albert Mehrabian, *Nonverbal Communication* (Chicago, IL: Aldine-Atherton Company, 1972), pp. 23–38.

[9] "The Anatomy of a Message," *Ford's Insider* (1981), pp. 4–9.

[10] Paul Ekman and Wallace V. Friesan, "Hand Movements," *Journal of Communication* 22 (1972), pp. 353–358.

[11] Based on Edward T. Hall, "Proxemics: A Study of Man's Spatial Relationships," from *Man's Image in Medicine and Anthropology* (New York: International Universities Press, 1963).

[12] William M. Pride and O. Jeff Harris, "Psychological Barriers in the Upward Flow of Communication," *Atlanta Economic Review* 21 (March 1971), pp. 30–32. See also "Organization Charts as a

Management Tool," http://management.about.com/cs/general-management/a/orgcharts_2.htm. Accessed May 3, 2008.

[13] Keith Davis, "Management Communication and the Grapevine," *Harvard Business Review* 31 (September–October 1953), pp. 45–47.

[14] O. Jeff Harris and Sandra J. Hartman, *Human Behavior at Work* (New York: West Publishing Company, 1992), pp. 270–271.

[15] Karan Ronin, "5 Common Body Language Mistakes on International Business Trips," January 22, 2014. http://www.executive-impressions.com/blog/5-body-language-mistakes-international-business-trips.

[16] Edward T. Hall, "How Cultures Collide," *Psychology Today* 10 (July 1976), pp. 66–74. See also Edward T. Hall, *Beyond Culture* (Garden City, NY: Doubleday, 1976).

[17] Based on Dulek, Fielden, and Hill, "International Communication," pp. 21–22.

Chapter 7

[1] Jon L. Pierce and John Newstrom, *Leaders and the Leadership Process* (Burr Ridge, IL: McGraw-Hill Irwin, 2008), pp. 158–163.

[2] G. E. Myers and M. T. Myers, *The Dynamics of Human Communication* (New York: McGraw-Hill, 1973), pp. 125–127.

[3] V. W. Tuchman, "Developmental Sequences in Small Groups," *Psychological Bulletin* 63 (May 1965), pp. 384–399.

[4] Ibid., pp. 386–389. See also A. C. Kowitz and T. J. Knutson, *Decision-Making in Small Groups: The Search for Alternatives* (Boston, MA: Allyn & Bacon, 1980).

[5] Feldman, "Development and Enforcement of Group Norms," pp. 49–53.

[6] https://highered.mheducation.com/sites/dl/free/0073010189/228359/groupthink2.html (From the First Edition of *A First Look at Communication Theory* by Em Griffin, © 1991, McGraw-Hill, Inc.)

[7] Robert R. Blake and Jane S. Mouton, "Don't Let Group Norms Stifle Creativity," *Personnel* 62 (August 1985), pp. 28–33.

[8] J. Richard Hackman and Charles G. Morris, "Improving Group Performance Effectiveness," in *Advances in Experimental Social Psychology*, ed. Leonard Berkowitz (New York: Academic Press, 1975), p. 345.

[9] Peter Piven, "Increasing Your Project Team's Effectiveness." Coxe Leadership Group, 2008. www.coxegroup.com/articles/effectiveness.html (retrieved May 4, 2008).

[10] These three categories are based on Dr. Marlin S. Potash, *Hidden Agendas* (New York: Dell Publishing, 1990), p. 56. See also Roberta Shaler, "The Queen and Her Bobble-Heads: Uncovering 'Hidden' Agendas," http://hodu.com/queen.shtml (retrieved May 4, 2008).

[11] Richard L. Daft and Dorothy Marcic, *Understanding Management*, 5th ed. (Mason, OH: Thompson South-Western, 2006), pp. 412–413.

[12] Warren Bennis and Burt Nanus, *Leaders: The Strategies for Taking Charge* (New York: Harper & Row, 1986), pp. 19–26.

[13] Rosabeth Moss Kanter, "The New Management Work," *Harvard Business Review*, November/December 1989, pp. 85–92.

[14] Robert R. Blake and Jane S. Mouton, "A Comparative Analysis of Situationalism and 9.9 Management by Principle," *Organizational Dynamics*, Spring 1982, pp. 20–43.

[15] Afsaneh Nahavandi, *The Art and Science of Leadership*, 4th ed. (Upper Saddle River, NJ: Prentice Hall, 2007), pp. 99–112.

[16] Gary A. Yukl and C. M. Falbe, "The Importance of Different Power Sources in Downward and Lateral Relations," *Journal of Applied Psychology* 76 (1991), pp. 416–423. See also Gary Yukl, *Leadership in Organizations*, 6th ed. (Upper Saddle River, NJ: Prentice Hall, 2005).

[17] Nahavandi, *Art and Science of Leadership*, pp. 184–190. See also John P. Kotter, *John P. Kotter on What Leaders Really Do* (Boston, MA: Harvard Business Review Books, 1999), pp. 143–172.

[18] Harvey Robbins and Michael Finley, *The New WHY TEAMS DON'T WORK: What Goes Wrong and How to Make It Right* (San Francisco, CA: Berret-Kohler Publishers 2000). See also Rosemary Batt, "Work Organization, Technology and Performance in Customer Service and Sales," *Industrial and Labor Relations Review* 52 (July 1999), pp. 539–563 (retrieved July 15, 2005), http://www.hrzone.com/articles/teams_tqm_or_taylorism.html. See also "Work Team Skills and Productivity," Center for Collaborative Organizations (Center for the Study of Work Teams), University of North Texas (retrieved May 18, 2008). http://www.workteams.unt.edu/research.htm.

[19] These defining factors are based on E. Thomas Moran and J. Fredericks Volkwein, "The Cultural Approach to the Formation of Organizational Climate," *Human Relations*, January 1992, p. 20.

[20] Stewart R. Segall, "Reflections of Your Management Style," *Supervisory Management* 36 (February 1991), pp. 1–2.

[21] E. Thomas Moran and J. Fredericks Volwein, pp. 22–47. See also: R. M. Guion, "A Note on Organizational Climate," *Organizational Behavior and Human Performance* 9 (1973), pp. 120–125.

[22] Sharon L. Kubiak et al., "Making People an Organization's Most Important Resource," *Business* 40 (October–December 1990), p. 33.

[23] For more on stories in corporate cultures, see Thomas J. Peters and Nancy K. Austin, *A Passion for Excellence* (New York: Random House, 1985), pp. 278–293.

[24] Paul Hellman (1992), op. cit., p. 63.

[25] Edgar Schein, "How Founders/Leaders Embed and Transmit Culture" (retrieved July 12, 2005) http://www.tnellen.com/ted/tc/schein.html. See also: Edgar Schein, *Organizational Culture and Leadership*, 3rd ed. (New York, Jossey-Bass, 2004).

[26] These qualities of the "New Corporate Culture" are based in part on: Joseph D. O'Brian, "The 'New Corporate Culture': Mainly Just Common Sense," *Supervisory Management* 39 (January 1992), p. 9.

[27] Marshall Sashkin and Richard L. Williams, "Does Fairness Make a Difference?" *Organizational Dynamics* 19 (Autumn 1990), pp. 56–58.

[28] For information on the psychological contract, see Edgar Schein, *Organizational Psychology* (Englewood Cliffs, NJ: Prentice Hall, 1980).

Chapter 8

[1] Daniel Goleman, Paul Kaufman, and Michael Ray, *The Creative Spirit* (New York: Dutton, 1992), pp. 72–79.

[2] Daniel Goleman, *Emotional Intelligence* (New York: Bantam Books, 1995), p. 34.

474   REFERENCES

[3] Goleman, *Emotional Intelligence,* pp. 8, 291–296.

[4] Allen Farnham, "Are You Smart Enough to Keep Your Job?" *Fortune,* January 15, 1996, pp. 34–42. See also "Leading by Feel: Be Realistic," *Harvard Business Review,* January 2004, p. 28.

[5] Goleman, *Working with Emotional Intelligence,* pp. 26–28.

[6] Robert Sternberg, *Successful Intelligence* (New York: Simon & Schuster, 1996), also retold in Daniel Goleman, *Working with Emotional Intelligence* (New York: Bantam Books, 1998), p. 22.

[7] Ibid., pp. 24–27.

[8] Mark Daniel, *Self-Scoring Emotional Intelligence Tests* (New York: Sterling Publishing, 2000), pp. 1–2.

[9] Daniel Goleman, Richard Boyatzis, and Annie McKee, *Primal Leadership: Realizing the Power of Emotional Intelligence* (Boston: Harvard Business School Publishing, 2002). pp. 105–109.

[10] Richard E. Boyatzis, "Developing Emotional Intelligence Competencies," in Joseph Ciarrochi and John Mayer (eds.), *Applying Emotional Intelligence* (New York: Psychology Press, 2007), pp. 29–30.

[11] Cf. Boyatzis, pp. 30–31.

[12] Goldman, Boyatzis, and McKee, *Primal Leadership,* pp. 107–118.

[13] Matthew McKay, Martha Davis, and Patrick Fanning, *Thoughts and Feelings: Taking Control of Your Moods and Your Life* (Oakland, CA: New Harbinger Publications, 2007), pp. 233–234.

[14] These four characteristics of anger are based on Gilian Butler and Tony Hope, *Managing Your Mind,* 2nd ed. (New York: Oxford University Press, 2007), pp. 171–173.

[15] Daniel Goleman, *Emotional Intelligence* (New York: Bantam Books, 1995), p. 65.

[16] These steps were drawn in part from Butler and Hope, *Managing Your Mind,* p. 178.

[17] Jim Tamm, *Radical Collaboration* (New York: HarperCollins, 2005), pp. 123–159.

[18] Shirzad Chamine, "Positive Intelligence," http://www.positiveintelligence.com/ (retrieved June 2, 2017).

[19] Marina Krakovsky, "Shirzad Chamine: How to Defeat Your Internal Saboteurs," Stanford Graduate School of Business, posted September 9, 2013, https://www.gsb.stanford.edu/insights/shirzad-chamine-how-defeat-your-internal-saboteurs (retrieved June 2, 2017).

[20] "Positive Intelligence and PQ," Sources of Insight, http://sourcesofinsight.com/positive-intelligence-and-pq/ (posted 2012, retrieved June 2, 2017).

[21] Lydia Dishman, "How to Quiet the Negative Thoughts That Are Killing Your Career," *Fast Company,* posted June 12, 2012, https://www.fastcompany.com/1839905/how-quiet-negative-thoughts-are-killing-your-career (retrieved June 2, 2017).

[22] Muriel James and Dorothy Jongeward, *Born to Win* (Reading, MA: Addison-Wesley, 1973), op. cit., pp. 69–70.

[23] Gerald M. Goldhaber and Marylynn Goldhaber, *Transactional Analysis* (Boston, MA: Allyn & Bacon, 1976), p. 180.

[24] Maurice F. Villere, Thomas S. O'Connor, and William J. Quain, "Games Nobody Wins: Transactional Analysis for the Hospitality Industry," *The Cornell University H.R.A. Quarterly* 24 (November 1983), p. 72.

[25] "Of Frogs and Princes," http://frogsandprinces.dawntreader.net/games.html, accessed July 12, 2005. See also Ian Stewart and Vann Joines, *TA Today: A New Introduction to Transactional Analysis* (Chapel Hill, NC: Lifespace Publishing, 1991).

[26] Villere, O'Connor, and Quain, "Games Nobody Wins," p. 75.

[27] This example is adapted from Linda L. Phillips, *Film Guide for "Transactional Analysis"* (New York: McGraw-Hill, Films, 1977), p. 6.

[28] Villere, O'Connor, and Quain, "Games Nobody Wins," p. 77.

Chapter 9

[1] Robert M. Fulmer, *Practical Human Relations* (Homewood, IL: Richard Irwin Company, 1983), pp. 292–293.

[2] Edward A. Charlesworth and Ronald G. Nathan, *Stress Management: A Comprehensive Guide to Wellness* (New York: Ballantine Books, 1985), pp. 178–181.

[3] Shad Helmstetter, *You Can Excel in Times of Change* (New York: Simon & Schuster, 1991), p. 46.

[4] Bernadine Kreis and Alice Pattie, *Up from Grief: Patterns of Recovery* (New York: The Seabury Press, 1969), pp. 11–23.

[5] William Bridges, *Transitions: Making Sense of Life's Changes* (Reading, MA: Addison-Wesley, 1980), pp. 90–99.

[6] Gail Sheehy, *Pathfinders: Overcoming the Crises of Adult Life and Finding Your Own Path to Well-Being* (New York: William Morrow, 1981), pp. 313–314.

[7] Bridges, *Transitions,* p. 112.

[8] Kreis and Pattie, *Up from Grief,* p. 36.

[9] L. John Mason, *Stress Passages: Surviving Life's Transitions Gracefully* (Berkeley, CA: Celestial Arts, 1988), pp. 230–232.

[10] These six steps are based on Helmstetter, *You Can Excel in Times of Change,* pp. 145–180.

[11] Prosci, "What Is Change Management?" https://www.prosci.com/change-management/what-is-change-management (retrieved June 2, 2017).

[12] John Paul Kotter, *Leading Change* (Cambridge, MA: Harvard Review Press, 1996, 2012).

[13] Kurt Lewin, *Field Theory and Social Science* (New York: Harper and Row, 1964), especially Chapters 9 and 10.

[14] Ibid., p. 10.

[15] Leonard D. Goodstein and W. Warner Burke, "Creating Successful Organizational Change," *Organizational Dynamics* 19 (Spring 1991), pp. 9–11.

[16] Ibid., p. 10.

[17] Peter B. Vaill, *Learning as a Way of Being: Strategies for Surviving in a World of Permanent White Water* (San Francisco: Jossey-Bass, 1996), pp. 47–78.

[18] Kurt Lewin, "Group Decisions and Social Change," in *Readings in Social Psychology* (New York: Holt, Rinehart & Winston, 1952); and Kurt Lewin, "Fronteerism Group Dynamics: Concept, Method, and Reality in Social Science," *Human Relations* 1 (1974), pp. 5–41.

[19] Ibid.

20 James Brian Quinn, *Strategies for Change: Logical Incrementalism* (Homewood, IL: Richard Irwin, 1980). Cf. "Logical Incrementalism," www.12manage.com/description_logical_incrementalism.html (accessed May 18, 2008).

21 James Brian Quinn, "Strategic Change: 'Logical Incrementalism,'" *Sloan Management Review* 30 (Summer 1989), pp. 45–59.

22 For more information on the role of the leader in organizational change, see David A. Nadir and Michael L. Tushman, "Beyond the Charismatic Leader: Leadership and Organizational Change," *California Management Review* 32 (Winter 1990), pp. 77–97.

23 Brendan McGuigan, "What Is Kaizen?" published by Conjecture Corporation, November 29, 2012 (accessed March 17, 2013 at www.wisegeek.org). Norman Bodek, *How to Do Kaizen: A New Path to Innovation—Empowering Everyone to Be a Problem Solver* (Vancouver, WA, US: PCS Press, 2010). https://en.wikipedia.org/wiki/Kaizen (accessed 3/17/2013).

24 Stephen P. Robbins and Tim A. Judge, *Organizational Behavior: Concepts, Controversies, and Applications* (Englewood Cliffs, NJ: Prentice Hall, 2007), pp. 665–691.

25 Harry Levinson, "Easing the Pain of Personal Loss," *Harvard Business Review* 50 (September–October 1972), pp. 80–88.

Chapter 10

1 Ross L. Mooney, "Groundwork for Creative Research," in Clark E. Moustakas (ed.), *The Self: Explorations in Personal Growth* (New York: Harper & Row, 1956), p. 264.

2 Mihalyi Csikszentmihalyi, *Creativity: Flow and the Psychology of Discovery and Invention* (New York: HarperCollins Publishers, 1996).

3 "On Creativity," *Omni* 11 (April 1989), pp. 112–119.

4 L. Terman and M. H. Oden, *Genetic Studies of Genius:* Vol. 5. *The Gifted Group at Mid-Life* (Stanford, CA: Stanford University Press, 1959).

5 Arthur Koestler, *The Act of Creation* (New York: Macmillan, 1964), pp. 124–145.

6 Jacob Bronowski, *The Ascent of Man* (Boston, MA: Little, Brown, 1973), pp. 118–119.

7 Ibid., pp. 137–141.

8 Edward Hoffman, *The Right to Be Human: A Biography of Abraham Maslow* (Los Angeles: Jeremy P. Tarcher, 1988), p. 238.

9 James L. Adams, *Conceptual Blockbusting: A Guide to Better Ideas* (Cambridge, MA: Perseus Books, 2001), pp. 25–33.

10 From Samuel Wood and Ellen Wood, *The World of Psychology*, 3rd ed. (Needham Heights, MA: Allyn & Bacon, 1999).

11 Graham Wallas, *The Art of Thought* (Orlando, FL: Harcourt Brace, 1926).

12 Ibid.

13 Roger von Oech, *A Whack on the Side of the Head: How You Can Be More Creative* (New York: Business Plus, 2008), p. 142.

14 Graham Wallas, *The Art of Thought*. (London: Jonathan Cape, 1926), pp. 80–81.

15 Daniel Goleman, Paul Kaufman, and Michael Ray, *The Creative Spirit* (New York: Dutton, 1992).

16 L. Juang, D. V. Krasikova, and D. Liu. (2016). "I Can Do It, So Can You: The Role of Leader Creative Self-Efficacy in Facilitating Follower Creativity." *Organizational Behavior and Human Decision Processes*, 132, 49–62. DOI: 10.1016/j.obhdp.2015.12.002.

17 Siân Harrington, "Exclusive: Employees Want Financial Rewards for Innovation But Employers are Slow on the Uptake," *HR Magazine,* July 29, 2010, http://www.hrmagazine.co.uk/article-details/exclusive-employees-want-financial-rewards-for-innovation-but-employers-are-slow-on-the-uptake.

18 Laurie Tarkan, "Work Hard, Play Harder: Fun at Work Boosts Creativity, Productivity," FoxNews.com, Health @ Work (http://www.foxnews.com/health September 15, 2012; accessed March 18, 2013).

19 For a full discussion of the brainstorming process, see Adams, *Conceptual Blockbusting*, pp. 160–173.

20 Teresa M. Amabile, "The Motivation to Be Creative," in Scott G. Isaaksen (ed.), *Frontiers of Creativity Research* (Buffalo, NY: Bearly Press, 1987), pp. 229–230.

21 Ibid.

22 Cleese, "And Now for Something Completely Different," p. 50.

23 Parachin, "Seven Ways to Fire Up Your Creativity," pp. 3–4.

24 von Oech, *A Whack on the Side of the Head*, p. 21.

25 Jimmy Calano and Jeff Salzman, "Ten Ways to Fire Up Your Creativity," *Working Woman* 14, July 1989, pp. 94–95.

26 Ibid., p. 95.

27 von Oech, *A Whack on the Side of the Head*, p. 93.

28 Teresa Amabile, *The Social Psychology of Creativity* (New York: Springer-Verlag, 1983).

29 Robert Epstein, "Capturing Creativity," *Psychology Today,* July/August 1996, pp. 29, 41–43, 75–78.

30 Reprinted by permission of Warner Books/New York. From Roger von Oech, *A Whack on the Side of the Head: How You Can Be More Creative* (New York: Business Plus, 2008).

31 Bob Eberle, "Scamper On," in *Gifted Education: A Resource Guide for Teachers*, Ministry of Education, British Columbia, Canada, 1987, posted 2007, www.bced.gov.bc.ca/specialed/gifted/process.htm (retrieved May 31, 2008).

32 Epstein, "*Capturing Creativity*," p. 3.

33 3M Corporation, "Post-it, the Whole Story," www.mmm.com/us/office/postit/pastpresent/history_ws.html (retrieved June 1, 2008).

Chapter 11

1 Coalition of Services Industries, Jobs Across America: Services Lead Employment 2016, https://servicescoalition.org/jobs/ (retrieved June 20, 2016).

2 Peter Coffee, "Service Economy Brings New Technology Demands," *E-Week.Com,* December 13, 2004, pp. 1–3, www.eweek.com (retrieved August 20, 2008).

3 L. L. Putnam and M. S. Poole, "Conflict and Negotiation," in F. M. Jablin, L. L. Putnam, K. H. Roberts, and L. W. Porter (eds.), *Handbook of Organizational Communication: An Interdisciplinary Perspective* (Newbury Park, CA: Sage Publications, 1987), pp. 549–589.

476 REFERENCES

[4] Stephen P. Robbins, *Organizational Behavior: Concepts, Controversies, and Applications* (Englewood Cliffs, NJ: Prentice Hall, 1993), p. 445.

[5] Much of the material on sources of conflict is adapted from John Stewart and Carole Logan, *Together: Communicating Interpersonally* (New York: McGraw-Hill, 1993), pp. 347–377.

[6] These questions are excerpted and adapted from Stephen Goldberg, Eric Green, and Frank Sander, *Dispute Resolution* (Boston, MA: Little, Brown, and Company, 1985), pp. 545–550. See also Howard Raiffa, *The Art and Science of Negotiation* (Cambridge, MA: Belknap Press, 1982), pp. 14–22.

[7] Edward Glassman, "Selling Your Ideas to Management," *Supervisory Management* 36 (October 1991), p. 9.

[8] Barry L. Reece and Rhonda Brandt, *Effective Human Relations in Organizations* (Boston, MA: Houghton Mifflin Company, 2005), pp. 313–314.

[9] Gini Graham Scott, *Resolving Conflict with Others and Within Yourself* (Oakland, CA: New Harbinger Publications, 1990), p. 159.

[10] Edward Glassman, "Understanding and Supervising Low Conformers," *Supervisory Management* 35 (May 1990), p. 10.

[11] Ibid.

[12] This section is adapted from Teresa Brady, "When a Jealous Co-Worker Is Giving You a Hard Time," *Supervisory Management* 36 (June 1991), p. 5.

[13] Robert M. Bramson, *Coping with Difficult People* (Garden City, NY: Anchor Press, 1981), p. 70.

[14] Ibid., pp. 71–72.

[15] Adapted from ibid., pp. 72–76.

[16] Graham Scott, *Resolving Conflict with Others and Within Yourself,* pp. 160–161.

[17] Joseph T. Straub, "Dealing with Complainers, Whiners, and General Malcontents," *Supervisory Management* 37 (July 1992), pp. 1–2.

[18] Adapted from ibid., pp. 161–163.

[19] Reece and Brandt, *Effective Human Relations in Organizations,* pp. 313–314.

[20] Andrew E. Schwartz, "How to Handle Conflict Between Employees," *Supervisory Management* 37 (June 1992), p. 9.

Chapter 12

[1] Hans Selye, "The Stress Concept Today," in I. I. Kutash et al. (eds.), *Handbook on Stress and Anxiety* (San Francisco, CA: Jossey-Bass, 1980).

[2] Ibid.

[3] Allen Kanner, James Coyne, Catherine Schaefer, and Richard Lazarus, "A Comparison of Two Models of Stress Measurement: Daily Hassles and Uplifts Versus Major Life Events," *Journal of Behavioral Medicine* 4 (1981), pp. 1–39.

[4] Deborah L. Plummer and Steve Slane, "Patterns of Coping in Racially Stressful Situations," *Journal of Black Psychology* 22 (1996), pp. 302–315. See also American Psychological Association Press Release, "Racial Discrimination Has Different Mental Health Effects on Asians Depending on Ethnic Identity, Age and Birthplace, Study Shows," posted May 8, 2008, www.apa.org/releases/asianhealth0508.html (retrieved June 1, 2008).

[5] Spencer Rathus, *Essentials of Psychology* (Fort Worth, TX: Harcourt College Publishers, Inc., 2001), Chapter 11.

[6] Daniel Sanders, "Researchers Find Out Why Some Stress Is Good for You," Berkeley News, http://news.berkeley.edu/2013/04/16/researchers-find-out-why-some-stress-is-good-for-you/Posted April 16, 2013. Retrieved June 20, 2017.

[7] Ibid.

[8] Albert Ellis and R. A. Harper, *A New Guide to Rational Living* (Hollywood, CA: Wilshire, 1975). See also Albert Ellis, "The Basic Clinical Theory of Rational-Emotive Therapy," in A. Ellis and R. Grieger (eds.), *Handbook of Rational-Emotive Therapy* (New York: Springer, 1977); Albert Ellis, "Cognition and Affect in Emotional Disturbance," *American Psychologist* 40 (1985), pp. 471–472; and Albert Ellis, "The Impossibility of Achieving Consistently Good Mental Health," *American Psychologist* 42 (1987), pp. 364–375.

[9] The Albert Ellis Institute, http://albertellis.org/.

[10] Kay Devine, Trish Reay, Linda Stainton, and Ruth Collins-Nakai, "Downsizing Outcomes: Better a Victim Than a Survivor?" *Human Resource Management,* Summer 2003, pp. 109–124, www.gpworldwide.com/quick/oct2003/art5.asp (retrieved July 18, 2005). See also Joanne Sujansky, "The ABC's of Employee Trust," KeyGroup.com, www.keygrp.com/articles/article-abcoftrust.html (retrieved July 18, 2005); and "Stress in the Workplace," TheStressClinic.com, www.thestressclinic.com/news/Display.asp?ArticleName=StressAtWork (retrieved July 18, 2005).

[11] Ibid.

[12] Ibid.

[13] Ibid. See also Salvatore Maddi, "The Story of Hardiness: Twenty Years of Theorizing, Research, and Practice," *Consulting Psychology Journal: Practice and Research* 51 (2002), pp. 83–94. See also American Psychological Association Help Center, "The Road to Resilience" and "Resilience in a Time of War," www.apahelpcenter.org/featuredtopics/feature.php?id=6 (retrieved May 29, 2008).

[14] Hans Selye, *The Stress of Life* (rev. ed.) (New York: McGraw-Hill, 1976). See also Hans Selye, *Stress Without Distress* (New York: Harper & Rowe, 1974).

[15] Suzanne C. Segerstrom and Gregory E. Miller, "Psychological Stress and the Human Immune System: A Meta-Analytic Study of 30 Years of Inquiry," *Psychological Bulletin* 130 (4), American Psychological Association, posted July 4, 2004, www.apa.org/releases/stress_immune.html (retrieved July 19, 2005).

[16] Jamie Talan, "Stress Can Strike Back 20 Years Later," *The Bend Bulletin/Newsday,* Bend, OR (November 26, 1993).

[17] James Brodzinski, Robert Scherer, and Karen Goyer, "Workplace Stress," *Personnel Administrator,* July 1989. See also Nick Nykodym and Katie George, "Stress Busting on the Job," *Personnel,* July, 1989, pp. 56–59.

[18] Ibid. See also Robert Epstein, "Stress Busters," *Psychology Today,* March/April, 2000; and "Workplace Stress: It's Enough to Make Your Employees Sick," in *Success Performance Solutions,* www.super-solutions.com/RisingHealthCareCost_workplacestress.asp (retrieved June 1, 2008).

[19] Ibid. See also Ken Frenke, "Stress: An Economic Issue," Money Matters Online, Crown.Org., posted June, 2005, www.crown.org/newsletter/default.asp?issue=328&articleid=396 (retrieved July 19, 2005).

[20] Shelley Taylor, Lisa G. Aspinwall, Traci A. Giuliano, Gayle A. Dakof, Kathleen K. Reardon, "Storytelling and Coping with Stressful Events," *Journal of Applied Social Psychology* 23 (1993), pp. 703–733.

[21] Shari Caudron, "Humor Is Healthy in the Workplace," *Personnel Journal*, 1992, p. 71. See also C. W. Metcalf and Roma Felible, "Humor: An Antidote for Terminal Professionalism," *Industry Week*, July 20, 1992; Nykodym and George, "Stress Busting on the Job"; and Richard Maturi, "Stress Can Be Beaten," *Industry Week*, July 20, 1992.

[22] Spencer Rathus, *Essentials of Psychology*.

[23] Nykodym and George, "Stress Busting on the Job." See also Richard Maturi, "Stress Can Be Beaten," and Brodzinski, Scherer, and Goyer, "Workplace Stress."

[24] Edwin Locke, *A Guide to Effective Study* (New York: Springer Publishing Company, 1975). See also David Burns, M.D., *Ten Days to Self-Esteem* (New York: Quill-William Morrow, 1993).

Chapter 13

[1] Don Peppers and Martha Rogers, "Customers Don't Grow on Trees," *Fast Company Magazine*, July 2005, p. 25.

[2] Michael LeBoeuf, *How to Win Customers and Keep Them for Life* (New York: Putnam, 1987), pp. 38–40.

[3] Ibid., pp. 39–40.

[4] Matt Mansfield, *Small Business Trends*, "Customer Retention Statistics—The Ultimate Collection for Small Business" https://smallbiztrends.com/2016/10/customer-retention-statistics.html (posted October 25, 2016; retrieved June 20, 2017).

[5] Michael Roennevig, *AZCentral*, "The Top Reasons Why Customers Give Repeat Business," http://yourbusiness.azcentral.com/top-reasons-customers-give-repeat-business-7098.html (retrieved June 20, 2017).

[6] John Tschohl, "Customer Service Importance," *Supervision*, February 1991, p. 9.

[7] Ibid., pp. 9–11.

[8] Jerry Plymire, "Complaints as Opportunities," *The Journal of Service Marketing*, Spring 1991, p. 39.

[9] William B. Martin, *Quality Customer Service: The Art of Treating Customers as Guests* (Los Altos, CA: Crisp Publications, 1987), p. 9.

[10] Donna Earl, "What Is Internal Customer Service? A Definition and a Case Study," Donna Earl Training, 2008, www.donnaearltraining.com/Articles/InternalCustomerService.html (retrieved June 14, 2008).

[11] Shep Hyken, "Internal Customer Service," www.hyken.com/Article_10.html (retrieved June 14, 2008).

[12] Shep Hyken, "Internal Customer Service," *Shep Hyken: Create a Customer Service Culture*, 2008. www.hyken.com.

[13] Lane Baldwin, "Serving Internal Customers," Business Solutions, http://customerservicezone.com/cgi-bin/links/jump.cgi?ID=821 (retrieved June 14, 2008).

[14] Steven A. Eggland and John W. Williams, *Human Relations at Work* (Cincinnati, OH: South-Western Publishing, 1987), pp. 152–153.

[15] Norm Brodsky, "How to Lose Customers," *Inc.*, July 2005, pp. 49–50.

[16] Much of the following material on getting customers to complain is based on Oren Harari, "Nourishing the Complaint Process," *Management Review*, February 1992, pp. 41–43. See also Jerry Plymire, "Transforming Complaints into Opportunities," *Supervisory Management*, June 1990, pp. 11–12.

[17] Bill Gates, *Business at the Speed of Thought* (New York: Warner Books, 1999), pp. 267–271.

[18] Plymire, "Transforming Complaints into Opportunities," pp. 11–12.

[19] National Ethics Association, *Customer Service Ethics: Beware the Dark Side*, December 9, 2011 (accessed March 21, 2013 at http://www.ethics.net).

[20] Don Knauss, "The Role of Business Ethics in Relationships with Customers," January 19, 2012 (accessed March 21, 2013 at www.forbes.com).

[21] Andrew J. DuBrin, *Contemporary Applied Management Skills for Managers* (Burr Ridge, IL: Richard D. Irwin, 1994), p. 134.

[22] LeBoeuf, *How to Win Customers and Keep Them for Life*, pp. 48–49.

[23] Martin, *Quality Customer Service*, p. 37.

[24] LeBoeuf, *How to Win Customers and Keep Them for Life*, pp. 48–50.

[25] Debra R. Levine, "Diffuse the Angry Customer," *Transportation and Distribution*, January 1992, p. 27.

[26] Ibid., pp. 27–28.

[27] LeBoeuf, *How to Win Customers and Keep Them for Life*, p. 95.

[28] These examples are based on Martin, *Quality Customer Service*, p. 63.

Chapter 14

[1] Lennie Copeland, "Learning to Manage a Multicultural Work Force," *Training* (May 1988), pp. 48–56.

[2] Ann C. Wendt and William M. Sloanaker, "Confronting and Preventing Employment Discrimination," *Supervision* 52 (March 1991), pp. 3–5.

[3] David Myers, *Social Psychology*, 6th ed. (New York: McGraw-Hill, 1999), Chapter 9.

[4] Claire Renzetti and Daniel Curran, *Women, Men, and Society*, 5th ed. (Boston, MA: Pearson Education Co., 2003). See also Linda Lindsey, *Gender Roles: A Sociological Perspective*, 4th ed. (Upper Saddle River, NJ: Pearson Prentice Hall, 2005) and Margaret L. Anderson, *Thinking About Women*, 6th ed. (Boston, MA: Allyn & Bacon, 2003).

[5] Ibid. Myers, *Social Psychology*.

[6] Ibid.

[7] Jon Corzine, "Corzine, Brownback Renew Call to End Genocide in Darfur, Introduce 'Darfur Accountability Act.'" Press release of Senator Jon Corzine, posted March 2, 2005, http://corzine.senate.gov/press_office/record.cfm?id=232683 (retrieved July 20, 2005). See also "Darfur Conflict," Wikipedia.com, http://en.wikipedia.org/wiki/Darfur_conflict (retrieved July 20, 2005).

478   REFERENCES

[8] United Nations News Centre, "Attacks Against Rohingya 'A Ploy' to Drive Them Away; Prevent Their Return—UN Rights Chief," http://www.un.org/apps/news/story.asp?NewsID=57856#.WiWsn VWnHX4 (published Oct. 11, 2017, retrieved Dec. 4, 2017).

[9] Bureau of Labor Statistics, U.S. Department of Labor, "Unemployment Rates By Age, Sex, Race, and Hispanic or Latino Ethnicity," February 2013 at: http://www.bls.gov/opub/ted/2013 /ted_20130312.htm (visited July 2017).

[10] See "Employment Situation Summary," compiled by the Bureau of Labor Statistics, U.S. Department of Labor, www.bls.gov/news .release/empsit.nr0.htm (retrieved June 15, 2008).

[11] Jeffrey H. Greenhaus, Saroj Parasuramam, and Wayne M. Wormly, "Effects of Race on Organizational Experience, Job Performance, Evaluations, and Career Outcomes," *Academy of Management Journal,* March 1990, pp. 64–83. See also Joan Ferrante, *Sociology: A Global Perspective,* 5th ed. (Belmont, CA: Thomson Wadsworth Publishing, 2003).

[12] Resume of Congressional Activity, United States Senate, http://www. senate.gov/pagelayout/reference/two_column_table/Resumes.htm (retrieved April 1, 2013).

[13] Liz Roman Gallese, "Why Women Aren't Making It to the Top," *Across the Board,* April 1991, pp. 18–22.

[14] "Black and Hispanic Women are Paid Substantially Less Than White Men," Economic Policy Institute, by Elise Gould and Jessica Schieder, March 7, 2017. Visited July 2017 at http://www.epi.org /publication/black-and-hispanic-women-are-hit-particularly-hard -by-the-gender-wage-gap/

[15] Andrea Sachs, "Excess Baggage Is Not a Firing Offense," *Time,* March 25, 1991, p. 50.

[16] Ibid.

[17] "Give Me Shelter: Discrimination Against Gay & Lesbian Workers," *Nolo's Legal Encyclopedia* (Nolo.com, Inc., 2000), www.nolo.com /encyclopedia/arYmp/gay_les.html.

[18] http://www.catalyst.org/knowledge/lesbian-gay-bisexual-trans gender-workplace-issues#footnote12_8dqqet7 (visited July 2017).

[19] Michael R. Carrell and Frank E. Kuzmits, "Amended ADEA's Effects on HR Strategies Remain Dubious," *Personnel Journal,* May 1987, p. 112.

[20] Paula C. Morrow, James C. McElroy, Bernard G. Stamper, and Mark A. Wilson, "The Effects of Physical Attractiveness and Other Demographic Characteristics on Promotion Decisions," *Journal of Management,* December 1990, pp. 724–736.

[21] Irene Pave, "They Won't Take It Anymore," *Across the Board,* November 1990, pp. 19–23.

[22] Zachary A. Dowdy, "Fired Workers Awarded 6.7M," *Boston Globe,* Boston Globe Online (Metro Region, p. B01, September 24, 1998), www.civiljustice.com/fired_wo.html.

[23] A "U.S. Equal Employment Opportunity Commission: An Overview," U.S. Equal Employment Opportunity Commission (1999), www.eeoc.gov/overview.html.

[24] Age Discrimination in Employment Act (Includes concurrent charges with Title VII, ADA and EPA) FY 1997–FY 2012, accessed April 4, 2013, from http://www.eeoc.gov.

[25] Patricia M. Buhler, "Hiring the Disabled—The Solution to Our Problem," *Supervision,* June 1991, p. 17. See also "Disability

Facts," Courage Center, www.courage.org/about/tips.asp?id=9 (retrieved July 20, 2005).

[26] George E. Stevens, "Exploding the Myths About Hiring the Handicapped," *Personnel,* December 1986, p. 57.

[27] Mary W. Adelman, "Does Your Facility Comply with the Disability Act?" *Management Review,* June 1992, pp. 37–41.

[28] U.S. Equal Opportunity Employment Commission (EEOC), "Religion-Based Charges FY 1997–FY 2016" accessed at http:// www.eeoc.gov/eeoc/statistics/enforcement/religion.cfm on April 4, 2013.

[29] Barbara Kate Repa, "Religious Discrimination: Keeping the Faith at Work," *Nolo's Legal Encyclopedia* (Nolo.com, Inc., 2000), www.nolo.com/encyclopedia/articles/emp/emp10.html (retrieved June 15, 2008).

[30] Ibid.

[31] Kelly Flynn, "Protecting the Team from Sexual Harassment," *Supervision,* December 1991, pp. 6–8. See also www.mspb.gov /sites/mspb/pages/Public%20Affairs.aspx (retrieved June 16, 2008).

[32] Ibid, pp. 6–7. See also Steve Nelson, "Message from the Chairman," Silver Anniversary Edition, a publication of the U.S. Merit Systems Protection Board, Office of Policy and Evaluation, posted Summer 2004, www.mspb.gov/studies/ newsletters/04sumnws/04sumnws.htm#Sexual (retrieved July 21, 2005).

[33] Barbara Kate Repa, "Equal Pay for Equal Work," *Nolo's Legal Encyclopedia* (Nolo.com, Inc., 2000), www.nolo.com/encyclope dia/articles/emp/emp11.html.

[34] Alan Deutschman, "Dealing with Sexual Harassment," *Fortune,* November 4, 1991, pp. 145–146.

[35] Barbara Kate Repa, "Much Ado About the Sterile Workplace," *Nolo's Legal Encyclopedia* (2000), www.nolo.com/encyclopedia /articles/emp/sterile.html.

[36] Gordon Allport, *The Nature of Prejudice* (Garden City, NY: Anchor Books, 1954), p. 139.

[37] Ibid.

[38] Myers, *Social Psychology,* Chapter 9.

[39] Kathryn E. Lewis and Pamela R. Johnson, "Preventing Sexual Harassment Complaints Based on Hostile Work Environments," *SAM Advanced Management Journal,* Spring 1991, pp. 21–26.

[40] Robert K. McCalla, "Stopping Sexual Harassment Before It Begins," *Management Review,* April 1991, p. 46.

Chapter 15

[1] Joseph Massie and John Douglas, *Managing: A Contemporary Introduction* (Englewood Cliffs, NJ: Prentice Hall, 1992), p. 78.

[2] T. J. Murray, "Ethics Programs: Just a Pretty Face?" *Business Month,* September 1987, pp. 30–32. See also Sandra Salmans, "Suddenly Business Schools Tackle Ethics," *New York Times,* August 2, 1987, pp. 64–69.

[3] Robert A. Cooke, *Business Ethics: A Perspective* (Chicago, IL: Arthur Anderson and Co., 1988).

4 Don A. Moore, Daylian M. Cain, George Loewenstein, and Max Bazerman, *Conflicts of Interest: Challenges and Solutions in Business, Law, Medicine, and Public Policy* (New York: Cambridge University Press, 2005), pp. 37–88.

5 PC Computing, www.zdnet.com/pccomp. Accessed June 15, 2008.

6 Ibid.

7 Texas Instruments, Inc., *Ethics in the Business of TI* (Dallas, TX: Texas Instruments, 1977).

8 George A. Steiner and John F. Steiner, *Business, Government, and Society* (New York: Random House, 1985), pp. 150–151.

9 G. F. Cavanaugh, Dennis J. Moberg, and Carlos Moore, "The Ethics of Organizational Politics," *Academy of Management Journal,* June 1981, pp. 363–374.

10 Justin Longenecker, Joseph McKinney, and Carlos Moore, "Egotism and Independence: Entrepreneurial Ethics," *Organizational Dynamics,* Winter 1988, pp. 64–77.

11 Immanuel Kant, "To the Metaphysic of Morals," in *The Critique of Pure Reason and Other Ethical Treatises* (Chicago, IL: University of Chicago Press, 1988), pp. 392–394.

12 Bernard Williams, *Ethics and the Limits of Philosophy* (Cambridge, MA: Harvard University Press, 1985), pp. 61–64.

13 Saul W. Gellerman, "Why 'Good' Managers Make Bad Ethical Choices," *Harvard Business Review,* July–August, 1986, p. 88.

14 See David Callahan, *The Cheating Culture: Why More Americans Are Doing Wrong to Get Ahead* (Orlando, FL: Harcourt, Inc., 2004).

15 Robert Levering, "Can Companies Trust Their Employees?" *Business and Society Review,* Spring 1992, pp. 8–12.

16 O. C. Ferrell and Gareth Gardiner, *In Pursuit of Ethics: Tough Choices in the World of Work* (Springfield, IL: Smith Collins, 1991), pp. 79–80.

17 *Life Application Bible* (Wheaton, IL: Tyndale House Publishers, 1991), p. 1823 (Luke 10:30–35).

18 Ferrell and Gardiner, 1991, *In Pursuit of Ethics,* p. 28.

19 Robert A. Cooke, "Danger Signs of Unethical Behavior: How to Determine if Your Firm Is at Ethical Risk," *Journal of Business Ethics,* 1991, pp. 249–253.

20 Kent Hodgson, "Adapting Ethical Decisions to a Global Marketplace," *Management Review,* May 1992, p. 54.

21 Courtland Bovee and John Thill, *Business in Action,* 3rd ed. (Upper Saddle River, NJ: Pearson Prentice Hall, 2005), pp. 53–56.

22 Silvia Olivares, *Harley Davidson blogspot,* "Ethics and Social Responsibility," http://harleydavidsonus.blogspot.com/2012/09/chapter-3-ethics-and-social.html (posted Sept. 18, 2012; retrieved June 20, 2017).

23 Harley-Davidson Home Site, http://investor.harley-davidson.com/downloads/CG_financialcodes.pdf. Accessed June 20, 2017.

24 Don Hellriegel and John Slocum, *Management,* 7th ed. (Mason, OH: South-Western Publishing Company, 1996).

25 Courtland Bovee and John Thill, *Business in Action,* 3rd ed. (Upper Saddle River, NJ: Pearson Prentice Hall, 2005), p. 75.

26 Lloyd–LaFollette Act, MedLibrary.Org, http://medlibrary.org/medwiki/Lloyd-La_Follette_Act (retrieved June 15, 2008).

27 Survival Tips for Whistleblowers," Government Accountability Project, www.whistleblower.org/www/Tips.htm.

28 Adapted from Richard P. Nielsen, "Changing Unethical Organizational Behavior," *Executive,* May 1989, pp. 123–130.

29 Government Accountability Project, "Program Highlight: Pipefitter Case Ends in Triumph," posted September 2, 2005, www.whistleblower.org/template/page.cfm?page_id=68 (retrieved June 15, 2008).

30 Matthew L. Wald, "Nuclear Waste Believed Threat to River," *New York Times,* October 11, 1997. See also "The Hanford Pipefitters' Story," Government Accountability Project, www.whistleblower.org/template/page.cfm?page_id=134 (retrieved July 2005).

31 David Ewing, *Freedom Inside the Organization* (New York: McGraw-Hill, 1977).

32 Sally Seymour, "The Case of the Willful Whistle-Blower," *Harvard Business Review* January/February 1988, pp. 103–109.

33 Glenn Coleman, "Ethics Communication and Education," Texas Instruments; printed in *Bottom Line/Business,* September 1, 1995. See also Mary Ellen Guffey, www.westwords.com/guffey/ethitest.html.

34 Andrew W. Singer, "Ethics: Are Standards Lower Overseas?" *Across the Board,* September 1991, pp. 31–34.

35 Bowen H. McCoy, "The Parable of the Sadhu," *Harvard Business Review,* September/October 1983, pp. 103–108.

36 This story is adapted from Lawrence Kohlberg, "The Development of Children's Orientations Towards a Moral Order: I. Sequence in the Development of Moral Thought," *Vita Humana,* 1963, pp. 18–19.

Chapter 16

1 University of Pennsylvania, "Performance and Staff Development Program," http://www.hr.upenn.edu/staffRelations/performance/Default.aspx (retrieved June 24, 2008).

2 eHow Business Editor, "How to Improve Company Morale without Spending Money," www.ehow.com/how_2045950_morale-without-spending.html(retrieved June 24, 2008).

3 Dan Neuharth, "Top 20 Self-Sabotaging Behaviors," Secrets You Keep from Yourself, http://www.secretswekeep.com/the_self-sabotage_top_20.htm (retrieved June 24, 2008).

4 Jeff Nesbit, *US News and World Report,* "The Staggering Costs, Monetary and Otherwise, of Substance Abuse," https://www.usnews.com/news/at-the-edge/articles/2016-12-19/drug-and-alcohol-abuse-cost-taxpayers-442b-annually-new-surgeon-generals-report-finds (posted Dec. 19, 2016; retrieved July 3, 2017).

5 "Alcoholism and Drug Dependence Are America's Number One Health Problem," National Council on Alcoholism and Drug Dependence, Inc., posted June 2002 (retrieved June 22, 2008), http://www.ncadd.org/facts/numberoneprob.html#10.

6 National Drug-Free Workplace Alliance, http://www.ndwa.org/statistics.php (retrieved July 3, 2017).

7 Ibid.

480   REFERENCES

[8] "Reducing Substance Abuse in the Workplace," Work Drug Free, Oregon Department of Human Services, retrieved July 23, 2005, http://www.workdrugfree.org/reducingSubstanceAbuse/reducing SubstanceAbuse.asp. See also "The U.S. Department of Labor Drug Free Workplace Conference Briefing Book," U.S. Department of Labor, July 10, 2003 (retrieved July 23, 2005), http://www.dol .gov.

[9] Ibid.

[10] Mario Alonso, "When an Employee Has Personal Problems," *Supervisory Management,* April 1990, p. 3, and see also David G. Schramm, Ph.D., *The Family in America: A Journal of Public Policy,* "Counting the Cost of Divorce: What Those Who Know Better Rarely Acknowledge," http://familyinamerica.org/journals/fall-2009 /counting-cost-divorce-what-those-who-know-better-rarely -acknowledge/#.WVqXdYTyvX4 (retrieved July 3, 2017).

[11] Katarzyna Wandycz, "Divorce Kills," *Forbes,* October 25, 1993.

[12] Jennifer Joseph, "HMOs Target Family Violence," ABC News (November 12, 1999), http://abcnews.go.gom?sections/living/ DailyNews/domesticviolenceplans.html. See also "Costs of Inti- mate Partner Violence Against Women in the United States," U.S. Department of Health and Human Services, Center for Disease Control and Prevention, Injury Center, posting reviewed August 5, 2004 (retrieved July 22, 2005) http://www.cdc.gov/ncipc/pub -res/ipv_cost/02_introduction.htm.

[13] National Domestic Violence Hotline, http://www.ndvh.org/ ndvh2.html. See also "Costs of Intimate Partner Violence Against Women in the United States," U.S. Department of Health and Human Services, Centers for Disease Control and Prevention, Injury Center, posting reviewed August 5, 2004 (retrieved July 22, 2005), http://www.cdc.gov/ncipc/pub-res /ipv_cost/02_introduction.htm.

[14] Deborah Amos, "Victims of Violence: Victims of Domestic Violence Now Get Help from Employers," ABC News (June 5, 2000), http://abcnews.go.com/onair/WorldNe . . . 05_CL _domesticviolence_feature.html. See also: "Costs of Intimate Partner Violence Against Women in the United States," U.S. Department of Health and Human Services, Centers for Disease Control and Prevention, Injury Center, posting reviewed August 5, 2004 (retrieved July 22, 2005), http://www .cdc.gov/ncipc/pub-res/ipv_cost/02_introduction.htm. See also: Robert Pearl, M.D., "Domestic Violence: The Secret Killer That Costs $8.3 Billion Annually," *Forbes,* https://www.forbes.com /sites/robertpearl/2013/12/05/domestic-violence-the-secret- killer-that-costs-8-3-billion-annually/#d6a6b234681f, (posted December 5, 2013; retrieved July 3, 2017).

[15] National Domestic Violence Hotline, http://www.ndvh.org/ ndvh2.html.

[16] Los Angeles County Sheriff's Department, "The Domestic Vio- lence Handbook . . . A Victim's Guide," http://walnut.lasheriff.org /women.html.

[17] Janet Deming, "Rescuing Workers in Violent Families," *HR Magazine,* July 1991.

[18] Kay James, Commission Chair, "National Gambling Impact Study Commission Final Report," National Gambling Impact Study Commission, revised August 3, 1999 (retrieved July 22, 2005), http://govinfo.library.unt.edu/ngisc/index.html.

[19] U.S. Department of Labor, Bureau of Labor Statistics, http:// stats.bls.gov/ (May 24, 2000). See also: "Employee Assistance Programs," U.S. Department of Health and Human Services, and Substance Abuse and Mental Health Services Administra- tion, Clearinghouse for Alcohol and Drug Information, posted November 9, 2000 (retrieved June 22, 2008), http://www .health.org/workplace/fedagencies/employee_assistance _programs.aspx.

[20] Ibid.

[21] VITAL Work-Life Inc., "Why Offer an EAP?" http://vitalworklife. com/fororganizations/offer-eap/ (retrieved July 3, 2017).

[22] Ibid.

[23] Christy Marshall, "Getting the Drugs Out," *Business Month,* May 1989.

[24] Harris Sussman, website articles, "Diversity Questions and Answers column," "The Next Big Thing: People Over 60," and "Review of Workforce 2020," postings updated July 11, 2005 (retrieved July 25, 2005), http://sussman.org/.

[25] Lynn Martin, "Drug-Free Policy: Key to Success for Small Busi- nesses," *HR Focus,* September 1992, p. 23.

[26] Roger Thompson, "Anti-Drug Programs Tailored to Small and Mid-Sized Firms," *Nation's Business,* September 1992, p. 12.

[27] National Caregivers Library, "Fast Facts About Working Care- givers," http://www.caregiverslibrary.org/for-employers/fast- facts.aspx (retrieved July 3, 2017).

[28] Kim Parker and Eileen Patten, *Pew Research Center,* "The Sandwich Generation: Rising Financial Burdens for Middle-Aged Americans," http://www.pewsocialtrends.org/2013/01/30/the -sandwich-generation/ (posted Jan. 30, 2013; retrieved June 20, 2017).

[29] Karen Matthes, "A Coming of Age for Intergenerational Care," *HR Focus,* June 1993, p. 10. See also Roger Crisman, media contact for Work Life Benefits, "The Sandwich Generation Is in a Pickle," Accor Services, posted April 9, 2002 (retrieved June 22, 2008). http://www.wlb.com/en/worklifebenefitsnews/ pressreleases/2002/04_09_2002.asp; Belden, Russonello, and Stewart, "In the Middle: A Report on Multicultural Boom- ers Coping with Family and Aging Issues," Research/Strategy/ Management, American Association of Retired People, posted July, 2001 (retrieved June 22, 2008), http://www.aarp.org/ research/housing-mobility/caregiving/Articles/aresearch-import- 789-D17446.html.

[30] Ibid.

[31] Denis Waitley, *Psychology of Success* (Boston, MA: Richard D. Irwin, Inc., 1993). See also Denis Waitley, *Seeds of Greatness: The Ten Best-Kept Secrets of Total Success* (New York: Pocket Books, 1983), Denis Waitley and Reni L. Witt, *The Joy of Work- ing* (New York: Dodd, Mead, and Company, 1985), Denis Waitley, *Empires of the Mind* (New York: William Morrow and Company, Inc., 1995), and current articles posted on Waitley's website at http://www.deniswaitley.com.

[32] Ibid.

[33] Joan Harvey, and Cynthia Katz, *If I'm So Successful, Why Do I Feel Like a Fake?* (New York: St. Martin's Press, 1985).

REFERENCES   **481**

[34] Martin Seligman, *Authentic Happiness* (New York: The Free Press, 2002). See also the "Reflective Happiness" website at http://www.reflectivehappiness.com/, or the "Positive Psychology" or "Authentic Happiness" websites at http://www.authen tichappiness.org/; Lisa G. Aspinwall and Ursula M. Staudinger (eds.), *A Psychology of Human Strengths: Fundamental Questions and Future Directions for a Positive Psychology* (Washington, DC: The American Psychological Association, 2003); Claudia Wallis,

"The New Science of Happiness," *Time,* January 17, 2005 (also linked to http://www.reflectivehappiness.com/).

[35] Richard Bolles, *What Color Is Your Parachute?* (Berkeley, CA: Ten Speed Press, 2005). See also Bolles' online supplements at http://www.jobhuntersbible.com/ (retrieved August 20, 2013).

[36] American Psychiatric Association, *Diagnostic Manual of Mental Disorders,* 4th ed. (Washington, DC, 1994).

index

Pages with examples are indicated with *e*, footnotes and reference notes are indicated with *n*, and figures are indicated with *f*.

Biographies, 37
Black Girls Code (BGC), 372
Blair, Tony, 254
Blake, Robert R., 473*n*
Blind pane, in Johari Window, 54*f*, 55
Bloomberg Business, 9
BLS. *See* U.S. Bureau of Labor Statistics (BLS)
BMW, 411
Bodek, Norman, 475*n*
Body language, 145, 198
Bolles, Richard, 450, 481*n*
Bonding, with customers, 349–350
Boss massaging, defined, 405
Bottom line, 440
Bottoming out, 227*f*, 229
Bottom-line economy thinking, 86
Boudreau, George T., 469*n*
Boudreau, John W., 469*n*
Bovee, Courtland, 479*n*
Boyatzis, Richard, 199, 200, 474*n*
Brady, Teresa, 476*n*
Brainstorming, 263–264, 296
Bramson, Robert M., 476*n*
Brandt, Rhonda, 476*n*
Bridges, William, 227, 228, 474*n*
Britain, 373. *See also* England
Brockner, Joel, 472*n*
Brodsky, Norm, 340, 477*n*
Brodzinski, James, 476*n*, 477*n*
Bronowski, Jacob, 475*n*
Brooks, B. David, 469*n*
Brown, Susan, 262*f*
Brown v. Board of Education, 368
Bubble of space, 150
Bufka, Lynne, 318
Buhler, Patricia M., 478*n*
Bump, Philip, 468*n*
Bureaucracy, defined, 14
Burke, Brian, 472*n*
Burke, W. Warner, 474*n*
Burnham, David, 472*n*
Burnout, 321, 321*f*
Burns, David, 477*n*
Burns, Robert, 52, 55, 72
Bushnell, Nolan, 268*e*
Bussenius, C. E., 141*n*
Butler, Gillian, 474*n*
Buy-in, defined, 39

C

Cain, Daylian M., 479*n*
Calano, Jimmy, 475*n*
Callahan, David, 87, 471*n*, 479*n*
Campbell Soup, 437
Cappello, Sherry, 377
Carlin, George, 88*f*
Carnegie, Dale, 67, 470*n*
Carrell, Michael R., 478*n*
Carrey, Jim, 88*f*
Carrol, Dan, 377*n*
Carver, C. S., 470*n*
Casey, Karen, 58*n*
Catastrophize, defined, 311
Caterpillar Inc., 437
Catlett, Joyce, 469*n*
Caudron, Shari, 477*n*
Cavanaugh, G. F., 479*n*
Centers for Disease Control (CDC), 377
Challenge, in hardy personality, 315, 323
Challenger (Space Shuttle), 169*e*

Chamine, Shirzad, 205–207, 474*n*
Chan, M. Y., 470*n*
Change agent, 236–237
Change plan, 235
Changes
    dealing with, 231*f*
    as fact of life, 224
    OD and, 239–240
    organizational (*See* Organizational change)
    pace of, 237
    personal, 226–230, 240
    rebellion and, 237
    resisting, 236–238, 238*f*, 241
    seven major life, 224–226
    seven stages of personal, 227–230
    stress and, 226, 322–323
    success and, 440
    technology and, 231
    as wrong, 237
Chapman, Elwood N., 471*n*
Charismatic power, 174, 175
Charlesworth, Edward A., 474*n*
Chartier, Emile, 268, 270
Cheating, 86–87, 91, 258
Cheating Culture, The (Callahan), 87
Chevron Corporation, 437
Child labor laws, 15
Children, 440, 441
China
    annual growth rate of, 7
    ethics in, 406, 410*e*
Chinese, 7
Chopik, William J., 470*n*
Chronic illness, 319
Chronic stress, 318, 319
Chronic stressors, 307, 309
Ciarrochi, Joseph, 474*n*
Civil Rights Act, 368, 378, 379, 381
Civil rights movement, 369
Clark, K. C., 470*n*
Clayton, Victoria, 469*n*
Cleese, John, 267, 475*n*
Cliché conversation, as level of self-disclosure, 60–61, 61*f*
Clinton, Bill, 254
Closed mode, defined, 266
Code of ethics, 401–403. *See also* Ethical code
Coercive power, 174
Coffee, Peter, 475*n*
Cognitive appraisal, 310, 313
Cognitive categorization, 370, 373
Cognitive dissonance, 90–92
Cognitive (thinking) causes of prejudice, 369*f*, 370
Cohen, R. D., 470*n*
Coleman, Glenn, 479*n*
Colgate-Palmolive, 411
Collaboration approach, 297
Collaborator, 288*f*, 290
Collective habits of thought, defined, 256
College degree, 7
Collins-Nakai, Ruth, 476*n*
Commitments, in hardy personality, 315, 323
Common sense, defined, 9
Communication
    change and, 241
    conflict and, 20, 297–298
    conscious, 138, 138*f*
    defined, 11
    effective, 20
    with empathy, 289*f*
    face-to-face, 142
    factors of, 138*f*
    failures in, 140

gut-level, 61*f*, 62–63
high-context, 157
horizontal, 151
intercultural, 152–155
international, 152–155
leadership and, 171
leadership styles and, 172–174
levels related to disclosure, 60–63
listening and, 138, 141–143
miscommunication and, 138–140
nonverbal, 147, 198 (*See also* Nonverbals)
nonverbal messages in (*See* Nonverbal messages)
online, 139–140
organizational, 151–152
peak, 61*f*, 62
productivity and, 427
timing of messages in (*See* Timing)
unconscious, 138, 138*f*
vertical, 151
without words, 145–146
Communication channels, 290
Communication habits, 142
Communication skills
    development of, 11, 20
    for new job applicants, 5
Community, burnout and, 321*f*
Community roles, 109
Company towns, 12
Comparison, 323
Compensating, defined, 32
Competence
    emotional, 197, 198
    personal, 198
    productivity and, 427
    social, 198, 200
Competition
    creativity and, 252
    economic, 376
    ethics and, 405
    increased, 7
    prejudice and, 373
Competitiveness, 39
Competitor, 288, 288*f*, 291
Complainers, 292–293, 342
Complaints, 342–344
Completion, in seven-step recovery diagram, 227*f*, 229–230
Compliance, 347
Compromise, 287, 290, 295, 398, 406
Compromiser, 288, 288*f*, 290, 291
Compromising style, 288*f*
Compulsive gambling, 435
Concern, logical incrementalism and, 235
Concession bargaining, 295
Concessions, 295. *See also* Compromise
Conditional positive regard, 29, 34, 35*f*
Confidence, success and, 442–443
Conflict
    anger and, 201
    approach-approach, 308
    approach-avoid, 308
    avoid-avoid, 308, 309
    communication and, 20, 297–298
    constructive, 280
    content, 281–283, 282*f*
    defined, 280
    destructive, 280
    dysfunctional, 280
    ethical, 406
    family, 436
    functional, 280
    group values, 89

492   INDEX

Credits